COHABITING WITH SPIRITS

The Biography of a Marriage in Mayotte

Possession aptly describes the explicit manifestations of spirits when they temporarily displace individuals by assuming control of their bodies and minds, but the word does not account for what it means to cohabit with them. *Cohabiting with Spirits* offers an intimate portrait of the intertwined lives of a married couple together with the various spirits who came to possess each of them. Set against the backdrop of the island of Mayotte during the twentieth century, the book paints a vivid picture of the couple's lives, navigating the demands of their respective spirits while practising an art of cohabitation, both with the spirits and with each other.

While studies of spirit possession often focus on ceremonial practices and dramatic performances of spirit mediums in trance, Michael Lambek shifts the focus to explore what it can be like to cohabit with spirits. The book examines the ways in which various spirits entered the lives of this married couple and how their presence shaped the hosts' careers as healers, leaving lasting impacts on their domestic and personal lives. Based on rich ethnographic research conducted over the course of several decades, *Cohabiting with Spirits* presents a rare biography of "ordinary" Africans in the twentieth century and celebrates the resilience of a strong marriage.

(Anthropological Horizons)

MICHAEL LAMBEK is a professor and Canada Research Chair emeritus in the Department of Anthropology at the University of Toronto.

ANTHROPOLOGICAL HORIZONS

Editor: Michael Lambek, University of Toronto

This series, begun in 1991, focuses on theoretically informed ethnographic works addressing issues of mind and body, knowledge and power, equality and inequality, the individual and the collective. Interdisciplinary in its perspective, the series makes a unique contribution in several other academic disciplines: women's studies, history, philosophy, psychology, political science, and sociology.

For a list of the books published in this series, see page 323.

Cohabiting with Spirits

The Biography of a Marriage in Mayotte

MICHAEL LAMBEK

UNIVERSITY OF TORONTO PRESS
Toronto Buffalo London

ISBN 978-1-4875-5961-8 (cloth)   ISBN 978-1-4875-5964-9 (EPUB)
ISBN 978-1-4875-5962-5 (paper)   ISBN 978-1-4875-5963-2 (PDF)

Anthropological Horizons

Library and Archives Canada Cataloguing in Publication

Title: Cohabiting with spirits : the biography of a marriage in Mayotte /
  Michael Lambek.
Names: Lambek, Michael, author
Series: Anthropological horizons.
Description: Series statement: Anthropological horizons | Includes
  bibliographical references and index.
Identifiers: Canadiana (print) 20240490401 | Canadiana (ebook) 2024049041X |
  ISBN 9781487559618 (cloth) | ISBN 9781487559625 (paper) |
  ISBN 9781487559632 (PDF) | ISBN 9781487559649 (EPUB)
Subjects: LCSH: Spirit possession – Mayotte – History – 20th century. | LCSH:
  Marriage – Mayotte – History – 20th century. | LCSH: Married people –
  Mayotte – History – 20th century. | LCSH: Mayotte – Social life and
  customs – 20th century.
Classification: LCC BL482 .L36 2025 | DDC 133.909694/5 – dc23

Cover design: Louise OFarrell
Cover image: Weeding the rice crop, Mayotte, 1975. Photo courtesy of the
author, Michael Lambek.

We wish to acknowledge the land on which the University of Toronto Press
operates. This land is the traditional territory of the Wendat, the Anishnaabeg,
the Haudenosaunee, the Métis, and the Mississaugas of the Credit First
Nation.

University of Toronto Press acknowledges the financial support of the
Government of Canada, the Canada Council for the Arts, and the Ontario Arts
Council, an agency of the Government of Ontario, for its publishing activities.

Canada Council   Conseil des Arts
for the Arts   du Canada

ONTARIO ARTS COUNCIL
CONSEIL DES ARTS DE L'ONTARIO
an Ontario government agency
un organisme du gouvernement de l'Ontario

Funded by the   Financé par le
Government   gouvernement
of Canada   du Canada

Canadä

Our object, being what it is, is the other in ourselves and ourself in the other.
– Hans Loewald (2000, 297)

We should respect in the Other the same mystery we expect others to respect in ourselves.
– Vincent Crapanzano (1985, 152)

Contents

Part Four: Scenes from a Marriage

Part Five: Final Matters

Photos appear on pages 288–91

Photos

Dramatis Personae

Tumbu Vita
Mohedja Salim

Their children, in order of birth:
  Nuriaty, eldest daughter, raised by Dady Nuriaty
  Mariam, second daughter
  Haza, third daughter, raised by Tumbu's cousin
  Ali, first son
  Amiaty, fourth daughter
  Mwanesha, fifth daughter
  Maulida, second son, raised by Nuriaty

Rae Samba, Mohedja's mother
Samba, Mohedja's older half-brother
Asman, Mohedja's full brother

Dady Nuriaty, Tumbu's mother
Saidu, Tumbu's older full brother

Malidy Juma, a fundi of patros
Musy Matwar, a trumba fundi in Lombeni Kely
Mwana Sidy, a fundi of patros in Lombeni Be
Safy, a young male patros fundi in Lombeni Be

Toihan, a rejected suitor
Juma Abudu, a cosmologer and Tumbu's mother's half-brother
Amina, a young woman Ali wished to marry

Spirits cohabiting with Mohedja:
  Patros:
      Mze Nuru, a senior male
      Darwesh, a junior male
      Maimuna, an adult female

  Trumba:
      Ndramboeniarivu, or simply Ndramboeny, a mature older man
        and former Sakalava monarch from Madagascar, sometimes
        referred to as Grandfather (Dadilahy)
      Kos Vola, an adult Sakalava princess
      Kalu, a very young child, a servant girl
      Botu Changizy, a young male, one of a cohort of sailors,
        possibly of Creole background from Ile Sainte Marie, who
        drowned in a shipwreck between Madagascar and Mayotte
      Rasua, a spirit from Betsiuku, a Sakalava cemetery at which
        members of the royal Sakalava Bemihisatra line have been
        buried since the Merina and French colonial incursions
      A lulu kimaore, a spirit equivalent to the trumba but from the
        Mahorais-speaking sultanate in precolonial Mayotte

Spirits cohabiting with Tumbu:
  Mze Marwan, an adult male patros
  Mze Rihu, an older male patros
  Mze Drudrudru, an adult male patros

  Fanimbaly, a male kakanoru

COHABITING WITH SPIRITS

PART ONE

Introductions

Chapter One

Cohabiting

This book recounts the lives of two people, Tumbu Vita and Mohedja Salim, a married couple who lived through much of the twentieth century on the island of Mayotte. During their childhood and young adulthood, Mayotte was an impoverished colony, neglected by the French metropole, but from the mid-1970s onward Mayotte began moving in stages towards becoming a full overseas département of France. Tumbu and Mohedja were not actively involved in the popular politics that led to this development; they were concerned with making a living, raising children and being part of a broader family, overcoming illness, being good citizens of their community, and working as healers. But they did not engage in these activities by themselves. They cohabited with several other beings, beings that, in a comparative language, anthropologists have come to call "spirits." The story I tell is of their lives intertwined with these spirits.

I describe the subject of the book as cohabiting with spirits. This is a redescription of what has been called in the literature, not least by me, "spirit possession." This redescription does not discount the previous description but it changes the focus and frame.

"Possession" is an apt term for the explicit manifestations of spirits in the episodes during which they take over the bodies and minds of people, temporarily displacing them. Tumbu once memorably likened the experience to a coup d'état. We can say that the human hosts, as I call them, enter a state of trance or dissociation such that they are absent from the scene. This is often dramatic, both in the physical movements as the spirit enters or leaves a host's body, and in the ways in which spirits make their presence and their difference from their host manifest by changes in voice, demeanour, comportment, clothing, language, and so on. Spirits want onlookers to know that they are who they are – in the first instance, that they are other than their human hosts. Their performance is often intense and flamboyant, especially when they appear in public.

To focus on public episodes of what I continue to call "possession" is important, but it can too easily ignore the background, namely the significance of the spirits in the lives of their hosts and the long-term relationships built up between them. Spirits are part of the local world or "behavioural environment" (Hallowell 1955). They arrive and demand to cohabit with human hosts who are often initially reluctant to receive them; they sometimes intrude, like unwelcome guests. However, forced hospitality transitions into mutual acceptance and learning to get along together. Cohabitation is continuous and only infrequently interrupted by episodes of active possession. Once the correct rituals have taken place – rituals that can be described, depending on context or perspective, as a cure, an initiation, or an annunciation – the relationship becomes mostly positive. The spirits are invited from time to time to displace their hosts and speak through them, and sometimes they come on their own. There develops an addition and then possibly an integration of other voices, other persons, with the self of the host in the living of a life for oneself and with others. The spirits become entwined in the biographies of their hosts and their families; they figure in daily life and practice, and also in informal autobiography and memory, as people reflect on their lives in retrospection and in prospection. I call this an art of living with spirits, or rather, I describe cohabitation with spirits as an art of living. This is analogous to the description, say, of philosophy as an art of living (Nehamas 1998).

This book recounts the cohabitation of two primary hosts, a married couple, with their respective spirits. It shows how Mohedja and Tumbu lived with the spirits who demanded to be received by them and how they practised an art of living with the spirits, of cohabiting with them and with each other.

Cohabitation entails mutual acknowledgment between a given host and spirit. But it is not purely an individual matter; spirits become a part of the lives of their hosts' families as well. Cohabitation enables certain kinds of marital and domestic encounters, and it shapes the lives of family members with one another. The hosts and their family members lead their lives in the presence of the spirits and through that presence. In a sense, then, spouses and other family members also cohabit with the spirits. Moreover, the relationships among family members as mediated by the presence of the spirits in their midst are not simply social in an objective or public sense but characterized by intersubjectivity and currents of unconscious identification, projection, and introjection. The spirits open new possibilities for reflecting, communicating, acting, working, playing, and loving. One could say that cohabitation becomes an integral part of kinship.

Being actively possessed by spirits is far from random; it has a grammar, a tacit set of criteria, rules, and constraints. This grammar differs from place to place, whether in Mayotte, Madagascar, Zanzibar, or elsewhere.[1] As with the grammar of a language or the conventions underlying a literary or artistic genre, an infinite number of things can be said and done with it. Each life is unique, and each host and host family cohabit according to their particular circumstances and character. As in any biography, the particulars matter, and as in any creative genre, some artists are more skilled or more imaginative and original than others. I follow the lives of hosts whom I consider to have mastered the art of living with spirits. This art has both creative and ethical dimensions.

In the following chapter, I will expand on who the spirits are and what I mean by the term. I retain the word "spirit," despite the unfortunate Christian connotations of spirit and spirituality. "Meta-persons" (Sahlins 2017) would be a neutral alternative, but it is clumsy and removed from local understanding. "Beings" is too broad and carries unnecessary Heideggerian connotations.[2] When speaking of a spirit in the third person whose gender is unspecified, I use the masculine pronoun, since the majority of the spirits who appear are gendered male. Conversely, I use feminine pronouns to refer to hosts whose gender is unspecified, since more women than men host spirits. I retain the word "possession" when the spirit is manifesting directly in someone's body and speaking and acting through them.[3] From a naturalist perspective, active possession could be understood as occurring in a state of trance or dissociation, or simply in an altered state of consciousness on the part of the host. I will speak of someone entering or leaving trance. I refer to the humans who receive the spirits and become actively possessed as hosts, although, as I have indicated, the spirits themselves are not exactly guests. Occasionally I use the word "medium." Each of these terms – spirits, possession, trance, dissociation, host, medium – come with problems, but they are the best I can do. For reasons of efficiency, when I write of cohabitation, the meaning "with spirits" is implied.[4]

Although I speak about cohabitation and possession in general, my account draws on specific ethnographic material. What I describe in Mayotte resembles cohabitation from Zanzibar through Madagascar, albeit not precisely, and shares features with phenomena across North and West Africa, the Caribbean, Latin America, and much of Asia. It is up to ethnographers of those places to decide how well my description of cohabitation applies there. The subjects of this book are speakers of a dialect of Malagasy called Kibushy, who made up, during the course of Tumbu and Mohedja's lives, about 40 per cent of the population of Mayotte.[5] Speakers of the majority language, Shimaore, had similar relations with spirits. Two kinds of spirits with whom people in Mayotte cohabit – trumba and kakanoru – hail from Madagascar and are also found extensively there. Inhabitants of Mayotte are pious Muslims, and the other main class of spirits – patros – has strong affinities and connections with spirits found in Islamic East and Northeast Africa.

The redescription of spirit possession as cohabitation resonates with some of the earlier work on the subject, but the emphasis of most recent studies has been on transformation through ritual. Much of this work is powerful but the focus is on episodic events and performances rather than on ordinary life or the life course.[6]

I first carried out fieldwork in the island of Mayotte for fourteen months during 1975–6. I spent most of that time in the pair of neighbouring villages I refer to as Lombeni Kely and Lombeni Be, which forms in many respects a single community. I have revisited eleven times, for periods ranging from two weeks to four months.[7] The villages were inhabited by subsistence cultivators whose ascendants had acquired a foothold in the wake of failed colonial plantations. The founders were a mix of people originally from Madagascar and East Africa. They had all come to speak Kibushy, a northern dialect of Malagasy inflected with Comorian and Arabic words, and had become practising Muslims, albeit still somewhat insecure in their knowledge of Islam. They built a complex exchange system that bound community residents to one other in the enactment of reciprocal and obligatory ceremonies of reproduction. In 1975, the villages were without electricity or running water and were reached by an hour's steep walk from the road or by canoe in the lagoon. Houses then were built of wattle and daub or raffia palm. Most inhabitants were mistrustful of Europeans, at once subordinate to French authority and actively campaigning to become equal, as full French citizens. This goal was reached, after a series of intermediate stages, in 2011 when Mayotte became a full overseas département of France. By then the village was served with electricity and running water and accessed by a paved road with lots of traffic. Citizens of Mayotte now hold French passports and membership in the EU. Political incorporation was accompanied by enormous changes in infrastructure, education, and opportunity but has also had destructive consequences. The most obvious has been the flooding of the island with informal migrants, well beyond the political will and the ecological or infrastructural capacity to support them. (Lambek 2018; Riccio 2022). Cohabitation with spirits continues (Bouffart 2009; Heslon 2022, 2023).

On my initial scouting of Lombeni as a place to reside, I met Mohedja Salim and Tumbu Vita. They were a married couple who became my close friends and patient instructors. They came to see themselves as my parents, but our relationship was both less and more than that. I rented a small wattle and daub house from Tumbu's maternal half-brother and his wife, but I contributed to the domestic budget and ate my daily meals with Tumbu and Mohedja. Of all the villagers, they were the most patient as I struggled to understand, and to make myself understood, in Kibushy. They accepted me, took my work seriously, and actively encouraged my socialization in the community. After some weeks, I discovered they each hosted several spirits. Over the course of the year, I learned a great deal about spirits, and I accompanied each of them as they managed ceremonies and treated spirit-related illnesses and a range of other problems faced by their clients. From the first, I was struck by the intimacy cohabitation enabled. The spirits made a difference in how they related to themselves and to each other, in their marriage and in the life of their family. It is this story I tell in this book.

Tumbu and Mohedja have already figured extensively in my writing. Our relationships were characterized by deep commitment – indeed, that commitment was one of the things that the spirits who cohabited with them ensured – and they were particularly open with me. My account here is based on knowing them across twenty-six years, that is, from 1975 to 2001, my last visit three years before their deaths in 2004. They knew I was writing books, but they could not have anticipated everything I would put into them or where they would circulate. Given the personal nature of these accounts and the fact that their adult children might not wish to be identified, I have decided, regretfully, to continue to refer to them (as to all other people in this book) by pseudonyms. I also take the liberty of calling them by personal names for the ease of readers, but in Mayotte they would have been addressed and referred to most frequently by teknonyms: Baba ny Nuriaty and Nindry (or Mama) ny Nuriaty, translating to father and mother of Nuriaty, their eldest daughter, respectively. Nuriaty herself came to be called mother of her own eldest child. I have decided not to use pseudonyms for the spirits.

Tumbu and Mohedja were by no means the only members of the community to cohabit with spirits, but they were the people I came to know best and most intimately. I think too that they drew on their relations with their spirits more creatively than did many others. Other hosts

enter the narrative, as well as people who never received spirits themselves but lived among them. In effect, each of Tumbu and Mohedja's
children cohabited with their parents' spirits. The spirits looked out for
them but also made demands on them. Two of their seven children who
lived to adulthood received spirits as well. Like the other siblings, I
cohabited with the spirits without receiving any directly; I have never
become actively possessed myself.

The spirits came to make a difference in my life, enriching my experience, deepening my relations with Mohedja and Tumbu, and providing
the basis for my doctoral dissertation, two of my previous books, and
numerous articles.[8] I draw on that material once again, most extensively
from some of the articles, but here figure and ground are reversed. In
this work I no longer objectify "spirit possession" as an institution or
tradition to be analysed from the outside and illustrated by means of
examples, nor do I use it to further think abstractly about philosophical
questions like mind/body. Instead, I explore more directly and comprehensively how people live with spirits, their active presence in and
across the lives of actual persons and families. The incidents now gain
their relevance from their relation to each other – hence, the shift in
conceptualization from "spirit possession" to cohabitation. I show the
potential of cohabitation as it plays out in the lives of a married couple,
and I explore the living of their lives in cohabitation with spirits.

I want to write as directly as possible, with little anthropological
jargon or nods to theory or comparative ethnography. The underlying
theoretical approach should be plain enough, but this is an account of
people's lives, and lives are lived and recounted, not theorized. I have
made many theoretical interventions elsewhere concerning spirit possession, and I continue to assume them. But I take the incidents I used
elsewhere (sometimes with different pseudonyms) to illustrate or make
theoretical points and to compose from them the full lives of the main
protagonists.

In places I draw lightly on psychoanalytic ideas in order to illuminate but not overdetermine the account. The ideas come not directly
from Freud on drive theory, but rather from the sort of mature object
relations theory well described by Steven Mitchell (1988a) and others.
The point is not to explain cohabitation by means of psychoanalysis,
but rather to suggest that each tradition or form of life can speak to
the other. Each illuminates the lives of its subjects, and their subjects
draw respectively from them to live and illuminate their own lives. The
main point I draw from psychoanalysis is how cohabitation with one
spirit rather than another might be motivated by largely unconscious
identifications with other salient humans, in a dialectic of projection

and introjection. I take seriously both psychoanalyst Hans Loewald's remark that "our object, being what it is, is the other in ourselves and ourself in the other" (2000, 297) and anthropologist Vincent Crapanzano's admonition that "we should respect in the Other the same mystery we expect others to respect in ourselves" (1985, 152). A discussion of psychoanalysis itself is reserved for the postscript.

On my first return to Mayotte, during the dry post-harvest season of 1980, Tumbu, with characteristic acuity and generosity, observed that given the commitment I had shown in returning, people would now be much readier to talk about their private affairs. Tumbu said that if I did not push, I would learn all sorts of things. What ethnographer could ask for a better mentor? Indeed, I proceeded to have an incredibly rich few weeks. Tumbu also told me – more than once – that I should call up the spirits who cohabited with Mohedja, and should do so before the onset of Ramadan, which was imminent. I had made friends with the spirits in 1975–6, and they would be insulted if I didn't greet them on my return. And so I arranged a time with Mohedja. It was evident that she and Tumbu had already discussed the matter with each other.

12 July 1980. After a supper of rice and fresh fish poached in a broth fragrant with lemon, tomato, and turmeric, we called the spirits. We sat in the small hut where Tumbu and Mohedja slept since their recently married daughter had moved into their own larger house and until Tumbu could complete a new one. Mohedja set up the brazier, gave me the *embuku* (the resinous cone that emits the incense that Malagasy spirits, trumba, respond to) and told me to speak. Placing the incense on the smoldering flame, I asked the trumba to rise gently (*moramora*). There was a long transition. The aromatic smoke rose from the brazier and filled the small room. Mohedja sat on a mat laid over the dirt floor in front of the incense, yawning and turning her head away from me. She coughed and stretched until the senior male trumba, Ndramboeniarivu (Lord of the People a Thousandfold), arrived, displacing Mohedja herself. I will shorten his name to Ndramboeny (Lord of the People). Mohedja's eyes became glazed and dull, her posture erect. The spirit moved up from the floor to sit above us on the bed.

Ndramboeny greeted Tumbu informally: "*Akore haly*, Tumbu?" ("How are you, Tumbu?"). Tumbu explained that I had come to greet him.

Ndramboeny told me he was glad we were good friends and that I hadn't abandoned the relationship once I had what I wanted. He was pleased (*ravrav*) that I had returned to visit, and he wished me nothing but good. He added that he followed me wherever I went.

Ndramboeny said he rose originally in Mohedja because he liked her. But he remarked that he was prohibited chili pepper (*fady pilypily*) and would fight with Mohedja if she didn't stop eating it. He said he felt compassion for her, and so was reminding her gently at first; he didn't want to cause any more illness. Tumbu had treated him well and Mohedja should too. Later, when Mohedja returned to herself, she said that she had eaten chili pepper the previous day and it had made her ill. She really liked hot food, and every once in a while she couldn't resist it, but she was always sick afterwards.

Ndramboeny continued that he had many dietary prohibitions, such that Mohedja couldn't eat from a dish that children had eaten from or from any dish previously started by someone else. But he said he went easy on this since Mohedja was raising small children.

Tumbu then asked Ndramboeny for advice about the new house that he and Mohedja were planning, and whether the astrologer from F— (Mohedja's brother) was correct in his ascertainment of an auspicious time for starting construction.

There was a transition as Ndramboeny left, his place taken by Kos Vola, an adult female trumba who also lived with Mohedja. Kos Vola, who covered her face with a veil and held an ebony staff embossed with bands of silver, said approximately the same things to me as Ndramboeny had and she asked Tumbu what was up in the family (*mraba*).

Then Mohedja's child trumba, Kalu, rose. Speaking with a thick lisp, she too said she was very happy I had remained friends. She asked me for food and then complained about having to ask first; she declared she wouldn't eat since she had to ask. Why didn't Tumbu and Mohedja feed her once in a while on their own initiative? She said she hadn't been invited to a single meal since I left [in 1976]. Tumbu retorted that neither she nor the other trumba ever came to visit anymore; he frequently left incense by the bedside in order to see them in his sleep, but they didn't appear. Mohedja did the same, with similar results. Kalu replied that this was because Tumbu had forgotten to give them occasional gifts. Tumbu acknowledged to me that she was speaking the truth. He and Mohedja had been so pleased with their recent economic success that they had been neglecting the spirits. He promised to call her for a meal during the month after Ramadan.

In telling each of the spirits why I called them, Tumbu stressed the importance of enduring social relationships and commitments and how I had remained a friend. This was in part an ethical lesson directed at me. The spirits, in turn, emphasized how glad they were that I had not forgotten them and had come all this way to see them again, even after completing my dissertation and getting a job. In sum, the first part of each conversation concerned the maintenance of our relationships, speaking to my future actions as well as present and past ones. My relationships with the spirits did not demand active possession on my part. The spirits spoke to my cohabitation with them and, of course, with Mohedja and Tumbu. The second part of each conversation concerned practical matters between the spirits and Tumbu and Mohedja. Ndramboeny raised an ostensible tension that had arisen in his relationship with Mohedja. If they were to cohabit peaceably, she had to respect his prohibitions. He was willing to comprise on one but expected her to submit to the other. The senior spirits each asked after the well-being of the family and Tumbu inquired about the new house he and Mohedja were building, a matter of some urgency and anxiety on his part. And while the child spirit was entirely in character in her petulance and expression of gluttony, here too the message was about mutual acknowledgment and reciprocity in the course of living together.

The next day I called Tumbu's spirits before Ramadan started that evening, after which the spirits, out of respect for Islam, would no longer be available for the month.

I asked the spirits to rise and chat and then was silent. Tumbu picked up the incense burner (now filled with *uban*, the incense used both for Muslim prayer and to call patros, spirits indigenous to Mayotte) and started murmuring to himself in the rhythmic undertone that was appropriate for calling spirits and that I never quite mastered: "Come, wherever you are, from north, south, east, or west.... Come, show yourself to us today. Come gently and don't fight." Tumbu stretched, scratched, and yawned. His eyes stood out, showing the whites, and he stared with great intensity. It was his patros, Mze Marwan, who, after greeting me, said I would see him again in my dreams at home, five days after returning to Canada. He would take on the appearance of Tumbu. The spirit was intense, staring at me and speaking forcefully. He was replaced by Mze Rihu, who explained that the spirits who rose in Tumbu gave their names right away because Tumbu had a *nyora mahery*, a strong destiny or constitution. Both spirits spoke positively of Tumbu. Mze Rihu said he entered Tumbu precisely because of his strong constitution. He called Tumbu his *mwanafundi*, his student or apprentice, and observed that Tumbu couldn't do much on his own.[9]

Both patros drank cologne from the bottle before speaking much. They addressed Mohedja informally by her first name, rather than by her teknonym. Mohedja told them about the plans for the new house and received assurance that things would go well.

When he came to himself, Tumbu said he felt that the spirits had fully entered his body (*lulu niditry an'nengin tsara be* – i.e., that he had been in a deep trance). He remarked that this was not always the case for him.

Rather than call up Mohedja's patros (the previous night, Tumbu had said it was too much for Mohedja's body to take), Tumbu took the bottle of cologne, held it over the incense smoke, and spoke to her patros, explaining it was my gift to them. They would rise after Ramadan to drink.

That night, the patros Mze Nuru spoke to Mohedja in her sleep and told her to ask me whether I wasn't angry or sad he hadn't risen to greet me directly. I assured her to tell him I wasn't. Mze Nuru also instructed Mohedja to tell me that he had seen my gift of cologne and thanked me for it.

Calling up spirits requires some effort and is often painful for the host. Tumbu and Mohedja took advantage of the occasion not simply to confirm the bonds between me and the spirits, but to gain reassurance and advice about a matter of great practical concern to them at the time, namely the construction of their new house. The spirits spoke positively about their respective hosts, indicating harmonious relations and perhaps self-love or self-approval. This was a time when Tumbu and Mohedja were living well and feeling relatively good about things. They wanted to relieve their anxiety over their house plans, but the very fact that they were able to put the plans into motion showed progress towards a long-awaited goal, achieved with the cooperation of the spirits.

Regarding the house, Tumbu had been to F— to call up Mze Rihu in Samba, Mohedja's well-respected older brother. Mze Rihu had cohabited with Samba long before he also moved in with Tumbu. Tumbu explained that he wanted to ask the spirit directly and to have a good, straightforward conversation about it – so he didn't draw upon Mze Rihu in himself (whether in his sleep or by letting Mze Rihu speak through him to a third party, such as Mohedja). Speaking from Samba, Mze Rihu said they should hold a *kuitimia*, a commemorative blessing for deceased kin, and he also issued a *wakat*, an auspicious time, for placing the first piece of wooden frame for the house. Once the spirit had left, Samba, who was himself an astrologer, checked his books and came up with an identical result. To be absolutely confident, Tumbu took the opportunity to check this advice with Mohedja's senior male trumba, who said it was fine as long as the day was not an astrologically inauspicious one (*nuhus*). The following night, Mohedja discussed it again, this time with Mze Rihu risen in Tumbu. It is noteworthy that while Tumbu had sought reassurance from the spirit elsewhere, now it was the spirit speaking through him who gave that assurance. There is a circulation and redundancy of communication, with an amplification of effect.

These exchanges manifest cohabitation. It is cohabitation not only of humans with spirits, but of humans with each other through the mediation of spirits, in a common world and ideally to mutual ends. Cohabitation is based on intersubjectivity that requires forms of mutual acknowledgment – evident in these conversations between the hosts and spirits.

Non-human others, or meta-persons, can be imagined in all kinds of ways. In the Western Indian Ocean region, some of them are understood, on the order of humans, as discrete, named individuals, each having specific traits associated with their respective age, gender, and status. Moreover, they are understood as persons in a forensic sense, namely that what they say and do at one time has consequences for how they are understood subsequently: they are accountable for their words and acts. Although the appearances of individual spirits are discontinuous, their relationships with hosts and their families are continuous; they pick up where they left off, as they did with me after an absence of four years. Spirits and humans are expected to acknowledge each other and to maintain the commitments and promises they make to each other. When the spirits are not actually present, the commitments remain embodied, largely in the prohibitions that the host maintains.

Hosts can invite the spirits' presence or leave them messages over incense. Spirits can speak directly to their hosts in dreams. But when spirits are actively present, hosts and spirits speak to each other through intermediaries, trusted others. The other may be a healer or a spouse or close family member. The other is someone trusted by the host, and their relations with and through the spirits build further trust. This was certainly how things unfolded between Mohedja, Tumbu, and me.

Acknowledging the personhood of spirits shifts the focus from periodic public episodes of possession, with all their drama, force, and wit, to the longer perspective of cohabitation, of living with significant others. It is this description or frame that I bring to the fore.

I take the spirit world as it was found in Mayotte and show what people in Mayotte made of and with it, and especially what Tumbu and Mohedja made of and with it over the course of their lives. For those who take it up, the phenomenon that anthropologists have objectified as spirit possession becomes implicitly an art of living. It is first and foremost an art of living *with* spirits, rather than of being only temporarily possessed *by* them. Episodes of manifest possession – when a spirit temporarily displaces the host and speaks and acts through their body – are significant, but living *with* spirits indicates that it is less a matter of being taken over by a force beyond one's rational control than it is a broader kind of reception. Spirits afford an opportunity with respect to how one acknowledges their presence and engages the relationship.

In Mayotte, people who go often into states of trance do so based on their long-term arrangements with particular spirits – relationships akin to marriage or affinity, but also to kinship in a deeper and less purely contractual sense than might be implied by the former terms. Ideally, the relationships become ones of "diffuse enduring solidarity" (Schneider 1968) or "mutuality of being" (Sahlins 2013), although they remain somewhat ambiguous insofar as spirits are fundamentally amoral and somewhat more powerful and less predictable than human kin (Lambek 1980).

A spirit who rises periodically in a human host also develops relationships with those close to the host, as Ndramboeny, who rose in Mohedja, did with Tumbu and as he began to do with me. People often say there is a spirit in the extended family (*mraba*) to indicate that the relationship is not only with the host but with all members of the family. Spirits can become part of the family; as Diego Malara (2022, 23) writes of spirits in Ethiopia, they are "not external to relationships, but inherent to kinship networks."

That Tumbu and Mohedja introduced me to the spirits with whom they cohabited indicated their commitment to stronger and more intimate relations with me, as part of a family that included Ndramboeny, Mze Marwan, et al. among its members. These relationships continued over the course of Tumbu and Mohedja's lives, especially as they let me attend consultations with people seeking advice or assistance from them and as they served as my teachers in understanding the aetiologies of illness and the means of diagnosis and cure, but also as they held private conversations within the family or even privately and directly with me.

Cohabitation is a more capacious concept than possession insofar as a given individual's relationship with spirits is broader and more continuous than the temporary episodes of possession. As noted, it applies to those who are not actively possessed as well. Mohedja cohabited with the spirits who possessed Tumbu and Tumbu cohabited with the spirits who possessed Mohedja. Their children also cohabited with the spirits who possessed their parents, and the longer and better I knew Tumbu and Mohedja, the more I came to know and live with these spirits as well, albeit not as intimately as they did. Their respective spirits could also be said to cohabit with each other.

Often a given spirit developed relationships with several human hosts. Mze Marwan had a long-standing relationship with Mwana Sidy, an older woman in Lombeni. Their mutual relationship with Mze Marwan provided a connection between Tumbu and Mwana, who were otherwise unrelated. Over time, Mze Marwan came to possess Tumbu and Mohedja's eldest daughter, as well as a cousin living in another village. The fact that each of them hosted Mze Marwan added another strand to their relations with one another. This, in turn, added a dimension to Mohedja's relationships with them and with their spouses as well. My relationship with Mze Marwan also extended to his presence in Tumbu's daughter and cousin. We could all have been said to cohabit.

Cohabitation indicates the ordinariness of what has been called spirit possession, as well as its integration within the everyday domestic lives and concerns of the mediums and their families and with their life projects. The relationships the spirits developed with Tumbu and Mohedja and their family were for a lifetime, and they were significant even when the spirits were not directly manifest and displacing them. Cohabitation is an integral part of both their subjective experience and their objective practice.

To say I place the phenomena under a different description is not to say the former description is wrong; indeed, it is still useful in certain respects, and I continue to speak of possession in what follows. It is rather that the new description offers a reorientation and a shift in focus and perspective. As Elizabeth Anscombe (1963) convincingly showed, any act can be put under multiple descriptions that need not challenge so much as complement one other in the sense of offering further understanding of what is going on, but each with distinct and differing implications for what we speak of as intentionality, motivation, responsibility, and agency. Cohabitation, as a description, displaces some of the weight that "possession" inevitably gives to episodes of dissociation and looks rather at the forms of life in which such episodes are meaningful and of which they are a part.

Cohabitation with other beings is widespread across the globe. Marshall Sahlins (2017) has written about the prevalence of what he calls meta-persons or meta-humans. Robert Orsi (2005) writes about what he calls companionship between individual Italian Catholics and particular saints. This is not romantic. For Sahlins it is political, historically anticipating forms of human hierarchy rather than merely reflecting them. For Orsi it can be painful. He writes, "What the saint seems to have offered [my grandmother] was companionship on a bitter and confusing journey – bitterness and confusion to which the saint's own stories had contributed. My grandmother asked no grace of Gemma other than that of accompaniment, no miracle beyond the recognition of shared lives. But the sharing was costly."[10]

What I mean by cohabitation can be further enhanced by reference to a distinction that Tim Ingold makes between an assemblage of things simply added together and what he calls "correspondence." He captures this in the contrast between "and" and "with." Thus, "filiation is not the connection of parent *and* child, it is the life of parent *with* child…. Just as in musical counterpoint, parts are not components that are added to one another but movements that carry on *alongside* one another, so too, in the human family, lives lived in counterpoint are not 'and … and … and' but 'with … with … with.' And in answering – or responding – to one another, they co-respond." Ingold continues, "It follows that the relations that make up the whole are not *between* but *along*. Between-ness gives us the idea of interaction, a reciprocal back-and-forth exchange between subject positions. The along-ness of correspondence, by contrast, does not go back and forth but side by side, like companions walking together or playing music together. And the thing about walking and playing is that they do not issue from a position but continually pull the performer out of it" (Ingold 2018, 160).

If one aim of the book is to explore what happens when spirit possession is redescribed as cohabitation, a second is to offer a close look at the lives of two people. It is rare to find biographies of Africans, and even rarer, biographies of people who were not famous. These are lives lived in Mayotte prior to departmentalization and may show contemporary citizens of Mayotte the ways in which their grandparents and great-grandparents lived. I am concerned with what mattered to Tumbu and Mohedja and with how they made things matter; with the texture of their lives and their engagement in life; with what engaged their attention, energy, and imagination. I hope to show the affordances of spirits – beings who, at first glance, seem to disrupt or interrupt their lives – for the enrichment of their lives, their lives with one another, adding moral complexity and insight, confidence, vitality, irony, play, and sometimes pleasure, sometimes aggression, sometimes pain.

This is not a functionalist or causal argument. In living alongside spirits, and in intimate relations with the spirits and with each other, Mohedja and Tumbu have been shaped by their proximity and mutual relationships – the humans by the spirits and equally the spirits by the humans. Rather than either abstracting and objectifying spirit possession as a cultural system or extracting specific instances of pathology encountered and resolved, I explore how cohabitation unfolds over the life course of distinct subjects, each with their own hopes and troubles, their own ways of expressing joy and pain, certainty and uncertainty, likes and dislikes, love and aggression, their own personal identifications and internal conflicts, their own character and voice. The ethnography could thus be described as person-centred, but with the caveat that at the heart of my account is not one person but persons alongside each other.[11]

Additionally, when I say cohabiting with spirits, I mean also cohabiting with the concept of spirits and the genre of spirit cohabitation. This genre enables the shaping of subjectivities for those attracted to it in specific ways. In living with spirits, people do certain things and are moved by certain things, and in doing and being moved, they live their lives and grow as persons. Doing and being are intertwined. They happen within the worlds people inhabit, worlds that include means to transcend particular givens, whether temporarily or over the longer term.

What, then, did Mohedja and Tumbu make of and with spirits? How did the spirits arrive and why these spirits in particular? How were they moved by them and how did they move with them? What kind of life is it that acknowledges the presence of spirits and periodic interruption by them? What kind of selfhood? How do spirits articulate personal conflict, uncertainty, ambivalence, and desire?

Some of these questions are easier to answer than others. Or perhaps some of them are merely better phrased. But the answers cannot be rushed. To understand cohabitation, I add two dimensions that are often missing in accounts of spirit possession. The first is a life course dimension. This will not show a history of trauma culminating in possession; nor will it explain possession according to dominant Western ontogenetic models. Examining the course of possession over the lives of hosts, the different times at which they gained spirits, the enlargement of the cast, and changes in deployment from youth to old age shows adaptation and growth.

The second dimension is that of daily practice within a moving present. In this respect, the account resembles the practice of psychoanalysis more than popular conceptions of it. It shows people working through personal, domestic, and work issues (spheres that cannot be readily distinguished), living their lives on a daily, ongoing basis, rather than uncovering some deep secret or initial event that set everything in motion. I take people's accounts of past events as a field of practice contiguous with the present. The emphasis is on how they produce their lives (and not merely the representations of their lives) rather than simply being the products of those lives. I describe the presence of spirits in the exigencies, concerns, and projects of life in Mayotte, how two people lived with spirits, and the import of cohabitation for daily life. In fact, the diachronic and synchronic dimensions are fused; accounts of practice form episodes in the life course narratives and it was in the course of daily practice that my subjects recalled and understood past events in their lives.

This corresponds as well to how I collected the material. Except for a brief experiment in 1992 in eliciting taped life histories, I simply listened and took extensive notes as people spoke for and about themselves, whether to each other or to me. These were for the most part informal conversations, initiated as often by Tumbu or Mohedja as by me. And sometimes it was one of the spirits who came of their own accord to speak to me. In other words, the accounts of their lives, and my understanding of them, emerged, piece by piece, from the midst of things rather than as the result of deliberately standing back and trying to elicit the whole.

The result is a book that does not conform to the genre of "life history" as it has manifest in anthropology. A life history is generally drawn from the taped account of a single speaker over one or several settings who responds to open-ended questions on the part of the anthropologist. This does not correspond to my method, insofar as I can be said to have followed one.

Indeed, most of the material was not collected with a "life history" framework in mind and there were few leading questions. I did not ask questions like, "What do you consider your greatest strength? Your most important achievement?" There were no questions of the "How do you feel about … ?" sort. I don't even know how to ask such questions in Kibushy. For the most part, my questions were in response to what Mohedja or Tumbu said or did, rather than ordered systematically as though in an interview. Significant events came up contingently. The pain caused by the entry of one spirit led Mohedja to reminisce about the entry of prior spirits, and so forth. This in turn led me to ask questions, but they were primarily ones of clarification and determined by a context in which Mohedja took the lead.

In other words, the material is based primarily on their ongoing reflection and construction of their lives through daily conversation and practice – on life as it was lived, rather than interviews about it. Furthermore, I collected their reminiscences at different points in their lives, across the changes taking place in their life circumstances and in Mayotte more broadly. Each of them took up certain themes and discussed the same events over my different visits. One could say that the result is a conjunction of the repetition of the transference with the inexorable motion of the life course. And, as in any recollection of a life, the versions were not always consistent. All this speaks to what Ian Hacking has called the indeterminacy of the past.

"Biography," Jean and John Comaroff have remarked, "is anything but innocent" (1992, 25). They observe that biography or life history as a genre implies a concept of self with roots in "the Cartesian 'I,' an image of a self-conscious being freed from the webs of enchantment and possessed of the capacity to gaze out at, and measure, the world.... Life-histories bespeak a notion of the human career as an ordered progression of acts and events," exhibiting "a modernist fantasy about society and selfhood according to which everyone is, potentially, in control of his or her destiny in a world made by the actions of autonomous 'agents'" (26). While Mohedja and Tumbu are evidently *not* "freed from the webs of enchantment," they certainly *are* "possessed of the capacity to gaze out at, and measure, the world." They could see their lives as a progression of events when the question was put to them, but they were not in the habit of objectifying themselves or their lives such that a life history could be readily constructed. They did not see themselves in control of their destinies or as fully autonomous agents, but they did not deny their agency either. In fact, one could say that the ways in which they cohabited with spirits expressed the relative weight of agency and patiency that they understood in their lives, adding to that the force of God's will, the working of astrological destiny, and the attacks of sorcery cast against them.

My account is a secondary reworking of the significance of spirits in their lives, shaped by the way I received their accounts, yet with my own attempt at narrative coherence (and, no doubt, "modernist fantasy"). I write about their lives neither in fully chronological order, nor fully in the order I heard things, but return to events and periods from different perspectives and with respect to different themes. In the end, the divisions by chapter are thematic, meant to be read as parts of a recursive and emerging whole. But the wholeness of experience is always compromised by the linearity of narrative; short of writing poetry, there is little one can do to get around this. In the interests of space, rhythm, and coherence, I have collapsed some of their accounts when they did not differ substantially from one another, and I have not always fully contextualized them. Such compromises are inevitable; any biographic account must itself be a form of condensation, interpretation, and rewriting. Inconsistencies are also evident. These may be attributed to two general factors. First are my limitations as a recorder – what questions I thought to ask at the time, my concentration at the moment, my facility or lack of facility with the language, my appreciation of the broader context – and of course, Mohedja's and Tumbu's judgment about how all these factors should shape how they spoke to me at that moment. Second is the fact that the stories went in and out of salience for them, both according to their distance from them in years and according to other factors I can only guess at, such as what event from the past a particular experience in the present might evoke.

For the most part, I have chosen to write in the past tense, since the events and conversations took place some time ago and both Mohedja and Tumbu are deceased. Mayotte has also undergone radical change since the periods I write about. However, this should not be taken to mean that the practices and relationships I describe are all outdated. Spirits may or may not keep up with the times, but they have not disappeared, and they continue to cohabit with new generations in Mayotte.

I considered separating my accounts of Mohedja and Tumbu. They are two distinct people so should they not have distinct life histories? But to do so would be to violate the very insight to which their stories give rise, namely the fact of cohabitation, the ways in which persons and lives in Mayotte are intertwined with one another. The dense thicket of connections that make up their long marriage cannot be pruned to the model of Western individualism without gross distortion. And it is not simply Mohedja and Tumbu who are in question but also their relations with the spirits who possessed each of them respectively, yet cohabited, in effect, with both, and whose presence contributed to and mediated their relations with one another.

In its grounding in listening rather than interviewing, the ethnographic method pursued here is more akin to the psychoanalytic method than it is to positivist conceptions of social science. However, I was not trained to listen psychoanalytically and there were none of the controls of the psychoanalytic situation. While some conversations of spirits and healers with their clients do bear a resemblance to the psychoanalytic setting, the conversations on which the book is based differ from psychoanalysis in that they do not emerge from a ritual of regularly scheduled and private sessions (compare Crapanzano 1985, 2010), but rather from opportunistic encounters whenever Mohedja or Tumbu happened to be free and interested in talking.

Like certain recent accounts of the analytic setting, I take what is reproduced here to be a collaborative production. What people told me does not exist in some neutral objective space in their memories, but is in part a product of our interaction and of what caught their and my attention. It is certain that in such circumstances the ethnographer benefits from being both a relative outsider and an object of a positive transference and must carry the obligations that come with this, including acknowledgment of counter-transference (Crapanzano 1985; Obeyesekere 1984). Yet people were neither as free from the entailments of ordinary conversation as are analysands, nor as vulnerable. If the material is of any quality, it is due in part to their trust and interest in me as an interlocutor. (I am not bragging here; I simply do not report on the people with whom I was unable to develop this kind of relationship.)

Transference works both ways. I found Mohedja and Tumbu to be exceptional people and people whom I could trust. They raised a large family and also fostered numerous children who were not their own. I may have been the first *vazaha* (European), but I was not the first adult whom they had taken in as a kind of foster son, and I enjoyed and benefitted from their care. I was compelled by their happy marriage and respect for each other, and I no doubt idealized them.

They were also active and interested in all areas of community life. Without a school education, Tumbu served as the first local assistant mayor under the system of *communes* that the French administration established. Around the same time, Mohedja was selected by the village women as their chief, responsible for managing the complex distribution of food at major ceremonies. All this was their own doing; they began marriage with neither social capital nor economic means. They were conscientious, disciplined, hard-working, generous, and civic-minded, and also highly perceptive, intelligent, thoughtful, and self-reflective. They were outgoing and engaged in joking relations, but more contained, less extroverted, and less pushy or verbally aggressive than many of their neighbours. They were complex people with strong and healthy characters. I was strongly attracted to them.

Mohedja and Tumbu have figured at great length in several of my books and articles, and it might be supposed that my understanding of possession is biased in that it develops from my knowledge of two people who may be eccentric or exceptional. However, their cohabitation with spirits fits with what I know about many other families. I have a lot of case material from other people.[12] The reason that I draw less from other people is partly that my knowledge of them is less complete and consistent. With Tumbu and Mohedja I can build a richer picture. I saw them daily and knew them better than other people.

I owe them very much. They were there at the beginning, they developed the best understanding of and sympathy for my goals, and they were very patient, especially when I was struggling with the language. They showed concern for my well-being. And they were reflective and open about their experiences. Tumbu once remarked that in the past he had been like me and asked questions about what trumba were. People said they were spirits (*lulu*) of dead people, but he wasn't fully convinced. He said, "*ary*" – a word that means, "so they say."

In sum, the book is about cohabitation with spirits as an art or vehicle for living one's life, as Mohedja and Tumbu lived theirs. Turned the other way, the book serves as the portrait of an articulate man and woman, a married couple, who lived in this part of Africa in the twentieth century and whose relationship with each other was enriched, and mediated by, their relationships with the spirits with whom they came to cohabit. This book follows their lives, sometimes peaceful, sometimes troubled, as they recounted them, as they lived them, and as I came to understand them.

Chapter Two

Acknowledging Spirits

What about the beings I have referred to as "spirits"? The spirits in question are conceived in Mayotte and in both neighbouring Madagascar and the Swahili coast as separate, individuated persons. They are not all of a single kind or species, but Kibushy speakers in Mayotte understand them with respect to the generic concept of *lulu*, a Malagasy word, and the concepts of *djinn* and *shetwan*, from Arabic. The main species are *trumba* and *kakanoru*, from Malagasy, and *patros*, from Shimaore, the Bantu language spoken by the majority of citizens of Mayotte. It is significant that the words are drawn from several languages, indicating that they are not fully commensurable with one another. In anthropology they are all referred to as spirits, but they do not fit well with the associations of the word "spirit" or "spirits" in ordinary English, nor with that of "demons," nor with the incommensurable French concepts, *esprits* and *diables*. In fact, no translation of noumenal beings is adequate, and this holds for the words Kibushy borrows from Malagasy and Arabic as well. I note the neutral terms "meta-persons" and "meta-humans," proposed by Sahlins (2017), or "quasi-persons" (Austin 1970), but will stick with "spirits."

More immediately relevant in Mayotte is the specific kind or species of spirit at issue and whether it is one of the kinds that cohabit positively with humans. Ndramboeny and Kos Vola, whom we met in the last chapter, are trumba. Trumba are manifestations of people who were once alive but who, with appropriate treatment at burial, are able to return to visit the living, thereby enjoying a kind of half-life. Many trumba are former Sakalava monarchs and can be identified with actual historical figures. Known as Toakafo when he was alive, Ndramboeny reigned over northwest Madagascar c. 1710–33 (Vérin 1986, 110–11). Kos Vola was a Sakalava princess, possibly a wife of Andriantsoly, and would have lived in the early 1800s. Kalu presents herself in Mayotte as a young child, but she is a former servant or slave of Sakalava royalty. Youthful trumba are sailors who drowned in the employ of the monarchs.

Mze Nuru, Mze Marwan, and Mze Rihu are patros, indigenous inhabitants of Mayotte, living in underwater villages near the shoreline. Their villages tend to be near former sites of human habitation, and they refer in a vague way to the history of the island. Nevertheless, they are understood to be djinn, hence a part of Islamic tradition. As such, they are not deceased humans but beings distinct from humans, albeit parallel to them in some respects. Like trumba, patros have personal identities, are distinguished as male or female, and exist in relations of kinship to one another. Mze Rihu, who rose in Tumbu, is the older brother of Mze Nuru, who cohabited with Mohedja. Patros are different from humans in other ways, notably in their predilection for drinking cologne or, when they have the opportunity, the blood of freshly slaughtered goats. They have Arabic personal names, like djinn found elsewhere in the Muslim world. "Mze" is a Swahili honourific, equivalent to Sir or Mister.

Patros and trumba are therefore quite different in kind and origin, coming from different historical traditions and, one might say, different ontologies. A given person or household may be visited by one or more of each, but they rise on different occasions, by means of different incense and different music. They do not interact or interfere with one another except on rare occasions when their demands conflict. And yet their relationships with humans are similar. There are also other kinds of meta-humans who establish similar relations with humans, some of whom will appear later.

Patros and trumba are both described as lulu, and patros are also spoken of as djinn. Additionally, there are nameless and unindividuated spirits, shetwan, who are simply evil and can make people quarrel or engage in other anti-social activity and sometimes render them mad. An Islamic scholar in the village explained that lulu come from bright flames and shetwan from black smoke. Lulu are made of light and are themselves weightless. Shetwan, he said in a mix of languages, are "kafiry direct," straight unbelievers, associated with the devil (Iblis) and very, very bad. They hang around latrines and other dirty places and can catch you unawares. If one is caught by a shetwan, the state of possession (or simply dissociation) is continuous and the cure is a matter of exorcism, permanent removal of the spirit. Although the word "shetwan" was sometimes used in place of lulu or djinn, shetwan are conceptually different from lulu and are not central to this book, except for one episode in chapter 7.

In coming into presence, the spirits (*lulu*) manifest a taste for life. And they live it to the full, as it were, drinking, eating, dancing, and wearing fine clothes. They are forceful, zesty, assertive, and attentive. They expand the lives of their hosts and enable them to indulge vicariously in a wider range of tastes and actions than might otherwise be available, albeit simultaneously restricting their consumption to a narrower range, by means of what I once translated as "taboos" and now prefer to call restrictions, prohibitions, or interdictions.

Why do I say my translations of "spirits" (*lulu, djinn, shetwan, trumba, patros, kakanoru*, etc.) or "taboos" (*fady*) are inadequate? Simply for the reason that Wittgenstein reproached Frazer (2020). These words do not play the same role in our respective ways of life and the reverberations they have in the lives of most English speakers have little to do with the Kibushy words or concepts. North American readers sometimes first respond to my work by saying how "spiritual" my subjects are. In fact, nothing could be further from the truth when it comes to trumba, patros, and other spirits. People in Mayotte approach the connotations of "spiritual" when performing (through recitation, song, drumming, and dance) sacred Muslim compositions, genres quite apart from most of the spirits I write about here – except for lulu of the Maulida, who rise when their hosts are overcome with the beauty of performance (see chapter 14 and Lambek 1993). Furthermore, there is no neutral word in English into which we can translate these terms because there is no common autonomous object to which they refer (as would be case in the translation of Kibushy *mwaru* or Malagasy *pisu* to "cat"). That the terms are untranslatable into one another is indicated by their diverse sources in Malagasy, Arabic, and Shimaore.

Rather than "spiritual" in some other-worldly (religious, metaphysical, refined, paranormal, etc.) sense, the spirits in question are part of the earthly everydayness of things, intervening in the personal and domestic lives of their hosts. That said, the spirits are also vehicles of imagination, affording the possibility to see one's life from outside, as it were, to contextualize it with respect to the possibility of other lives, of being someone else.

~

From the perspective of the human protagonists, individual spirits choose to develop a relationship with them, after which the host can be said to "have a spirit" (*misy lulu*). This means that the spirit on occasion rises to their head (*manunga an luha*) and speaks and acts through them, effectively displacing them for the duration of their appearance. In these periods, when their own consciousness is displaced, the hosts are *menziky lulu*, subjected to, or impassioned by, the spirit. The anthropological term for this has been "possession." Paul Christopher Johnson (2014b) has queried this usage, linking it to Western concepts of liberalism, slave ownership, and possessive individualism. Nevertheless, in the Malagasy world, the ambiguity concerning who is possessed by whom (the spirit by the host or vice versa) is apt. In fact, *menziky* is a political concept, indicating "ruled by," rather than an economic one.[1] As I noted, Tumbu once described the onset of trance as a "coup d'état."

On another occasion Tumbu explained that spirits are like wind (*tsiku*). A spirit can enter you and pump up your body until you are full, like a bicycle pump. It fills your veins (*huzatra*) and when your body is full you lose your consciousness (*dzery*). It is not the flesh of the spirit that enters you, just its breath or wind. When it leaves, your body deflates. He added that some people keep some awareness but cannot help themselves from giving way to the speech of the spirit. He likened it to people who are drunk and remain conscious but removed from what they are saying. Others speak without consciousness of what they are saying. Tumbu said that he himself sometimes retained some awareness and sometime not, but it was always the spirit who "makes me speak" (*mampivulanga zahu*), that is, speaks through him. If you're stubborn and refuse the spirit's entry, it will bother you. In the past, he concluded, he hadn't fully believed in possession until a spirit forced its way into him.

It is more commonly said of spirits that they sit or reside (*mipetraka*) with someone or within a family, or indeed that they cohabit (*mipetraka mahala raiky* – literally, reside together, in one place).

Both trumba and patros develop personal relations with select humans, relationships that can begin in childhood (long before an individual is actively possessed or even recognizes that a spirit is present) and last until shortly before the death of the host. These relationships between host and spirit are continuous beyond episodes of active possession. For some people who cohabit with spirits, active episodes are extremely rare, possibly even non-existent, and for all hosts, they are circumscribed and occur most often on request made by or through the host, but sometimes spontaneously, especially at ceremonies where many spirits are invited and rise to dance and enjoy themselves in company. Most of the time the presence of the spirit is muted, like a friend or relative whom we think about only periodically but who is in our lives. The spirits are not strictly absent when not manifest; they are not visible most of the time, but they see and hear what their hosts are up to, and they are easily offended. Their proximity is manifest in the observance of their prohibitions.

While much of the fascination for outsiders is what goes on internally during active states of "possession" or "submission," this is in fact something of a black box, since from the perspective of the host, the state is most often one of a loss of ordinary consciousness and subsequent amnesia of what took place. The neurological condition is not my concern. I consider it a form of dissociation, stronger than the ordinary dissociation that happens when we are distracted, captivated by a film, unaware of where we have put the keys, or engrossed in states that psychologist Mihaly Csikszentmihalyi (2008) called flow, when we are so captivated by what we are doing that we are oblivious to what is outside of it, like a mountain climber for whom pausing to look down and wonder what they are doing on that cliff might be fatal. Dissociation is evidently a human capacity, one that in its more radical form some societies draw from to produce meaningful genres of activity. They do so by giving the dissociated state its own life, grammar, and awareness. Anthropologists have called these activities "spirit possession," but such generalization and abstraction can conceal as much as it reveals. No two cultural formations need be alike, not only in their social expression, but in their neurological and psychological dimensions. The San trance dance is unlike the appearance of individuated persons among Malagasy speakers; charismatic, often collective, possession by the Pentecostal Holy Spirit is different again. I am not interested in generalizing about the neurological phenomena so much as in showing what people in one society can make of the capacity for productive dissociation.

Daniel Barenboim says of music (much as Clifford Geertz did) that it only exists in the world when and as it is played. Barenboim says further, "If you are really able to concentrate totally on it, to grab the sound and hold onto it the way you hold onto a rope when you go mountaineering, and if you stay fully attached to the sounds as they develop, as they unfold, you are basically coming out of time. You must be able to do it with all your faculties, physical and psychic, with total concentration. And suddenly, Beethoven's Fifth Symphony takes 33 minutes, and for those 33 minutes you are out of physical reality. Music gives you the physical and metaphysical possibility of totally detaching yourself from the world. As if you were able to fly."[2]

Dissociation broadly understood is even more pervasive and significant than described thus far. Speaking of the human "eternal struggle against both fusion and isolation," psychoanalyst Margaret Mahler writes, "For the more or less normal [sic] adult, the experience of being both fully 'in' and at the same time basically separate from the 'world out there' is among the givens of life that are taken for granted. Consciousness of self and absorption without awareness of self are the two polarities between which we move, with varying ease and with varying degrees of alternation or simultaneity.... As is the case with any intrapsychic process, this one reverberates throughout the life cycle." (Mahler 1986, 223, as cited by Chodorow 1989, 10).

The continuous and embodied aspects of cohabitation can be seen through the responses to the restrictions that spirits place on their hosts. Recall that in the brief conversation with me, one of Mohedja's spirits took time to complain that she was not attending to the dietary restrictions he required. Recognizing and maintaining a given spirit's prohibitions (*fady*) are central to the practice of cohabitation. These prohibitions are salient features of the spirit's identity and a common idiom or register through which to both maintain and express the relationship between host and spirit.

The more spirits with whom you cohabit, the more restrictions. Like most other people cohabiting with trumba, Mohedja could not go to work in her fields on Tuesdays and would fall sick if she did so. Nor could she buy things, open a suitcase, take out money on a Tuesday, or practise any activities involving the trumba. At first, Mohedja said, she refused to obey these prohibitions, but she got sick and so changed her mind.

These restrictions formed one of the primary vehicles through which Mohedja both experienced and recounted her day-to-day relationships with the spirits. Cohabitation manifests both materially and discursively through the maintenance by the host of the restrictions imposed by the spirits. Ignoring the restrictions and suffering for it is a way in which the reality of the spirit's presence is confirmed.

Each kind of spirit has characteristic food and drink that they consume, but this affects the hosts only when they are in trance and replaced by the spirit. For the rest of the time, as they cohabit, relations are marked not by which foods the spirits consume but by which they do not. If there is a food that a given spirit refuses, whether because of the kind of spirit he is or because of his individual history, then the host must also refrain from it. If the host does not, the spirit gets angry, and the host falls sick. This has several implications. First, insofar as spirit and host share the prohibition, the fact of their cohabitation is emphasized and there is even a suggestion of their unity or identification with one another, that they "operate as a singular body" (Bamford 2007, 101).[3] But second, insofar as the host falls sick when she ignores the prohibitions – which she may do out of ignorance, or in order to experiment to see if the restrictions are truly necessary, or perhaps simply because she is desirous of the food in question, or because she fails to pay sufficient attention – this signifies the difference or separation between spirit and host insofar as it is the former who punishes the latter.

In short, where common observance signifies respectful cohabitation and a sharing of the same body, ignoring the restriction marks the separateness of their identities and the conflict between them, or even the harm imposed on the host by the impatient or demanding spirit. In the course of living together, host and spirit come to take on each other's interests – the host absorbing the spirit's restrictions and the spirit taking on the host's personal and domestic concerns – such that they come to have more and more in common. The prohibitions not only signify and enact cohabitation, and are sometimes the only signs of the spirit's continuous presence, but they also indicate the bond between them, the quality of the relationship at a given time, and the consideration the parties show each other.

This tension between difference and commonality, or even identification, is central to life with spirits in Mayotte. It encompasses some of the tension I will describe between the local model of spirits as autonomous beings and a model that sees a spirit's presence, acts, and statements as products of the host's creativity and motivations. This tension is condensed in the way that prohibitions and their transgressions are manifest, but it will be expressed in much more elaborated fashion over the course of the book.

Restrictions also mark the identities of the individual trumba. Each trumba has his own food prohibitions and day of the week when activities are restricted. In Madagascar these are explicitly linked to the day on which the historical person who became a trumba died and the food he ate that might have poisoned him. A person cohabiting with several spirits might have several days when they cannot accomplish certain tasks and so might have to bargain with the spirits to reduce the number.

Restrictions also mark status distinctions among the trumba themselves. In general, the higher the status of a given trumba, the more the restrictions. No one hosting a senior trumba can eat chicken and each individual spirit adds restrictions of his own. Mohedja's youthful male trumba (*changizy*) rejects only one species each of shellfish and fish. These are minimal restrictions. The child trumba, former servants or slaves in Madagascar, are marked precisely by an absence of restrictions, a sign of their lack of status or ancestry. Mohedja said that as far as she knew, her child spirit, Kalu, had no restrictions at all – at least, for as long as they had been cohabiting, Kalu had never asked to observe any. In Madagascar this would indicate someone of slave background who didn't know or couldn't acknowledge their ancestry and likewise someone less concerned with purity. In sharp contrast to the senior spirits, the child spirits indulge in chicken. As a host to senior trumba, Mohedja could not eat chicken without getting sick. But when she was actively possessed by Kalu, chicken was precisely what she did eat – and with relish, gluttony, and no ill effects.

All hosts to senior trumba must restrict their activity on Tuesdays. But labour restrictions encompass a broader range. In the past there was a prohibition across Mayotte against cultivating rice fields on Wednesdays, indicating everyone's deep connection to the land and obligation to maintaining its fertility. During my fieldwork few people maintained this restriction, but they did keep to an Islamic injunction against cultivation on Fridays, enabling them to attend the Friday noon prayer. Both the Wednesday and Friday prohibitions were solely against the cultivation of rice and not against other crops. Tumbu explained that this was because only rice was used in Muslim sacrificial meals.

While restrictions were imposed by the spirits and every host of a given spirit in principle maintained the same restrictions, each host also personalized her response, according to how stringently she observed them, how she responded to transgressing them, whether she managed to reach a compromise with the spirit, or how far she elaborated their significance.

Some trumba would not let their hosts even raise chickens to lay eggs. Mohedja said she refused to believe this and had kept a laying hen. For three months she was sick, and the eggs were no good. Then the hen died and she herself had to be washed in medicine before she got well. Since then, she accepted the prohibition. In 1985, one of Mohedja's daughters observed that her mother's trumba didn't permit Mohedja even to close the hen house in the evenings. Nor could she let chickens stray into her own house, sweep up chicken or goat manure, or raise kittens. This had to do with avoiding what is unclean. Mohedja herself explained she could not raise kittens because they defecate in the house. However, the deleterious effects of ignoring these restrictions rebounded not on Mohedja alone, but also on the animals. If she raised kittens or goats or chickens, they wouldn't flourish (*havy tsy manzary*). Thus the children looked after the animals and had to do all the sweeping. The only animal let into the house was the adult cat.

The principle behind this operated just as well for people who were not cohabiting with spirits. Experience showed what they could not eat or do. Mohedja observed that when Tumbu first gave their son Ali primary responsibility for looking after their cattle, the animals got sick. Tumbu asked Mohedja's patros whether the cause was sorcery against them, but Mze Nuru said no, that Ali simply couldn't raise livestock. The goats he attempted to look after also became sick. It was not that he didn't know how to look after them but that it simply didn't work out. Mohedja thought it was probably due to an incompatible astrological destiny (*nyora*). In fact, as Tumbu aged, Ali did successfully take over responsibility for the cattle.

The prohibition against consuming chicken was one of the strongest restrictions facing those who cohabited with senior trumba and one that admitted no compromise. Mohedja felt sick just dishing out a meal of chicken prepared for men who were uttering a prayer over the household. She attributed her malaise the next day to the trumba's anger. People with many restrictions, especially those concerning meat, suffered, said Mohedja. In the past she used to long for chicken, but eventually she was no longer tempted when she saw others enjoying it.

In 1976, Mohedja insisted that she was unable to keep her trumba's prohibition against eating from the same plate as small children. At first it made her very sick. She would drink a little cologne (*marash*) with white clay (*tany futsy*) as purification and would then feel better. She became more used to it and no longer felt sick. But hot pepper (*pilypily*) continued to make her ill, although it had not done so before she began cohabiting with the trumba.

In the 1980s, Mohedja acquired a new trumba who had a restriction against goats. Her repeated entanglements with spirits not only negatively limited her diet but positively decreased her domestic labour. The restrictions reinforced her connections with family members, notably their care, as they looked after the goats and kept them away from her. What is critical is cohabitation not only with spirits, but with human others.

Cohabitating with spirits could be taken as a form of life in Wittgenstein's sense. As philosopher Juliet Floyd (2020, 126) observes, *Lebensformen* "are not exactly objects of description but fields of philosophical exploration." This book is first of all a work of description, but it is also implicitly a philosophical exploration, raising questions of what it means to be more than one, to take that up seriously and explicitly, but also with irony – irony in the philosophical senses of acknowledging "both/and" and of knowing that one does not (fully) know. In the remainder of this chapter, I confront some of these issues before turning to a more purely descriptive account.

The issues are simultaneously psychological ones. I take up a psychoanalytic perspective in the postscript. Here I will say only that the personality and degree of inner conflict and psychological maturity of a given host shape how she accepts and cohabits with spirits. Not everyone has the means to safely articulate more than one persona. Conversely, I suggest that cohabiting can generate internal growth. Accepting the active presence of spirits in one's life provides a set of affordances comparable not only to performing as an actor or writing fiction, but also to participating in long-term psychotherapy.[4] Cohabitation has implications for becoming the person one is and being the person one has become, for oneself and with others. And if philosophy and psychoanalysis offer insights into cohabitation, so cohabitation might in turn offer insights to these traditions of thought.

Thinking about possession as continuous cohabitation rather than exclusively as episodic dramatic performance shifts the weight somewhat away from the question of who is "really" acting or speaking. It is as though an actor lives with her character off-stage as well as on, the writer with his character within the novel and outside it. One can say cohabitation enables people to live alongside themselves, to speak as distinct persons, in distinct voices, and thereby cohabit with themselves. Spirits are formally invited into hosts on specific occasions and hosts give way to spirits, but the relations between hosts and spirits are more porous than this suggests; spirits are somehow always (already and thereafter) a part of their hosts, though it is far less clear that the hosts are somehow always a part of the spirits, who visit and cohabit with other hosts elsewhere. In other words, the difference or separation between humans and spirits is simultaneously explicitly established and implicitly transcended. The spirit speaking and acting through my body is simultaneously me and not me – or rather, simultaneously not-me and not-not-me.[5] But contrary to how it might appear, the separation that is maintained inside the frame is transcended outside it; that is to say, if the presence of the spirit is manifest during the performance of possession and thus marked in distinction to the absent human host, then outside of the performance frame, when the host has returned to herself, the spirit remains latent. It is always possible that the agent behind my acts or condition is not me but the spirit. Such possible recursion is an aspect of the ambiguous quality of spirit cohabitation.

People in Mayotte do not set out consciously to cohabit with spirits or become possessed and they may try to ignore the signs and fight against it. It may take time to learn that they are cohabiting with a spirit and to acknowledge that fact. Once they do accept the presence of spirits in their lives, they negotiate with them so that the situation is livable for each side. The presence of the spirit is fully realized through the sequence of curing rituals during which the spirit, host, host's family, and the public acknowledge one other and acknowledge the relationship that has been established. When in active possession, the host temporarily gives up her voice and agency to that of the spirit. But in a complementary description, another reading, can one say that this ostensibly different voice is another inflection contributing to the host's voice and agency overall? If the spirit's demand is ultimately "Acknowledge *me!*" who is that "me" in question?

Just as possession entails the ostensible paradox of speaking in or with more than one voice, as host and as spirit, as me and as not-me – who is, perhaps, not-not-me – so too writing about it as an anthropologist requires at least two voices: taking it as it is and as my subjects experience it, understanding it, speaking of the spirits as autonomous beings, fully distinct from their hosts; and yet also stepping back and interpreting the spirits as human constructions and their voices as inflections of their hosts. Neither description would be valid on its own; both are necessary.

People have often asked me – both in Mayotte and Madagascar and at home – whether I "believe" in spirits. This is actually two questions (at least): whether I take them as ontologically real, that is, as existing autonomously from human thought about them; and whether I take the performances of possession as sincere. But framing the question as one of belief is unhelpful. Spirits are evidently real when they are right in front of you, asserting their presence. They are socially real, and in that sense no different from other features of the social world.[6] The performances are as sincere (or not) as those of piety or gender, parenting, or friendship. The issue is not one of belief but one of acknowledgment (Cavell 1996).

It is a question of acknowledging the presence of the spirits and their call upon us, but also their force and scope. The latter terms are drawn from a distinction made by Geertz: "By 'force' I mean the thoroughness with which ... a pattern is internalized in the personalities of the individuals who adopt it, its centrality or marginality in their lives.... By 'scope,' on the other hand, I mean the range of social contexts within which religious considerations are regarded as having more or less direct relevance."[7] This book attends to the presence and call, and the

force and scope, that spirits have in the lives of their human cohabitants, albeit stronger in some than in others.[8]

I write of the spirits as autonomous beings, beings who choose to
cohabit with people or not, who enter them calmly or violently, and
who remain stubbornly silent or speak their own mind. This is how
people in Mayotte describe them. One cannot understand anything
about how people cohabit with spirits or what their significance is if
one does not accept their social reality. However, I simultaneously take
a second position and understand their speech and action as humanly
motivated, refractions of their hosts and creative appropriations of
their character.

In the past I have been accused of naive New Ageism for the former
position and what one anonymous referee, well before the so-called
ontological turn in anthropology, memorably called "ontological imperialism," for the latter position. My response to the former critics is
to argue for the significance of a hermeneutic position, as laid out in
philosophy by Hans-Georg Gadamer and in anthropology by Clifford
Geertz. Geertz famously illustrated his point by means of the difference between involuntary twitches and meaningful winks (1973). My
response to the latter critics is also to take a hermeneutic position; I can
only interpret foreign actions by the terms available in my own (expanding) world. Were I not to do so I would leave the practices incompre-
hensible, thin, or mysterious at best, and I would also be indulging
romantic and exoticist fantasy. Instead of acknowledging and respect-
ing the difference or distance between their world and mine, I would
be exaggerating and mystifying it. Speaking more broadly, one could
underline, with Dipesh Chakrabarty (2000), the importance of maintaining both enchanted and disenchanted modes of understanding.

I hope the presence of both ways of looking at things does not con-
fuse the narrative. The very concept of thickness, as drawn by Geertz
from Gilbert Ryle, acknowledges that in any human action many things
are going on at once. In the language of Ryle's contemporary, Elizabeth
Anscombe (1963), one and the same action can be put under multiple
descriptions: a man who is moving his arm up and down can be said to
be pumping water, but should that water contain something harmful,
he is simultaneously poisoning the household. Each description under
which we put the action may be valid, and each has its uses. Questions
of intentionality or agency enter each description differently.

Putting an act or event under more than one description need not
imply that the one falsifies the other, as when we describe someone
simultaneously as moving his mouth and vocal cords, applying the
rules of grammar, speaking, asserting confidently that it is raining,

lying about that, and so forth. Actors themselves might put their actions under multiple descriptions.

Ryle and Geertz's wink offers a particularly apt comparison with active possession by a spirit. We see the human face and the performance, hear the words, but there is ambiguity between the message and the meta-message. It is as if the speaker or actor is putting his or her own actions under more than one description, more and less ostensible. What is critical is the plurality and delicate orchestration of voice. It is as if the actor or speaker is offering a commentary on the act or message at the same time as they are carrying it out – as if the speaker were simultaneously winking. The act or message is sincere, but simultaneously, the gap or contrast between the message and the meta-message ("this is not me speaking"), and the meta-meta-message ("perhaps it is not not-me speaking either"), is one of irony. Possession, one could say, affords a unique means of delivery that is simultaneously sincere and ironic. At least, this is how I have received it.[9]

As an anthropologist, I begin with the descriptions under which the people I converse with put their actions. Indeed, I try to record them "in the act" of putting specific acts under description. Acts can be placed under description by speakers, by their recipients, and by neutral observers. One explicit way that actors do so is by means of performative utterances, as described by J.L. Austin, in such phrases as "I promise," "I apologize," and so forth. But one can also put one's acts under description in more subtle fashion, by means of meta-messages that can elaborate, reinforce, complicate, undermine, or contradict the message or act itself.

The descriptions under which people put their acts are deeply interesting in their own right. At the same time, and without rendering those descriptions invalid, I sometimes add additional levels of description that might, of necessity, be invisible to the immediate participants, similar to how we are not conscious of using grammar as we speak. So, for example, I draw on Austin's account of the illocutionary function of speaking, in which to say something is to do something; this is sometimes explicit and evident to speakers, as when they utter an oath or a promise, but not always so. Sometimes the illocutionary force is hidden or mystified such that what is a product of human action is perceived to be natural or carried out beyond human agency. The converse is also possible, such that what is beyond human agency is claimed to be the product of an intentional human act.

The judgment as to under what description to place a given act can be an ethical one (that is to say, it can be put under a further description as "ethical"). Was a positive remark a compliment or flattery? Was the failure to greet me an act of absent-mindedness or a deliberate slight? Was the boss's invitation, to a new employee, for a drink after work a friendly outreach or potential harassment? I consider ethnographic writing no less subject to ethical judgment than it is to aesthetic or intellectual judgment, and the ethics lies in just this: exercising judgment over the kind of descriptions acts and persons are placed under and establishing a careful balance between different levels of description.

The description under which I place the relationship between spirits and humans in Mayotte is evidently one of cohabitation in addition to possession or subjection. Cohabitation is about living together. It is about daily life, ordinary life. The chapters that follow recount episodes from the lives of spirit mediums in Mayotte. Cohabitation with spirits is not the only aspect of the lives described, but the narrative shows the presence of spirits within ordinary life – making a living, raising children, getting along or quarrelling with one another. Indeed, the spirits who cohabit are fully part of ordinary life. Their presence elaborates, sometimes complicates, and sometimes simplifies social relationships. Spirits manifest pain but also joy and security.

This account thus departs from most work on spirit possession by focusing on its ordinariness – that is, locating it in the ordinary, in the everyday world of its practitioners. Episodes of possession can be dramatic, and spirits can be disruptive and disconcerting, but in whatever ontological position we place them, spirits speak to the real, to what is in front of them.

To speak of the ordinary is not to discount the uncanny. As a form of life, cohabitation in Mayotte is an ordinary way of making things strange, or of acknowledging strangeness, but equally of reabsorbing the alien into the familiar. Cohabitation manifests both the *Heimlich* and the *Unheimlich*. The latter is often translated as "the uncanny" but could also be "unease." Ease, unease, and disease readily dissolve into or refract and recall one another.[10]

Moreover, as Veena Das emphasizes, the ordinary is constituted by doubt and despair, as well as by habit, common sense, self-assurance, and happiness. The intercession of spirits exposes and acknowledges human vulnerability and subjection and yet simultaneously offers repair and partial transcendence. Das (2020) writes of the "texture of life," in which modes of experience and attention are interwoven with one another. Students of Das, like Bhrigupati Singh (2015) and Marco

Motta (2019), provide a more active metaphor, speaking of rhythm and intensity, the pulse, tempo, and vibrancy of life. Spirits certainly heighten this.

As an account of the lives of Tumbu and Mohedja, this is also partly an account of my life, as I too cohabited with them and with their cohabiting spirits for a time and they have lived alongside me, even when I was not in Mayotte, in my memory and imagination, much as the spirits suggested they would. They are all – Tumbu and Mohedja, Mze Nuru and Mze Marwan – present in my life.

I do not see this world with spirits as an ontology radically distinct from the naturalistic one that I inhabit. Ontology is slippery. Spirits are conceived in Mayotte as exotic beings, different from living humans. When they manifest, they are visibly – powerfully – other than human, but no less in the world. Anthropologists might say they are meta-humans, meta-persons, or even simply beings, or meta-beings. But if they are extraordinary beings, they come to play a role in ordinary life, in the ordinary lives of people who cohabit with them. Over the course of what could be called a "cure" or an "initiation" – which is a stabiliza-tion and public recognition of the identity of a given spirit in relation to a given host – one of the things that happens is a partial socializa-tion of the spirit, such that the spirit comes to acknowledge the human concerns of the host and often becomes a friend, mentor, or ally. At the same time, the host recognizes the otherness, power, and unpredictabil-ity of the spirit.[11] Life continues, now in the company of this ambiguous other.

My position is not one of pointing to radical ontological differ-ence. I accept the social reality of the spirits and their cohabitation with humans. In greeting the spirits, I was acknowledging their exis-tence, their reality. In Wittgenstein's terms, I participated in the form of life and the language games of my subjects. I can step outside these games as well – not to a position of neutrality, outside the world of human activity and imagination, but into other games, like the game of anthropology.

In this way I shift between proximity with my subjects and dis-tance from them. But I must add that one of the first lessons I gained was how, by means of the spirits, Mohedja and Tumbu brought me into closer proximity, offering a kind of intimacy. This was a risk on their part and a gift. They pressed me to ask myself whether I could acknowledge these voices and what it would mean to hear them and to respond to them as distinct persons and yet as persons closely attached to the humans I knew directly. Acknowledgment of the spirits enabled us to grow closer and understand each other better than we might have otherwise. The spirits opened a common world rather than indexing a radically different one.[12] One can learn to cohabit with spirits as much as one can with difficult human guests (like anthropologists), and one can learn to appreciate spirits as much as one can learn to appreciate a new or foreign art form.

That their alterity is not so radical is found too in the modality of appreciating life that I call "irony." More often the distinction is made between belief or knowledge and disbelief or scepticism. I phrase the issue less as one of scepticism than as one of irony – a tacit, never spoken sense that the spirits with whom "I" cohabit might not be beings fully distinct from me and that, after all, they speak with my voice, or rather, with one of my voices, or perhaps I sometimes speak in their voice. This irony is not the kind we associate with sarcasm but of acknowledging unknowability.

Here is another way to put these matters. Having acknowledged that much of the action concerning spirits is shaped by cultural models and scenarios, themselves located within a wider field of incommensurable discourses, it remains to understand the deep personal investment that some people have in cohabitation, what it means for them, with what (tacit or preconscious) motivations they approach the cultural characters and scenarios, and what they receive from them, what the characters and texts return to subjectivity. In sum, it remains to develop a dialectical understanding of the relationship between objectification and subjectification, to grasp the movement between the cultural models and the participants' subjectivity, and how each contributes to the other.[13] This is a matter of how hosts bring their experience, interests, and motivations to bear in receiving and performing as spirits, and the ways in which such practice reverberates on their subjectivity. Cultural models do not exist in some neutral space, but only insofar as they are lived out subjectively, always in the process of becoming objective, always in the process of becoming subjective.

What I explore in this book is the way practice is subjectively informed and likewise how, through practice, subjectivity is transformed. I understand living as a relational activity in which the self is formed always in relation to others, others who in Mayotte include cohabiting spirits. Cohabitation is shaped by and contributes to relational issues prevalent in the lives of its subjects, issues whose meanings move across the spectrum from the unconscious to the conscious and from the intersubjective to the interpersonal. And insofar as living is relational, so it has an ethical dimension. Although agency often appears concealed or even denied, cohabitation and manifest possession are "passive actions" that entail the exercise of practical wisdom with respect to oneself and others.

This is not to discount what I have described in earlier work (Lambek 1981) as possession's amoral quality. The spirits are sometimes presented as stupendously – heroically – amoral, ready for anything. The spirit who blesses you may also be chuckling about eating your liver. The spirit who serves as the dispassionate healer one minute is reeling drunkenly across the dance floor the next. This Dionysian aspect of possession is one of its most appealing qualities, one of the things that make it so much fun to perform and to watch, and at the same time, fundamentally disconcerting. It adds humour, pathos, suspense, and violence to the picture. But how does this jibe with the argument I make in this book?

The key lies, I think, in the fact that cohabitation works at more than one level. At one level, it is a series of performances in which the spirits come together to celebrate, carouse, and acknowledge one another, manifesting themselves as distinct from humans and sometimes provoking them. Here the delicious and possibly disturbing amorality of the spirits is front and centre. But at another level, it is not "mere" performance but reality – it is the thing that the performance is about. That is to say, it operates directly at the level of the selfhood and relationships of the hosts. It is their selfhood, refractions of it, at work and at issue in the practice of the hosts. People active in possession are at one level enacting a cultural performance; but at another level, the enactment is part of who they are. An actress performs specific roles and we do not, usually, mistake her for the characters. But we would not deny that she is an actress and that an account of her life and her selfhood must include the fact of her performing as one. (The same holds for an anthropologist, or a professor.) Possession is self-constitutive. And here I think that the frank exploration of the amoral, or rather the taking on of an amoral attitude, may be precisely an avenue with which to build character: not to build morality understood in the sense in which Nietzsche despised it, as adherence to an imposed code or norm, but character as acting with integrity and insight in acknowledgment of alternatives. This is an ethical understanding that is perspectival rather than absolutist. The spirits offer a means of understanding the world through an amoral (not immoral!) perspective and through accepting one's own desires and ambivalence. Such working through is accomplished here (to the degree that it is accomplished) via the mimesis of spirit possession as well as by means of talk, somewhat akin to psychoanalysis.

Chapter Three

Tumbu: The Search for Livelihood and Land

I began thinking about this book several decades ago. In 1992, I sat down with Mohedja and Tumbu separately, as well as with two younger, unrelated hosts, and asked each of them to tell me about their lives. They were each rather nonplussed at the question, in part because I did not know how to phrase it well.

I gave little direction and what they each understood me to ask about was quite illuminating. Mohedja focused on her reproductive history, beginning with a list of her births, naming the living children but also noting the ones who had died. She then recounted marrying off her daughters and circumcising her sons, the achievements of social reproduction expected of all adults in Mayotte. I'll describe this in chapter 9. Tumbu focused on how he secured the family's livelihood. Throughout his adulthood, Tumbu was preoccupied with acquiring land, both on which to reside securely and on which to cultivate subsistence and cash crops and raise a few cattle, as well as to pass on to their children.

Despite differences in emphasis, Mohedja and Tumbu each independently recounted how they had gone through life together, cooperating on their joint projects, domestic and economic. Mohedja was part of Tumbu's narrative about the purchase of fields and the growing of crops, and Tumbu was part of Mohedja's story about raising their children to social adulthood and becoming grandparents who could choose how much to assist their children in producing the ceremonies of social reproduction for their grandchildren. Both were talking about social reproduction, about building something and building it together.

In 1992, Tumbu spoke with satisfaction about the various ways he had made his living, how he and Mohedja had made a good marriage, and how, as a result of hard work and God's help, they had built a rich life together. Since his recent return from a pilgrimage to Mecca, he was tired and had decided to retire, passing on the responsibility for his fields and cattle to his son Ali and anticipating that the resources would be shared among all his children upon his death.

I begin with an account of Tumbu's life, drawing from both what he said on tape and what I learned in other contexts. The narrative here is chronological; in later chapters I delve into specific events.

When in 1975 I first moved into the village of Lombeni Kely, Tumbu and Mohedja appeared well established and secure. Not only did Tumbu hold the position of *chef de village*, which was why I was directed to him in the first place, but as both his mother and Mohedja's mother lived in the village, I assumed they had each spent their entire lives there. It took time to correct these assumptions.

While some villages in Mayotte dated back several centuries to when Mayotte was a small sultanate within the greater Swahili maritime world, others were the product of late-nineteenth or early twentieth-century migration from various parts of coastal Madagascar, and others again, like Lombeni, were a product of the gradual dismantling of the large plantations that had begun with French occupation in 1841. There had been slavery during the precolonial era and the plantation system subsequently drew on captured and coerced labour from the East African coast. Much of the land was assigned the property of French and Réunionnais colonists, but as the sugar economy failed and many owners sought to leave, they sold off their large tracts of land in pieces to former employees where they could subsist for themselves. Some people banded together in small groups of friends or acquaintances to collect sufficient money to buy property and it was associations (*sociés*) like these that formed the nuclei of both Lombeni Kely and Lombeni Be. The original members of the associations were not necessarily one another's kin though they often became so through marriage in subsequent generations. Rights to ownership were passed on bilaterally. Village residents were thus either owners or people affiliated with the owners and their descendants by kinship, marriage, or friendship, who were granted permission to reside there. Tumbu and Mohedja were each well connected by kinship and extremely active in village affairs, but in 1975 neither of them had the status of owners. Mohedja had ownership status through her father in her village of birth, a long day's walk distant, while Tumbu had ownership status nowhere.

Tumbu's father, Vita, had been a migrant from the island of Mwali. He was briefly married to Tumbu's mother, Nuriaty, in Lombeni Kely, and they had two sons together, Saidu and Tumbu. Vita and Nuriaty divorced when Tumbu was an infant. Vita declared that he did not want his ex-wife raising his son, so Tumbu was passed on to Nuriaty's mother, Amina, who looked after him in an adjacent settlement a few minutes' walk away. Amina's parents had been born in East Africa (Mrima) or of East African parents and Tumbu recalled that Amina spoke an African language as well as Kibushy. Neither Amina nor Nuriaty's father, also of African background, were village owners. After divorcing Nuriaty's father, Amina remarried and had several children together with Seleman, a man also of African descent but who was one of the original purchasers of Lombeni Kely. They too divorced before Tumbu was born. So Tumbu grew up among maternal kin, some of whom – half-siblings of his mother, and their children – were owners in Lombeni Kely, and some of whom, like Tumbu, were not. In the time I knew them, Tumbu's mother's half-brother was the leading owner and most authoritative figure in Lombeni Kely. He and Tumbu had a slightly uneasy relationship, while his adult children were rather aloof and unfriendly. One of Tumbu's goals was to become independent of them and an owner in his own right.

By 1980, he and Mohedja had purchased a small piece of land contiguous to the inhabited portion of Lombeni Kely from the descendant of an unrelated original owner who had moved elsewhere. Henceforward they could consider themselves owners, fully at home. This was a major turning point for them and was why the initiation of the construction of their new house was a major issue and needed to be confirmed in triplicate, as it were (as described in chapter 1). The new house, on a plot carved from the steep hillside by Tumbu and constructed by him over the following year, was more substantial than anything they had lived in previously. It had two rooms on a cement base that extended to a large veranda with a corrugated metal roof. But most importantly, it was on land from which no one could remove them. They intended to live there for the duration of their lives together and in fact did so. Mohedja died suddenly on the veranda in 2004 and Tumbu a few months later. Adjacent to their house and on the hillside above it, Tumbu built houses for several of their daughters, forming a new quarter of the village.

Youth

Tumbu's mother's ascendants, and I assume his father's, came from East Africa. Tumbu's mother, Dady (Granny) Nuriaty, spoke a bit of an East African language she called KiMrima (possibly Makoa), and she occasionally prepared a thick yam porridge that was an African dish not part of local cuisine. Dady Nuriaty once told me what her father's father had told her about Mrima: people were enticed onto boats by the French with offers of sugar or drinks and then taken to Mayotte. In Mayotte her grandfather married a woman from near his original home. He had a lunar-shaped incision on his forehead and a pierced septum, and he worked as a mason.

Tumbu was raised by his grandmother, Amina. He depicted Amina as tall, strong, and an extremely hard worker, cultivating her own rice fields and as active and outspoken as a man. She made Tumbu work hard too and expected him to do much of the cooking, as she was raising no daughters or granddaughters. She was mean-tempered (*mashiaka*) and everyone was afraid of her. He did not suffer for food or clothing, but he had to work. Tumbu gratefully attributed to her his own work ethic. Their village was small and finally disappeared during the powerful cyclone Disseli (in 1934), whereupon Tumbu and his grandmother moved up the ridge to Lombeni Kely. Tumbu had many maternal kin in Lombeni Kely but no paternal kin, with the exception of his older brother, Saidu, and a younger half-brother in Lombeni Be. Tumbu saw little of his father growing up. Nor were spirits a significant part of his youth. Amina cohabited with two trumba, one of whom was subsequently hosted by her daughter, Dady Nuriaty's younger half-sister. Tumbu's mother's father also hosted a spirit. But Tumbu's mother, who lived to a ripe old age, dying in the early 1980s, never did. Nor did Saidu or any of Tumbu's half-siblings. Tumbu therefore attributed the presence of spirits in his own life not to family inheritance (*mwaratha*), as was the case for many hosts, but rather to his astrological destiny (*nyora*).

Tumbu attended Koranic school in Lombeni Kely until he had memorized the Qur'an. He quit his studies when, as he put it, he reached working age and his grandmother "could no longer afford to dress me." Tumbu was ashamed and tired of being hit and shouted at by her. He sold a large black goat to pay his Koranic teacher and also gave him a bottle of cologne. The teacher in turn held a *shijabu*, a small blessing ritual for him. Tumbu then moved to the semi-urbanized coastal strip (*Aranta*), some distance from Lombeni, where he worked as a servant – a "*boy*," Tumbu said – for two years for an Anjouanais official and then five years for a Frenchman. In truth, Tumbu was still a boy himself, in early adolescence. He shared a bachelor's house with another youth and ate sometimes at his employer's and sometimes at the house of a mother's brother (*zama*) who had married nearby. Tumbu was comfortable with his aunt by marriage (*zena*) and continued eating there once she and his uncle separated, giving her money and helping her cultivate. She was very kind to him. By 1942, when the English arrived to replace the Vichy French regime, Tumbu said he was already a man.

During World War II, local men were being drafted into the army and once Tumbu turned sixteen, he too was draftable. Having heard horror stories about the war, Tumbu did not wish to go. In some consternation, he called up a trumba hosted by an elderly woman in town to ask for assistance. The trumba advised him to rub chili pepper in his eyes immediately before the army medical exam and this worked to grant him an exemption.

He subsequently followed an employer to the neighbouring island of Anjouan (Nzwani) where, after a year, he struck out on his own. He worked as a pedlar, hiking the mountainous island with a friend. When the police stopped and challenged them for selling without a permit and their wholesaler refused to purchase one for them, and moreover didn't pay him fairly, Tumbu took a job in public works, then as an orderly. After a certain time, his mother's brother, who had moved to Diego Suarez (Antsiranana, northern Madagascar), sent him the fare to join him but insisted Tumbu travel via Mayotte to see his family first. Tumbu was ashamed to visit home at the time because he had nothing to show for his ventures. His uncle said, in that case, to return the fare, but Tumbu had already spent it. After that, Tumbu began to save, supplementing his salary by working weekends in house construction, and he purchased clothing with which he could return home proudly. He also sent money home, which his older brother used to purchase a cow for him, which Tumbu later used in his wedding to Mohedja. After three and a half years in Anjouan, Tumbu fell sick and realized it was time to go home. He waited for his last paycheck and then set sail by dhow (*butry*).

Arriving back in Lombeni Kely, Tumbu immediately thought to leave again, this time to join his mother's brother in Diego. But Tumbu's mother, Dady Nuriaty, made a fuss. She said his younger half-brother was already married and had a child, and that he should settle down too. She engaged him to Mohedja, and he became agreeable (*malemy*). They married and started having children, Tumbu explained, so he never had the opportunity to go to Madagascar (*Bushin*). In the event, it was his older full brother, Saidu, who went to Diego a few years later and stayed there.

Marriage

Mohedja's background was quite different, of Malagasy ancestry on both sides, and not descended from African indentured labourers. She once said that both parents came from Antalaotra stock (a term for Islamicized Malagasy seafarers). Mohedja's mother was one of three sisters who had agreed to leave the established village in which they were born and where they had rights as owners, to marry men from Lombeni. This was counter to the pattern that became common of men marrying into their wives' villages. The eldest sister was married for a time to the same Seleman to whom Tumbu's grandmother had been married and they had a daughter, considerably older than Mohedja, who resided in Lombeni Kely. This daughter, whom Mohedja called "older sibling" (zuky), and her children had ownership status there.

Mohedja's mother, known by the teknonym Rae Samba (mother of Samba), had spent some years with her sisters in Lombeni, but for most of her adult life she was married to a succession of four men in F—. Sometime after Mohedja reached menarche (which happened at age fifteen, she told me), Rae Samba and her last husband separated and Rae Samba took herself and her two younger children to Lombeni Kely.

And so it was in Lombeni Kely, around 1948, that Tumbu and Mohedja, each newly arrived in the community, met and very soon were engaged and married. Mohedja would have been around eighteen and Tumbu perhaps twenty-three. He estimated he had spent some ten years away. The match was agreed upon before Tumbu even had the time to purchase clothes and jewellery for the bride, as was expected. He gave Rae Samba 300 CFA francs, which in those days was considered a lot of money and perhaps more than the village had ever seen spent on a wedding before. Rae Samba in turn slaughtered a goat and a cow. Tumbu gave Mohedja a few pieces of silver jewellery; this was a time before people gave gold.

Tumbu and Mohedja barely knew each other. Mohedja was older than most girls to marry. Unlike many, she was permitted by her mother to choose her husband, or at least to reject men who displeased her, of which there were several suitors. Tumbu said Mohedja was happy to marry him and did not tell him until much later that she had been in love with a previous fiancé in F— and had suffered much grief when the engagement was abruptly broken off by the young man's father. Thus, as will become more apparent later, Mohedja's emotions at the time were quite complicated and the union was not assured of success. Nevertheless, unlike most marriages in Mayotte, it did not break up but proved happy and long-lasting. They got along well, respected each other, and thought alike on most issues. As their son Ali once said to me, his parents had a lot of luck (bahaty) in their marriage. But, of course, there was a more to it than luck. In fact, the marriage survived much bad luck, including infant deaths and serious illness on the part

of both husband and wife. But there was good will, effort, and cooperation on both parts. Moreover, Tumbu and Mohedja were not alone but
came to cohabit with a series of spirits who joined them and strength-
ened the marriage.

The first thing any household needs is to achieve a livelihood and,
beyond that, to acquire some economic security. Beginning with no
land of their own, the couple worked extremely hard and planned carefully until, by the time I first met them, they had acquired property and
were gaining an income from cash crops, notably ylang ylang, which,
at the time, was quite remunerative if you had the land and put in the
labour.

A decade later, in 1985, they could look with satisfaction at their
achievements. They had by the standards of the time (subsequently to
change radically) a solid two-room house, with a shaded terrace, plas-
tered walls, and metal roof, on their own piece of land. Tumbu had also
completed the house of his brother Saidu's daughter, a young woman
who had been raised by Tumbu's mother ever since she had fetched
the girl from Madagascar. After the cyclone Hamisy the French government gave 200 francs to everyone whose roof was blown off and 2,000
francs to everyone whose walls had fallen in. Tumbu's niece asked for
reimbursement since her grandmother's house had been destroyed.
With the allotment, Tumbu bought tin roofing quickly, before the
money could be used up on food, he said. Sometime after, he built the
house. That left him with one last daughter to build for.

Back in 1948, circumstances were different. The couple engaged in
subsistence cultivation of dry rice on land about an hour's walk from
Lombeni that was owned by one of the remaining French plantations.
Tumbu also raised a few cattle there and cut timber into boards for
a modest remuneration. They built a two-room house of raffia palm
(*mavañaty*) in Lombeni Kely, adjacent to that of Mohedja's older classificatory sister, who was an owner. Some years they lived on their fields
during the growing season, returning to the village for the rest of the
time. The cattle flourished under Tumbu's care and at one point he had
as many as fifteen. They had sheep and goats, ducks in a duck pond,
and as many as thirty or forty chickens.

Mohedja gave birth to four children during this time: first Nuriaty,
then Mariam, then two sons who each died in childhood. This was also
the period during which several spirits arrived and made them sick,

but they began cultivating relations and learning to live with them. Kos Vola, a senior female trumba, had already joined Mohedja before her marriage. Botu Changizy, a young male trumba first rose in Mohedja while she was pregnant with Nuriaty. Mze Nuru, the senior patros, had joined Mohedja at their marriage, she told me later, but he first rose only some months after Nuriaty was born. They held his annunciation ceremony (*azulahy*) a few years later. Kalu, the child trumba, arrived while Mohedja was nursing Mariam, around 1952, and it was then as well that the senior patros, Mze Marwan, entered Tumbu. After this, the youthful Darwesh, a patros who had entered Mohedja together with Mze Nuru, put in his appearance. They held the full ceremony for Mze Marwan and Tumbu began to learn how to cure. I will describe the emergence of these spirits and the relations among them more fully in later chapters.

After assisting them with Mze Marwan's ceremony, Tumbu's brother, Saidu, left for Diego in Madagascar, where he lived from then on. Repeatedly falling sick, losing all their animals, and considering themselves the victims of sorcery in Lombeni Kely, Tumbu and Mohedja decided to relocate. So Mohedja's mother, Rae Samba, and Rae Samba's childless older sister put in a request for a plot of land, and they all moved out, resettling on a remote hillside a full day's journey on foot from Lombeni. This plot of 5.5 ha, at a place known as Red Rock, was eventually purchased by Rae Samba together with her older sister and that woman's husband, who was from a Sharif family in Anjouan. Mohedja and Tumbu spent a decade in Red Rock, from the late 1950s through the late 1960s, together with the old people as well as Mohedja's full brother Asman and his family. They returned to Lombeni Kely for ceremonial events, staying a week or two at a time, but did not pass the full post-harvest period in Lombeni (as did many cultivators who moved seasonally). At times, two to three years went by before they visited, except for brief trips for funerals and to maintain their house in Lombeni, which they kept locked up. They did, however, continue to consider Lombeni Kely their home.

Mohedja was pregnant with her third daughter, Haza, when they set off for Red Rock. Haza and then her brother Ali were born there. Two more sons followed who died in infancy and then their younger sister, Amiaty. Haza was sent back to be raised by a cousin of Tumbu's in Lombeni (chapter 9) and Ali was eventually boarded with an older cousin there as well. While living at Red Rock, Mohedja's senior trumba, Ndramboeniarivu, arrived and Tumbu received two additional patros. During their years at Red Rock, Tumbu studied sorcery extraction and both he and Mohedja learned more about medicine and curing. Their own health gradually improved.

The husband of Mohedja's mother's sister, the Sharif, knew a good deal about Islam and when they lived at Red Rock the old man would talk of nothing else but the Msahaf (Qur'an). He explained many things concerning God to Tumbu, including the relation of spirits to God. Tumbu said that since that time he stopped being afraid of many things. He regretted that the Sharif was already old and going blind.

After eleven years had passed, Tumbu said to Mohedja, "Let's go home. The grandmothers have aged, and I want the opportunity to purchase our own land." The Sharif had died, and Tumbu had heard that the large plantation at H— was beginning to sell off pieces of fertile land. This was attractive because it was much closer to Lombeni than Red Rock and it would belong to Tumbu rather than his mother-in-law. Mohedja also wanted to take her mother home to better look after her. And so Tumbu and Mohedja returned to Lombeni along with Mohedja's mother and her older sister. Mohedja's brother Asman, with his wife and children, stayed on for some years at Red Rock before returning to Lombeni. They took over full ownership of the plot there, but there were no quarrels about it, as Tumbu and his children acquired land of their own.

Tumbu was successful in his acquisition of land, purchasing three distinct parcels. On first hearing that the plantation was selling plots, Tumbu wrote Saidu in Madagascar and urged him to buy since Tumbu did not yet have the means. Saidu sent money and they paid off the first plot little by little. At the time, one hectare was selling for 400 CFA francs and Tumbu managed to acquire ten hectares in Saidu's name. The first year back, Tumbu and Mohedja planted their rice on company land, but by the second year they were able to plant on Saidu's plot. Tumbu kept his cows there, cleared some forest, and planted ylang ylang, which required three years of growth before it was ready to be harvested. The ylang ylang was planted in the early 1970s and they had started harvesting the flowers by my first visit in 1975. Ylang ylang paid well but required a good deal of labour. The flowers bloomed about twice a month and had to be picked rapidly by hand and then cooked in a homemade still, which had to be kept stoked with firewood. Before constructing his own still, Tumbu rented time at one. Distillation produced an essence or oil that was highly valued in the French perfume industry. The oil came in different densities, which were evaluated and measured by the middlemen who purchased it.

This new piece of land belonged to Saidu, but Tumbu paid the annual tax on it and was able to use it in Saidu's absence. Tumbu was also able to purchase two plots of land of his own, a smaller one of 1.5 ha and a somewhat larger one of 7 ha for 500 CFA francs/ha. He once told me that he sold an ox to make the down payment and provided supplementary payments of copra and cinnamon bark. Another time he said that when he had built his herd of cattle to nine head, he sold all but one to buy the larger field. He saw that there was less and less space to keep cattle and he realized that land was a better investment.

All this land required heavy work to clear it and Tumbu often spent time alone on it. During this period, he gained another spirit, a kakanoru, associated with forests, as I describe in chapter 13. The family spent two agricultural seasons on the largest property, with the herd growing again, until a man nearby was killed by a cattle thief. This frightened Mohedja who insisted they relocate back home. Tumbu had planted ylang ylang on the smaller properties as well and finished off the payment in ylang ylang oil. Paying in kind, Tumbu was dependent on market value and the seller's assessment of the quality of the oil, but at the final payment, he was pleasantly surprised to receive 1,500 CFA francs back. At the time, Ali was his only living son and Tumbu placed the last pieces of land in his name, with the admonition that it was to be shared among all the siblings. Tumbu paid the annual land tax on both the larger properties (plots under five hectares were then untaxed) until he was too old to work, after which Ali took over the obligation.

Tumbu reflected that he had had luck in acquiring the fields but admitted that he also made use of *politiky* – that is, he spent much time buttering up the various Europeans to sell to him. Tumbu was also fortunate to purchase when he did. By the 1980s there was hardly any land available, and the price had risen, up to 3,000 francs/ha plus the cost of the surveyor. (In February 1976, currency changed from the CFA franc to the French franc, and from January 2001 to the euro.) At least one of the French plantations eventually rejuvenated its remaining property under the ownership of Guerlain, a French perfume company, planting twenty hectares with ylang ylang. Guerlain even named one of its perfumes Mayotte ("Mayotte Guerlain for Women," n.d.).

Ylang ylang proved to be extremely remunerative for over a decade although the demand, and hence the price, fluctuated unpredictably. During the prefecture of Jean Marie Coussirou (1976–8) there were periods when Tumbu was able to harvest weekly and flowers were abundant, amounting to between 200 kg and 400 kg per picking. From 400 kg of flowers, he was able to produce about two litres of *extra*, two litres of *premier*, and two litres of *troisième*, as the respective densities of oil were called. This came to about 200 francs for each litre of *extra*, 60–70 francs for the *premier*, and less for the *troisième*, for up to approximately 3,000 francs per month. Tumbu described this as a time when there was a great market. During the appointments of subsequent prefects, prices declined and the middlemen stopped buying *troisième* entirely. In 1985, depending on the season and the weather, Tumbu received between 1,000 and 2,000 francs per month for the ylang ylang.

The money was shared with workers who helped in weeding and pruning the trees, collecting the firewood, and cooking the oil. At first Tumbu took half the proceeds and let the other workers split the rest. Once Ali married, he split evenly with him. Flower pickers, who were women, were paid varying rates depending on the employer and might each pick between 9–30 kg per day for a daily yield from several pickers of 100–200 kg. Ali gave his wife 2–3 francs per kilogram whereas another man paid his wife nothing since, as the couple told me, they "consumed the profits together." The wife said she preferred it that way as she "received what she asked for." These two wives were sisters and when they picked for their father, they each received only one franc per kilogram. Pickers were in high demand and Tumbu often faced a labour shortage. Ylang ylang production was remunerative, but it remained a continuous source of anxiety. The production cycle was demanding, disrupting Tumbu's ability to participate in the ceremonies he was expected to attend and to carry out all his kin obligations, and requiring his own intense labour plus access to additional labour and firewood.

Ylang ylang partially commoditized labour relations in the village and initiated something of a class division in Lombeni between families who got in early and those who had to work for others. Moreover, subsistence land that had been readily available on an annual basis for use by friends and kin grew scarcer. With the money he was bringing in, Tumbu planned a trip to Mecca but put it off to pay for Ali's wedding. Next, he thought of buying a truck, which would have been useful for transport (replacing his mule) and could have also earned a rental income. However, prices were rising steeply, rice yields rapidly declining, and material needs growing. Tumbu used earnings from ylang ylang to purchase food for the family and also to prepare the weddings of his remaining daughters. For each daughter, including the daughter of his brother in Madagascar, Tumbu had to provide a house. This took both cash and a good deal of labour time. In addition, the houses had to be furnished, and over the years that he married off his daughters, the requirements for adequate furnishing (as for house construction materials) escalated, while revenue from ylang ylang sharply declined. Eventually Tumbu did go to Mecca, sponsored by the government. On his return, his health in decline, he declared himself retired and left management of the ylang ylang to Ali. Ali continued to give his parents some money and, together with his sister Nuriaty, opened a small shop. Ali also managed to purchase a second-hand pickup truck through money earned by working for a Frenchman. By 1993, Tumbu explained, he no longer worked full time and it was now Ali who sold the ylang ylang oil and gave some of the proceeds to his father, rather than the reverse. Tumbu reflected that he had made Ali used to hard work since he was small.

Aside from ylang ylang, there were other cash crops that people cultivated in varying amounts and whose prices also fluctuated. In 1980, dried vanilla pods were selling for 20–30 francs per kilogram. Tumbu produced only 10–20 kg, whereas a half-brother produced a good deal more. Vanilla is labour intensive as the plants must be pollinated by hand. In 1980, Tumbu sold 40–50 kg of coffee beans for 15 francs/kg. In 1985, Mohedja sold 18 kg of coffee beans at 10 francs/kg. She declared it a lot of work for little money as the beans needed to be picked, dried, husked, and winnowed before sale.

In 1980, Tumbu contemplated investing in a fishing canoe, carving it himself and buying a motor for it. Tumbu knew little of fishing, but he would have rented the boat to a fisherman and received both the canoe's and the motor's shares of the profits, not to mention a secure supply of fish. He never managed this. In 1985, on a very lucky night, a fisherman in the lagoon could make 600 francs; but you had to catch 7.8 kg of fish just to break even on the gasoline. Fish cost 14 francs/kg if you met the fishermen bringing in the catch at dawn, or more if already frozen.

Village prices for other foodstuffs were also high. In 1985, a medium-sized chicken cost 18 francs; imported rice was fixed by the government at 4.30 francs/kg; coconuts, used to make cooking oil and in food preparation, 50 centimes each; tomatoes 10 francs/kg; sugar 5–6 francs/kg; and beef 25–8 francs/kg. The materials for a government-designed two-room house were 2,600 francs. A trip to Mecca cost 7,000 francs – an amount that could be reached by selling two large head of cattle.

In 1975–6, Tumbu and Mohedja let several other kin and friends cultivate dry rice alongside them on one of their land holdings. They asked no more than a nominal return of a bushel-sized basket of ripe stalks of rice. By 1985, the land was no longer sufficiently fertile for rice but still fine for bananas, manioc, pineapples, and vegetables. They still grew some rice at the other properties but were shifting to bananas. The land was also a source of firewood and coconuts and a place to graze cattle, an activity Tumbu continued so long as he was physically able. In 1975, he was starting to rebuild the herd so that he would have enough animals for his next two daughters' marriages (at that point the girls were aged about eight and three ...). Until the countryside became insecure due to the influx of migrants, raising cattle was one of the best means of growing and storing capital. But it was always risky as animals died or got lost.

Being able to support one's family was not a straightforward matter and demanded both planning and flexibility and the willingness to face the odds that any given investment strategy might not play out in the short or long term. Tumbu handled the risks well. He rightly declared himself pleased that he was able to provide for his children and to leave them an inheritance. Where he failed was in providing them a French education. He had for many years only one son, on whom he relied for labour, and his older daughters were already married and parents themselves before schooling became available. However, several grand-children have since been successful and gone on to white-collar careers.

An achievement that gave Tumbu unqualified satisfaction was becoming an owner in Lombeni. Until then, his plan had been to move the family out of the village entirely and onto one of his purchased tracts, even though they were at some distance from the village. Shortly before 1980, a piece of unoccupied land that was part of the original tract of Lombeni Kely came up for sale by the non-resident descendant of one of the original members of the *socié*. Tumbu and Mohedja seized the opportunity. They joined with some of Tumbu's closest kin to com-bine resources to meet the purchase price and then divided house plots among themselves. It cost Tumbu and Mohedja 800 francs for one hect-are. In 1980, as the communications with the spirits indicated, they were anxious concerning the construction of the new house and eager to move from the plot on which they had lived until then. They knew that some of Tumbu's cousins who were already owners wanted the plot for their own children and were ready to insult them and even try to remove them. Tumbu recognized that legally his relatives did not have a case, since the government had reclassified the tract as a village rather than private property, but he did not wish to quarrel with them and preferred to move before things came to a head.

During the period in which Tumbu and Mohedja returned from Red Rock and built their estate, they did not neglect either their civic responsibilities or the spirits. They completed their obligations in the village ceremonial system by sponsoring the public wedding of Nuri-aty, Ali's circumcision, and mortuary rituals, first for Rae Samba and then in 1985 for Tumbu's mother, as well as multiple smaller and non-obligatory affairs.

Having started from a position of relatively low status, Tumbu became recognized as a highly competent elder (*ulu be*). He shared responsibility for village collective endeavours and expenditures. People often came to him for advice, and little was done in Lombeni Kely without consulting him. Tumbu worked for some years as *chef de village* and then as *adjoint maire* when the village was linked into a larger administrative unit (*commune*), and so he had some idea of how the system worked. After a five-year term as *adjoint maire*, he stepped down because, he said, it took too much time away from cultivation. He received 450 francs per month for the office.

Mohedja served for a time as *chef tanana*, head of the community of village women in Lombeni Kely, responsible for overseeing internal affairs, especially the collection, cooking, and distribution of food at life cycle and public events. After one ceremony, Mohedja admitted she was exhausted. She hadn't slept all night and said that during these affairs she could not eat, her stomach too tense and her intestines overactive. Supervising food distribution was an especially delicate business.

As *chef*, Mohedja chaired women's formal discussions, spoke as their representative, and was responsible for organizing and overseeing collective events. Mohedja observed that sometimes it forced her to voice opinions for which she could be criticized. One year, on the day of the local New Year celebration (*mwaka*), she spoke to the gathered villagers on behalf of the women. For two years the women had wanted to host a Muslim festivity to which they could invite other villages, but the men had never acted on it. The women had met together a month previously and decided they would definitely hold such an event in the coming year. The senior man agreed and Mohedja then asked the women to speak, that is, to decide what kind of festivity they wanted. They told her to choose and so she announced that they would hold a *mulidy* (a male dance celebrating the Prophet, selected because it was a genre for which the village had at the time strong instructors). The male spokesman then suggested the village provide a cow, to which the women replied that one would not be sufficient. One man suggested contributions of 100 francs per household. Mohedja said no: two cows and 200 francs per household. The men then said it would be up to the women to collect the money, to which Mohedja agreed. As she told me later, it would go much quicker that way because women were readier to give the money.

That night, Mohedja and Tumbu talked it over. Tumbu was shocked at the amount and suggested 150 francs per household. Mohedja countered by saying that each male age group should provide a cow.

People in Mayotte practised Sunni Islam (of the Sha'fi branch). Tumbu and Mohedja were each committed Muslims. Both of them could recite from the Qur'an and they were familiar with the Arabic script, albeit not able to translate. In the early years of our acquaintance, Mohedja sent me letters in Kibushy written in Arabic script. Tumbu prayed regularly for as long as I knew him. He went to the mosque daily and was one of the most loyal attendants in the village. He said it was worse to go on and off than not to go at all. Tumbu's uncle never attended, claiming he had too much work and not enough time. But, as Tumbu was asked by his own teacher, when will you have the time? Tumbu said one must steel oneself to go all the time. At the dawn prayer in 1975, there was sometimes only Tumbu and one old man. When others came, Tumbu was often embarrassed for them because they prayed half asleep. For years he was one of the few men to stay on in the mosque after the *swala* (regular prayer) to recite the *wathifa*, the chant (*dhikr*) of the Sha-thuly (Shadhuliyya) brotherhood with which he identified. At Ramadan and other occasions, he often served as the *imam* for nightly prayer. Mohedja prayed at home until she reached menopause, when she too began to pray at the mosque. Many women, especially younger ones, did not pray, in part because while rearing children their clothes were never clean enough. In 1995, Mohedja rose for dawn prayer and then recited from prayer books at home until others were up. At night she prayed at home so as not to leave her grandchildren alone. She was also a devotee of the Maulida Shengy, a woman's performance comparable to the Sufi dances performed by men. Both Mohedja and Tumbu tried to increase their religious knowledge, albeit without succumbing to the teachings of the latest reformist preachers and, unlike many, without showing off their piety or moralizing to others.[1]

Tumbu spent several years preparing for a pilgrimage to Mecca. Although he had to put it off when Ali married, he later acquired the money necessary for a return ticket from the sale of ylang ylang and two cows as well as government sponsorship. He made the hadj around 1990, together with a small group guided from Mayotte. However, the trip did not turn out as expected. In Mecca, he was inadvertently separated from his companions and did not return home with them; eventually, after some misadventure, he turned up. His health was never the same after.

In 1975, Tumbu and Mohedja lived very modestly, but since that time they achieved what they wanted: marriages and houses for their children, a decent house on a plot of their own, sufficient land to pass on to their children, and, for a period, reasonable health. They enjoyed the loyalty and support of their adult children. Although none of their children received a French education, which was a necessary condition for a white-collar, well-paying job and for insight into how to gain the increasing benefits of the French system, one of their granddaughters was among the first to acquire an office job and other grandchildren have succeeded since. (Today, a great-granddaughter is a high school English teacher.) During the 1990s, they adapted well to the changes rapidly taking place in Mayotte; alongside the improved infrastructure – paved roads, electricity, running water – there were much higher food prices, more taxes to pay, and personal bank accounts into which the small state benefits were deposited.

By the 1990s, Mohedja and Tumbu felt they had done their part; the rest was up to the young people to make what they could of their lives and the opportunities presented them. The generations succeed each other in Mayotte, the elderly ideally giving way gracefully to those who follow. Mohedja and Tumbu enjoyed the affection of their grandchildren, but the latter, as was customary, often treated them informally, without the respect due parents. When I visited in 1992, I brought several cloth bags and satchels as gifts. I offered Tumbu first choice, and he selected the best one, a leather knapsack. I handed out the others and reserved the smaller presents for the adolescent grandchildren. By the time I was due to leave, I did not see the knapsack anywhere. When I inquired, Tumbu replied good-humouredly that one of his grandsons, having spotted the knapsack and remarking that it would be perfect for school, had simply appropriated it.

PART TWO

Arrivals of the Spirits

Chapter Four

Mohedja: Kos Vola and the Line of Women

Mohedja's mother, known in the 1970s as Rae Samba (Mother of Samba), came from a large family of Malagasy descent from the village of M—. Most women married in the village of their parents, but Rae Samba and her older sisters left home in their youth. After a brief marriage in Lombeni, where she gave birth to Mohedja's beloved older half-brother, Samba, Rae Samba got remarried in a distant village, called F—. The couple divorced and Rae Samba returned briefly to Lombeni until Salim, Mohedja's father, married her and took her and Samba back to F—, where Salim was an "owner" (*tompin*). This was originally a polygynous marriage; the other wife lived in a different village. Salim and Rae Samba were married eleven years before Rae Samba gave birth to another son, Asman, and a year later to Mohedja, when Rae Samba was already close to forty. Mohedja was born in her father's village, sometime between 1930 and 1933. Salim died when Mohedja was very young and Mohedja barely remembered him. She recalled him as kind and very popular; many people came to establish fictive kin ties with him and there were always a lot of people around. Rae Samba remained in F— where her next husband joined her. Mohedja grew up in F—, closely attached to her mother but identifying also as a member of her father's family, and through this connection had local rights to land. F— was one of the few villages in Mayotte at the time to offer primary schooling and Mohedja acquired some knowledge of reading and writing in French, although when I met her, she certainly didn't speak it. She was, however, able to use this learning to help Tumbu ensure that they were not cheated when it came to economic transactions.

I do not know much about Mohedja's childhood; childhood was not a subject that adults appeared to reflect on or talk about readily, even when asked. She described her mother as kind but ready to shout at her when Mohedja did something bad, just like Mohedja's own parenting style. Although Mohedja had to cope with the arrival and departure of two stepfathers (one who stayed four years and the next for five), her childhood was characterized overall by its continuity. I knew Rae Samba in her last years, and I can imagine that her style of mothering was similar to Mohedja's – firm but warm, predictable, and steady. In old age, Rae Samba was a modest, shy person, but someone who knew her own mind. She and Mohedja were close and Mohedja, as her only daughter, looked after her needs faithfully. Mohedja often compared her favourably to Tumbu's mother, a feisty woman with a sharp tongue, of whose child-rearing methods and general disposition Mohedja thoroughly disapproved.

Mohedja was her mother's youngest child and only daughter. She had two older brothers, Samba and Asman, the latter a full brother, and an older paternal half-sister. Her maternal half-brother, Samba, was a key figure in her life. He was well over a dozen years older than Mohedja and began having children of his own when she was still a girl. As an adult, she maintained warm relations with both her father's kin in F— and her mother's kin in M—. Occasionally she visited her paternal half-sister who lived in what was then the closest thing to a town (Aranta).

Mohedja wasn't happy with her mother's move to Lombeni Kely. Although she and her mother had occasionally visited Rae Samba's older sister there, she wasn't used to the place. It took her some time to feel at home and at first, she didn't think she would want to live there permanently. But, as she said, she got married in Lombeni and began to have children and so she stayed. In 1980, she still spoke of F— as the village where she was an owner and where she was "related to everyone." Her father had left a field there, with coffee and vanilla. Her kin used it, but they encouraged her to return and share it. She liked to visit. When I asked why she didn't move to F—, she replied that if her husband truly loved her, he would follow, but that she would miss her children too much; their spouses would not permit them to make the move too. In later years, especially after the death of Samba in F— and after she and Tumbu had purchased land of their own in Lombeni and had become secure there, the subject of return no longer came up.

Rae Samba cohabited with two spirits. When Mohedja told me this she remarked how astonished she was at how many spirits she herself had come to have. Rae Samba was visited by a senior female trumba from Madagascar named Kos Vola and by a female mrewa. Mrewa were spirits from Zanzibar who were no longer prevalent in Mayotte by the 1970s. The mrewa spoke Kingudja (Swahili). Rae Samba's family never held the ceremony for her mrewa and no one else received the spirit until 2007, when the mrewa announced her presence in Mohedja's daughter Mariam. Some mrewa left their host once the ceremony was over. They ordered a toy-sized canoe which was launched with the various kinds of foods the spirit had requested for the ceremony and the mrewa sailed away. Mohedja did not know where to.

Kos Vola had been a Sakalava princess in life. She held a beautiful ebony staff embossed with silver, draped a white cloth over her face, and uttered breathy sighs.[1] Rae Samba worked as a healer through Kos Vola but also on her own and helped women conceive and get through pregnancy. Rae Samba taught Mohedja, and Mohedja in turn taught Nuriaty, when she came to ask her. The other children were not interested in learning. Mohedja laughed and said they could still come and ask her, so long as she remained alive. She tried to warn them that once she was gone, the knowledge would disappear too, but they did not seem to care.

Kos Vola was the first spirit to actively possess Mohedja. Although Kos Vola did not rise in Mohedja until after her engagement to Tumbu, Mohedja told me that she had cohabited with the spirit ever since she was a little girl. She knew this because she remembered feeling sick whenever she ate chicken or chili pepper (foods which are prohibited by the spirit and which would have been forbidden to her mother). Her mother had cohabited with Kos Vola and completed all her ceremonies well before Mohedja was born.

Despite the spirit's presence, and even occasionally vomiting blood after eating chicken, Mohedja said she simply paid no attention as a child – not until after she moved to Lombeni. One day, when her mother had returned to F— to tell the relatives there about Mohedja's upcoming marriage to Tumbu, there was a blessing ceremony held in Lombeni at which a large cock was sacrificed. Mohedja partook of the food and immediately suffered strong stomach pain. She went to lie down in her empty house. The last thing she fully remembered was getting up to vomit. Mohedja shouted without knowing it and then saw a crowd gathered around her. She was very embarrassed. The senior trumba fundi (master, teacher, curer) gave her a mixture of honey, cologne, and kaolin to drink. This immediately calmed her. Since it was trumba medicine, people began to suspect she had a trumba. The fundi told her never to eat chicken again, a restriction she largely kept. She learned the spirit was Kos Vola much later during the ceremony at which the spirit announced her name.

I asked why she had been embarrassed. Mohedja struggled a bit and admitted she could not really put it into words. People are always embarrassed when a spirit first appears. Once a spirit has stopped making you sick and started helping the family then you might be pleased, but earlier it makes you sick.

The embarrassment has partly to do with the sense of exposure and loss of self-control under possession. You have to wait until the spirit leaves to learn what "you" did and often this is contrary to your own social persona. The fact that it was the spirit and not "you" who did those things never seems completely satisfactory and indeed the clarity of the distinction is undermined by the talk of embarrassment. At the very least, it throws into question the relationship between the body and the self. The resort to an idiom of pain or sickness underlines the fact that possession is involuntary, that what happens to the host is quite independent of her will. Yet the embarrassment comes from the fact that it is still her body.

Mohedja described herself during the first appearance of the trumba as *atiseriña*. This describes the condition when a spirit only partially rises in you; you are conscious of what is going on but cannot help yourself from crying, shouting, etc. Mohedja remembered how she could not keep quiet when the trumba first made her sick, the day she ate chicken. Of subsequent entries of the spirit, she remembered nothing. Likewise, at the original onsets of her other spirits, she was not conscious and had no memory.

Despite this account, on other occasions, Mohedja remarked that Kos Vola was the only one of her spirits who did not cause her suffering when she first arrived. She speculated that perhaps she was born with her. She thus distinguished entry into a relationship – what we might call "latent cohabitation" – from the first moment of rising in her head, when the spirit is fully manifest. She was pointing as well to the fact that most of her spirits first entered her in association with an illness she was suffering at the time. Whereas the nausea at eating chicken was just a sign of the spirit's displeasure at her having broken the prohibition, other spirits announced their arrival with actual illness.

Mohedja indicated that her connection with Kos Vola was long-standing, deep, and consistently positive. Her symptoms were merely hints of the spirit's presence. Rather than being determined by some external factor or by happenstance, Kos Vola's presence was closely linked to her relationship with her mother, emerging out of her childhood, and possibly even the womb, as a part of her own identity as her mother's daughter.[2] I would say that their cohabitation with the same spirit was indicative and expressive of profound mutual identification. Mother and daughter shared a fundamental aspect of personhood. Just as any daughter incorporates aspects of her mother, so did Mohedja; here one modality was given articulation in the cultural idiom of spirit possession, objectified – or rather, personified – and embodied as Kos Vola. The first embodied signs – queasiness on eating foods she knew were forbidden to her mother – developed into a public display of nausea and loss of consciousness and later cohered in the voice and presence of the spirit, coordinated with the spirit's voice and presence in her mother, and finally legitimated in a series of public rituals.

The timing of Kos Vola's appearance in Mohedja, that is, her first episode of dissociation, was significant. She had only recently moved to Lombeni, and her mother had briefly left her there for a trip back to F— to announce her forthcoming marriage. Mohedja had been removed from her close kin and her village. Her mother was newly divorced from her stepfather, and most significantly, Mohedja's engagement to a boy she had known in F— had been suddenly broken off to be replaced with an engagement to Tumbu, a man who, at the time, and despite her acquiescence, she barely knew.[3] They were married within a month of the engagement, Kos Vola having risen in the interim. Thus, at a moment of perceived abandonment and anxiety about the future, Mohedja affirmed the link to her mother along an intensely personal dimension and claimed her past. Feeling vulnerable, she incorporated for herself the strong and nurturant trumba whom she had experienced in her mother.

Kos Vola was the only spirit to enter and rise in Mohedja before her marriage. Despite the continuity with her mother articulated via Kos Vola, Mohedja subsequently developed her autonomy, becoming possessed by additional spirits after her marriage to Tumbu. She received three other trumba while her mother was still alive, and another subsequently, as well as several patros, of whom her mother had none.

After her marriage, it was at first the patros rather than trumba who made her sick. Several years later, when she and Tumbu were living at their fields at Red Rock, Mohedja fell ill again. The elderly Sharif (descendant of the Prophet), who was married to her mother's sister and living with them at Red Rock, was a diviner. He said the medicine she had received would have no effect on her; since she was suffering from a trumba, she needed treatment by a fundi (healer) who had a trumba herself. So Mohedja made the long trek back to Lombeni. It was a very slow trip since she was ill and could not walk at normal speed. When she arrived, she went to see Musy Matwar, an older woman who had become the leading trumba fundi in the village. There Kos Vola rose and said she wanted to hold her first ceremony. Kos Vola specifically asked for Musy Matwar rather than Rae Samba as manager of the ceremony. Accordingly, the first ceremony for Kos Vola, called a *fanuing*, was held, and a couple of years after that was the major ceremony, the *rombu be,* at which Kos Vola announced her name publicly. At the final ceremony for Kos Vola, the *valu hataka,* a senior male trumba, Ndramboeny, who had arrived in the meantime, was also given his major ceremony (chapter 7). This was shortly before my first arrival.

~

The morning after a large trumba ceremony held for an elderly man of Lombeni in August 1985, Mohedja remarked how happy she had been not to have entered trance immediately, as she usually did at these events, but to have had the opportunity to observe the proceedings. Watching her daughter Nuriaty, Mohedja could see that Nuriaty was possessed by her own senior male trumba, Ndramboeny, although he had not yet announced his name. Once Nuriaty switched from him to a youthful trumba spirit, Ndramboeny entered Mohedja, and she went into trance for the rest of the night.

Although Mohedja presented this scene as the product of her good fortune and left the agency to the trumba, it demonstrates the way succession and sharing of spirits is negotiated between the parties. It was Mohedja's abstention from possession that enabled Nuriaty to perform as Ndramboeny; had Mohedja entered trance and Ndramboeny manifested his presence within her, he could not have manifest simultaneously in Nuriaty. This is one means by which the presence of the spirit in the younger woman is tacitly affirmed by the older. This follows from a basic property of spirits as they are understood in Mayotte, namely that while a given spirit may have a relationship with more than one host, it can manifest itself (via trance) in only one place at a time. Thus, while Mohedja could not determine that her daughters received this or that spirit, she could tacitly suggest the identity and express or withhold her permission when they showed signs of possession. In effect, the identity of the spirit was negotiated and confirmed between them. In a similar fashion, the presence of Kos Vola in Mohedja must have occurred with the tacit permission or encouragement of Rae Samba. Thus, if sharing a spirit with her mother is a sign of identification on the daughter's part, it cannot work if the identification is not acknowledged – that is, if the identification is not mutual, part of a two-way process, reciprocated by the mother. One could describe this as the working through of intersubjectivity.

The rule of silence over the name of a spirit who has not yet held their public ceremony is critical here. Cases where the name remained unspoken were often ones where the identity of the spirit was truly ambiguous. But more generally, the silence was also determined by the subjective reality that until the name was announced and the identity of the spirit was publicly established and legitimated, it was, in fact, not fully separate from the inner processes of the host – processes through which she was coming to terms with who the spirit was or would be and thus which of her relational components or issues would be manifest. The intersubjective aspects also needed confirmation. Nuriaty was tacitly testing Mohedja to see whether possession by Ndramboeny would be acceptable to her.[4] Once accepted there was a tacit and private understanding between mother and daughter.

In addition, the way a host shifts during performance between one of her spirits and another provides subtle messages regarding personal identity, which in turn are linked to public models of social status and hierarchy. Thus, Ndramboeny pre-empted Kos Vola and, in Mohedja's case, as she explained, neither of her senior spirits approved of the presence of the carousing youthful spirit, Botu Changizy. Nuriaty, on the other hand, as a younger woman, spent more hours of the ceremony possessed by her carouser spirit than by her senior one. While male carouser spirits drink and dance, senior male trumba sit upright or pace assertively. Kos Vola, a female elder, covered her face with a cloth on public occasions, behind which she made cooing noises.[5] Her demeanour was thus more contained and self-effacing than that of the male spirits, although she too could intervene in human affairs. I saw Kos Vola alternate with Ndramboeny and Botu Changizy in Mohedja during night-long trumba ceremonies. However, as Mohedja grew older, and especially as she began to take on the responsibility of managing the ceremonies of clients, Ndramboeny took proportionately more and more of her time (chapter 7).

A moment like this, reviewing events that took place during a public ceremony, enabled Mohedja to reflect on her possession history. Mohedja spoke about Kos Vola as an inherited spirit, *lulu ny mwaratha*, and retold the story of her arrival and first appearance. She also remarked that while the Grandfather (Ndramboeny) had not come to her as a spirit of her family, *lulu ny mraba*, he was showing every sign of continuing there (as evident in his cohabitation with Nuriaty). Finally, she reflected that since the arrival of Ndramboeny, Kos Vola did not visit as often.

Each time she spoke about her spirits, Mohedja transformed embodied performance into narrative. Whether or not her inability to eat chicken extended back to early childhood and preceded more robust signs of possession, as her account suggests, the narrative had relevance to her self-understanding and a coherence of its own, and it could shift subtly according to context and over time. Thus, like any form of remembering, stories about the onset and practices of her spirits provided the opportunity to rethink the present in light of the past and vice versa. In this manner, lines of continuity and coherence were continuously rewoven. Selfhood is realized (in all senses of the term) by means of this intertwined, ongoing practice of both narrative and enactment.

Through most of her adult life, Mohedja and her mother shared Kos Vola. Rae Samba was a curer and maintained clients who came to do *trambuñu* medicine under Kos Vola. *Trambuñu* (protective) medicine was performed for women having difficulty producing live offspring, that is, women who suffered from miscarriages, stillbirths, or infant mortality. After two or more such experiences, a woman would likely seek out either an astrologer (*mwalim dunia*) or a senior spirit known to perform *trambuñu*. There were various ways to do *trambuñu* medicine, but all entailed being placed under the protection of either a spirit or an astrologer. The treatment enacted a kind of contract in which the practitioner pledged to vouchsafe the well-being of the woman's next or current offspring. In a sense, the powerful and knowledgeable spirit or astrologer acted as the guarantor or trustee of the children. The parents carried out their part by observing various restrictions, such as avoiding quarrels, adultery, and funerals, and by acknowledging the curer. The proscriptions were meant for both parents, although, as Mohedja remarked, perhaps only the mothers proved able to stick to them. Mohedja added that each case and its treatment was particular.

> *April 1976.* An older woman, Zaina, explained why she had undergone *trambuñu*. If a woman's husband was born while his mother was taking the medicine, then the wife should also take it for the first birth of an offspring with him. If the child was male, then his spouse in turn would have to undergo it. Though it was primarily trumba medicine, Zaina was supervised by her father's patros spirit. The process was not a big deal. The main restrictions were to avoid large crowds and not commit adultery, which could have killed the infant. She couldn't eat chicken, nor the flesh of young, nursing animals. Treatment ended by cutting open a newly finished mat and pouring medicine through a cloth over the mother's head. The practitioner kept the cloth and mat that the client provided.

Other proscriptions included avoiding funerals, not eating at an event where many pots were used, abstaining from fish caught with poison, abstaining from chili pepper, not arguing, and not watching others argue. Some people viewed the prohibitions as more difficult to maintain than did Zaina. Thus, a client who had successfully given birth came to Kos Vola in order to reduce her restrictions. However, the latter said it was too early to do so since the client was pregnant again.

Others emphasized that *trambuñu* was needed because a woman suffered from an illness caused by a "bad thing" (*raha ratsy*), sometimes known as *tambavy*, which came to eat the offspring conceived or scare them to death, whether alive or in the womb. This was an evil spirit, neither patros nor trumba. Here is how one young woman from Lombeni Be described her condition. She said a *tambavy* had long been bothering her. She saw it in her sleep, a male who came to talk with her and sometimes slept with her. If she was pregnant at the time, the child died. The *tambavy* had visited since she was a girl (i.e., from before her marriage), but she never said anything about it. Her first child, a boy, died; then she had a miscarriage, then another child who died, then another miscarriage. People asked her: didn't she see anything when she slept? Then she spoke up. She didn't have the dream while she was carrying her two oldest living children (a girl, six, and boy, three), but it returned during the subsequent pregnancy. Since she'd taken *trambuñu* medicine, the spirit returned in her sleep, but she refused him or saw him tied up. Her youngest daughter was now eighteen months. She contracted the medicine with a patros spirit in Safy, a young male medium, and maintained taboos against quarrelling and adultery; after attending a funeral she had to wash her hands and change her clothes before holding her child. She didn't eat fish caught with poison or beef if she hadn't seen the cow's ear. She had to keep the taboos in order for the patros to keep the *tambavy* away. Her husband was also not permitted to commit adultery or to quarrel, though he could speak badly to her and, if so, she had to keep quiet in return. She said that were she to use contraception, she would go to Safy to stop the medicine and the taboos. The treatment always included a medicated bath of some sort (in fresh water if the fundi was a trumba, in the sea if it was a patros) and was generally accompanied by amulets and a *shijabu* (Muslim prayer ceremony). The bad spirit left as a result of the medicine, but if you didn't keep the restrictions it would return.

Another woman said that at each new birth one informs the fundi, who then picks new medicine. When the baby's navel is healed, infant and mother wash in the medicine; this is how *trambuñu* continues from child to child. Safy himself added that the *tambavy* was an evil spirit that didn't like children. It took the shape of a donkey or other animal or of a man to sleep with a woman in her dreams. She might see the spirit as her husband. The dream was pleasurable. For a difficult case, the woman was placed in a pit with a white cloth over the top and a chicken killed above her head.

From these accounts the illness seems to concern sex that doesn't lead to procreative outcome; the product of the sexual act and the act itself is usurped, seized, and controlled by the evil spirit. The evil spirit can in turn be controlled by a stronger spirit or curer, but such control works only so long as the couple also control themselves, control their own sexuality (don't practice adultery), control their anger, and keep their distance from death. It is interesting, in addition, that the need to be under a healer's supervision is passed on to a woman from her husband. The taboos speak to the marital union and the role of both parties in procreation; the woman herself is not blamed as the source of reproductive failure (though it could always be said that she had not the strength of will to maintain the prohibitions).

Children born under *trambuñu* could not eat fish caught with fish poison (*hamu*), food from cooking fires placed too near each other, or food from a funeral. Mohedja explained that the prohibitions were removed when the children could walk, in case they wandered off and inadvertently ate something they shouldn't; a child under the prohibition who broke it would suffer. It is evident from this that the prohibition is not considered "natural" but a product of its ritual instantiation; it speaks to social relations, not natural cause and effect. The mother's prohibitions were normally also terminated once toddlers could move on their own and away from the mother. Since the child could no longer maintain the prohibitions, said Mohedja, why should the mother? The argument linking termination of the prohibitions to separation issues emphasizes how *trambuñu* medicine refers to identification between mother and child. In a similar vein, Safy said that the restrictions imposed on children had to be removed before boys were circumcised or girls matured, otherwise they became slow or half-witted (*dabadaba, luha tsy fenu*).

Here is how the conclusion of Mohedja's *trambuñu* treatment with her daughter Mwanesha took place.[6]

15 October 1975. Mwanesha was quite ill during her first year of life. She is now almost two, over the danger period, healthier and stronger, and able to walk, so they remove the prohibitions kept since her birth. Mohedja buys a two-metre length of white cloth that Kos Vola requested, brings a bucket of water to her mother's, and pounds herbal medicine. Following

Rae Samba's instructions, Tumbu digs four holes in a square pattern in the dirt in front of her house and plants four poles, about waist height. The white cloth is tied over them as a canopy. Rae Samba lights incense and speaks over it in a low voice, explaining that we have gathered to remove the restrictions. Her half-finished mat is placed on the ground under the canopy. Mohedja and Mwanesha sit on it, Mohedja wearing just a single cloth and the baby naked. Rae Samba calls in Mohedja's adult daughter Mariam to help. Water is poured into a large bowl full of medicinal leaves, which in turn is poured over the canopy drenching the mother and child beneath. Mohedja then dresses and gives her mother a small bottle of cologne and 200 CFA francs. Mariam was told to shake out the cloth in running water in order to remove and disperse the evil. Long ago, they say, the restrictions would have been removed in a much more elaborate manner with a big trumba ceremony and lots of liquor. Today the medicine was leaves, cologne, and white clay; honey – the remaining critical ingredient in northern Malagasy purification recipes – was unavailable.

Despite the termination of the prohibitions once a child had passed the age at which infant mortality was common, the child's relationship with the guarantor was a lifelong affair. The practitioner had to be notified when the child was circumcised or married. Likewise, when the child born under *trambuñu* reached childbearing age, the relationship was renewed for the next generation – that is, if either member of a newly married couple had been born under *trambuñu*, they should renew it for the sake of their own procreative ability.

If the fundi who performed and guaranteed the first *trambuñu* was no longer living, the parents had to seek his or her successor. In the case of a spirit guarantor, this meant searching for a medium who cohabited with the same spirit as the one under whom the previous contract had been established. In other words, the relationship entered into with a given spirit did not end when the host died, but was transmitted to whoever succeeded her as host to the same spirit. In this way *trambuñu* provided significant chains of continuity. Sometimes the clients were kin, but often they were strangers to the host, arriving from a distant village in order to renew their relationship with a particular spirit.

The transmission of the role of guarantor of *trambuñu* meant that the implications of Mohedja's cohabitation with Kos Vola developed over time. In 1975, Mohedja's daughter Mariam observed jokingly that when Kos Vola wanted to make medicine, she rose in Rae Samba, but when she wanted to dance, she entered Mohedja. Yet a few months later, Kos Vola rose in Rae Samba and announced that from then on, the medicine she had started with her clients was to be continued via Mohedja. Over the years, Mohedja had observed her mother performing *trambuñu* treatments, and since childhood she had learned the medicines both directly from her mother and from Kos Vola when Rae Samba was actively possessed. Now it was Mohedja who would actively host Kos Vola to pursue the work. Rae Samba was also teaching her medical knowledge to her granddaughter Mariam, with whom she was close. This was a relation between people, not spirits, and Mariam gave her grandmother some money for the instruction. Mariam was not able to do much because she had no trumba of her own. However, Mariam anticipated that when the old woman died, Kos Vola would visit her in her sleep and explain more. Mohedja already knew all the medicines, having shared the trumba with her mother for many years.

Rae Samba herself had had trouble giving birth and children who died. She had gone to her brother-in-law, a well-known cosmologer for *trambuñu*; he died before the treatment ended, so his son took over as the guarantor even though he was not a cosmologer. By the time Mohedja needed the medicine, she sought it from her own mother. She depended here not merely on her mother but on her mother's trumba, Kos Vola, to oversee the protection of her children. Yet this was a spirit with whom she too already cohabited. Thus, in a sense she was in the process of introjecting the very source of strength onto whom she was projecting her dependency needs. *She had idealized a person whom she was becoming.* It is precisely this process that leads me to argue that possession can be a source of growth.

While I have been elaborating the strong maternal links implied by Kos Vola, the spirit herself was not explicitly identified with Rae Samba by Mohedja. The connection was rather that both mother and daughter hosted the same spirit. Tumbu explained that Kos Vola was Mohedja's *rahavavy*, a term used between two women to refer to siblingship in the broad sense (as identified by Kelly 1977) of people who are related to each other by their common relations to a third party. Co-wives who get along with one another are *rahavavy*, as are the wives of a pair of brothers.[7] *Rahavavy* has a positive connotation and is also used between women friends. It implies an egalitarian relationship between equivalent female parties, as opposed to the terminology for older/younger siblings (*zuky/zandry*), where sex is irrelevant, or the terms for cross-sex siblings, *anadahy/anabavy* (female and male speakers, respectively), or the equivalent term between men, *rahalahy*. In sum, while projecting her idealization onto the spirit, Mohedja is also asserting her equality with her.

In 1975, Mohedja's mother was very old and quite feeble, yet *trambuñu* clients seeking out Kos Vola were still directed her way by Mohedja. Neither Mohedja nor Tumbu scorned her activity or tried to intervene. However, the transmission of responsibility for supervising the *trambuñu* medicine did take place, as follows.

On 4 December 1975, Mohedja was asked to help treat a couple who had arrived that morning from another village to consult Rae Samba. Mohedja replied, "Thanks for telling me, but there's no need for everyone to participate." The young woman was having a difficult pregnancy. They came to Rae Samba because when the husband's mother had had difficulty with her pregnancies and when she was carrying him, she had been treated by Kos Vola in Rae Samba for *trambuñu*. Now that the wife was concerned, they figured it was because the trumba was angry that she had not been notified of their marriage. The sponsor of this kind of reproductive medicine had a lifelong claim for recognition of her work from the children who represented its successful outcome.

Even though Mohedja shared the same trumba, she explained that the client could not go directly to her. As long as Rae Samba was living, clients had to go to their own healer. However, when Kos Vola rose in Rae Samba, she told the clients that in the future they should seek her in Mohedja and that Rae Samba herself was now too old to handle such things. Kos Vola instructed Mohedja to collect the medicines for them. Kos Vola had indeed been angry not to have been informed of their marriage, and they were told that in the future they should send their news and direct their requests through Mohedja.

On 17 March 1976, Kos Vola rose again in Rae Samba to announce that Rae Samba was now too old to work and would no longer be available for curing; henceforward, all treatments that Kos Vola had started with clients were to be continued through Mohedja. The spirit also announced that her goods, notably the handsome staff (*angira*) banded with silver, were to be transferred from Rae Samba's keeping to Mohedja's.[8] The critical point was that Kos Vola, speaking from Rae Samba, herself initiated the transition. As a result, Mohedja gained both the right and the responsibility to take over the work. In addition, the continuity of their practice was assured.

When Rae Samba died in the late 1970s, a significant portion of her identity, as well as her most valuable item of portable material property, had already been passed on to her daughter. This transmission had been initiated and legitimated by the mother and internalized by the daughter. As the sole successor to her mother's spirit and authority at that time, Mohedja acquired an immediate group of clients, including the members of her mother's kindred. All of them, kin or not, who had engaged in *trambuñu* medicine with her mother now looked to her as their fundi.

Mohedja herself had been born under a *trambuñu* arrangement with her mother's sister's husband, an astrologer. And Mohedja had placed several of her offspring, from Ali through Amiaty and Mwanesha, under the *trambuñu* medicine of Kos Vola in Rae Samba. Kos Vola therefore had to be informed at their life cycle rituals. After Rae Samba's death, this happened via Mohedja herself. When Amiaty was engaged, Kos Vola was called up in Mohedja, and she subsequently rose of her own accord and cried with joy at Amiaty's wedding.

Mohedja performed *trambuñu* both as the trumba Kos Vola and as the patros Mze Nuru (succeeding her deceased patros fundi, Malidy Juma), and by the 1980s she had done so for many people. The spirits were not interchangeable. Each client worked with the particular spirit with whom she had a relationship; as noted, often their identity was determined by the history of the client's parents' or in-laws' practice. These vertical connections could be of long-standing and brought to Mohedja people whom she herself had never previously met. Thus in 1985 Mohedja was visited by a woman from a distant village for treatment because her husband had been under *trambuñu* medicine as an infant with Rae Samba decades earlier. His mother had told him that Rae Samba was his family fundi and he had come to her for medicine before his marriage. Similarly, another client had received *trambuñu* treatment previously with Mze Nuru in Malidy Juma. The fundis received notification and gifts at the subsequent life cycle rites of their clients and their clients' children, and this right was also passed on between the generations of curers.

On 7 July 1985, Tamamy, the daughter of Mohedja's full brother, Asman, came seeking medicine from Kos Vola. Tamamy's mother had received *trambuñu* medicine with Kos Vola in Rae Samba when Tamamy was born. Thus, there was a link between her children and Kos Vola. While this link was established via Rae Samba, it continued through Mohedja, at least until such time as Kos Vola rose in one of Asman's offspring as well, as eventually Kos Vola rose in Tamamy herself. In a sense, Kos Vola had become a fundi of the family (*mraba*) for the descendants of Rae Samba. As a fundi, Kos Vola was someone who took on the responsibility of looking out for the family, warning the members of danger, assisting them in their endeavors, and healing them when they were sick. Mohedja, as the spirit's host, had taken over her mother's place as the focal point for her brothers' families. As time passed and the family branches grew apart, Kos Vola began to show signs of appearing in at least one daughter of each of Rae Samba's two sons.

Mohedja did not know whether Rae Samba's mother had also cohabited with Kos Vola. (As her mother was rather old when Mohedja was born, she did not know her grandparents.) She also did not know how long her mother had cohabited with Kos Vola, but at least for as long as she could remember. Mohedja just laughed when I asked whether one of her own daughters cohabited with Kos Vola yet. It does not do to mention possession that has not yet been made public and it is especially wrong to identify spirits by name until they have had the chance to do so themselves at the public annunciation which forms the climax of possession ceremonies (Lambek 1981). My suspicion that Kos Vola would appear in Mohedja's daughter Mariam was not confirmed until close to Mohedja's death.

Spirits not only articulated vertical kinship ties, but they could connect hosts who were otherwise unrelated. A woman in another village who cohabited with Kos Vola sometimes came to call her in Mohedja. Mohedja always put her off because she did not like the woman. But if two people who shared a spirit trusted each other, they could each call the spirit in the other person and thus speak face-to-face with the spirit who otherwise spoke through them.

In the mid-1970s, Mohedja's responsibilities extended to caring for both her mother, Rae Samba, and her mother's elder sister, who had no surviving descendants. Each of the women, who were very old at this time, cooked her own food for as long as she was able, though Mohedja had to ensure they had something to prepare each day. When they were sick, and later when they suffered dementia, Mohedja shouldered more of the care, although she was able to delegate certain tasks to her own grandchildren.

Mohedja's adult daughters, Rae Samba's grandchildren, preferred to emphasize their joking relationships with the old women. They teased them and privately told me they were a nuisance. When Rae Samba had trouble during the night, Mohedja's daughters would fetch Mohedja, but they would not attend to the old lady themselves. Rae Samba in turn insisted that only Mohedja take care of her. During the harvest season of 1974, the family camped out in their fields. Every night Mohedja would dream there was something wrong with her mother, and in the morning, she would rush back to check on her. Thus in 1975 (to my good fortune) they had decided not to reside in the fields. There were many days on which Mohedja did not go out to cultivate and she turned down other excursions out of concern for the women. She felt quite tied down.

The elderly women themselves resisted the decline in their social worth. Whenever they fell ill, they insisted the cause was sorcery and appealed for counter-medicine. Yet, Mohedja said, she remembered her mother being sick on and off ever since she was a little girl; now her medical problems were simply compounded by old age. Mohedja once consulted a diviner at her mother's urgent request. He concluded that the problem was not sorcery, nor evil eye, nor spirit possession, but merely "came from God." Mohedja was not surprised, but the old woman resisted the diagnosis. Sorcery would have implied a finite illness and the promise of a cure. Even more important, I think, it would have suggested that she remained socially significant enough for someone to bother attacking her. Sorcery implied ongoing social relationships, thus her continued existence as a valued person.

Mohedja told her mother the diviner had said it was not sorcery. On hearing this, Rae Samba jumped out of bed and was soon cooking rice. Mohedja felt that if she had not mentioned it her mother would still be in bed, complaining. And she added: "Imagine an old woman attacked by sorcery! People have no reason to do sorcery against a poor old lady, she has nothing anyone covets. When one gets to be that old one should recognize the inevitability of sickness." She laughed about her mother and "big mother" (*nindry be*, mother's older sister). The latter announced that she would live to be a hundred and that she would clear a field that year if she were not sick. She called for Tumbu, presumably to extract sorcery. By saying they were subject to sorcery the old women were claiming to still be part of things.

A day before her final illness, Rae Samba called for Mohedja and reminded her how to raise her children. If they do something wrong, you should let them know; you can scold or shout at them, but no matter what they do to hurt you, you must never ever withdraw your blessing or affection (*rady*) from them. To do so would permanently harm their character. Rae Samba told her this on a Wednesday; by Thursday evening she fell very sick. Clearly, Mohedja said, Rae Samba knew she was dying and wanted to speak first.

In 1980, Mohedja described her mother's death, which had taken place during my absence. To understand her account, it is important to know that houses were primarily for married couples and composed of two rooms. When women got older, they would move into smaller one-room structures, leaving their house for the use of a married daughter or granddaughter. But although adults of different generations never shared the same house, it was considered essential for a parent to be brought to a daughter or son's house when they were close to death, and hence to die in the bosom of their family.

After five days of serious illness, during which her mother had stopped eating, Mohedja took Rae Samba into her own house. Mohedja sent for her brother Asman who was out at his field at Red Rock. She told him she thought their mother was dying and that he should send his son to fetch their older brother, Samba, in F—. Asman visited a week later and Mohedja begged him not to stay at Red Rock any longer. This illness was different from the previous ones, as Rae Samba had never stopped eating before. It would be bad if he had to be called with the news that his mother was already dead.

Asman returned to the field unconvinced and told his wife that they should continue cultivating. But when the wife heard that her mother-in-law was already in Mohedja's house, she insisted on returning to Lombeni at once. She declared that if Asman stayed away, people were not going to be able to say it was because of her! He followed her back to Lombeni and two days later they called their older brother. His entire family came from F—. Ten days after that, Rae Samba died. Her final illness had lasted twenty-two days, Mohedja added with precision. People came from all over for the funeral. The family stayed on through the Islamic sacrifice (*swadaka*) of the ninth day after the death. Some months later, Mohedja supplied a cow for the commemoration ritual (*mandeving*) and they held a Maulida performance (collective singing by women of the poem commemorating the Prophet) on her mother's behalf.

During the last illness, Rae Samba told Mohedja she was dying but Mohedja replied that she should not speak that way. Mohedja, Samba and his wife, and Rae Samba all slept in the "men's half" (*tapa lalahy*, the front room) of Mohedja's house. Tumbu slept in the couple's usual bed in the "women's half" (*tapa viavy*). Only on such occasions, when it was a matter of severe illness, could a brother and sister sleep near each other. Asman also slept there the last night. In fact, no one really slept, but ministered to Rae Samba throughout the night. She wanted to sit up and people had to support her.

After she died, Mohedja and Asman each took one of her beds. Mohedja divided her clothes; she gave a sheet to Samba and she and her adult daughters each took a few items. She kept two small cooking pots. There was nothing else. Kos Vola's goods had come to Mohedja before her mother died. Rae Samba's land passed de facto to Asman since he was the only one still cultivating it. Mohedja and Tumbu found Red Rock too far and had by then purchased their own land. Tumbu said there was never any quarrel about it.

Rae Samba's older sister, whom Mohedja had also been caring for, died three weeks later. They sent a son-in-law to call the people from F—. He drank palm wine in a village on the way, returned to Lombeni, and reported that the kin in F— had said, "We came for our own mother, but this one is not our mother." People from M— (the old woman's village of birth) arrived for the funeral, but no one from F—. A week later, the people in F— heard the news and one of them showed up very angry they had not been informed. The truth came out, but no one punished the miscreant.

The second old woman died in the house of a deceased sister's daughter. Mohedja asked her cousin to take her because she had already received her own mother. The cousin was reluctant, but Mohedja insisted, saying they would all be ashamed to let her die in her "shed" (*bangan*).

Mohedja was at peace with her mother when she died. The same was not true of her brother Asman, who had long had a drinking problem. Here is how Mohedja described it in 1976. (It makes an instructive comparison with Mohedja's sense of herself.)

Tumbu was one of the very few adult men Mohedja could think of who stopped drinking palm wine when he got married and he had not drunk at all since. In contrast, Asman was a particularly heavy drinker, a problem that kept him from the mosque and from most public affairs.[9] Before his marriage, his mother had tried to get him to stop, but to no avail. An older male neighbour dreamt that Asman's deceased father came and told him to stop, but the message fell on deaf ears. Another senior man had a similar dream, again to no effect. Then Asman himself, drunk, saw his father standing and watching him on the path late one night. Yet even so he kept on drinking. Faced with the heavy obligations to marry off his older children and hold his wife's spirit possession ceremonies, he nevertheless began drinking as soon as he awoke. He had no cash crops but earned a bit of money making and selling palm wine. He sold a cow and even spent part of the proceeds of this pre-eminent source of savings on drink. His wife never complained, as most would have, even when he kept a supply of palm wine in the house. In 1975, he began appearing drunk in public. His wife was embarrassed at this and asked Mohedja to talk to him. Although she very much disapproved of her brother's habit, Mohedja did not feel comfortable speaking to him and asked Tumbu to do so on her behalf. At one point her trumba Ndramboeny spoke up and told them to hold a *fatiha* (Muslim prayer) on behalf of their dead father and connected this with the drinking.[10]

Mohedja continued the story in 1980. On her deathbed, Rae Samba urged Asman to forgo drinking. This request had no immediate effect, but sometime later he fell from a palm tree he was tapping and broke a leg and an arm. He lay alone all night under the tree before he was found and then spent five months recuperating in bed. During this time, he had visions of his mother and father who were angry with him. He told Mohedja and she arranged a *fatiha* (prayer) with a ritual meal, calling in Tumbu to recite. Asman recovered and since then had not touched palm wine, even when tempted by others. He called it *haram* (forbidden by God); in fact, it took an act of God to convince him, concluded Mohedja. Since then, he prayed regularly as well.

Mohedja's relationship with Kos Vola recalls Margaret Trawick's remark that for Tamils, "spirit possession is a love relationship, or more precisely, a relationship of Desire…. The possessing other is often an elder kinsman or kinswoman."[11] In the embodied state of possession with Kos Vola, Mohedja was perhaps partially restored to the body of her mother. Their mutual relationship with the spirit provided a dynamic vehicle through which to experience this identification. The sense of wholeness is of course never complete; in a sense it is the yearning that is acknowledged in sharing a spirit with a parent. But the introjection of the spirit affords a deeper identification that offsets the need for the external other. Indeed, after Rae Samba's death, Kos Vola's visits to Mohedja became less frequent.

This was not simply a matter of mother and daughter. Mohedja was positioned as the nucleus of a set of relationships, overlapping with and succeeding her mother as host to Kos Vola, and supported other kin who looked to the spirit as a maternal figure. As Stephen Mitchell puts it, with respect to post-Freudian trends in psychoanalytic theory:

We are … shaped by and inevitably embedded within a matrix of relationships with other people, struggling both to maintain our ties to others and to differentiate ourselves from them. In this vision the basic unit of study is not the individual as a separate entity whose desires clash with an external reality, but an interactional field within which the individual arises and struggles to make contact and to articulate himself [*sic*]. Desire is experienced always in the context of relatedness, and it is that context which defines its meaning. Mind is composed of relational configurations. The person is comprehensible only within this tapestry of relationships, past and present…. In this perspective the figure is always in the tapestry, and the threads of the tapestry (via identifications and introjections) are always in the figure. (1988a, 3)[12]

Chapter Five

Mze Nuru: Affirmation and Identification

As a couple, Tumbu's and Mohedja's lives were intertwined, and their possession histories shaped by each other. In this chapter, I describe Mohedja's initial cohabitation with Mze Nuru; in the next, I describe Tumbu's cohabitation with Mze Marwan. I think of these as "moves" and "responses," not in the sense of a game with rules and competition, but rather as a kind of open dance. Cohabitation with their spirits enabled Mohedja and Tumbu to perform a kind of dance with each other, a dance that took them through over fifty years of marriage. The presence of the spirits also afforded what I call a polylogue, adding new voices and new channels and levels of intimacy between them, as well as providing opportunities for distancing themselves from each other when circumstances seemed to warrant it.

In their dance, Mohedja more often took the lead. She hosted more spirits than Tumbu and they appeared more regularly on the domestic scene and took a more active role in family life than did Tumbu's. Tumbu himself was as likely to defer to and talk about the spirits who entered Mohedja as he was the spirits who entered him. Tumbu drew on the spirits he hosted to practise outside the immediate family as a curer (Lambek 1993). But the difference was only relative: Mohedja received clients outside the family as well, and Tumbu's accommodation with spirits was closely tied to his concerns for Mohedja. They dwelt together. Their cohabitation was mostly harmonious but, as among any close group of people, marked by occasional conflict.

Tumbu and Mohedja's marriage was fortuitous. As Mohedja grew to adolescence, she rejected every suitor who came to call. Finally, her parents suggested engaging her to her stepfather's son from a pre-vious marriage. This proved agreeable to both young people and arrangements were made. They were engaged for some three years. However, before the wedding could take place, Mohedja's mother separated from her husband and moved with Mohedja to Lombeni. At first, Mohedja's stepfather – now former stepfather – remained in agreement about Mohedja's engagement to his son and so Rae Samba went ahead with preparations for the wedding. When the suitor's father came to discuss the details, Rae Samba was absent, visiting kin elsewhere. He became angry and abruptly told Rae Samba's older sis-ter that the marriage with his son was off. Rae Samba, on her return, did not seem to take it much amiss, saying someone else would come along, but the young people were extremely upset. In recounting this, Mohedja pointed out that in the past an engagement was never pur-sued without the acquiescence of the suitors' parents. By 1980, that was no longer always the case; a boy no longer depended on his father's permission.

When Mohedja arrived in Lombeni Kely with her mother, it was the month after Ramadan. A number of men came courting, including Tumbu's two paternal brothers and even his mother's brother. Mohedja rejected all of them. Rae Samba was tolerant and left the choice to her; unlike many mothers, she did not seem nervous that her daughter would lose her virginity before marriage. However, the only person Mohedja had agreed to marry was the son of her former stepfather, suddenly no longer available.

The month they were to have been married was the very month that Tumbu arrived back in Lombeni from his sojourn in Anjouan. Tumbu and Mohedja had never met before but as his mother urged him to marry, he asked her to inquire whether Mohedja would agree, and she did so. I asked Mohedja why she had agreed, and she replied that she was already grown; her age-mates had all married and some had given birth. They were engaged within two months of Tumbu's return. When her previous fiancé discovered that Mohedja was marrying someone else, he wrote her grief-stricken, saying he could not stay in Mayotte any longer and he left the island.

As described in chapter 4, it was during the brief engagement to Tumbu that Kos Vola first rose in Mohedja.

Tumbu and Mohedja married within the same month of their engage-ment, around 1948. Tumbu supplied a cow for the feast and purchased clothing and jewellery for Mohedja that he had saved for in Anjouan. Mohedja had no house (it was the bride's father's duty to build one and it was usually prepared before the marriage) and so they spent the first three and a half years in the house of Mohedja's older female first cousin, which the latter lent them.

Mohedja was very attractive, with an oval face, broad forehead, and unblemished café-au-lait skin. When I knew her, she was neither thin nor unduly fat, unlike many of the women. I did not realize how short she was until I developed a photo taken of us standing together at the end of my first stay. She was not vain, but when she went to town she wore brightly patterned and currently fashionable cloth wraps and put on her gold jewellery and two gold teeth caps. Tumbu was even shorter than Mohedja but very strong. He may have experienced some prejudice because of his dark skin, indicating African (Makua) origins. Some people of more clearly Malagasy descent liked to boast that they would not let their daughters marry men from families like Tumbu's, a sentiment whose time has long since passed. But it was never a consideration for either Mohedja or her mother. Mohedja and Tumbu did not refer to their respective appearance, but it was clear that Mohedja was light-skinned and Tumbu dark, a binary distinction that was relevant only in the neutral selection by divination of auspicious curers for particular cases.

In describing the onset of their marriage, neither Mohedja nor Tumbu spoke about romantic love or passion. Mohedja appeared to have been thinking about her previous fiancé and Tumbu about his lost opportunities for further travel, but they settled into the practical arrangements of a local household. Only a small proportion of people in Lombeni found the "right" union on their first try; most men and women of their generation and the succeeding one had multiple successive spouses. Tumbu once attempted a polygynous marriage, as I will describe in a later chapter, but it proved very brief – "a day or so," as he put it.

Tumbu and Mohedja worked towards common goals and celebrated common achievements. They grew increasingly intimate, evincing mutual respect and solicitousness, and often seeming to know exactly what the other was thinking. They sometimes spoke of themselves as *ulu raiky*, literally "one person." A key factor in this development was their cohabitation with spirits from early in the marriage and their growing mutual interest in them.

Mohedja's Lead: Mze Nuru and the Elder Brother

Mohedja said she was only the second person in Lombeni Kely to acquire a patros. There were already plenty of patros in F— and before her move to Lombeni, she used to attend the ceremonies and watch the dancing. But she was afraid to eat the cakes because she had been told that if she did so, she too would get a patros.

Her patros first entered at the birth of her first child, Nuriaty, which took place within the first two years of marriage. Mohedja recalled she fell ill a week after giving birth. She was very sick for six months and no one could cure her. She was bedridden and so ill that often she did not know the time of day or who was talking to her. They tried all sorts of cures, Muslim prayer rituals (*shijabu*) and sacrifices (*swadaka*), but to no avail. People feared for her life and Mohedja herself thought she was going to die.[1]

Finally, her older [maternal half-] brother, Samba, arrived from F—. Mze Rihu, the spirit with whom he cohabited, rose and said the stars were against Samba himself being the curer, that he was not astrologically compatible (*mwafaka*). At this, Mohedja became even more despondent and was sure she was going to die, since Samba was already a strong and well-known healer and she had known Mze Rihu since childhood. But Samba said that he would try anyway, lest it be said that he had refused to help his little sister. He made her an amulet and fed her medicine composed of a handwritten Koranic verse dissolved in water (*singa*). The spirit [in Mohedja] tore off the amulet. But for the first time in six months Mohedja was able to get up.

Two days later, she was as sick as before. Mze Rihu then advised them to seek Malidy Juma as the curer. Tumbu fetched him in Lombeni Kely. Malidy's patros, Mze Nuru, rose and announced that Mohedja was being bothered by a spirit who would rise. Mohedja laughed over this as she told me, since it turned out that it was Mze Nuru himself who was entering her, though he did not say so at the time.

On his first visit, Malidy extracted a *sairy* and gave her medicine to drink. The *sairy*, a small packet filled with dirt and sharp objects, is the material manifestation of both sorcery and its removal (Lambek 1993), but Mohedja was certain when she spoke to me that there had been no sorcery in this case. Senior spirits, she said, especially those intending to manifest themselves as healers in their hosts, generally entered people of their own accord [rather than being sent by sorcerers], making them sick. In the case of patros, they required the removal of a *sairy* before they stopped making the host sick and rose to her head.

In marking the distinction between spirits sent by sorcerers and those coming of their own accord, Mohedja was, in a sense, suggesting that the spirit was ego-syntonic, that its arrival was acceptable and even desirable, even if not consciously intentional, that the spirit was there to support her and not to harm her.[2] It is unlikely that she knew at the time that the spirit would become a curer (fundi), but it appears that she and her curers were attempting to transform the setback of her illness into something positive. She recognized, at least with hindsight, that right from the start of her marriage, with the birth of her first child, she was setting the stage for a life and career based on cohabitation.

The declaration by Mze Rihu that Samba was astrologically incompatible with a successful cure could have been the result of a simple astrological calculation. However, it may well have been made because Samba was close kin and was himself frightened that Mohedja might die. His suggestion of Malidy Juma as the curer in his stead was a positive one and subject to multiple motivations. Malidy Juma was a classificatory brother of Samba, though no direct relation of Mohedja's, and he was living in Lombeni at the time. He was also the trusted curer who had presided over Samba's own patros ceremony. And finally, he cohabited himself with Mze Nuru.

> Malidy Juma said he would return in a week and that in the meantime they were to cook a red chicken, setting aside the blood, make a cake, and acquire a red cloth. Gradually during that week, Mohedja improved until she was able to get out of bed and even walk about a little – after six months! At the end of the week, Malidy returned, together with the other leading patros fundi from Lombeni Be. They asked her spirit to rise. She'd never been actively possessed (*menziky*) before. She was at a loss (*kushanga*). How would she be *menziky*? What should she do? They lit incense and called the spirit. At first it didn't come. Then a spirit rose in Malidy Juma. She was still at a loss. Finally, the spirit left Malidy and then she began to feel "my body not quite right" (*neñku kara tsy manzary*), like fainting. And then I remembered nothing else. Later they told me I drank blood [from the sacrificed chicken]. One is completely unaware. If one knew what one was doing, one wouldn't do it. But one doesn't know anything."

> This event was sufficient to constitute the *ishima* (courtesy), the first ceremony of a possession cure (normally it is a public event, but Malidy's approach was somewhat idiosyncratic). Malidy asked the spirit what he wanted for the *azulahy be*, the large confirmatory ceremony, and the spirit replied, a red goat. Malidy gave Mohedja more medicine and she became well and was soon going out to the fields again.

> The spirit had said that Mohedja should hold a public ceremony (*azulahy*), on its behalf. But Tumbu, who did not yet have a spirit himself and was not interested in them, didn't support the idea. And so, a year passed and Mohedja fell sick again, not as badly as before, but sick. Tumbu continued to ignore the need for the ceremony. Finally, Mohedja lit some incense, and spoke directly to the spirit, saying that if he wanted his ceremony, he was bothering the wrong person since she did not have the means. The spirit had better do something about Tumbu, since it was he

rather than she herself who was the obstacle. Two days later [in another version, "that very night"], Tumbu fell ill. He went to a diviner, though without informing Mohedja. The diviner told him told that his wife's spirit lay behind his illness; he had broken his promise to the spirit and should hold the ceremony. Immediately he rushed off to S— and returned with a large red goat. Mohedja was astonished and asked what it was for. Tumbu replied that the goat was for her ceremony, and then she knew that her trick had worked. But to that day [5 January 1976, some twenty-three years after the event], she had never told Tumbu what she had done, for fear of him accusing her of having tried to commit sorcery against him.

The two of them went to Malidy Juma to schedule the ceremony. By this time, Malidy had remarried and gone to live in K—, a village not too distant from Lombeni. When Malidy's spirit rose, Tumbu also asked what medicine he needed to cure himself. The spirit replied that holding the *azulahy* for Mohedja's patros would be sufficient, nothing else was necessary. Tumbu asked a second time, to be very sure he didn't need any medicine of his own. [This remark was characteristic of Mohedja's precision in reporting such matters.] Then they collected the accoutrements they needed for the ceremony and set aside rice to make cakes for the guests.

Before her ceremony, Mohedja went to Lombeni Be to invite people who hosted patros. But they laughed at her and said they wouldn't come since she didn't really have a patros. The reason they thought this was that throughout the prior year, whenever they had held patros ceremonies, Mohedja had not attended or joined in, as people with spirits are wont to do. She heard the drums from afar but never felt moved to follow them, nor did her patros rise at the sound. Neither she nor they knew that on the spirit's first appearance, Malidy Juma had specifically instructed him not to go dancing at other peoples' patros ceremonies.

Mohedja grew discouraged and she thought to herself that maybe they were right that she didn't have a patros after all. On the night of her ceremony, very few people attended. The people in Lombeni Kely came to watch but none of them had patros yet. They urged her patros to rise, singing and clapping, but nothing happened and Mohedja kept thinking that maybe the Lombeni Be people were right. Finally, she overheard a guest from another village say that the whole thing was a waste of time and there was no patros. They had never heard of a patros who asked for a ceremony and then refused to rise to celebrate it! Mohedja was upset and embarrassed. People were getting tired and wanted to go off to sleep.

All this time, Malidy Juma had been actively possessed and Mze Nuru had been chatting with Tumbu and others. Now the spirit said he was leaving, and people said that if he left, that would be the end of it. But the instant Mze Nuru left Malidy Juma [he went out of trance], a spirit rose in Mohedja [she went into trance]! They gave the spirit his medicine and the spirit whispered to the fundi the time at which he wished to announce his name [the climax of the ceremony and a moment always kept in suspense]. People danced until, at the appointed hour, the spirit was washed in medicine and emerged on the plaza to announce his name. He was Mze Nuru, the same spirit who cohabited with her fundi, Malidy.

Then the others understood why her patros had not risen earlier. It was already present in Malidy, and a spirit cannot be in two places at once. The reason they had not thought of this before was that they were all still quite inexperienced at dealing with patros.

It was only then that she learned Mze Nuru's name. She said that she had not known the spirit's identity in Malidy Juma either. Mohedja concluded of the ceremony that "one could say it was the fundi treating himself (*ary fundi mitaha neñiny*)!"

I have used this story elsewhere (Lambek 2007) to illustrate the suspense of an emerging identity, the rule-bound nature of the dramatic process, and most importantly, the way a host learns to acknowledge the reality of her cohabitation with a spirit. What is also striking here is the way in which Mohedja unconsciously predetermined who her spirit would be. It was she, with the assistance and tacit acquiescence and perhaps prompting of Malidy, who had subconsciously identified her emerging cohabitant, who had, in a sense, taken control of things, even from an apparent state of illness and subjection. Not only had she demonstrated autonomy in selecting the spirit, but, as we will see, the particular identity she selected was critical in her self-construction. The instant switch of the spirit from Malidy's body to Mohedja's further indicated how they co-constructed the identity of the spirit as Mze Nuru and how Malidy authorized Mze Nuru's presence in Mohedja.

Mohedja's ostensible ignorance of the spirit's identity, and her doubts as to whether she even had a spirit, all the while acting in such a manner as to make it an absolute certainty, was not typical of possession cases. Sometimes the host and her healers already knew the name, but the spirit reserved the right to announce it himself on the occasion of his ceremony. Sometimes the name remained unknown until its revelation at the height of the ceremony, when the patros stepped up on a chair to identify himself.[3] Had the spirit heard others speaking his name before this, he would have been angry and asked people whether they thought he didn't even know his own name and that they had to go around revealing it themselves. This attitude, enunciated explicitly by Mohedja, and evident in the actions of many spirits, indicates at once both the general problem of finding and settling on an identity and the pride of "self-discovery," as it were. To reveal a spirit's name before he did so himself was to shame him and to violate the intimate connection between a host and her cohabiting spirit.

Malidy Juma was a rather idiosyncratic curer. After Mohedja's first ceremony (*ishima*), he advised Mze Nuru not to go dancing at the ceremonies of other patros. Mohedja followed this advice, without any ill effect. One of the main activities of patros is to dance, eat, and enjoy themselves at each other's ceremonies. But Mze Nuru, with the encouragement of Malidy, was reserved. This presumably corresponded to a reserve in Mohedja's character, though the younger spirits, who rose later and less frequently in Mohedja, certainly did not abstain from carousing.

In her recounting, Mohedja also portrayed herself – and the community – as ignorant of the way patros worked. She was learning what it might signify that she was not in trance while her fundi was, even if we can surmise that unconsciously she already knew this. She was learning what it meant to share a spirit with another host. At the same time, she was taking something of a risk; the ceremony could have failed, exactly as she had feared. But the risk and its upshot added to her own growing confidence as a host and fundi herself.

I think that both the sequence of events and their subsequent narration served to convince Mohedja of both the reality of the cohabitation and the identity of the spirit. They showed her transcending her own uncertainty.

I heard about Mohedja's initial illness several times. Once, Mohedja presented Mze Nuru's arrival in a somewhat different and more elaborated fashion. Instead of emphasizing how each of her spirits made her sick at the outset, she singled out those who were beneficent from the beginning. In this version, it was the young patros Darwesh (see chapter 8) who entered her and made her sick. They fetched Malidy Juma to administer medicine and, during the treatment, his cohabiting spirit, Mze Nuru, took the opportunity to transfer himself to Mohedja as well. Mze Nuru himself did not make her sick. In other words, while the spirits arrived directly after each other, it was Darwesh who made her ill, while Mze Nuru, in fact, put the illness on hold. In this way, Mze Nuru was portrayed as consistently beneficent, a view that corresponded with her subsequent experience.

Tumbu's versions of events did not discount any of this. In December 1975, he explained that Mohedja had been sick from the beginning of their marriage. She was treated a first time and Mze Nuru rose; treated a second time and Darwesh rose. Malidy Juma managed the ceremonies for both spirits. In 1980, Tumbu clarified that Mze Nuru and Darwesh had entered Mohedja at about the same time, but that Darwesh did not actually rise in her until much later. The ceremony for Mze Nuru took place before they moved to Red Rock while Darwesh's was held only sometime after they returned to Lombeni for good.

Comparing alternate versions of the arrival of Mze Nuru is not simply a matter of recording the actual sequences of events in order to see which is correct. Each narrative was true for Mohedja at the time she recounted it and shaped it for a particular listener and context. Moreover, the nature of spirits is such that new versions may always be constructed retroactively. Mohedja was sick and Mze Nuru rose. Darwesh rose only a few years later. But with hindsight, it became apparent to her that Darwesh had actually entered her first – and caused her illness – but remained silent until well after Mze Nuru had risen, held his *azulahy*, and gone on to assist the family and Mohedja herself. As Tumbu finally remarked to me when I was puzzling over these sequences, one cannot know for certain when a spirit first enters or engages with you – only when it first rises.

The critical point was that since his arrival, Mze Nuru had been a positive influence, a sort of parental or older sibling figure in the family, perhaps an ego ideal. In that sense, the comparison with Kos Vola, the trumba who came to her from her mother, is appropriate. Each of these spirits who were to cohabit with Mohedja – Kos Vola and Mze Nuru – indexed vertical connections, links to senior relatives with whom she had strong positive associations, namely, her mother and, as I will show, her considerably older brother, Samba, respectively. Likewise, her account emphasized her positive identification with the curer Malidy Juma, also closely linked to Samba.

Mohedja also pointed out that while some spirits had caused her less trouble than others, any of them could act up at any time. There were periods, she said, when she spent a whole month coughing. This was caused by one or the other cohabiting spirits, and cough medicine only aggravated it. When a cohabiting spirit got angry for some reason, he could leave you in a lot of discomfort. Living together with someone was not always easy.

The identification of Mze Nuru, destined to be the most trusted spirit of the household, was not accidental. Mze Nuru was not only the same spirit to cohabit with the admired curer, Malidy Juma, but he was also the younger full sibling of Mze Rihu, the spirit who cohabited with Mohedja's beloved older half-brother, Samba – a man she looked up to and trusted and who had been originally called in to treat her.

Samba had been born in Lombeni but was taken to F— when their mother, Rae Samba, married Salim (Mohedja's father). Salim decided to marry Samba to the daughter of his sister in F—. Samba's wife was thus Mohedja's first cousin. Samba had acquired Mze Rihu before Mohedja and her mother left F— for Lombeni. Mohedja recalled having seen Samba with the spirit since her early childhood, for as long as she could remember. Mohedja returned to F— shortly after her marriage in order to attend Samba's patros ceremony (*azulahy*), in which the identity of Mze Rihu was publicly announced and legitimated. But Samba was already a fundi of spirits well before the ceremony. He was also a respected astrologer (*mwalim dunia*) and Mze Rihu, when cohabiting with Samba, manifested as an astrologer as well.

Samba (whom I never met) was one of the few older men I heard Mohedja speak about in unqualifiedly positive terms. She was a good deal less sanguine about her second older brother, Asman, her only full sibling, who had also come to live in Lombeni, and who was a mild-mannered and rather ineffective person. Recall that Mohedja's father died when she was quite young, whereas Samba had remained a stable presence throughout her childhood and youth. Samba was, I think, a kind of idealized father figure for her. It was not uncommon for parent-less siblings to address one of their number as father or mother and to look to that person for social and material support. However, Mohedja herself said Samba was not a father for her in this sense since they themselves did not share paternity. That followed the cultural logic in Mayotte, but I mean it in an emotional and possibly unconscious sense. Samba was a man upon whom Mohedja allowed herself to direct her dependency feelings.

This was confirmed in 2000 when Mohedja described her reaction to Samba's death. This was very sudden. When one of his sons came to inform her, she did not believe him at first. On the ride to F— she kept thinking to herself, "What am I going to do if it is true? I depend on him for everything." When she saw his body, she fainted.

For Mohedja, then, the identity of Mze Nuru was multiply motivated. On the one hand, it affirmed her connection to the brother she admired and, through him, to her home village, F—. A woman's brother was a source of security should a marriage not work out. Had Mohedja and Tumbu quarrelled, she could always have returned to F—. Indeed, her relatives there kept asking her to do so. Shortly after they were married and before Mohedja had given birth, Mohedja and Tumbu began fostering Zara, a daughter of Samba's. Some twenty years later, when Zara's marriage to a cross-cousin in Lombeni was in difficulty, she did retire to F—, where she had not lived since infancy, until her husband made things up to her and coaxed her back.

Mohedja was not only affirming links with her brother, but in partially identifying with him, she was also striking out as her own person. Mze Nuru was the younger sibling of Samba's patros, but nonetheless a senior, authoritative, and knowledgeable spirit in his own right. Both siblings – Mze Rihu and Mze Nuru – were said to cohabit with very few hosts and when they did so, they always appeared as fundis.

If Mohedja looked up to Samba and possibly idealized him, cohabiting with Mze Nuru in effect served to internalize and partially introject him. Indeed, she once told me that she saw Mze Nuru in her dreams with a face like that of Samba. She became, in a sense, a refraction of her own father imago; or rather, her father – as she imagined him – became a part of herself.[4]

Mze Nuru was also the very spirit who cohabited with Malidy Juma, who had been Samba's curer and would become her curer, and who was another person whom she admired and who mediated the connection with her brother. Mohedja called Malidy zuky (older sibling) as well. Cohabitation with the same spirit was again a form both of identification and of autonomy. In time, she would not need these impressive men since she had internalized the spirit for herself. Mature individuation works by means of connection.[5]

From the account above, it appears that the identity of the spirit may also have been enabled and motivated by Samba's actions in directing Mohedja to Malidy Juma. In other words, Samba's refusal to take the case and his recommendation of his own colleague and fundi may have been a tacit message to Mohedja about who her spirit might turn out to be – that is, Mohedja was identifying with Mze Nuru with the permission, and possibly at the tacit suggestion, of her brother.

It is a reasonable question why she did not take on her brother's spirit, Mze Rihu. Perhaps such proximity was too dangerous, with undertones of competition or even incest. By taking on the younger sibling, she maintained the relationship she had with Samba.

Mze Nuru's arrival was not simply an internal matter for Mohedja, but rather enabled her to look out for her family and start a career as a curer. Mohedja told me that Mze Nuru started rising to give advice to the family and began healing people as soon as they held his confirmation ceremony (*azulahy*) and he announced his name. After the ceremony, Malidy Juma said, "Your spirit already knows medicines, but you don't yet." So Malidy came to teach Mohedja, and she paid him for the lessons. Tumbu's response will follow.

Mohedja went on to cohabit with several other spirits, but Mze Nuru remained the most consistent and reliable. He cared for Mohedja and her family with attention and compassion.

Chapter Six

Mze Marwan and Mze Rihu: Consolidation and Cooperation

Tumbu recalled how his illnesses interfered with his productive activities. Long ago, early in their marriage, he and Mohedja were prosperous, with sheep, goats, chickens, and ducks. He tended up to fifteen head of cattle that he kept on a plot of land they rented from a nearby plantation. These included animals brought by Mohedja (and hence belonging to her) and those belonging to his elder brother. Then, shortly after their second daughter, Mariam, was born (c. 1953), Tumbu became ill and could not take care of the livestock; many died. However, the loss of the animals was not simply a consequence of Tumbu's inability to care for them. As he reflected, sometimes, if God makes you sick, the worst of the affliction will be taken out on your livestock, killing them but letting you live.

While God was the ultimate source of his trouble, the proximate one was sorcery. The animals died and both Tumbu and Mohedja were afflicted with spirits. Tumbu was very sick (*marary maresaka*) when Mze Marwan wanted to enter him. Tumbu thought he would die. He felt sick throughout his body, from mid-afternoon through the night, with a high fever. There were days when he just stayed home and could do no work. Mze Marwan kept him sick, off and on, for three years; they thought it was simply a disease (*areting*) and tried treatment after treatment to no avail (*nañan audy ata vaha*).

In 1992, Tumbu recounted how he had been quite shaken to finally realize he had a spirit. He went to a fundi for treatment in S—. Her patros rose and said he would heal Tumbu, but only if Tumbu gave him a cow (either sex). Tumbu's herd was thriving then, and he agreed. He was told to come back in three days' time, in the evening, with kin. And so, he returned with Mohedja and his mother. The curer prepared medicine, lit a fire, and covered him with a cloth so he could inhale the medicine. After some time, his body began to shake, as though he were frightened or shivering. He began to heat up until he could no longer cope. "I can remember until the moment I transformed, under the cloth. I thrashed about like someone very angry. They held me and from that moment I didn't know anything [lost consciousness]. They said I struggled hard until finally a spirit rose and demanded to know why they had called him." The spirit then said he rejected taking medicine from the patros of the healer in S— and wanted treatment from Mwana Sidy, an unrelated older woman in Lombeni Be.

Another time I heard that the cure worked only when the fundi in S— turned eventually to "bad medicine" (*audy ratsy*), the kind used to drive out an evil spirit, in contrast to the fragrant medicine used to coax a spirit to be amenable to living together with the host in peace. It was only when Tumbu inhaled acrid smoke that the spirit finally rose, agreed to speak with them, and declared that he wanted Mwana Sidy to administer the ceremony.

In any case, the next day, early in the morning, the healer from S— arrived to claim her animal and Tumbu gave her a small male calf. Tumbu then went to Mwana Sidy. At first, she called the spirit to no avail. "He didn't want to rise," said Tumbu. "I was in pain all over my body, but the spirit didn't come. Because he didn't want to." Eventually they gave him sufficient medicine so that the spirit rose. He asked for cakes and a black goat for his initiatory ceremony. Tumbu was still sick then but not so badly that he could not get up in the mornings and go to work. He only felt ill by mid-afternoon when he came home, bathed, and went to pray. He was able to find someone in a distant village who was selling a black goat and brought it home. They held the ceremony in Lombeni Be, at Mwana Sidy's, where she and her husband cohabited with several patros. It was then that Mze Marwan announced his name.

Tumbu explained that the healer was Mwana Sidy rather than the fundi in S— or Malidy Juma because that was who the spirit asked for. Spirits very often are treated by one fundi and then at the last minute call for another fundi to manage their ceremony. This often makes the first curer angry. The first curer complains that they have done all the work and now will not receive the money, cakes, and other benefits that come with the ceremony. But there is really nothing one can do about it. Such fundis, said Tumbu, were in any case more interested in the material rewards of the business than in curing people. And anyhow, he said, it worked out more or less evenly in the end, since these fundis would get clients coming to them for their ceremony in the same way.

The choice of fundi was again not random. Mohedja recalled in 1980 that unlike a recent *azulahy* at which Mze Marwan danced all night in Tumbu's body, at Tumbu's own ceremony the spirit rose only briefly in him, then switched to Mwana, in whom he danced all night, and then rose again in Tumbu just before dawn, to announce his name. He was Mze Marwan, the very spirit who already cohabited with Mwana Sidy. As Tumbu explained to me, this was why Mze Marwan had demanded that Mwana Sidy officiate the ceremony. In other words, though Tumbu did not originally know the identity of his patros, the spirit had basically demanded that he treat himself. Mze Marwan officiated in the ceremony marking his new residence with Tumbu. By selecting Mwana Sidy as the curer, Mze Marwan was in effect making a statement about the strength of his presence with and for Tumbu.

Mze Marwan's appearance initiated a long collaboration between Tumbu and Mwana and her husband. They were a generation older, among the first in the area to develop patros spirits, and the main orchestrators of patros ceremonies in Lombeni Kely. It may not be coincidental that Mwana Sidy's husband had also been for a short time married to Tumbu's mother. The two women had been co-wives and the man was thus a former stepfather to Tumbu. The husband (deceased by the time I first arrived) had been a significant patros fundi and his main spirit moved on to cohabit with many of his and Mwana Sidy's descendants.

At subsequent events, Mze Marwan would slip with ease between Tumbu and Mwana. When Marwan took the face (*sora*) of Mwana in Tumbu's dreams, it meant that Marwan was in a good mood and had come to talk. When he took another face, he came to fight. Marwan was not as strong a curer in Mwana as he became in Tumbu. Mwana never learned how to extract sorcery or to divine as Tumbu did. Yet because Marwan had been in Mwana much longer than in himself, Tumbu extended courtesy to her. Whenever he was mildly ill, he asked her help to collect plant medicine and he invited her to all the spirit ceremonies he managed. They developed a tradition of inviting each other to the ceremonies they oversaw. However, Tumbu pointed out that some people who shared a spirit did not get along. Each wanted the spirit to himself or herself and was jealous of the other's knowledge since the spirit did not make each of its hosts fundis equally.

In 1975, I participated in a cure Tumbu orchestrated for one of his younger female cousins who lived in another village. She and Tumbu had a close relationship. The spirit demanded that the *azulahy* be held in Lombeni Kely and that Mwana be invited. Once again, the spirit turned out to be Mze Marwan. The cousin became an active curer, eventually moving her practice to La Réunion. Mze Marwan also moved in with Tumbu's daughter Nuriaty and in later years she began to take over his caseload as Tumbu gradually withdrew. Unlike in Tumbu's case, Mze

Marwan's entry in his cousin and daughter made them only mildly ill. In 1975, Tumbu described Mze Marwan as already quite an old man; in entering his young cousin, he said, Marwan was like an elder who marries a young virgin bride, seeking someone with more vigour. Another time, he described Marwan as a young adult with a strong destiny (*zaza misy nyora*).

Mze Marwan's cohabitation with several cooperating hosts was quite different from that of Mze Nuru, who himself explained to me (long after Malidy's death) that he cohabited with no one else in Lombeni and did not like to cohabit with many people. We were attending the ceremony for Tumbu's cousin at the time. Nuriaty was dancing with a spirit who had not yet given his name. Mze Nuru observed that he knew the identity of the spirit (Mze Marwan) but could not mention it before the spirit himself had the chance to do so at the naming ceremony Nuriaty would produce for him. However, he asserted, it was certainly not Mze Nuru himself, as indeed it could not have been, as both spirits were present at once.

When I questioned why Mze Nuru had not moved on to one of Mohedja's adult children, I was told that it was characteristic of this spirit that he entered only one member of a family at a time. Tumbu explained that Mze Nuru was interested in their daughter Mariam but would only begin to cohabit directly with her when Mohedja herself was near death. As we'll see later, this prediction came to pass.

Tumbu attributed the fact that he received spirits to his destiny (*nyora*). The word *nyora* also refers to one's constitution, as a product or facet of destiny. Tumbu described his constitution as *mahery*, meaning tough, strong, resistant, or resilient. It was this toughness that led to the protracted struggle when Mze Marwan first wanted to enter his body. He could fight back and was able to withstand Mze Marwan's entry and so the spirit pushed harder. The struggle was a difficult one, lasting three years, until the fundi in S— finally enabled the spirit to rise. Once the spirit was installed, the strength of Tumbu's *nyora* became an asset, enabling him to learn to extract sorcery and to perform as a sorcery extractor, a practice in which one has to be able to confront and withstand the spirits sent to attack one's clients.

Tumbu here drew from a pair of concepts central in Mayotte. The terms in question are *malemy* and *mahery*. According to context, they can mean, respectively, soft and hard, weak and strong, receptive and resistant, pliable and stubborn, sensitive and tough. *Mahery* can also mean difficult and *malemy* can mean easy, flexible, or readily agreeable. People's destiny and character may be ascertained as either *malemy* or *mahery*. The distinctions are not absolute, and the terms do not carry the identical values associated with the English translations. Tumbu saw himself as *mahery* in comparison to Mohedja. This meant that she was more vulnerable to the arrival of spirits, but also that she was able to live with them more easily than he could. He could withstand the anger of bad spirits (not the possessing kind) whom he extracted from clients in curing them of sorcery more easily than she could. She knew how to extract sorcery, but it affected her more. She was more sensitive, more receptive. But by the same token, when a spirit was determined to enter him, Tumbu would fight back harder and sustain more injury in the process than might Mohedja.

This difference in constitution implicated their respective practice. When he taught Mohedja medicine, Malidy Juma warned her not to practise as a sorcery extractor, as her constitution was *malemy*. This meant she was vulnerable to the advent and attacks of spirits and extraction would make her sick all the time.

In 1975, Tumbu suggested that spirits tend to follow their principals (*tompin*, hosts) in character or constitution. They are soft if the host is soft, quarrelsome if the host is quarrelsome, and so on. But at the same time, a spirit can transform his host, turning someone who was not previously a fundi into one. Tumbu said this was what happened in his case. In 1985, he added a different but not incompatible explanation for his career as a curer, attributing his development to his teachers. Tumbu then confirmed that he learned how to remove sorcery from Mze Nuru, both when he appeared in Mohedja and when he rose in Malidy Juma. And from the latter he learned also how to return sorcery packages (*sairy*) to the person who sent them, and even how to initiate sorcery.

Sorcery can be extracted from clients either by a knowledgeable *patros* or by the knowledgeable host of such a spirit. Some practitioners can perform an extraction only when they are under direct possession by their *patros* – that is, it is always the *patros* who carries it out. In Tumbu's case, however, sometimes Mze Marwan performed the extraction, but more frequently Tumbu did so directly himself. This was a skill he had to learn from someone.

Tumbu's decision to become a curer and sorcery extractor happened through the suggestions and intervention of both Mze Nuru and Mohedja herself. In fact, Tumbu explained, he had three teachers – Malidy Juma, Mze Nuru, and then eventually Mze Marwan – who taught him directly. As Tumbu recounted it, Mze Nuru rose in Mohedja and proposed to Tumbu that the two of them practise medicine and treat people together. Mze Nuru urged Tumbu to hold the *azulahy* for Mze Marwan quickly so that they could start. They had already begun working together before Tumbu ever received a spirit of his own. He accompanied Mze Nuru into the forest (*añala*), where the spirit instructed him on medicinal plants. Mze Nuru organized *azulahy*s and performed other kinds of medicine while possessing Mohedja. But when there was a task for which Mze Nuru considered Mohedja too vulnerable (*malemy*), he asked Tumbu to take over. In particular, Mze Nuru speaking through Mohedja told Tumbu that he (Mze Nuru) would not extract *sairy* while he was possessing her and that Tumbu should not let Mohedja extract on her own as she was too vulnerable (*malemy*).

This was a pattern with Mohedja. When she was torn about doing something, one of her spirits would rise and ask Tumbu or someone else close to her to tell her to desist. Occasionally I served as the intermediary between Mze Nuru and Mohedja myself.

In a conversation in 1985, Tumbu said that Mze Nuru knew how to extract sorcery when he possessed Mohedja. Mohedja herself wanted to learn from him but Tumbu agreed with Mze Nuru's request to learn in her place. Her constitution (*nyora*) was far too sensitive (*malemy*) and she would internalize everything too deeply, not have sufficient detachment, and thus continually get ill. Perhaps one could say that Mohedja's emotional empathy enabled her to understand others' problems, but it also made her vulnerable to sharing them. Tumbu himself refused to extract sorcery at night because the spirit would follow him home and either make him suffer or affect Mohedja or one of the children. Often, they would cry out during the night after he had performed an extraction.

Mohedja generally agreed with Tumbu on these points. She told me that Malidy had told her early on that her constitution was too *malemy* (sensitive, receptive) to extract sorcery packets (*sairy*). (*Sairy* are extracted from an ailing body part or sometimes from the ground.) And that was why he went on to teach the art to Tumbu. But she must have been ambivalent about this and sometimes phrased things differently. In a conversation in April 1976, Mohedja said she was capable of extracting sorcery but simply chose not to do so. Mze Nuru had taught her in her sleep by taking her along to extract with him. She affirmed that she had subsequently conducted an extraction herself. The reason she no longer did so was not that she was too *malemy* to fight off the spirits after an extraction, but because she was too young, and because extraction was not an appropriate activity for women. (However, a few other women did extract.) The reason was not one of vulnerable *nyora*, but that women should not be going off to different villages as the job demanded. She said she was too young to do curing of any kind, yet she evidently did a good deal. On a case within Lombeni Kely that very week she treated a neighbour's infant but passed on the extraction of sorcery to Tumbu.

Whatever the reason, it seems clear that Mohedja wanted Tumbu to join in her practice and to carry out tasks that would complement hers, especially travelling to clients in other villages.

Mze Nuru put things this way. Speaking to me through Mohedja in late January 1976, he said that while Mohedja was very knowledgeable, she did not like to practise as a healer. When Malidy was alive and wanted to make her his apprentice, he took her to observe his cases and taught her a lot. (This was what Tumbu was doing with me at the time.) Mze Nuru affirmed that Mohedja knew everything, even how to extract sorcery, and that in the early days Mze Nuru did so while possessing Mohedja. She learned all this before Tumbu knew any of it. On this occasion, Mze Nuru said that Tumbu had started learning from Malidy Juma at his own initiative. Yet, Mze Nuru remarked, it could be that Mohedja still knew more than Tumbu did and occasionally advised him. Mohedja would work with clients when they came to her but was embarrassed to go beyond Lombeni to practise.

Mze Nuru added that "he himself" (Mze Nuru) did *not* have a soft constitution and was perfectly capable of extracting sorcery and fighting off the spirits who were its bearers and that he had done so in the past. Mohedja was exposed to any unpleasantness only should the extracted spirits come to fight when he, Mze Nuru, happened to be away somewhere else.

Mze Nuru went on to say that Mohedja often did not listen to the advice he gave her, that she could be quite obstinate. Sometimes he preferred to tell her things through third parties (as he was then speaking to me). She often complained that she did not like to be possessed and that it was bad to be accompanied by spirits, and yet he, Mze Nuru, had never caused her any trouble since the original illness when he first entered her.

One could say that Mohedja was of two minds about these matters. But note also a sense of self-love and of confidence, even bravado.

As she grew older, Mohedja became less embarrassed to work as a curer, but she never again performed a sorcery extraction.

Tumbu himself acknowledged Mze Nuru and gave him precedence. He described Mze Nuru as *hodary*, strong and responsible, in the sense of reliable, someone you could count on. He said further that Mze Nuru was a good, well-disposed person. Spirits in general were bad, but this one had a good disposition (*lulu ratsy fo i tsara fañahy*). Mohedja, explained Tumbu, did not have to study with anyone. She became a fundi more directly; the spirits who rose in her were already fundis in their own right and taught her themselves. Tumbu himself studied with Malidy Juma in order to learn to extract sorcery. He explained that one has to study with someone if one is going to extract in person, that is, without being in a state of active possession at the time. But if one extracts only when taken over by a spirit, one does not need to study how to do it.

Tumbu emphasized what a good person Mze Nuru was. Unlike other spirits who might fight and make you ill directly if you did something that displeased them, Mze Nuru would always come and tell you first and only get irritated when you did not follow his advice. Tumbu listened to him, following his advice and carrying out his requests. Mze Nuru, he said, was a *mwalim* (diviner, cosmologer), at least as he appeared in Mohedja.

It was Mze Nuru who initiated Tumbu's curing career and who urged him to study with Malidy, in order to both heal himself and learn to treat others. And so Tumbu went to K— to study with Malidy Juma. He explained that he was careful to make friends with him and establish a relationship of trust such that he came to call Malidy "older sibling" (*zuky*). Malidy agreed to teach him what he knew. Malidy liked him because he learned fast. Tumbu was also friends with Mze Nuru; Tumbu observed that if you are friends with a person, you will get along with their cohabiting spirits as well. When Tumbu needed advice at home he could always just call upon Mze Nuru in Mohedja, since Malidy and Mohedja shared him. But Tumbu often travelled to K— from Red Rock (it was not too far away) or Malidy visited them. This was around 1960 when Tumbu was in his early thirties and he and Mohedja had been married for over a decade.

Sometimes Mze Nuru would rise in Mohedja and tell Tumbu to go to K— the following day. When Tumbu arrived in K— Mze Nuru would immediately rise in Malidy Juma and say, "Let's get to work!" There was no need for lighting incense and spending time calling the spirit to rise; the spirit was expecting him. This, said Tumbu, was why he was certain that Mze Nuru was an actual spirit.

Tumbu admitted he was puzzled why when his own spirit, Marwan, told him to go to Mwana Sidy, he had to light incense and specifically call up the spirit. And then when Marwan rose in Mwana he would ask Tumbu what he wanted. Tumbu would reply in consternation, "But it was you who called for me!" Tumbu said that in fact the experiences of most hosts were similar, making Mze Nuru's understanding all the more impressive.

All of this shows the close relationships that prevailed among Mohedja, Tumbu, Malidy, and Mze Nuru and how effective and astute Malidy was.

In effect, the triangular relationship between Mohedja, her brother, and Tumbu was redrawn in another form by means of Mohedja's fundi, Malidy Juma, who subsequently became Tumbu's teacher as well and whose spirit was Mze Nuru. This was facilitated by the arrival of Tumbu's most active patros, Mze Marwan.

Despite Mze Nuru's remarks, back in the 1950s, Mohedja herself had not been sufficiently confident to work as a healer. When Tumbu began to think about becoming a healer himself, he found himself cohabiting with Mze Marwan, albeit not without an intense struggle. This might have been a competitive move on Tumbu's part, but it was also an affirmative one; his relationship with Mohedja became one of cooperating equals as well as mutual affection. This is a structural process that was common to a relatively small proportion of marital unions in Mayotte: in a successful, long-lasting marriage, the relationship between spouses took on in practice the kind of solidarity and durability that characterized the cross-sibling relationship in principle. Spouses came to be trusted in the way that siblings were. To draw on the language of Marshall Sahlins (2013), with respect to kinship, the relationship between Mohedja and Tumbu became increasingly one of "mutuality of being." Indeed, as already noted, they often spoke in that fashion as being *ulu raiky*, one person. Their intimacy was not only with respect to their own personal matters but to the issues their clients brought them and how they discussed them in private and discerned what to tell their clients in turn.

Tumbu also considered himself Malidy's successor. In December 1975, he remarked that he had been Malidy Juma's favourite student/ apprentice (*mwanafundi*). He was always careful to follow Malidy exactly and never to counter or attempt to undermine him, and so it was to him that Malidy Juma bequeathed his practice. But he deferred to Mze Nuru, adding that it was really Mze Nuru who knew the cures. When Tumbu dreamt of Mze Nuru he had the appearance of Malidy.

By the time Malidy Juma died, Tumbu had learned what the older man had to teach. But Tumbu added that Mze Nuru continued to know more than he did, and he continued to ask him for further instruction, from this point forwards exclusively in Mohedja. As Mohedja fell sick when she took on the most difficult cases herself, Tumbu handled them, but taking advice from Mze Nuru. In this way they made a good team.

Once Tumbu's relations with his own spirits were well established, he began to receive instruction from them as well. Tumbu had received a handwritten notebook of *nyora* (astrological constellations and their respective impact on destiny) from Malidy Juma. However, as he explained in 1985, his own spirits also taught him astrological calculations (*hisabu*) in his sleep. He often dreamt the night before clients came and was thereby prepared by his spirits to expect them. The dreams signalled what the client's problem was and whether he would be successful at the cure. If he dreamt of fighting, the case would be difficult. If he lost in the dream or was unable to beat his opponent, he would not take the case. If he won but not without a "sweat," the case would be hard and need a big offering (*swadaka*) from the client. If he won easily and the opponent ran off quickly, the cure would be easy. In the event he was not pre-advised, he would look intently at the client's face and listen to what he or she had to say and would soon be able to evaluate the situation. Tumbu frequently also received advice concerning clients from Mohedja's dreams.

Tumbu received two further patros while they were living at Red Rock. His account of their arrival illustrates how they considerably thickened the relationship between him and Mohedja.

Mze Drudrudru arrived as a result of a quarrel over their plot of farmland on which Tumbu and his in-laws were cultivating dry rice, coconuts, coffee, black pepper, vanilla, and various subsistence crops. Tumbu explained that a man who was cultivating an adjacent plot had his eyes on expanding to include theirs as well. The man planned to apply for a property deed and brought a surveyor to take measurements. Mohedja and Tumbu were raising a daughter of her brother Samba, named Zara. Zara was then a young adolescent and very pretty. So, the man said to Tumbu that if he gave him Zara in marriage, he would let them have the land. Tumbu smoothly replied, "But why didn't you say so first? That will not be difficult to arrange." The man asked whether Tumbu had the authority to give Zara in marriage and Tumbu assured him that he did. So, they went together to the surveyor and asked him to put the application in the name of Mohedja's mother and full brother, Asman, who were cultivating there with them. The surveyor was agreeable and measured out 5.5 ha. Tumbu and Asman then rushed across the island to the land office to register the title, bribing the agent with 25 kg of rice to overlook the neighbour's prior request. Meanwhile the man had no idea they had gone ahead and was very surprised when he was informed. He raced to the land office, but it was too late. When he asked for Zara, they told him he would have to go and put the request to Samba, her biological father, living in F—. They had had of course no intention to give him Zara in marriage; the man was much older than Zara and she had no interest in him. Instead, they engaged her to a cross-cousin in Lombeni Kely (with whom she has since had a long and happy marriage).

The man was very angry and planted sorcery in their field so that they would not flourish. He was aiming at Tumbu, who was the one who had tricked him, but it was Mohedja, being more vulnerable (*malemy*), who caught it and she fell gravely ill. Tumbu rushed to his uncle, the senior astrologer in Lombeni Kely. He provided medicine, which expelled the sorcery-bearing spirit from Mohedja. Mohedja recovered but the result was that the spirit transferred himself to Tumbu! The spirit made Tumbu very sick and then rose and requested Mze Nuru in Malidy Juma as his fundi. On the application of some herbal medicine, he simply announced his name: Mze Drudrudru, from Mjiny Kwale, the site of an ancient coastal village, known as home to eels and snakes. He did not require a public ceremony, but only a red chicken and cakes, a meal which he shared at home with Mze Nuru.

This, said Tumbu, with some amusement, was what happened to him as a result of the trick he had played on the man who had wanted his in-laws' fields. Once the fields were secured, Tumbu left Red Rock for Lombeni in order to acquire fields of his own. But the arrival of Mze Drudrudru provided another opportunity for him to study with Malidy. Tumbu would visit him in K— and sleep over in order to receive further instruction. There, both Malidy Juma himself and Mze Nuru taught him. And when he returned home, the teaching from Mze Nuru would continue as he rose in Mohedja. Mze Nuru, said Tumbu, was a great fundi and taught him all matters concerning spirits. He taught him both from Malidy Juma in K— and from Mohedja at home. At night they would converse together.

Shortly after the arrival of Mze Drudrudru, while they still lived at Red Rock, another patros came to cohabit with Tumbu. This was Mze Rihu, the same spirit who cohabited with Mohedja's brother, Samba. Mze Rihu rose in Samba and announced that he would also cohabit with Tumbu. The reasoning was as follows: just as Samba was Mohedja's older brother, so was Mze Rihu Mze Nuru's older brother. He was concerned that he could not always attend to Mohedja while she lived out at Red Rock. Mze Rihu said that for serious matters Tumbu should come to F— to seek him out in Samba but that for lesser concerns, he should ask Mze Rihu for advice directly and Mze Rihu would then rise (in Tumbu) and know what to do.

There was another factor in Mze Rihu's arrival in Tumbu. The Shehu who was married to Rae Samba's older sister with whom they lived together at Red Rock had called upon Mze Rihu in Samba to serve as guardian of their fields (Tumbu used the French word *guardien*). If a thief came along, the spirit would take hold of him and make him sick. Tumbu, together with the Shehu's son, once harvested some black pepper without the old man's knowledge and laid it out on rocks to dry, in order to sell it. Mze Rihu grabbed hold of Tumbu and unexpectedly rose in him, claiming that Tumbu had stolen the pepper. Tumbu had not done so but merely collected it. It was the Shehu's son who had proposed to Tumbu that they dry and sell the pepper corns, but the spirit attacked only Tumbu.

It was this incident that prompted Tumbu to go to F— where he learned of Mze Rihu's plan to cohabit with him. That way, said Mze Rihu, Tumbu would not always have to go seek advice in F— but could find it at home.

Tumbu laughed in narrating the story. Mze Rihu bothered only him, not the Shehu's son, but he did not actually make Tumbu sick either. It was, in a way, an act of friendship. It also seems to show that spirits have a sense of humour.

By cohabiting with Mze Rihu, the patros who possessed Samba, Tumbu brought him directly into the household. The cohabitation confirmed his deep entry into his wife's family and an identification with her brother, one that the latter could easily have challenged had he wanted. The appearance of Mze Rihu had the practical result of making his authority available to the household even while Samba lived at some distance.

However, Mze Rihu never dominated or displaced the centrality of Mze Nuru in the family and Tumbu never fully replaced his brother-in-law as a figure of authority and respect. Perhaps his presence had not been strongly motivated but was largely at the suggestion of Samba himself. During the time I knew them, Mze Rihu was not a central figure in Tumbu's practice, and I don't think he ever was. It was the connection via Mze Drudrudru with Malidy Juma that proved more significant. Even there, however, it was Mze Marwan who proved the central spirit for Tumbu's practice and who was the main spirit of Tumbu's to continue to learn from Malidy and from Mze Nuru.

In sum, it is evident that the arrival and integration of the two main patros spirits, Mze Nuru and Mze Marwan, consolidated respectively Mohedja and Tumbu's positions as curers and thickened the ties between them. Mze Nuru was hosted by Mohedja but developed close relations with Tumbu, while Mze Marwan was hosted by Tumbu and developed close relations with Mohedja. Both Mohedja and Mze Nuru played significant roles in fostering the development of Tumbu's career and continued to provide advice and assist his practice. Tumbu and Mze Marwan likewise supported Mohedja's practice. The two spirits also knew and acknowledged each other. They cooperated in protecting the household and in curing its members as well as the various clients who came seeking assistance from any one of them.

Here is a brief illustration of their cooperation in curing activities.[1] One day in April 1976, a neighbouring couple came to Mohedja to treat their sick child. They selected Mohedja because a diviner had told them the child's destiny (*nyora*) called for a light-skinned curer. They called up Mze Nuru for a consultation and the spirit told them to provide a red chicken as an offering and to hold a ceremony to remove evil eye (*dzitzo*). Mohedja told me later that she did not know how to extract evil eye and so Mze Nuru would do it. A week later, Mohedja picked medicine at a crossroads as instructed by Mze Nuru in a dream. As part of the cure, Mze Nuru recited (*midzor*) a prayer from the Qur'an, something not expected of women or of spirits, but he did so anyway. He invited Tumbu to utter the closing *fatiha*, the most sacred verse. Mze Nuru also asked Tumbu to extract sorcery from the client's household, which Mze Marwan then rose to do. However, a few days later, the infant's condition worsened and he died.

The death led to a discussion with Mohedja about dreams. Mohedja told me she always knew in advance when she became ill. She would dream of it and a few days later she would be lying sick in bed. However, I discovered that by no means were all her dreams communications from her spirits. It turned out that both Mohedja and Musy Matwar, a fellow healer and elder relative of the infant, had had dreams portending the death of the infant. Mohedja explained that some people, but by no means the majority, had dreams that gave portents of things about to happen. Both she and her friend had such dreams. She said she did not know where they came from and had not thought about the question before. She did not think they came from the spirits. Perhaps they came directly from God, but in any case, these dreams were quite different from those in which her spirits came to teach her things, to tell her which medicines to use, to warn her of clients who were about to visit Tumbu or herself, and so on. They were also different from those dreams that had their source in one's *rohu* (soul, mind), such as when one dreamt of someone whom one was missing. Many of her dreams, Mohedja said, were personal of this kind, being neither portents nor related to curing. She said she never had a night when she failed to dream.

Mohedja's portent dreams took the following form. If she dreamt something good, then something bad would happen, and vice versa. But there were people, she said, for whom when they dreamt something good, something good would follow. It was as if each person had her own dream logic or code. Mohedja said she understood her dreams because when, as a young woman, she first started having portent dreams, she kept track of their content and of what happened in the waking world immediately afterwards. After a period of time, she was able to draw conclusions regarding the pattern of her dreams. She did not write any of this down but just observed it to herself. This illustrates how Mohedja kept track of her life and experience.

Mohedja's dreams bespoke an active engagement with the world, with consequences for those around her. The dreaming activity was not entirely pre-reflective. It was precisely her reflection – and indeed her methodical empiricism – that allowed her to reach her conclusions. Both the dreaming and the reflecting upon it were intrinsic parts of her practice. There was an ethical quality in the attentiveness of her dreamwork. Mohedja did not recount her dreams about the likely death of the infant to any of the baby's relatives while the baby was still alive, though she did tell Tumbu and me about them when the baby relapsed and shortly before he died. Musy told Mohedja her own dream about the baby's imminent death during the night they were lying in the house to keep watch over him. Mohedja waited until morning, getting well out of earshot of the infant's grandmother, before telling Musy hers. The whispered conversations between the curers expressed their intimacy and solidarity, and also their circumspection vis-à-vis the mother.

Mohedja and Tumbu's Polylogue

If Mze Nuru cohabited with Mohedja and Mze Marwan cohabited with Tumbu, it was also the case that Mohedja had a distinct relationship with Mze Marwan and the other spirits who cohabited with Tumbu, much as Tumbu had with Mze Nuru and the other spirits who cohabited with Mohedja. It was striking to hear the senior spirits in Mohedja address Tumbu by his first name and conversely for the senior spirits in Tumbu addressing Mohedja. Such appellation of adults was rare; it was only children who were addressed by their first names and, even then, not always. More commonly, adults were addressed and referred to by a teknonym – "father of Nuriaty," "older sibling of Ali," etc. In old age, either the personal name was used, preceded by the term for Grandmother or Grandfather, or a nickname was applied.

Mohedja and Tumbu addressed each other's spirits respectfully and generally not by name or kin term. However, they sometimes referred to the spirits by kin terms. Tumbu referred to Kos Vola as Mohedja's *rahavavy*, a term for co-wives, female friends, and the wives of brothers. Conversely, Mze Marwan was Tumbu's *rahalahy*, male friend, and the term used between husbands of sisters. *Rahavavy* and *rahalahy* indicate the equivalence or status equality between two people of the same sex. Spirit and host are not understood as spouses to each other. On the other hand, Tumbu might refer to Mze Nuru as *rahalahy* with the implication that they had equivalent relations to Mohedja. When I asked Mohedja what term she might use to refer to Mze Marwan, she said she did not know, but possibly brother-in-law. She did not say spouse. Conversely though, Tumbu said he could call Kos Vola a spouse (*vady*). In fact, he addressed her by the more intimate term *mwana kely*; literally, this means "little woman," but Tumbu paraphrased it as *viavy tsara* (good/beautiful woman), a term of endearment. I never heard him refer to Mohedja herself so fondly, though perhaps he did so in private. In general, it was uncommon for spouses to state or show affection publicly.

Many people called the spirits cohabiting with their parents "fundi" and people sometimes referred to spouses' spirits as *mwanzan* (friend). Mze Nuru himself emphasized in a conversation with me in early 1976 that he was particularly good friends with Tumbu. Tumbu had given him many gifts over the years, and they got along well. They cooperated, and he – Mze Nuru – helped Tumbu whenever he could. Mze Nuru said he also got along with Mze Marwan, but less well. Mze Nuru said that Mze Marwan could be bad; he was too quick to anger, and he manifested this by making Tumbu sick. When Tumbu first became ill, before Marwan had risen, Mze Nuru fought with Marwan every day (via medicine Mze Nuru was giving Tumbu). Later, they got along better, but Mze Nuru still did not like the things Mze Marwan was apt to do when he got angry.

At its most direct and intimate, the communication between Tumbu and Mohedja and their respective spirits was something I was not privy to. But sometimes it could be indirect and mediated across alternate channels. In late 1975, Mohedja was suffering stomach pain. Tumbu was treating his cousin, with whom Mze Marwan had also begun to cohabit. One day when we were visiting the cousin in her village, Tumbu took the opportunity to ask Mze Marwan, risen in his cousin, the cause of Mohedja's pain. The patros answered that it was Mohedja's trumba Ndramboeny who was angry because she was not following his prohibitions correctly. She ate all kinds of food and would eat in the fields without first washing her hands and also at home after handling her elderly incontinent mother's sister. Tumbu listened but told me that he was not prepared to say these things to Mohedja's face. One day when they were working together in the fields, he would diplomatically tell her to be careful. However, he would not mention the part about her mother's sister because Mohedja would say that he did not want her to look after her. Mze Marwan also announced that Mohedja was pregnant! Tumbu said he would not know whether this were true until he observed whether she missed a menstrual period.

Mohedja had been feeling sick every evening for some time. Her trumba, Ndramboeny, rose and diagnosed the problem differently, saying that sorcery had been implanted both in Mohedja's body and in her rice field. The trumba called for a light-skinned extractor, thereby ruling out Tumbu. A week later, Tumbu called in a healer who had learned sorcery extraction from Tumbu himself. The former apprentice extracted sorcery from Mohedja's body and Tumbu prepared a *singa* (a Qur'anic verse written in charcoal ink and washed off to make a drink) and also poured some medicine over Mohedja. The light-skinned healer, Tumbu, Mohedja, and I then walked to the bottom of the field, where Mohedja had been troubled by birds eating her crop. The healer removed a *sairy* from the field and Tumbu and Mohedja examined its contents: dirt, seeds, glass, and broken pieces of seashells.[2] Tumbu then sprinkled some medicated water over the field to purify it. He gave the healer 500 CFA francs and the latter returned him 150 CFA francs out of courtesy. Mohedja said later that her trumba had told her many times in dreams about the sorcery against her, but she had not believed it until she fell sick. The trumba communicated directly with her in her sleep and had not informed Tumbu.

The more spouses participated in each other's cures, the more trust was built. Both Mohedja and Tumbu made this explicit. For example, in 1985 Mohedja recounted how a woman client had approached her saying she wanted to hold an *azulahy*, but her husband would not let her. Mohedja replied that maybe her husband did not love her (*mitia*; "like" and "love" are not clearly distinguished). If he did, he would help her get well; when someone is sick, their spouse should treat them (*mitaha*). Mohedja noted how many of her own curing ceremonies Tumbu had helped her with. Similarly, Tumbu pointed out to a male client that since the man had sponsored his wife's *azulahy*, it was extremely unlikely that her patros would then lie to him. This was an indirect indication of Tumbu's confidence in the words of the spirits cohabiting with Mohedja.

In sum, the complex strands of their communication and therapeutic work, both between them, with their respective spirits, and via third parties, added a density to their relationship and enhanced the ways Mohedja and Tumbu were able to exhibit concern and compassion for one another as well as to speak with authority and objectivity. In their distinctiveness from the spouses themselves, the spirits offer means for protection, confidence, and communicating difficult messages. As subsequent chapters will show, the multiple channels enable the expression of conflict as well.[3]

Although I know their situation best, many other couples, albeit with less investment in curing, had good relations with each other's spirits. For example, shortly after his wedding one man brought a small number of cakes and a bottle of cologne to the spirit already cohabiting with his wife in order to introduce himself and make friends. He referred to the spirit as *rahalahy* (brother) or fundi. The spirit rose to warn of trouble in the household or told his wife in her sleep, and she then passed on the message to him if someone were after him or if there was sorcery. Occasionally, he and the spirit just chatted together. He and his wife called the spirit for help when he was subject to a legal action; they performed some medicine so that the requisite papers were lost in town, and the case was dismissed.

Another man was a patros fundi who had already held his ceremony in his home village before marrying in Lombeni. The spirit rose from time to time to talk or to treat people in the household, but in deference to his wife's wishes, the man did not pursue a healing practice in Lombeni. His wife also had spirits. He said they were kind and well disposed (*tsara fañahy*) and that his wife said the same about his spirits. He said that he and his wife trusted each other; neither was jealous, and neither chased after other partners. They had been married for sixteen years at the time he told me this.

Chapter Seven

Ndramboeny: Mohedja as a Curer

At the time that Tumbu was learning to live productively with his patros, Mohedja took a step further with her trumba. While they were residing at Red Rock, her senior male trumba arrived. At this time, she was also accommodating her youthful trumba, Botu Changizy, and her child trumba, Kalu, who had entered her some years earlier, though she did not know why. The trumba did not make her nearly as ill as the patros had. Junior trumba often accompanied senior ones and less import was given their arrival. Youthful trumba did not want much from their hosts – only liquor, Mohedja said. They did not require ceremonies of their own and could rise suddenly and give their names while the host was under treatment to accommodate a senior trumba.

Once they were established, both her senior trumba declared they did not like the youthful Botu entering Mohedja, so he rarely appeared. In contrast to the dignified elders, Botu arrived with a good deal of commotion, causing Mohedja to flail her arms and utter high-pitched screams. At a public event (*rombu*), this was a display that was viewed with nervousness and awe, but when Botu entered at home at night Tumbu told him to quiet down and come gently, saying, "We don't want all the neighbours to hear our private affairs, do we?" Botu liked to dance and drink; he disdained cologne as being "cold" and preferred hard liquor. When Tumbu remarked that he rarely visited, Botu retorted that was because all the other spirits were fed when they came but he never was. Why didn't they keep a bottle of liquor on hand for him?

The necessary conditions for becoming a trumba fundi included accommodating at least one senior trumba and going through a full sequence of trumba ceremonies oneself. The sequence was composed of three distinct events that could be widely separated in time, although, as happened with Ndramboeny, two of them could take place on the same day. The first phase, known as the *fanuing*, purified the client and infused her with medicine. It took place indoors and was not a public display, but it could include over twenty participants to assist in clapping, singing, and applying medicine. The second component, known as the *rombu be*, was a large public affair, requiring the purchase of a good deal of liquor and the slaughter of a cow. At this event, many trumba came to dance and many people to watch, and the client's trumba announced his name in public.[1] The third phase, the *valu hataka*, was a smaller version of the *rombu* and was the occasion at which the final "living arrangements" between the spirit and host, notably the restrictions to be observed by the host, were negotiated and confirmed. It was necessary to proceed through the *valu hataka* to become recognized as an autonomous trumba fundi. However, hosts who had not finished the ceremonial sequence but were experienced in trumba affairs could see clients informally and assist the fundis in the performance of their various tasks.

Sometime before Mohedja held her major ceremony (*rombu be*) for Kos Vola, another trumba began to visit her. He did not speak at first, but everyone could see it was not Kos Vola. Then, at the time of her *rombu be* (which took place in Lombeni but during the years they were living at Red Rock), he rose again and said he wanted his ceremony held concurrently. Tumbu replied that he was too late and should have spoken up earlier. Later, when the final ceremony (*valu hataka*) was planned for Kos Vola, the new arrival said that he would announce his name then. The trumba said he was in a hurry to get on with his medicine and since they did not have a cow available, he would be satisfied with a white goat and cloth for the occasion. So, whereas a cow had been sacrificed at Kos Vola's *rombu be*, this time only a goat was slaughtered. The goat sufficed for the simultaneous events for both trumba and there were no expensive purchases of liquor as were typically needed for a *rombu be*. The trumba was satisfied and did not require anything more.[2] This took place in 1974, the year before my first arrival.

The new trumba was Ndramboeniarivu, Lord of the People a Thousandfold (shortened by me to Ndramboeny), and often called "Grandfather" (*Dadilahy*). His presence was impressive. When he rose in Mohedja, he carried himself erect, draped a red cloth over his chest and shoulder, and held a tall spear. In Madagascar, Ndramboeny was remembered as a powerful but troubled monarch. Mohedja knew only the name of his home in Madagascar and that he was a former ruler.[3]

It was not clear what motivated his arrival, but like Mze Nuru, Ndramboeny was a spirit who appeared in very few hosts. No one else in Lombeni was then cohabiting with him and none of Mohedja's kin had done so. Mohedja herself said she had no idea exactly when or why he came. At the same time, Ndramboeny's presence connected her to his hosts and clients elsewhere and enabled Mohedja to expand her therapeutic activities in conjunction with the other women in Lombeni Kely who cohabited with related trumba. The establishment of a senior male trumba meant that Mohedja could take the lead in managing the ceremonies of clients who were also possessed by trumba. This she started to do in 1975. Moreover, as Tumbu was not visited by any trumba himself, this was a sphere of their marriage that Mohedja had for herself.

If the grandfather trumba did not require a full ceremony, he had another symbol of authority, namely the tall spear. Ndramboeny had previously cohabited with an elderly woman in M—, unrelated to Mohedja, who had recently died. When he first announced himself in Mohedja, Ndramboeny asked this woman's children to bring him one of two spears that belonged to him and were then in their keeping. Relatives of the deceased woman brought Ndramboeny his spear and subsequently came to seek advice and treatment from him in Mohedja. Ndramboeny said the second spear should remain in M—, thereby paving the way for his further cohabitation there. Ndramboeny thus established a new network for Mohedja, and indeed it led to the marriage of her daughter Haza to a son of the family in M—.

Ndramboeny arrived in Mohedja as a fundi who already had a reputation, and a clientele, a point that was reinforced by the provisioning of the spear. It is evident that by this time, Mohedja was quite certain of her ambition and capacity as a fundi and was "in a hurry" to get on with things.

When Ndramboeny was in active possession of Mohedja, he took on a dignified, erect, and self-assured demeanour, distinct from Mohedja's own presentation of self. I vividly recall the occasion of the sacrifice of a cow at the trumba ceremony of one of Mohedja's clients. Animal slaughter was an exclusively male activity with no women present as the cow was pulled to the ground, sliced across the neck, and butchered. There was always a good deal of masculine camaraderie and debate as the meat was cut and divided into appropriate portions for distribution. In this instance, Ndramboeny strode powerfully into the midst of the assembled men to oversee the process and authoritatively told them how to divide the meat (Lambek 1993, 369).

Tumbu pointed out that both Mohedja's senior trumba manifested as a fundi, and that, as with Mze Nuru, she mainly learned from them directly, rather than from a human intermediary. So, while she showed respect to her own trumba fundi, Musy Matwar, who orchestrated the ceremonies for Kos Vola and Ndramboeny, she did not learn directly from her. This was an intimate but delicate relationship and one that evolved over time.

2–3 September 1975. A woman came from M— to inquire whether Mohedja would serve as her trumba fundi and diagnose what was bothering her. This woman was the niece of a man who had married into Lombeni but she was unrelated to Mohedja. Significantly, Ndramboeny had cohabited with this man's late mother and Mohedja was the only other person the man knew who cohabited with him. The man had been attentive to Ndramboeny every time he rose at other people's trumba ceremonies, and when his niece became ill, he recommended that she come see Mohedja, trying, as he said, "to keep things within the family."

Ndramboeny rose and told the client that she was suffering from both sorcery and a trumba who was trying to cohabit with her. The woman replied that she wanted Mohedja to manage her cure. In that case, said Ndramboeny, Mohedja would have to request permission of her own fundi, Musy Matwar. Mohedja had not yet been given the right to practise autonomously. There was a small ceremony that needed to be performed before she could do so. I asked Ndramboeny about his treatment of Mohedja's niece, which I had observed the week before. He said that didn't count because Musy had been absent from the village at the time and in any case, the treatment in question had been a minor one.

Mohedja was now ready to become a trumba curer in her own right and she wished to do so in a correct and courteous manner that would affirm and solidify her ties with the other trumba adepts in the community. The next day, she invited Musy Matwar and told her both about the visitor from M— and about her intervention in her niece's case the previous week. The two women sat facing each other on a mat on the floor of Mohedja's house in the middle of a pleasant afternoon. Tumbu and I were also present. After some light joking, Mohedja put incense on the brazier and asked the fundi to come, gently and without trouble.

Musy burped several times, sighed, and yawned. Very soon, and with no symptoms of pain or any thrashing about, the trumba announced his presence with "eka" (so), shook our hands, and went to sit up on the bed. Mohedja bent her forehead to the spirit's shoulder, as one does with the senior trumba, and gave him a small bottle of cologne. The spirit offered me a sip of the cologne, remarking that he was not selfish [unlike me]. Tumbu explained to the trumba why he had been called. The spirit said, fine, but they should talk more about it. Adding more incense to the brazier, the spirit stuck the smoke in Mohedja's face, inviting Ndramboeny and asking him to come gently (*moramora*). The spirit continued to chat with Tumbu as Mohedja slowly entered trance, breathing hard.

Ndramboeny then shook our hands and joined the first trumba on the bed. "How are you, Tumbu?" said Ndramboeny. This startled me; Mohedja never addressed her husband in this manner; following custom, she called Tumbu by his teknonym, Baba ny Nuriaty. Status differences were marked throughout such interchanges. When people called up a trumba, they sat down on the mat; when the trumba arrived, he moved to a higher seat. Although Tumbu and I sat on chairs off to the side, through his mode of address, Ndramboeny clearly indicated his superiority to Tumbu.

The spirits petitioned God (*nangataka an'drañahary*), requesting that this step in Mohedja's life be propitious. The trumba in Musy told Tumbu to fetch medicinal leaves and then sorted through the pile, looking for samples of each kind of trumba medicine. Meanwhile, Tumbu and Ndramboeny held a whispered conversation outside. Following Ndramboeny's instructions, Tumbu put a thousand-CFA-franc note together with a bottle of cologne and a block of white clay in a dish. The items were offered to the trumba, although it was acknowledged that Musy herself would have use of them. Musy's trumba pressed the leaves and the bill between Ndramboeny's two hands, holding them between his own two hands, and said that one day soon Mohedja would go with Musy [i.e., each in person, not the spirits] to pick medicinal plants. Henceforward, Mohedja would be able to perform treatments without asking Musy first, although for complex matters she could continue to consult the senior fundi.

The trumba then pocketed the money and said goodbye. Musy switched rapidly to herself, moved back down to the mat, and reached up to shake hands with Ndramboeny [as they had not yet met that day]. Ndramboeny explained what had been decided, that Musy was to take Mohedja to the bush to look for plants. Musy then left and Ndramboeny conversed with Tumbu about treatment for the new client. Finally, Ndramboeny left as well, and Tumbu then repeated to Mohedja what had been decided. Without any public display, Mohedja had become an autonomous trumba fundi. Tumbu and Mohedja referred to what had transpired as *msara audy*. This was a payment to the fundi in order to be tested to ensure you know all the medicines. In other words, what was being passed on was not knowledge per se but the right to exercise it; and it was this authority that rendered the medicine efficacious.

Early one morning two weeks later, Musy took Mohedja off to the deep forest (*añala be*) to collect medicinal plants. Mohedja said she was afraid of going alone because of snakes [although natural historians denied there were any snakes to be found on Mayotte], but that big fundis were not afraid. Women cohabiting with spirits were readier to go into the forest than those without. Nevertheless, the two women returned without all the plants they had been seeking since some were "too far away, where one can go only if accompanied by a man." It was unclear whether this was a fear of encountering snakes or spirits in an isolated spot, or precisely a fear of encountering men. In any case, Mohedja brought back many species of leaves and twigs in her basket. I recorded that I didn't think she had let on to Musy that she already knew how to identify and collect the plants, but in retrospect I think I missed the point that the collecting trip was not about transmitting knowledge but rather about the collegiality of the two women and acknowledgment of the transmission of authority.

14 November 1975. When the woman from M— returned for treatment, Ndramboeny rose and convinced Musy's trumba to rise and help. Although Mohedja appeared to have set things up to develop her practice, she confided to me that she had been hoping that the trumba of the woman from M— would have asked for Musy rather than herself as the fundi. She was embarrassed at the thought of having to manage a trumba cure in front of a lot of people because she was still "too young" to do so. And in this case many outsiders would surely attend. This was her first big case on her own and the first with a client from outside Lombeni. Eventually, she conducted the *rombu be* successfully in M— without Musy's participation. The spirit who rose in the client was none other than Ndramboeny himself and he retained the second spear in M—.

The relationship between a given host and spirit was not static. At the onset of a possession history, the host and spirit were at pains to differentiate themselves from one another – the host because she was embarrassed, and the spirit because this was the only way his separate identity could be constituted. When the host became a curer, or the spirit manifested as one, there developed a productive tension between their respective voices. Mohedja's remarks expressed reticence and anxiety about what others would think about her, whereas Ndramboeny exhibited confidence and eagerness to forge ahead. As Mohedja grew in confidence, their respective voices came to work in harmony, as will be evident in the following descriptions of Mohedja's practice. Host and spirit sometimes grew even more closely identified with one another, the host gaining the benefit of the knowledge and power associated with her spirit without necessarily having to give way to him. This was the case with Musy Matwar. She barely had to enter trance and did so with very little commotion or change in mannerism. Her authority pervaded whichever identity she presented to the world.

In 1975, Musy was the leading figure of the group of trumba adepts in Lombeni Kely and had overseen the ceremonies of Mohedja and most of the others. Musy had been trained in trumba medicine by a woman of the previous generation, and she cohabited with senior male and female trumba. She had also gained extensive knowledge from a former husband who had been a diviner (*mwalim dunia*). Musy had a wide reputation, receiving clients from across the island. In 1985, she estimated that she made more from curing than from her government "pension" of fifty francs per month. However, by then she no longer liked to take new clients and often called upon Mohedja or one of the other women to assist her.

The solidarity among the women cohabiting with trumba in Lombeni Kely was striking. Although day-to-day relations in the village were often fraught, the atmosphere in trumba ceremonies was one of mutual concern among participants, physical proximity, emotional intimacy, and harmonious shifts and balance between moods, from warm solicitousness to enjoyment and broad humour. I once saw Ndramboeny "give away" Tumbu to a young woman who Mohedja thought had been rather foolish in sending off her own husband.[4]

For many years, Musy also held the office of leader of the women (*chef tanana*). This meant that she was responsible for organizing the collective work performed by the village women, ceremonies sponsored by the village or managed by the village on behalf of members paying their obligatory ceremonial feasts (*shungu*) (Lambek 1990, 2018). Musy was recognized to have performed the job with fairness and efficiency. She was well respected by the other women, who occasionally went so far as to organize work parties in her fields. There was no obligation to do so, but it was felt to be reciprocity well-earned. Moreover, Musy was elderly, widowed, and trying to support several female dependents without access to a regular supply of cash.

In becoming a healer, Mohedja moved from the passion of her own states of possession to the dispassion and compassion necessary for treating others. As Mze Nuru and as Ndramboeny, and even directly as herself with clients, Mohedja was calm, self-assured, concerned, yet somehow a little removed – exactly like a good physician or therapist.

Mohedja's three senior spirits – the patros, Mze Nuru, and the trumba, Kos Vola and Ndramboeny – each performed as curers, but in different cases, depending upon which of them the client requested. It was clear that the woman from M— approached Ndramboeny because he had been present in her family.

By 1985, Mohedja's trumba appeared to be in greater demand than her patros. I describe a few cases to show something of the scope and diversity of her activity. They are partial, but they demonstrate Mohedja's approach to diagnosis and the way the doubling of the fundi as host and spirit provided a context for communication that was broadly therapeutic. In the first case, Mohedja's niece Lidy consulted Kos Vola, who had cohabited with her grandmother. Although her condition was not diagnosed as incipient cohabitation, some years later, Lidy began to host Kos Vola as well.

> On 4 July 1985, Mohedja's sister-in-law came to consult Kos Vola about her daughter Lidy who has been sick since her marriage a year ago. Her whole body is ill, especially her abdomen. Don't I see how thin she is? Lidy also suffers from headaches and some mornings does not even get out of bed. The trumba asked whether she had had any bad dreams. Lidy said she saw someone trying to kill her with a knife or machete but could not recognize who, not even whether it was a man or woman. Kos Vola said this indicated sorcery. The trumba ordered plant medicines, which Lidy's father (Mohedja's brother Asman) then set out to collect. He too had learned to identify plants by helping his mother.

> On 7 July, the day before the treatment, Mohedja remarked that she didn't really want to practise but people kept coming and she couldn't turn them away. "Curing," she complained, "disturbs one's work. I have enough to do as it is."

> On 8 July, Tumbu extracted a sorcery packet from Lidy, and Mohedja then supervised the performance of a ceremony to remove *dzitso* (evil eye) caused by spirits. She asked Asman if he could recite the Yasin (a sura from the Qur'an). He was doubtful, so she called for a written copy. Then she joined her brother to stand reciting the prayer over Lidy. Asman read while she uttered it from memory. The act of praying over someone was quite unusual for a woman.

> Next, Mohedja bathed Lidy in herbal medicine designed to remove additional *dzitso* caused by humans. A *shijabu* (blessing) was then recited by a small group of men. Before she left, Mohedja instructed Lidy and her mother in the application of the remaining plant medicines, giving her a regime of inhaling at night and bathing in the morning for a week. Lidy was told to take note of her dreams during this time. This kind of

medicine would elicit the appearance in dreams of the people who were harming you.

In a subsequent dream, Lidy saw herself returning from the fields with her friends. They observed people emerging from a bush taxi. Lidy's cousin told her that her co-wife was looking at her and as she looked up, she saw the woman staring at her. Mohedja explained to me that the dream indicated that Lidy would be cured since the co-wife only looked at her and did not do anything more. She did not pass on this interpretation to Lidy because she assumed she could see it for herself. But perhaps the point of the cure was not so much to identify a sorcerer as to bring to consciousness Lidy's own role in the matter. In fact, it was Lidy who was the second wife, and she had insisted on marrying the man despite her parents' objections.

Lidy remained sick after the first round of medicine. Following a second round, she felt much better and slept well, without any bad dreams. On 20 July, she came to Mohedja for pain in the abdomen, supposedly unrelated to the previous condition. Mohedja felt her abdomen was stiff and recommended a plant that would help. Lidy returned for a week of massages. Here Mohedja worked on a straightforward "natural" illness without recourse to her trumba, nor was such recourse expected.

The next case illustrates the way Mohedja and Ndramboeny effectively worked and thought in tandem.

9 October 1985. Sua arrived this morning with her adolescent daughter and asked for a consultation. Sua was a woman in her early forties, the daughter of a cousin of Tumbu's. She said she "didn't know where to start." She had been sick for five years on and off and had received treatment from two previous curers. The problem was her abdomen (*kibu*).

"In what way?" asked Mohedja.

Sua described pain in her stomach, especially at night.

Mohedja asked, "You didn't go to the clinic?"

Sua continued that she was fighting with her husband and trying to throw him out. He had slept with another woman, lost his job, and did many little things that annoyed her. He hadn't given her any money for several weeks and she was afraid she couldn't even remunerate Mohedja. She added that she hadn't thought of coming to Mohedja until now. She went to a diviner some time ago who said she had "something in her head" (i.e., a spirit) and that the curer should be a light-coloured person to the south. So she went to Dady Zalia, another spirit fundi in Lombeni Kely, but without success. She had wanted to go to the clinic, but her daughter dreamt she would die there and persuaded her not to.

At this point, the daughter interjected that had her mother the sort of illness that could be treated at the clinic, it would have grown steadily worse, but instead it was something that came and went, now weaker, now stronger.

Sua said she was at the end of her rope.

Mohedja remarked that she had to go cook her fish that had been brought up from the beach an hour or two before.

Sua suggested that her daughter prepare the fish so that Sua could call up Mohedja's trumba, and Mohedja agreed.

Sua protested nervously that she didn't know how to speak over incense, but she managed. "Please come. I'm calling you sincerely, for a real problem. Don't be angry, come and if you cannot cure me, tell me where to go for help. Please come, fundi. Ignore the fact that my spouse isn't here but come anyway," she pleaded. She paused and added, "Come, fundi, come."

Ndramboeny arrived. "What's up?" he asked.

Sua lowered her forehead and greeted him politely. "I'm sick, my belly, and I'm fighting with my husband. I chase him out every night. We made a reconciliation, but I'm still angry. What's happening to me? Tell me everything, don't hide anything. My daughter had the idea to come here and find out from you. We asked my mother's brother's wife [Mohedja] and then called you and you came. Tell me all, conceal nothing. You can see so far."

Ndramboeny responded, "You want to be treated, yet you don't get along with your husband? Will you be able?"

"Yes."

"If you'll get along, lets pray to Andriamañitry ["God" in Malagasy and trumba usage, but not the local Kibushy word]. If not, what?"

"Perhaps I'll get medicine. I do like him, but I don't know what's going on. My rohu [feelings] has turned away. I've had no money."

"What do you want money for?"

Sua laughed.

Ndramboeny continued, "If he's done wrong, God will make him pay. You've told him what you think, so enough. What more should you fight about?"

"I'm listening to you."

"But you two are not in harmony [anareo tsy d'accord]. I can't help you if you two don't want to get along. If he didn't like/love you, he would have left after what you said to him. He must like you."

Sua asked, "But what do you think?"

Ndramboeny said, "He likes you."

Sua laughed, "Really?"

"I can't treat you if the two of you are not getting along."

"If you're *mwafaka* [effective, right for the case], you'll be able to."

"Didn't you do divination?"

"Yes. The effective curer is a person who lives to the south of me, fair-skinned. I went to Dady Zalia last year."

"Who told you to come here?"

"Halima had the same problem and she was cured [by you]. My daughter said to me, 'Why don't you go too? Go get help.' I'm sick and have loads of troubles [*mashaka mituburung*]. My daughter had the idea to come here. I will go to B— on Friday to tell my brother. He's always helped in these matters."

"Your problem can be treated. But get along with your husband first and come back together with him. I'm not prepared to treat you without your spouse."

"God willing. Have you seen what is bothering my belly?"

"I told you; I can treat it."

"Good. Can't you give me some medicine in the meantime? Isn't there some sorcery involved?"

"No, there is no sorcery."

"Is it only my own feelings [*rohuku tu*]?" Sua wondered. "He'll refuse to come because he has no money."

"So what shall we do?"

"I'm asking you. We'll come whenever you say. He listens to me. I'm angry with him, but he listens to me."

"You settle things with him first."

"He'll say he has no money. But if you tell us to come anyway, we will."

"So come tomorrow."

"We will. He works but has no money."

"So that's the way it is." Ndramboeny was ready to leave.

"God willing. Because I'm really sick. If he refuses, I'll get money from my brother and come myself on Sunday. I'll tell him today."

"All right. I've told you what needs to be done."

"Don't be angry, fundi. I'll bring you some cologne [*marash*] when I come."

"I don't drink cologne." [Unlike most spirits, Ndramboeny does not drink cologne.]

"What? Well, we'll come, God willing."

"Enough. I'm going. Go talk things over with your husband first. I'm not ready to say anything if the two of you aren't in agreement first."

"Yes."

Sua held Mohedja's infant granddaughter. Mohedja stretched, left trance, and exited the room.

Sua told me that she felt continually angry with her husband. When he touched her, her pulse beat faster (*rohu manyeñin*).

Mohedja returned. Sua told her what had been decided: She would return together with her husband, and they would call up the trumba again and he would tell them what to do next. She said she told Ndramboeny that he was right to demand her husband's presence but that she had no money to pay him. Ndramboeny had replied that she really was sick and should return anyway.

"Okay," said Mohedja.

Having prepared the fish, Sua's daughter then returned. Sua told her daughter, "Let's all come back together. The fundi told me I was sick but wasn't ready to do anything without the man present. I told him [the spirit] he was right. He told me the man would have left me already if he didn't like me."

There was some further talk about Mohedja's granddaughter and then the client left.

Mohedja clarified the situation for me. Sua had caught her husband with another woman. She had been shouting at him since to leave, but in fact she was frightened he would take her advice. Her words got out of control. Mohedja thus described Sua's ambivalence, caught between feelings of anger and betrayal and her strong wish to maintain and improve her marriage.

That evening, Mohedja added that she knew at once from the way Sua described her illness that a spirit who wished to cohabit was bothering her. Spirits manifest in various ways – in this case, abdominal problems. It feels as though you have something moving around inside you. Mohedja was once sick like this herself and thought she'd have to undergo an operation. But her daughter said to her, "Have you forgotten how spirits can make you feel?" She mixed a little kaolin and water, drank it, and immediately felt better. The symptoms never returned.

Mohedja also remarked that Sua's talk had been confused, that Sua had acted a little crazy (*adaladala*). Dady Zalia was not a fair-skinned person. Perhaps Sua went to her simply because she was kin. Sua had told me she was a bit afraid of Mohedja; this might partially have explained her nervous chatter. It seemed that Ndramboeny was somewhat irritated by Sua's indecisiveness.

Mohedja told me firmly that she would not treat Sua, or anyone else for that matter, unless their spouse were aware of it and in agreement. She said that a spouse has the right to accept or refuse any kind of treatment. Biomedicine might not be subject to this rule, but local treatment was. Throughout their conversation Ndramboeny attempted to stick to the procedure whereby the onset of possession is handled with the acknowledgment of the client's spouse. This was critical for future relationships between the spouse, the client, and the cohabiting spirits, especially because the spouse ought to be the main sponsor of the cure. In some cases, a sibling took this role, but Mohedja did not think that Sua could rely on her brother, and she also felt that Sua was not a particularly independent or capable person, the sort for whom an exception could be made. Ndramboeny was also sincere in stating that Sua's husband wished to help; around the same time, I heard him suggest to another client that the client's husband's refusal to help in that case meant he probably did not like her. The flip side of the obligation to have the spouse's acquiescence in order to initiate a cure is that it is the obligation of the spouse to assist an ailing partner. Mohedja pointed out to the client just how many of her own curing ceremonies Tumbu had helped her with.

One might see the fundi as a therapist acting in a conservative fashion, refusing to handle the case until Sua had accepted her husband for what he was and learned to get along with him. But it would be fairer to say the fundi was being realistic. Ndramboeny wanted the husband present at the consultation in order to make a more informed assessment of the marital relationship. He was reluctant to prognosticate without seeing how the husband reacted. Without her husband's initial support, Sua's cohabitation could go nowhere. Moreover, in her daily life as well, Sua had no other men upon whom she could rely. Her father was dead, her brother lived in a different village and was not well off, and her daughters were married to young men who had no money. Sua herself had been married several times and, if she were not careful, could have found herself husbandless again. Indeed, Mohedja sensed this anxiety in her. In requiring that relations between spouses be of a certain standard, spirit treatments helped assure that they reached that standard, that the relations between spouses were clarified. Although spirit cures were not directly about marital relationships, they provided a context in which relationships, if deficient, could be developed. But, before initiating a cure, a fundi had to ensure she had suitable ground with which to work.

More generally, consultation with a spirit provided an opening in which much communication was enabled, in which clients were freed from the normal constraints of expression. Not only did this provide the fundi with greater information, but it also began the therapeutic process as clients came to a more explicit realization of their feelings and as they began to reveal these to one another.

A good fundi like Mohedja or Ndramboeny was relatively quiet, facilitating the expression of the clients, listening to them, and limiting most of their remarks to what was necessary. In this case, Sua appeared confused, and the fundi wanted Sua to clarify her goals in her own mind before giving advice. The conversation gave her the space to begin to do that. Although the ostensive subject of the visit was abdominal pain that indicated a trumba, most of Sua's remarks were about her ambivalent feelings towards her husband. In the face of this ambivalence, the curer was suitably non-committal. The fundi's message was that if Sua were able to convince her husband to join her, the therapeutic context remained open and Ndramboeny well disposed towards them. This was classic non-directional, non-interventionist therapy.

I contend that the polyphony of the fundi – the fact that the fundi speaks in more than one voice – enhances the therapeutic potential of such interchanges. Here, it did so in at least three ways. First, the therapist became detached from her ordinary identity as Mohedja, fellow villager and kinswoman or affine. This enabled the client to speak more freely and listen more attentively. It also made the fundi freer to speak, separating her persona as therapist from her normal obligations, interests, and responsibilities. Mohedja was not herself responsible for what Ndramboeny said. This could be called a form of privileged discourse in the sense that messages are exempted from their ordinary relational implications and constraints.[5] Second, the split in the fundi between human host and powerful spirit channelled transference relations and encouraged feelings of dependency, love, and anger to rise to the surface of consciousness in a context in which they could be safely contained and possibly utilized or transcended. In both these respects, the person of the spirit was detached from that of the host. Third, the split created a communicational context that required redundancy. In the case described above, Sua recounted her troubles to Mohedja and then repeated them to the trumba. More important, she had to take what the trumba told her, the gist of what transpired between them, and repeat it to Mohedja. In doing so, clients come to acknowledge their acceptance of a spirit's message.

Not all Mohedja's therapeutic work was carried out in a formal context. For example, towards the end of a patros ceremony in 1975, Mohedja and Satuvy, the wife of Tumbu's half-brother, each possessed by a spirit, were singing nonsense together. When Satuvy's spirit abruptly left her, Mze Nuru immediately began to talk seriously to Satuvy herself, warning her that she was hurting her family. Satuvy hosted a trumba who had been promised a ceremony, but they had postponed it while planning the wedding of Satuvy's daughter. Mze Nuru explained that the trumba was angry with them and was the source of the delays and hassles over the wedding. He suggested they call up the trumba and explain the situation nicely to him.

In fact, Satuvy had been upset and depressed over the temporary cancellation of her daughter's wedding. The intervention might have provided a means for her to come to terms with the situation and move forwards constructively, especially if she had been feeling any responsibility over the matter. Mohedja could not have said this in her own voice and Satuvy would not have received it if she had. The alternate voice allowed interlocutors to cut through the niceties of polite social discourse and get straight to the heart of the matter. What transpired between Satuvy and Mze Nuru was based on the friendship between Mohedja and Satuvy, but had no direct implications for Mohedja's relations with Satuvy. Satuvy could give free rein to transference feelings and deference without significant social repercussion.

Therapeutic interactions are not always as neat as have been described. In the following instance, Mohedja began as the curer but new developments led others to take over, notably Safy, a young male curer with a different style from Mohedja. The case illustrates one of the more extreme manifestations of possession – precisely not cohabitation – found in Mayotte. This is a condition that I have encountered only rarely, but that twice led within a couple of weeks to death. The case described here ended happily, with a potential transformation into cohabitation.

13 August 1985. Early this morning, Athu came from Lombeni Be to ask Mohedja about trumba medicine for his wife Ruby. When Ruby was first sick, he went to Musy Matwar. She told him there were four trumba fundis in the village and that he should ask a diviner to confirm who would be effective (mwafaka). The diviner came up with Mohedja's name.

Mohedja replied that one could not do trumba medicine on a Tuesday and he should return in the evening. (Local days went from sundown to sundown.)

That evening, Athu returned with Ruby. Ruby had suffered abdominal pains for some time but didn't know if it was a problem with her reproductive or her digestive system. She had tried hospital medicine, namely shots of some kind, but they hadn't worked. A curer in Lombeni Be had also treated her without success. Finally, the patros cohabiting with that curer said the case needed a trumba fundi and through divination he had selected Mohedja.

Ruby called Ndramboeny over incense, asking him to come and talk so they could find out what was wrong. She said she had tried hospital and patros medicine; if the problem was sorcery, the trumba should tell her. They joked briefly that I had a trumba who should rise, then returned to the task at hand. "Come, Grandfather, we are desperate." They looked down at the floor.

Mohedja began to yawn and twist. She coughed and rubbed her leg. "Gently," said Ruby, "Don't come angrily. Please come and let's talk."

Ndramboeny rose, sat on the bed, and shook hands with us. The clients greeted him politely.

"What's up?" inquired the trumba.

Ruby: "I've been sick since last year."

Ndramboeny: "Tell me everything. What is your condition like? What do you see in your sleep?"

Ruby: "I was flying. I fell in the middle of a group of people but wasn't caught."

Ndramboeny: "Do you see yourself as male or female?"

Ruby: "Female."

Here Ndramboeny turned and asked me what the illness (*areting*) was. When I declined to comment, he continued, "Let us pray to God. But something must be removed in the meantime. We have to remove evil eye (*dzitso*)." Ndramboeny paused, then asked what day of the month it was, so as to schedule an auspicious day for treatment.

Athu then interjected something unexpected. "Is the condition both of ours or just hers?"

Ndramboeny: "Why?"

Athu: "People say it came from me and entered her."

Ndramboeny: "Ruby's the core of it. Let's treat her."

Athu: "People who marry form a couple. Each of them struggles."

Ndramboeny replied that Athu's illness was of a different kind. "But people shouldn't chatter too much [i.e., the trumba didn't want to speak about the source of the problem yet]. Let's just do Ruby's treatment in the meantime."

Athu: "If it was my other wife who did this to Ruby or me, I'll leave her."

Ndramboeny suggested that perhaps the co-wife had been given the wrong kind of medicine by her fundi. She had wanted medicine simply to make Athu forget Ruby and leave her. But they got sick instead.

Athu admitted they found a spell under the bed designed to give him the idea to leave Ruby.

Ndramboeny: "It was done quite a while ago."

Ruby: "Yes."

Ndramboeny: "So we'll need a *swadaka* (ritual offering). Both of you will need treatment." Ndramboeny repeated that they should not get him to say too much.

Athu: "So we're waiting to hear, fundi."

Ndramboeny: "Some things are hard to cure. They need a lot of treatment."

Athu: "Every illness according to its needs."

Ndramboeny: "Can you get a red chicken by tomorrow?"

Athu: "Male or female?"

Ndramboeny: "Male."

Athu: "Large?"

Ndramboeny: "Whichever."

Athu: "We'll have to look for one."

Ndramboeny: "If you don't find one you can bring a piece of red cloth instead."

Athu: "We'll look."

Ndramboeny: "This is for you, Ruby."

Athu: "If we bring it, will you remove what is in her?"

Ndramboeny: "Yes, this is Ruby's."

Athu: "So they're not together?"

Ndramboeny: "Do you want to be treated too?"

Athu: "If I'm sick."

Ndramboeny: "Let's do Ruby's treatment first and then we'll see about yours. If you can't find the chicken by tomorrow, Thursday will be okay. That's it."

Athu: "Yes."

Ndramboeny: "If you find the chicken, come tell us so that we can prepare the medicine. It needs to be picked in the countryside. Tell Mohedja to tell Tumbu since he will remove the stuff."

Athu had assumed until this point that we were talking only about the evil eye. But Ndramboeny corrected him; there was something else as well, namely sorcery, that had to be removed first.

Ndramboeny: "You'll get medicine of one kind first and then another later. I am going now. Don't be discouraged, you will be cured, God willing." Mohedja groaned a little and returned to the floor.

Mohedja asked, "So how are we?"

Athu: "Well, thanks to God."

Ruby: "Tell her about it."

Athu explained to Mohedja what the "Grandfather" had said. "Sorcery and evil eye are to be removed first."

Mohedja: "What's needed?"

Athu: "We have to look for a red chicken or cloth and will come tell you if we have it."

As the consultation ended, we began to chat informally. Athu's kidneys or lower back (*vania*) had been painful, ever since his second marriage the previous year to an older woman in the distant village of R—.

I asked Ruby whether she was angry.

"Yes," she said. "I threw him out of the house, clothes and all, but he returned."

"Couldn't you remove him?" I asked.

Mohedja interrupted, "Can't you see that Ruby still loves him? It's only the second marriage she doesn't like."

Ruby added, "We have boys' houses to build and daughters to marry off and he goes and spends his money on polygyny. Is that good? I say no!"

Athu asked me smilingly, "Do you judge her right?"

I backed off, saying it wasn't my affair.

Mohedja laughed and said firmly that polygyny was not good.

The next day, Athu showed up to say he had found a red chicken. Mohedja told him they would do the medicine the following morning but warned him to come very early before they left for their ylang ylang harvest. That morning, Tumbu removed a sorcery packet from Ruby's lower body and Mohedja removed human evil eye. Tumbu remarked that the sorcery was strong (*mahery*) and that the spirit would surely come to fight him hard that night. They gave Ruby plant medicine and told her to wash in it for a week and report her dreams.

This case demonstrates a point about divination well recognized from other African contexts. The conversation between the clients and spirits was open-ended. In effect, Athu and Ruby ended up telling the trumba what they thought the trouble was and they became more open about this as the conversation progressed. Ndramboeny refused to lead them and instead tried to keep up with their disclosures. In other words, the trumba provided a context in which the clients could speak freely and could discover an external authorization for their opinions. The clients read Ndramboeny's silences and evasions as positive agreement. Athu thus came to terms with a fact he had suspected but had not wanted to believe, namely, that sorcery from his second wife lay behind his own and Ruby's problems.

Athu's second marriage had been a sensitive one. Ruby was his cross-cousin. Athu had worked well with his mother's brother, Ruby's father, adjacent to whom they lived. This man was very angry about the second marriage and even Athu's older brother disapproved. There was thus a good deal of pressure on Athu to abandon the second marriage although it was already in its second year. In polygynous marriages, men alternate brief stays between the villages of their wives. At the time of their visit to Ndramboeny, it had been over twenty days since he had last visited the second wife in R— and people said that if he went back to her now, Ruby would leave him to go live with her mother in B—. Ruby had been sick ever since Athu's return to Lombeni from his last visit to the other wife.

On 17 August, I stopped by Ruby's and she told me to tell Mohedja that the medicine was working but that she had not had any dreams. Mohedja said, "Maybe it's just an ordinary illness" (i.e., without the complications of sorcery or possession). On the 18th, Mohedja visited Ruby and confirmed for herself. Trumba were specifically ruled out; if there were trumba, Ruby would have seen something in her dreams after taking the medicine. On the 23rd, Ruby came to Mohedja's for more plant medicine, saying she was feeling much better but not yet completely well.

And so, a few weeks later, we were shocked to hear that Ruby was actively possessed by a spirit who was singing and clapping without cease.

That evening, as he entered Ruby's house to assess the situation, the young male patros healer Safy was suddenly displaced by a patros who demanded to know who had sent the foreign spirit and why. Speaking through Ruby, the spirit said it had come for her *rohu* (i.e., to take her life).

"Only God can do that," replied the patros in Safy.

The next morning, I went to see what was happening. Ruby sat on a mat in the middle of a crowded room. A male cousin supported her back while her stepmother held her hands. Athu was speaking to the spirit, saying, "Tell us what you want." People warned me to stand back, saying that the spirit would fight and tear my clothes. The spirit breathed loudly, turning Ruby's head from side to side with rhythmical and forceful movements. The room was full of women and girls, more peering in through the windows and doors.

Grasping Ruby's shoulder, Safy inquired roughly, "Why are you acting like this? Who sent you?"

"Everyone here knows," replied the spirit. The spirit gave a garbled story about how a trumba had fetched him on Mt. X (a conspicuous mountain near the village inhabited by Athu's other wife) and that Athu was *d'accord* (in a positive relationship) with the person who sent it.

There was a lot of talk and coaxing. Safy told the spirit to speak straight and not cause mischief by dropping hints.

A patros risen in a female healer loudly interrogated Athu: "Do you have two wives?"

Athu: "I had two. I left one."

Patros: "When?"

Athu: "Long ago."

People held the spirit back each time he tried to stand. They were afraid of him, or at least showed a healthy respect. The spirit arched his back violently, they grabbed him, and Ruby's body sagged in their arms, a dead weight. The spirit alternated bursts of immense strength with complete laxity, and no warning of the shifts between them.

Safy massaged Ruby's shoulders and blew hard in each ear as the spirit seemed to leave and Ruby was put to bed, though Safy thought the spirit might return. As Safy and I left, he told me the spirit was just telling lies, laughing at us. The spirit knew that Safy knew this. The spirit was a patros who wanted to enter Ruby. He mentioned that Ruby already had a different patros, one that had held his ceremony some time ago.

Later in the day, Athu came to fetch Mohedja because her name had been on Ruby's lips. They brought her to the house and wanted to call up Ndramboeny, but Mohedja refused. She told them to go to a diviner first to see who was effective (*mwafaka*). She said that with such a "thick" illness she was not able to get involved unless the proper groundwork was done. In effect, she was not about to enter trance in public and possibly make a fool of herself in a case she might be unable to handle.

Mohedja told me privately that Ruby was mentally ill (*adala*), like a woman who had died in the village some weeks before. She said the spirit had been sent by the co-wife and that there was a rumour that the co-wife had come to Lombeni, to the house of a friend of Athu's. The friend had fetched Athu. She didn't know whether the couple had just talked, slept together, or what. Another rumour was that, despite his promise, Athu had returned (for whatever reason) to the other wife's village. Ruby had been cured, but then Athu had come home with another illness sent to Ruby by the co-wife.

Mohedja added that she was frightened by such a bad illness. And she was extremely put off by the behaviour of the people in Lombeni Be, crowding in to watch the spectacle, making stupid comments, and running away whenever the spirit made to move. She mentioned this several times over the next few days.

People were full of the story. One of my neighbours reported that Ruby kept tearing off her clothes so that they tied her wrists. It took several people to hold her down. The spirit had been sent to Ruby via Athu, though he must not have known it; Ruby had been sick ever since his return.

The following morning, I returned to Ruby's. Her mother, older sister, and stepfather had arrived. Ruby's wrist was limp; the spirit told someone it was broken. The person replied that she could not feel anything broken. The spirit retorted, "Cut it off!"

Ruby (or the spirit) was lying in bed, a few of her kin in the room, and visitors arriving to greet her. Mohedja had been by earlier but had already gone. The spirit had left during the night so that Ruby could eat and sleep, but he returned in full force at dawn. Ruby lay smiling slightly and tapping her hand on her mother's arm. A patros healer recited over incense and placed it under the bed.

The spirit had said it would leave Ruby once it received its *swadaka* – a red goat. They were looking for one. This turned out to be an untrue promise on the spirit's part, but it caused a lot of anxiety because it seemed to identify the spirit with the one who had caused the death of the crazy woman some weeks earlier; that spirit had asked for an identical *swadaka*. It could be that the other woman's episode – she had been Ruby's mother's stepdaughter – had put the whole thing in Ruby's head. That affair too had concerned a man who had wronged his wife.

The spirit asked for a red chicken to eat and said it would then leave.

"You're lying!" responded the patros curer decisively.

People listened to the spirit and at times tried to engage him in conversation, but they also remonstrated sternly. "Go away now so that Ruby can get something to eat."

"Where's the food? So, where's the food?"

"Do you have to see it before you leave?"

The spirit went off on a tangent. "Michel," it called to me, "Write 'wind.'"

Ruby's sister asked if her baby was breastfeeding. "Yes," replied Ruby.

Very suddenly, she rose from the bed in a single strong fluid motion, saying "*Allons!*"

Some people fled the room, others rushed to pin her down. The spirit fought as they tied amulets around Ruby's neck and arms, quietened once they were attached, and went completely limp when they carried her back to bed. The spirit didn't want the amulets and even tried to bite her cousin's hand during the struggle.

Athu was attentive, leaning over the bed. The spirit told him he was hungry.

People discussed how the whole thing had started. Around 3:00 p.m. the first day, Ruby had told Athu she was feeling sick. She said black birds were circling around her head. She did odd things. She took a pitcher and a mirror from one neighbour's house and left them at another's. She placed wet laundry, including Athu's trousers, on a bed at a neighbour's. The neighbours thought she had quarrelled with Athu and took her by the hand back home. Eventually people realized she was acting crazy.

The day was ill-omened (*nuhus*) so they waited to do the *swadaka* the next day. Athu also looked forward to the French doctor's weekly visit. The amulets had been written out by a fellow villager. He remarked how the amulets had weakened the spirit's hold and calmed the patient. Ruby lay quietly, though she looked disassociated.

I returned in the late afternoon. Ruby lay on her bed with her baby by her side, physically quiescent but babbling. The sheet was embroidered with the words in French, *Oh, ma chérie dort*. Female kin cleaned rice in a corner and a neighbour brought them fish. Safy looked in on the patient.

On 22 September we heard that Ruby had received plant medicine and that a chicken had been offered as *swadaka*. She was no longer talking irrationally. When I visited the next day, she seemed fine. Safy's patros had exorcised the spirit by forcing it to inhale bad-smelling steam. He told it to go find the person who had sent it. Her grandmother added that the person who sent it could give the spirit the promised red goat. The French doctor had come and forbidden Ruby salt; he gave her some medicine to take if her symptoms returned and told her to visit the clinic the following week. Athu said she was not yet completely cured and needed massaging. He announced loudly that he was not going back to the other wife. Ruby said she was not so sure. By 29 September, she was fully recovered.[6]

I hope to have accomplished two things in this chapter. The first was to illustrate Mohedja's development and style as a healer. The second was to show how therapy by means of spirits provides for the kind of conjunction of dispassion and compassion, or what Herbert Fingarette (1963, 245) calls "compassionate objectivity," similar to what psychotherapy advocates.[7]

Therapy in Mayotte includes embodied practices, like bathing in herbal medicines and massages, no less than the state of possession itself, but it is at base a communicative practice and one in which the good therapist mainly listens. Results are open-ended. Spirits and spirit mediums are not overdetermined in their actions and, as therapists, they do not ascribe overdetermination to their clients. In the best case, they produce the conditions by which they and their clients can continue to grow. Occasionally, as with Ruby, a more forceful intervention seems warranted, but that was not Mohedja's style.[8]

Chapter Eight

Darwesh and the Suitors

Mohedja's second patros, Darwesh, was a good deal younger than Mze Nuru. Although he arrived early in her marriage, at the same time as the senior patros, Mohedja stressed that he came to her in quite another way: he was sent to take her life (*rohu*). Darwesh was not successful at this, so he thought it best just to stay and get food by rising in her and asking for it.

I will explore the specific meaning of Darwesh for Mohedja, but I also want to use Darwesh to make some general points about the way in which cohabitation can be a vehicle for overcoming aggression and assault. I describe it as a kind of passive action in which the experience of onslaught from an external source is gradually internalized and transformed on the subject's own terms. Through the emergence of the spirit and his voice, the subject gains a means to articulate her concerns and take control of them. In both the subjective (intrapersonal) and objective (interpersonal) domains, possession enables a "working through" of issues.

In this account, I do not take sides in the heated discussion about the origins and conceptualization of trauma. We will see both external threats to her person and the characteristic way that Mohedja has of imagining and experiencing threat. These operate in dialectical relationship to each other; in some events in her life the external source has more force and in other events her relational concerns are primary. But cohabitation enables her to articulate her experience and move ahead.

Mohedja took her dreams as signs of the incipient arrival of another spirit. When Darwesh was first entering her, Mohedja dreamt that someone came into the room, went under the bed, and lifted it up so that she would fall off. One time, when Tumbu was not there, she shouted so loudly that her mother and her next-door neighbour rushed in to see what was wrong. Mohedja saw Darwesh as a boy. He wore only black shorts and a black hat. He tried to frighten her, but she was not frightened. It was then he went under the bed and lifted it up.

Dreams of flying were a more common sign that one was receiving a spirit. When spirits first entered her, Mohedja frequently dreamt she was flying. The spirits chased her and tried to catch and hit her. They fought together and she was able to fly away just in time. These dreams were unlike the ones she had once mature relations had been established with a spirit. In the latter, the spirits came of their own accord, in order to tell Mohedja something. But the dreams where she saw herself under attack, she affirmed, came not from the spirit, but from her *rohu* (soul), that is, directly from herself.

This is critical. In the dreams of attack, Mohedja was warning and protecting herself by fighting off the spirit. The fact that she was chased but not vanquished was a sign of the relationship to come – one in which the spirit could bring suffering but where, in the end, the host proved stronger. Cohabitation, in which the host was able to negotiate a relatively stable social relationship with her spirit, was thus very different from being overwhelmed (as Ruby was), going "crazy" (having a psychotic episode), and possibly even dying as a result of spirit attack. The dream was one of the first steps in the constitution of cohabitation, in which Mohedja came to realize that she was acquiring a spirit who would live adjacent and who would sometimes possess her, and in which she began to set the terms of that relationship. While the initial arrival of the spirit was experienced as beyond her control, the dream was an indication that the will of the host had become involved and that she was beginning to look out and care for herself.

This is an example of what I mean by passive action. The spirit is understood as an autonomous, external force, and possession as something that is happening to the host rather than an act initiated by her. And yet, exactly as Mohedja put it, it was the host's own *rohu* (soul, feelings, life force) that provided her with the dream and was beginning to exert control. If the spirit is a passion, it is one that quickly becomes subsumed within the host's agency, just as the host's voice and agency is subsumed in the spirit. While the spirit is always publicly distinguished from the person of the host, the subjective process is one in which the host is involved from the start.

5 January 1976, and subsequently. The person who sent Darwesh to kill Mohedja was Toihan, a man originally from Lombeni Be who called Mohedja's mother *angivavy* (father's sister), that is, he was Mohedja's distant cross-cousin. When Mohedja was still living in F—, Toihan and his mother came in order to procure an engagement between the young people. Mohedja did not like him from the first and refused outright. He sent her gifts, but she returned them all; she was not about to keep anything from someone she did not like! Much later, when she had moved to Lombeni Kely and already married Tumbu, Toihan still wanted to marry her. Once he even tried to rape her. She completely rejected him.

She became sick. When Malidy Juma extracted the sorcery from her body, Darwesh rose in Mohedja and announced he had been sent by Toihan in order to kill her. Toihan had promised Darwesh a red chicken and some cloth when the job was completed. But, announced Darwesh, since he had been unsuccessful in doing what was requested, he had decided to rise in Mohedja's head (*manunga an'luha*) instead. When Malidy asked what he wanted of her, he replied a patros ceremony (*azulahy*) with a white goat and white cloth. The ceremony was held some time thereafter. Since then, Darwesh rose only irregularly, much less often than Mze Nuru. He was a youth and at a patros ceremony he liked to dance and drink [goat's] blood. However, Mohedja's patros didn't go indiscriminately to amuse themselves at all patros ceremonies. Mohedja attended only ceremonies held by her relatives or those where she had been specifically invited by the host.

Darwesh hailed from an underwater village, Polé, "near the airport," and since his arrival he had taken Mohedja there to visit in her sleep. They walked together to the paved road, took a bush taxi to the airport, and a canoe from the beach out into the lagoon. The canoe started to spin and descended into the water. They entered a large town with cement houses and tin roofs [at the time Mohedja recounted this, such houses were rare among ordinary citizens of Mayotte and there were none in Lombeni]. The town was full of people, old and young. Darwesh took her to his mother's house, where she met his parents, who welcomed her as a guest. They cooked and she ate; the meal was rice and meat, not spirit food. She ate alone [as is fitting for a guest]. She saw many of his kin. When she had finished eating and chatting, she said her farewell. They rose in the canoe and took a bush taxi home. When they reached Lombeni, she woke up. She went on this trip frequently and Darwesh's family also visited her here in her sleep. She saw Darwesh in her dreams as a young man with nice features. She compared him to a young married man in the village.

Patros villages vary in size. Polé was very large, with many inhabitants who had never come and risen in people; were they to do so, said Mohedja, they would surely use up the entire population of Mayotte. Mze Nuru's village, by contrast, had few people. The buildings looked like shops and there were many animal pens. Mze Nuru's house was the only one inhabited and he lived alone. He was the only person she had ever seen there. He brought out food and they ate together. They flew there together, towards the human village of D—. Mze Nuru's town was on land, but deep in the bush. Mze Nuru had no children; perhaps he was not married. She hadn't seen the house of Mze Nuru's brother, Mze Rihu; Mze Rihu had no offspring either. His town was Faez, near L—; she had never been to these places in her waking life.

These stories were quite stereotypic, and I heard similar ones from other hosts to patros. The patros and their villages referred to past inhabitants and habitations of Mayotte, although this connection was never made explicit, and people were insistent that the patros were not deceased humans.[1] Many of their names are found in Arabic texts and correspond to the names of djinn reported on the African mainland. The name Mze Nuru itself is composed of the Swahili honorific Mze (Mister) and the Arabic word for light (*nur*). The patros towns showed signs of prosperity and mercantile connections of the precolonial period. The hospitality patterns were local ones.

What was expressed in these dream narratives was the establishment of strong positive relations with the spirits. Just as one would go to visit the family of a human friend, so too with the patros. Mohedja indicated a comfortable, though somewhat formal, relationship in which she was accepted by Darwesh's family. The visits to Mze Nuru's had perhaps a hint of incest fantasy; they described a situation in which her relationship to the spirit was intimate and singular, a fact which corresponded to the way she talked about Mze Nuru in other contexts. Overall, these dreams demonstrated Mohedja's good feelings about herself and the strength of her identifications with the respective spirits. As in the initial dreams of being chased, there was a passive quality. Mohedja was taken on a trip; she did not set out by herself. At the same time, the dreams may be understood as affirmations of the solidarity of her relations with her spirits and her sense of security with them.

In her relations with Darwesh, we see Mohedja triumph over a man who had been harassing her. (I never met Toihan, but that he was an unusually unpleasant person appeared confirmed by a rumour

I heard elsewhere that he had committed incest with his daughter.) The fear and real aggression Mohedja experienced against her person was internalized, but at the same time its force was mitigated and turned to her own interests. The black and red (strong colours apparent in his clothing in the dream and in the meal Toihan had provided him) were changed to white (a positive colour, in the sacrifice and clothing he requested). Darwesh rose infrequently to allow Mohedja her own chance to become an energetic, potentially dangerous young man, one who carried out boundary-violating acts like drinking blood but also befriended her, taking her on trips to meet his family. In the latter, he showed personal traits more characteristic of Mohedja – even-tempered, well-intentioned, hospitable – than of the menacing Toihan.

Mohedja thought Darwesh first arrived around the same time as Mze Nuru and may have been the cause of the illness that had originally been attributed to Mze Nuru. But he did not actively rise in her until some years later when Mze Nuru's ceremony had already been completed. Then Darwesh had a ceremony of his own. That Darwesh did not appear often in later life may have meant that the emotional salience of Toihan and the issues he represented had declined for Mohedja, perhaps resolved by the presence of Darwesh himself. Toihan lived elsewhere; she never saw him and, moreover, she had grown older and gone on with her life. By contrast, the frequently present Mze Nuru was based on identification with her brother, a much deeper, continuous, and more profound relationship than the trauma with Toihan, which the spirit helped her work through and move beyond.

In addition, Darwesh represented qualities of youthful male bravado, energy, and violence, which Mohedja did not wish to be a strong part of the persona she presented to the world. Unlike many hosts who tended to acquire junior spirits before they moved on to senior ones, in Mohedja's case, Mze Nuru's identification and ceremony took precedence over that of Darwesh. Like Darwesh, Mohedja's young male trumba, Botu Changizy, rose only rarely and then for relatively short periods during the heat of trumba ceremonies. The gravity of the senior spirits contained the exuberance of the junior ones. This appeared to be a matter of suppression rather than repression since there were moments at which the young males did appear. But overall, Mohedja preferred to act with calm and dignity. This was not true of all hosts, some of whom continued to perform as youthful, and at times outrageous, heavy-drinking male spirits until they were well on in years.[2]

Toihan was by no means the only rejected suitor in Mohedja's life. Persecution by such men was a motif that recurred several times, at least as she recounted her life in 1975–6. There were several incidents, about which she felt varying degrees of fear, anger, guilt, or desire. She handled the cases in different ways, not always by means of spirits.

Tumbu's cousin Hamidu was one of the men Mohedja had turned down before her marriage. Some years later, he tried to solicit an affair with her and always seemed to be following her around. One day she was harvesting rice alone in an isolated field. She heard a sudden noise and turning, saw Hamidu. He suggested they sleep together but she refused, reminding him that she was the wife of his *zandry* ([classificatory] younger brother). He tried to convince her, but she remained adamant. Then he came up and took her wrist, extracting the knife with which she had been cutting the rice stalks and putting it on the ground. She told him to stop. He took off his clothes and held both her hands, trying to force her to the ground. She put up a fight and finally he gave up. He started to leave, turning at the edge of the field to ask her one last time whether she was certain. After he left, she was frightened, starting at the slightest noise. She was afraid he might try to harm her physically. She returned to the village with an empty basket and no rice.

She did not know what to do; if she were to tell Tumbu it would lead to a fight. She thought hard about it and finally, after three days, decided to tell him. What decided it for her was the fact that this was his own cousin. She said to him, "Tell your older brother to leave me alone." Tumbu asked her what she meant, and she related the incident to him. It was night and the next morning Tumbu went to the mosque as usual; then went to Hamidu's house – Hamidu was married in Lombeni Be at the time – and went in and talked to him. There was no physical fight and Mohedja did not know what transpired between them. But since that time, Tumbu stopped taking an interest in Hamidu's affairs and Hamidu ceased to bother her.

28 July 1975, and subsequently. Mohedja emphasized that Darwesh was the only one of the spirits to cohabit with her who had been sent by a sorcerer expressly in order to kill her. Her other spirits each came on their own initiative, that is, because they were attracted to her on their own account. However, she had been the object of sorcery several times, and not always by the same attacker. These attacks sometimes manifested themselves in the form of spirits. But these were spirits who had to be removed or exorcized rather than accommodated.

Mohedja said she knew the identity of each culprit. Although the sorcery extractor was not permitted to identify the perpetrator by name, he described the person in such a way, male or female, light or dark-skinned, that she had a good idea who it was. In fact, in her descriptions of the attacks against her, she determined the identities of the perpetrators not through the loquacity of the healer, but by means of her dreams. She thought it right that the healer not identify the sorcerer, since this could lead to conflict, but in her own case, she always kept quiet about what she knew. She said she had no interest in retribution, although, as we will see, she was a master at indirect retaliation.

The first attack was caused by a man who wanted to marry her. She refused him and, when she married Tumbu, he was angry and wanted to see her dead. When she gave birth to her first child [Nuriaty], she fell very ill for six months. Her mother-in-law brought her up to her house to look after her. She was sick all over and her breasts were infected and gave no milk. The baby was nursed by Mohedja's mother and fed canned milk [see chapter 12]. Nobody knew what was wrong; some people said it might be a trumba. Her elder brother Samba came from F— and diagnosed sorcery. He extracted the sorcery and gave her medicine, and she became well. She learned the identity of her attacker when she dreamt of him fighting with her. [Note that this is a different version of the arrival of Darwesh and of the way Samba treated her first post-partum illness before handing over the treatment to Malidy Juma.]

The next attack happened when they were living out at their fields at Red Rock, where she knew practically no one. She fell very sick, delirious, could hardly tell day from night, couldn't speak, or eat or drink for fifteen days. The astrologer Juma Abudu was called in all the way from Lombeni, and he gave her medicine, but forbade the use of foul smoke, the usual remedy for driving out a spirit. Once he had exorcized the spirit [it was a generalized "evil spirit" rather than one who could come to possess people positively and by name], she was able to speak again and started getting better. Before she was fully recovered, she asked Tumbu to take her to F— where she consulted Mze Rihu, the patros cohabiting with her brother, Samba. [Recall, he was the older brother of Mohedja's own trusted Mze Nuru.] The patros said the source of her problem was sorcery [as the astrologer had not] and he removed it. Again, she saw the identity of the perpetrator in a dream, and again it was a man who had wanted to marry her, who had asked her to leave Tumbu when they were living at the fields, and whom she had refused.

At this point, Mohedja grew silent. We both laughed when I said I guessed she didn't want to tell me any more. Finally, she said she had been the victim of sorcery again, when she was pregnant with Mwanesha, who at the time we spoke was a toddler. Mohedja was already quite pregnant. The healer said the medicine wouldn't help if she took it at home because the sorcerer was close by. So she followed the healer to his house in a neighbouring village and stayed there while he extracted the sorcery and treated her with medicine. As soon as she was cured, she returned to Lombeni and gave birth at home. She said she didn't know the identity of the sorcerer, though the healer (Tumbu's former apprentice) surely did. Then she added that, again, it was a man who had asked her to marry him. I think she knew perfectly well who it was but didn't want to say because the event was recent, and the perpetrator was someone in the community whom I knew.

A year later, following the death of a woman in Lombeni who had suffered a post-partum psychosis, Mohedja again recalled the events that occurred when she lived in the fields. She said the cause of her illness had been an evil spirit, like that attributed to the illness of the woman who had just died, though her symptoms were different, and she hadn't thrashed about, as this woman had. She said she had no direct memory of the period of her illness but only heard about it later in conversation with her children. She was impaired for a month, could hardly see, and thought it was the end. Then she got better.

The source of the illness was "just a *lulu* (spirit)," of the sort to be found in the bush. But it had been sent by someone. Her patros rose and announced it, even giving the name of the perpetrator, so she was told later. Many people heard the spirit shout it out. The perpetrator also lived at the fields. For some years he had been after her to leave Tumbu and marry him. In the days when she was first falling sick, she had a dream. Someone came and told her not to eat anything that this man might offer her. He approached with something in his hand and invited her to eat. She refused, and he opened his hand and she saw meat. She refused until he tried to force her. He managed to get a tiny piece of it down her throat, though she spat out the rest. She gagged and gagged. Then she awoke. A few days later, she fell really ill.

During the period of recuperation, while Mohedja was lying in bed, the man came to visit [as was the polite thing to do]. Her children told him she was resting. They called out to her, and she pretended to be asleep, so he left again. She said she couldn't face him while she was still sick [i.e., she refused to be seen by him in the position of "victim"]. Much later, she saw him again and they just exchanged courtesies. She thought he had sent the spirit "because his longing for me could not be fulfilled." By killing her he would have removed the object of his longing.

Mohedja's account shows an interesting implication of the reluctance of the curer to reveal the identity of the sorcerer. The curer's reticence provides the victim the opportunity to construct her own interpretation, one which is consistent, meaningful, and psychologically relevant to her, and which will not be challenged in any public forum. Because it is not openly legitimated by the curer (however much he may encourage her to arrive at a particular identification), she could not very well publicly accuse her attacker, except via the enunciation of her spirit, even if she wanted to. Adaptation to the situation is thus usually restricted to the private domain; the victim fixes on someone appropriate and may make adjustments in her daily patterns of interaction, but she does not usually create an open social rupture. This fits the stated goal of avoiding conflict, but it also shifts the action from the collective arena to the inner scene. The fact of sorcery has social effects, but these may be subtle. Of greater consequence are the personal effects, the ways in which victims of sorcery internalize its meaning (or slough it off). In fact, of course, making a diagnosis and then an accusation of sorcery is itself part of the internal process of coming to terms with illness or misfortune and an expression of aggression on the part of the sufferer.[3]

19 May 1976. Tumbu gave me a different account of Mohedja's illness at the fields, placing it in an area of contestation that was more meaningful to him at the time than that of sexual coercion. Mohedja had just given birth. Her entire body became covered in sores. Tumbu brought seawater from a great distance [the fields were located on the slopes of one of the highest mountains on the island] to bathe her. He carried Mohedja all the way to the neighbouring village on his shoulders. He was crying; he thought she would die. Then he went to Lombeni to fetch the astrologer, his uncle Juma Abudu. Mohedja babbled for a day until she received some medicine; then she became *daba* (dumb, unresponsive). She was like a small child and just lay in bed and didn't see or hear anything. Eventually her hair fell out and her skin turned funny. Tumbu washed and cared for her for three months until finally she began to improve. He explained the cause of her illness as sorcery, but sorcery that was the product of a conflict over land.[4]

A man wanted their fields, but they had already planted long-term crops and were not about to give them up. The man tried to attack Tumbu with sorcery, but it struck Mohedja instead. [Remember that she had a more vulnerable disposition.] Tumbu actually saw him do it – saw him digging holes in their field one day. But at that time, he didn't know how sorcery was accomplished. Had he recognized what he had seen he would have gone and dug up what the man had planted, and everything would have been all right. Soon after, Mohedja went to the fields alone. She felt or heard something and was startled and the evil spirit [hired to convey the sorcery] took advantage of that moment of vulnerability and entered her.

Mohedja's illness was a crisis for both Tumbu and Mohedja and each of them gave a distinct reading of events. Each interpreted it in a way that was personally meaningful. Tumbu portrayed himself in a somewhat heroic light, urgently trying to save his wife. At the same time, however, he also accepted guilt for her condition. He was the intended victim, and it was his ignorance that failed to stop the sorcery's effects. This was a period when Tumbu himself was trying to acquire land, a difficult business which required access to both capital and the right social network, and a good deal of wily cleverness. The story also provided a rationalization for his growing interest in healing, especially curing sorcery.

The context in which Tumbu recounted these events was one in which he was attempting to cure the woman with the post-partum psychosis who subsequently died. He told me the story of Mohedja's illness to demonstrate his confidence in his approach to treatment and his long acquaintance with spirits and their peculiar, but to him no longer frightening, manner of appearance. He was also, no doubt, reassuring himself.

Tumbu's account is valid insofar as it is true to his experience. To be the intended victim of sorcery is to be socially significant, and both Mohedja and Tumbu were making this claim. Perhaps it was also a way to resolve feelings of guilt. In any case, it was in these contexts less a sign of paranoia than of ego strength. Moreover, they were able to build from the event insofar as it led them to recognize and develop their own talents as curers.

It is noteworthy that while some spirits arrived in their hosts as the result of attacks of sorcery perpetrated by others, once established, these same spirits provided a main source of protection against further sorcery and were also a channel through which sorcery accusations could be rendered explicit. There was a positive transformation, from having been a victim to wielding a sure means of defense, from anxiety and fear to articulate speech and action.

The presence of knowledgeable spirits in the household had implications for other family members as well. Sometimes one of the cohabiting spirits would rise of his own accord to warn the family about impending sorcery. In fact, spirits could help their friends through dreams even if they did not actively possess them. In other words, the confidence developed by the mediums in their spirits could diffuse to those around them.

21 July 1980. Shortly after my return to Lombeni, I had a dream in which a powerful local man, with whom I had never gotten along and who I felt was trying to manipulate me, tried to physically harm me. I was rather disconcerted by the dream and mentioned it to Mohedja and Tumbu. A few days later, Mohedja asked me whether I had had any more dreams since my report of the first one. She said that once one becomes friends with the spirits one can expect this sort of thing. Seeing people harming you is in fact a sign (*halama*) of the spirits' presence. They tell you everyone who has evil intentions towards you. I pointed out that I already knew that the man I saw in the dream didn't like me and that he had already tried to hamper my work. Mohedja felt this didn't discount the message. She regularly saw in her dreams the people who harboured evil intentions towards her. Sometimes she saw a sorcery packet buried in the courtyard; the next day she would go to the spot and dig it up. Or else the spirit told her in her sleep to get Tumbu to do it. One's enemies often appeared in dreams carrying a knife or machete. Tumbu also brought up my dream a few days later and said that when a person is in friendly association (*kuparan*) with spirits, they warn him about his enemies. This exemplifies cohabitation.

However, because people can become friendly with spirits who are in others, having a spirit is not always a guarantee of the security of the host. After describing various kinds of love potions, the young healer Safy explained that if either he or his wife fed something to each other, their respective spirits would cause them to vomit it up. On the other hand, his wife could call up his patros first and give him gifts in order to get him on her side before she fed Safy the potion. She would tell Safy that she and his spirit had talked about something else.

Both Mohedja and Tumbu had frequent dreams, especially when one or the other was working on a case.

24 March 1976. Mohedja told me that she always dreamt about Tumbu's cases but that she only informed him when he himself had told her about a particular client, otherwise she kept quiet. She mentioned that she didn't think that a client he was then treating would be cured. Usually after her dream, a response to the treatment followed quickly, but in this instance, she had started dreaming some days earlier. She saw two strange men come to the house. They were sitting by the back door, and she was in the kitchen shed. She called to them, asking who they were. One of them left and the other just sat there and didn't answer, even when she asked again. She could tell he was not from Mayotte but wasn't sure where he was from. He didn't answer any of her questions. He said he was a fundi but did not say what kind. Mohedja disliked him and told him to go be a fundi somewhere else. She was afraid of what he would do here. They struggled but she got the upper hand and propelled him out of the courtyard, where Tumbu sat watching her. She had such a dislike of the man that she kept on going, leading him all the way out of the village. She told me this man was clearly the fundi who had made the sorcery that was harming Tumbu's client. The other man, whose face she did not have a chance to examine, was probably the person on whose behalf it was done.

Mohedja recounted the dream to Tumbu, and this prompted him to ask his client for more detail. The client admitted that her troubles had begun while she was living on another island.

On another occasion, Mohedja dreamt that a prospective client couldn't be cured, so Tumbu did not take the case. Mohedja explained it was her cohabiting spirits who told her these things. It was a particular spirit who informed her at each dream, but all her cohabiting spirits did so at times. In the dream where she struggled with the two men, it was Ndramboeny who informed her, and in fact she saw herself actively possessed by him as she drove the men away.[5]

As noted in other chapters, Mohedja's dreams were not always warnings and not always sent by her cohabiting spirits.

One night in 1985, Mohedja dreamt she was living in her former house and that her neighbour, an elderly but since deceased brother-in-law, came and greeted her. When she asked how he was, he replied that ever since his death his adult children hadn't cared for him. "Oh," replied Mohedja. Then he left. This was his soul (*rohu*) speaking and bringing her the dream. The dream image looked just like him when he was alive.

The next morning Mohedja passed on the message to her (classificatory) elder sister, the widow, and their son. The widow replied that he had probably meant that they hadn't held a performance of a *daira* (a popular sufi dance) since his death (some six years earlier). He had really loved the *daira*. In fact, they had yet to hold the commemoration ceremony (*mandeving*) for him at which the *daira* would be performed. Mohedja told me that his sons drank palm wine and didn't care.

Mohedja had this dream on the anniversary of her brother-in-law's death – that is, at the beginning of the Islamic month in which he had died. Having passed on the message, she did not dream of him again in the days that followed.

As a woman, Mohedja's life experience was shaped by inhabiting a fertile body and one that was an object of male desire. She spent much of her adult life pregnant, and repeatedly suffered the risks of childbirth (chapter 9). While she did not speak of difficult pregnancies or labour, she often fell sick immediately after giving birth. She did not respond to sexual overtures in the way many of her suitors appeared to expect and she experienced their persistence as harassment. Many women have similar experiences; what distinguished Mohedja is what she made of them. I do not read her suffering as a product of inner conflict. Rather, I start with the external sources of her problems – sexual harassment and post-partum illness – and examine the ways she transcended them. The interesting psychological element lies in her mode of transforming these external obstacles and the suffering they brought.

One psychological response to her illness was aggression. The local model that suggested illness could be derived from sorcery provided a channel for aggressive impulses. As we have seen, it was Mohedja who identified the sorcerer and in so doing it was she who cast her hostility towards the suitor rather than elsewhere. Perhaps she feared her own unacknowledged desire, but more evident was straightforward retaliation to aggressive, improper, and unwelcome advances on his part.

Without resolving her unconscious motivation, I note a possible connection between her interpretation of harassment and another significant episode in her life, namely her first engagement, mentioned in chapter 5. She and her fiancé appear to have been in love. When his father cancelled their engagement, Mohedja was promised to Tumbu. By the time the original fiancé discovered what had happened, it was too late. Mohedja once revealed that her fiancé was so outraged by his father's behaviour that he deliberately made love to a virgin (a flagrant breach of morality in Mayotte) in order to shame his father. Then, mad with grief at losing Mohedja, and not being able to stand the thought of her with another man, he wrote her a final letter and left Mayotte forever.

Mohedja's sorcerers were each rejected suitors. So, one could hypothesize that Mohedja bore a repressed guilt for what happened to her original fiancé and what he had done. It is likely that when she agreed to marry Tumbu she did not know that her former fiancé was still ignorant of his father's action in breaking off their engagement. Each time since then that she rejected a suitor, however unsuitable he was, she was punished, perhaps even unconsciously identifying with the virgin violated by her former fiancé.

And yet, what was the result? After a period of suffering, she gained another spirit, another voice, another guardian, and greater confidence in those she had to help her. In a sense, she accepted the rejected suitor by incorporating and gradually identifying with him, rendering him acceptable by transforming him into the stronger and desirable figure of Darwesh. Loss became gain.

The interest of Mohedja's narratives lies less in what they may reveal about sexual desire or repression, or about projection of aggression onto others, or ambivalence about these matters, than about her resources and relational development. Mohedja negotiates between dependence and autonomy. She rejects male aggression yet needs strong male figures to admire, depend on, and sometimes herself become. The emergence of Darwesh and Mze Nuru demonstrates her ability to selectively reject or incorporate salient aspects of others and thereby transform her episodes of illness (whatever their etiology) into occasions for growth.[6]

Having incorporated the spirits, Mohedja could draw on them to develop rational and reliable responses to unwelcome exigencies. A clear instance of how she came to address unwanted male sexual aggression – and the difference having a spirit made – is evident in the following account, one that displays self-protection and self-love rather than aggression.

One afternoon in January 1976, I found myself in a conversation with Mze Nuru that left a deep impression on me and that formed one of the germs around which this book was conceived.

Mze Nuru rose of his own accord to tell the family to hold a Muslim blessing to ward off forthcoming illness but then decided to stay and speak with me alone. He began by telling me that of all the spirits with whom the family cohabited he was the one most concerned about their welfare. He then spoke about Mohedja, about how much curing she knew, about her and Tumbu's early relations with Malidy Juma (see chapters 5 and 6), and about how he, Mze Nuru, had never once caused Mohedja any trouble since he made her sick upon first entering her over twenty years earlier. And yet, Mze Nuru said, Mohedja sometimes didn't like to follow his advice, complained she didn't want to be possessed by spirits, and felt embarrassed to practise her therapeutic skills.

Continuing the theme of Mohedja's stubbornness, Mze Nuru asked me to pass on a message to Mohedja. He said she would not listen if he told her directly and that he did not wish to make use of the usual channel, namely Tumbu, because what he had to say would undoubtedly anger Tumbu. Mze Nuru asked me to tell Mohedja not to be so sure of herself.

Somewhat taken aback, I asked Mze Nuru what he meant. In reply, he recounted how Mohedja had been subject to sexual harassment a few days earlier. She had turned down her pursuer bluntly and been prepared to defend herself physically. Mze Nuru was concerned that Mohedja was no longer as young or as strong as she had been and should resort to other strategies in such circumstances, putting the man off more diplomatically in order to minimize the risk of attack.

When Mze Nuru left, I repeated his message to Mohedja. She appeared surprised that Mze Nuru suggested next time she plead sickness but listened with grave interest. She then recounted the incident in great detail and told me how frightened she had been. She described several other similar incidents and talked for well over an hour.

Two days earlier she was alone weeding in her fields when a man approached her and asked for fire. She indicated where it was, but he said he was too lazy to go and fetch it. She replied that was his business. He hung around and began to pester her; having some experience in these matters, she knew something was up. She kept on weeding but asked him his name and the name of his father, thinking it would be good to know, just in case. He asked the name of her husband, but she refused to tell him. He said they were alone, and wouldn't her husband be jealous if he knew. She replied that she didn't know whether he would be jealous, but that in any case it was he who had stopped to talk to her and not vice versa and she was only doing her weeding. He offered her money and said she could just take it as a gift, but she said no, why should I get something for nothing? I don't plan to give you what you want. He told her to give him her machete, but she refused. He took hold of her wrist, and she told him to let go. He did and began to walk away but then called her to join him. She refused and he returned. He raised his offer of money. He asked if she was sick. She replied that she wasn't sick at all. He said she had embarrassed him, that a woman who rejected him really embarrassed him and she should change her mind.

He came and stood very close to her as she was weeding. She told him to look out. He asked if she planned to cut his feet. She said no but that if he stood too close a swing of her machete might accidentally cut him. He mentioned committing suicide over his embarrassment, and she told him drily that he would get over it. Finally, he left and it was only then that she really began to be frightened. She was afraid he might be waiting to spring at her on the path home, so she decided to stay and weed. Finally, one of her grandsons came to weed his little patch and she was very glad to see him. After they had weeded awhile, she said she was tired and suggested they go home together.

When I reported this conversation in earlier publications, I pointed to the channels of communication possession set up. Mohedja was often quite laconic and at times diffident. Possession allowed her to broach a subject that was troubling her. It also enabled her to present two sides of an issue about which she felt genuine ambivalence – in this case, whether to respond to harassment with contempt or caution. Generalizing from this and other conversations with hosts and spirits, I concluded that possession enabled the expression of incompatible messages and, by adding new levels of communication, thickened the relationships between hosts and significant others, especially spouses.

All of this is true. But what I would add now is that the solicitude Mze Nuru showed for Mohedja's children and grandchildren was matched by the solicitude he showed for Mohedja herself. Stepping outside the possession idiom into a psychological one, we see a kind of internal conversation (albeit mediated by an external party such as myself) in which one part of the self responds to another part with criticism, but also solicitude and compassion. Although some stages of a history of cohabitation might appear self-punitive, here the strongest criticism Mze Nuru makes of Mohedja is her obstinacy. The harshness of the initial arrival of the spirit years earlier is replaced and transcended by a positive concern and a healthy narcissism. Perhaps when Tumbu says Mze Nuru is *hodary* (strong, solid, dependable), this is in part what he means. Mze Nuru is also an expression of Mohedja's confidence. Neither Mze Nuru nor Mohedja can prevent unwanted advances, but they are able to evaluate alternative responses to them. The spirit is someone who feels in control of things, confident about the advice he dispenses, positive about his ability and his record in helping the family and intervening on behalf of Mohedja. Despite the amoral characteristics of spirits in general, in cohabiting with Mohedja, Mze Nuru appears responsible and principled. For these reasons he gains Tumbu's and others' respect.

PART THREE

Family Matters

Chapter Nine

Raising Children

In 1992, when I asked Mohedja whether I could tape her life story, she was uncertain what to say. "Say anything you like," I said, "whatever is important to you." Mohedja recounted her accomplishments as a parent: the children she had given birth to, and the grandchildren, how she had seen to the circumcisions of the boys and the weddings of the girls. I was disappointed at what appeared to be a rather flat and formal account, but looking back at the informal conversations we had, reproduction of the family was indeed the central thread. Moreover, reproduction has been a central social value and the main trajectory around which community life has been organized in Mayotte.

By reproduction here I refer not only to the biological act of having children, but also to raising them and producing the rituals that transform them into social adults. What was marked were sponsorships of the circumcisions of sons and the first weddings of daughters. These events, together with commemorations of deceased parents, were critical not merely for those who underwent them, but as a primary means through which their sponsors participated in the system of public exchanges which constituted civic identity. Fulfilment of exchange obligations by means of the performance of reproductive rituals has been a central source of pride and the means by which equality among citizens was established. Conversely, failure to produce the ceremonies was a source of shame, rendering one less equal than other villagers and less fully connected to them (Lambek 2018). Mohedja and Tumbu were able to fulfil all their ceremonial obligations well before I met them.

Child fosterage enabled people without biological reproductive success to have access to children and sponsorship of their weddings and circumcisions. Infants were sometime given to be raised by others when their biological parents had difficulty keeping previous children alive. Parenting and fosterage were activities in which the intervention of spirits who lived with family members were critical.

> *27 January 1976.* I entered the house this morning to find Mariam tête-à-tête with Mohedja who seemed very reserved. I soon realized that it was not Mohedja but Mze Nuru who was present. Mariam, who is Mohedja and Tumbu's second daughter and was then in her early twenties, was seeking advice about her baby daughter. Mze Nuru picked up the infant, felt her carefully, and told Mariam to give her deworming medicine. Mze Nuru had risen of his own accord to urge the family to hold a Muslim blessing to ward off illness. Mze Nuru explained that for years he had come to Mohedja's family to warn them when something was up. When he saw something was imminent and in need of action, he just could not keep quiet. Other spirits might, but not Mze Nuru. Of course, the family could fail to take his advice, but they did so at their own risk. Spirits could see into the future and learn God's plans, but most refrained from helping people.

It is evident that Mze Nuru, like Mohedja herself, was vitally concerned with the well-being of the family. His spontaneous arrivals were in order to help family members. His relationship was not simply with Mohedja herself, but with her entire family. Moreover, Mze Nuru asserted an unqualifiedly beneficent attitude towards them. Not only did he have their interest at heart, he said, but no spirit in Lombeni worked better on behalf of his host's family. This was a very strong assertion of assurance and commitment. Conversely, however, Mze Nuru was but one of Mohedja's cohabiting spirits. As he implied, they did not all work quite as hard or as unambiguously on the family's behalf.

Mohedja gave birth to thirteen children. Five daughters and two sons grew to adulthood. The other six died in infancy or early childhood. Mohedja's reproductive period spanned some thirty years and overlapped with those of her four eldest children. Tumbu was the father of all Mohedja's children, and he had no children with other women.

In Mayotte it was seen as unproductive and even wrong to talk about the dead or to dwell on one's losses. Mohedja never referred spontaneously to the children who had died. Indeed, it was completely inadvertently that I learned she had had a baby who was born and died between two of my visits. If I asked her to list the number of children she had had, like other women, she would mention only the living. However, if asked for the number of births or pregnancies (*kibu*), she would list them all.

Childbirth in Mayotte during Mohedja's lifetime was risky. Many women, including Mohedja, recounted how after giving birth they fell seriously ill, describing high fevers and periods of delirium. Sometimes the advent of spirits was associated with these crises. But Mohedja was also proud of her competence and autonomy in pregnancy and child-birth. With the advent of French obstetrical care, she tested the new doctor's competence by deliberately lying about what month she was in to see if he could correct her (he did).

Mohedja once recounted to a sister-in-law and me how she had con-cealed a pregnancy from Tumbu simply to see how observant he was. It happened this way. An older male neighbour mentioned that he could never tell what month his wife was in. Tumbu responded that he could always tell when a woman became pregnant; there was no woman who could hide it from him. Mohedja overheard this and sometime later when she became pregnant, she decided to keep quiet about it. Tumbu suspected nothing. In her sixth month, she was suffering from a stomach ache and called in an old woman to massage her. The woman could not find any physical condition and reported to Tumbu that she saw nothing "except what's in the belly." Tumbu looked puzzled at this remark and became silent. After the woman left, he went to Mohedja and asked her if she was pregnant. At first, she tried to deny it but then Tumbu said he guessed she was keeping silent because he was not the father. Mohedja asked him if he had ever heard or seen her with another man. Tumbu then asked what month she was in, and she remained quiet. Tumbu appeared upset. He sat brooding for a while, and then went out to fetch firewood. On his return he would not eat. Finally, Mohedja took pity on him and told him she was in her sixth month. He did not believe her and said maybe she was in the second or third, but surely not the sixth. She invited him to keep count and, exactly on schedule, three months later she gave birth. Mohedja found the story amusing.

The sister-in-law responded that if you do not tell your husband you are missing your period, he will never notice it for himself. She said that once she did not tell her husband until the fifth month. But the reason was that she had earlier suffered a series of miscarriages and worried it would be the case again. Only once she had gained confidence did she tell her husband – and his reaction, like Tumbu's, was first to assume she had slept with someone else.

In 1980, in a conversation about changing birthing practices subse-quent to the advent of the clinic, both Mohedja and her daughter Mar-iam (who at the time, at about age twenty-nine, had six children – she has since given birth to six more, all living) acknowledged that they had each given birth enough and would have liked access to contraception. Unfortunately, they had heard that the contraceptive shots that were then offered (possibly experimentally) in Mayotte had bad effects – women bled heavily and later suffered in childbirth. Perhaps the bodies of people in Mayotte could not handle it, they speculated. Mohedja added that she was always afraid of having twins since both her mother and her mother's sister had given birth to twins and they died in infancy.

Mohedja's child-rearing activities were by no means coextensive with her childbearing. The first child she raised was a daughter of her brother Samba. She was not the primary caretaker for all her biological offspring but did raise several grandchildren. She also took in the children of friends for certain periods of time; although I was twenty-five in 1975, my incorporation in the household was not entirely unlike this. Before accepting me, Mohedja and Tumbu checked with their spirits.

Here are three letters Mohedja wrote to my mother during my early months in Lombeni. She dictated them to me in Kibushy and I translated them and sent them on.

30 July 1975

I, Mohedja, send greetings to you, Hanna. We here are well. I am writing you a letter to ask how you are and how your husband is. I, Mohedja, am well here, together with Michely [as I was called]. There are no problems; we live together fine. My husband Tumbu sends his greetings to you and to your husband. Here we are conversing well, laughing well, there is nothing the matter. I, Mohedja, am Michely's mother here in Lombeni. We are getting along well, there are no issues. He makes no trouble for me or my husband, thanks be to Allah.

2 September 1975

I, Mohedja, send you warm greetings. The letter you sent me has reached me, thank you. We here are well, there has not been any trouble. We are living well with Michely and he hasn't done anything bad yet. Thanks be to Allah. I want to tell you about my children. I have six – first Nuriaty, second Mariam, third Haza, fourth Ali, fifth Amiaty and sixth Mwanesha. These are my children here. Nuriaty has three children, all boys. Mariam has four children, a boy and three girls. Haza has two children, a boy and a girl. My mother is still alive but very old. My big mother [mother's older sister] is still alive but also very old. My father is dead. I have had children who have died.

We here are getting ready to fast Ramadan. Next month is Ramadan. People don't eat or drink [during the day] until the month of Ramadan is over. When that is over we will prepare the ground for planting; we plant rice, manioc, and bananas the month after next. That's what's going on here. There are no problems. Greetings to your husband, your children who are there, your grandmother, and to all your friends and family in the town. My husband, my mother, and my big mother all send their greetings. How many children do you have? Are you no longer giving birth? I hope you and your husband, and your family and friends, and your grandmother and children, are all well. [signed in Arabic writing] Mohedja Salim, Lombeni, Mayotte.

10 February 1976

Bismillah ir Rahman ir Rahim. I, Mohedja, have come to visit you. I heard your grandmother died so I have come to visit you and your husband and your children. [Visiting is the way of expressing condolence here.] How are you all? We here are well and there are not yet any issues, thanks to God. But here there has been a big windstorm, a cyclone, that destroyed bananas, manioc, and corn in the fields. In the village it broke houses and compound walls. Two houses collapsed. That's what happened here. Here we are already weeding the rice and corn. We have already begun to eat some of the corn. Greetings to you, to your husband, to Larry and Bernie [my brothers], and to your friends.

I find these letters quite remarkable. They are indicative of moral imagination and confidence and show how seriously she took her relationship with me and extended it outwards to my mother and the rest of my family.

Although common, the movement of children between households was often fraught, entailing ambivalence on the part of those who gave up their children as well as on the part of the children themselves. Some young women were happy to pass the responsibilities for childcare onto their elders, while others resented the decisions imposed by senior women upon them. Among women who were relatively equivalent in age, there was often some anxiety or resentment. Sometimes it was the need or desire of the foster mother that was the motivating factor; a woman might be childless, want a child to help with domestic tasks, or seek closer relations with the biological parents. At other times the consideration was the needs of the children – for example, if astrological calculations or experience showed they would not flourish at home, or perhaps to provide access to schooling. In many cases the decision was made easier by the intervention of the spirits. Each time Mohedja gave over a child, the emotional and practical circumstances were complex. Of her live children, Mohedja had given up her eldest daughter and both her sons in infancy and two of her other daughters in childhood. As they grew older, however, they each gravitated back towards her and Tumbu.

I briefly describe the circumstances of each of Mohedja's biological children, in order of birth and as she portrayed them. In what follows, it should be clear that Mohedja lived in the same compound as her mother, Rae Samba. Tumbu's mother, Dady Nuriaty, lived elsewhere in the same village. In listing the births to me, Mohedja did not supply the names of those who died.

Nuriaty, First Daughter

Mohedja became pregnant six months after her wedding. Nuriaty was her first child, born around 1950. In the past, personal names were selected according to the calculations of a trusted astrologer. Mohedja's brother Samba gave her daughter the auspicious name Fatima, but it was changed to Nuriaty, the name of Tumbu's mother, at the latter's request. Mohedja was sick after giving birth (as we have seen) and could not nurse, so Nuriaty was fed with milk from a cow of Tumbu's. One day the cow died. Mohedja's mother fed Nuriaty a rice gruel and Tumbu went and tied up his mother's cow, who also had a calf, in order to milk it. When his mother heard this, she went and untied her cow, saying in the village that the baby was undoubtedly trouble (*shonga*); it had already killed off Tumbu's cow by drinking her milk, but it was not going to do the same to hers.

Tumbu returned in the evening and was astonished to find the cow untethered. He mentioned it to his mother, but she said nothing. In the village he heard the story, and he returned to his mother, who admitted her action. Tumbu left in tears that his mother was more worried about the welfare of her cow than her grandchild. He set off immediately for town, where he purchased a bottle and canned milk. Mohedja's mother, Rae Samba, started manipulating her own breasts until they were able to give milk. From that time on she nursed Nuriaty, whose diet was supplemented with canned milk purchased by Tumbu.

When Nuriaty reached the age where she could walk, Tumbu's mother came and asked to raise her. People told Rae Samba not to agree.

She had gone to all the trouble of nursing and looking after the infant, and now, in return, she should at least have the benefit of Nuriaty as she reached the age when she could begin to do chores. But Rae Samba said that grandchildren should be shared among the grandparents, and she gave Nuriaty up.

Mariam, Second Daughter

Mariam, their second child, was raised by Mohedja. Mother and daughter developed a particularly close relationship. When Mariam was old enough to sit, Mohedja was bothered by a trumba. They held a ceremony, the trumba announced she was Kos Vola, and Mohedja improved. As an adult, Mariam visited her mother every morning, holding intimate conversations, and they often shared the same dreams. Mariam was also close to both Mze Nuru and Kos Vola.

A First Son

Mohedja was sick with swollen breasts, so she fed the baby with a bottle. The baby died around six months and Mohedja remained sick for at least a month longer.

A Second Son

When the boy turned about three or four, he became ill. Each of the diviners from whom Tumbu sought advice said he would recover only if the boy were moved away from their house. Tumbu asked his mother to take him, but she refused. As Mohedja's mother lived within the same compound, that was not an option. The boy grew sicker until finally Tumbu's mother took him. He died that same evening in her house.

Haza, Third Daughter

Several people asked to raise Mohedja's third daughter. The first was Mohedja's paternal half-sister, living in town. Mohedja valued her relationship with this woman but found her too severe (*mashiaka*) with children. She told the woman she had been to a diviner who had warned against the move. This was untrue but the woman accepted it without taking insult. Sometime later, Mohedja in turn took in the woman's daughter's son, whom she and Tumbu raised and were very close to until, when the boy was quite grown up, his mother asked for him back. He was dear enough to them, Mohedja said, that they would have financed his wedding.

Next, Mohedja's sister-in-law (Tumbu's maternal half-sister), who had no children at the time, asked for Haza. Mohedja thought she would not make a warm mother as she got angry frequently. Mohedja said she did not care what her sister-in-law thought and just turned her down flatly. The sister-in-law was extremely put out, particularly when soon after Mohedja acceded to the request by a childless first cousin of Tumbu and his sister's, with whom Haza had already developed a warm relationship. Mohedja thus preferred Tumbu's cousin over his sister; she said she did not know whether or not the affair caused Tumbu embarrassment.

When the sister-in-law did not get Haza, she asked another brother for his eldest daughter. The wife of this brother also refused, and Tumbu's sister was then really angry. When the next niece was born, she went off to her brother's, announced without ado that she was going to adopt, and returned for her as soon as she was able to walk.

Tumbu's cousin raised Haza "like a daughter she'd given birth to" and Mohedja did not interfere at all. They sponsored Haza's first marriage jointly. Later, Tumbu built Haza's house on a plot provided by the cousin. Haza addressed the cousin as "father's sister" (*angivavy*). As an adult, Haza moved to her husband's village and seemed to me the least emotionally attached to Mohedja of all her children.

Ali, First Living Son

Since the children who died had both been boys, it was determined that Mohedja was not able to raise sons. Derived from experience, this conclusion was validated on astrological grounds. Like many women in a similar condition, Mohedja herself was not deemed to be at fault, but her subsequent infant sons were given to others to raise. By the time Ali was born, they knew the situation. They performed *trambuñu* medicine (see chapter 4) and let him be raised mostly by Mohedja's mother.

There were then two children who died as infants, first a girl and then a boy.

Amiaty, Fourth Living Daughter

Amiaty, born in the late 1960s, was raised by Mohedja. I knew her as a child and was present at her wedding. It is with Amiaty that I have stayed since the death of her parents.

There was then another child who died as an infant.

Mwanesha, Fifth Living Daughter

In 1975, Mohedja was under protective medicine (*trambuñu*) on behalf of Mwanesha who was then less than two. Mwanesha was very beautiful with large brown eyes, but heavily infected with abdominal worms and quite dependent on her mother. The two of them were very close.

One day early in my stay, Mohedja appeared with splashes of brown paste on her face. I thought it might be makeup, but she said it was medicine. I asked whether she was sick. "No, I'm wearing it for Mwanesha." I asked whether Mwanesha was sick. "No, but she has been." As described in chapter 4, this was medicine used when a woman had had several failed pregnancies or children who died in infancy. It was applied during pregnancy and then to both mother and infant until the latter could walk. Mohedja said it should be applied daily but that she just "can't" do this, that is, it was too troublesome. Along with the paste, made from scraped wood and leaves, there were several restrictions (*fady*) that a mother had to observe. Mohedja abstained from attending funerals and eating the food prepared for them. Another woman in the compound had had a stillbirth and Mohedja could not help being nearby. That was why she applied the medicine today. Mohedja received the medicine and the restrictions from Kos Vola, who rose in her mother, and Mwanesha was, in effect, under the spirit's protection for the duration. At the time, Mohedja did not enlighten me that she shared Kos Vola herself. (I describe the completion of the treatment in chapter 4.)

Nine months later, Mohedja was faced with giving Mwanesha to one of Tumbu's clients who had asked for her in order to cement a relationship of siblingship she had proposed with Tumbu. This client was a relatively wealthy woman living in the heart of the large neighbouring village of S—. She had originally asked for Amiaty, a request that Mohedja turned down. Amiaty was nevertheless invited to spend the Eid holiday with her and had stayed longer than her parents anticipated. Now the woman was eagerly awaiting receipt of Mwanesha, a request Tumbu and Mohedja had finally agreed to because of the better opportunity for education (at the time, Lombeni still lacked a school).

Giving up Mwanesha was extremely difficult for Mohedja. This was how she handled it.

April 1976. On the night of 20 April, two weeks after the sacrifice of the goat and prayers on Mwanesha's behalf [chapter 4], Mze Nuru rose in Mohedja and instructed Tumbu that Mwanesha was to go to S— the day after next. Tumbu sent word to his new "sister." This was earlier than they had planned; they had been going to wait until Mwanesha was big enough to follow the woman to her fields.

The next day passed normally. On the following morning, the woman came for Mwanesha. Mohedja packed up her few items of clothing. Mwanesha walked off placidly with her "father's sister" (*angivavy*). Mohedja did not appear to pay attention, for fear of disturbing Mwanesha. After that, the subject was not brought up. One day a little granddaughter whom Mohedja was raising mentioned Mwanesha and was quickly hushed with the admonition: "you're making her cry." There was a convention that mentioning a missing person reminds that person of their loneliness. Mohedja heard a couple of reports that Mwanesha was doing fine; she said she would not stop in to visit for fear it would upset Mwanesha. I assumed this was for Mwanesha's sake. Tumbu too said he would only stop in when Mwanesha was thoroughly accustomed to her new surroundings.

One morning we walked past the woman's house in S—. Mohedja saw that Mwanesha was not in the courtyard and so risked calling out a greeting. The woman came to the gate and assured us all was well. We did not go in to see Mwanesha. That afternoon, as Mohedja was eating a cookie at Jon Breslar's (an anthropologist working in a village of Shimaore speakers whom we had dropped in to see), she sighed and said that ever since Mwanesha left she thought of her each time she ate something. Jon asked her why she had let Mwanesha go, and she replied that one cannot deny a request of this kind. She said that she would never give up a child to someone she thought was incompetent or disreputable (*tsy manzary*) or to someone who treated children too severely. In the case of Nuriaty, her grandmother had simply taken her. Mohedja would never have given her to her mother-in-law on her own accord since she was quick to anger, not warm with children, and, said Mohedja, did not really like to raise them.

Mohedja said she was satisfied that the woman in S— was capable and loving and that Mwanesha liked her. She also admitted that the reason she didn't want to visit Mwanesha was that if Mwanesha cried she would immediately sweep her into her arms and take her home, which she knew she could not do.

30 May. Mohedja and I went to S—. She said she wouldn't visit Mwanesha yet though I felt she wanted to. She led us down the street by the house and Mwanesha saw us and called out "Mama." We entered and Mohedja had Mwanesha formally greet her as children are taught to do and then asked her how she was in baby talk and told her repeatedly not to cry. The woman drew Mwanesha into her lap and Mohedja did not touch her. We left quickly. Mohedja said she had been worried Mwanesha would cry and then she would have wanted to take her home. That she hadn't cried was a sign she was being treated well and this made Mohedja feel better. We brought her some bread and Mwanesha asked where her father was. He had dropped in a few days earlier. Mohedja said it would only upset Mwanesha if we stayed longer. When I dropped by on my own on later occasions, Mwanesha greeted me and didn't ask about her parents. After each visit Mohedja asked me eagerly how Mwanesha was doing.

There are many points of interest in these poignant accounts: the use of diviners to ease an unpalatable decision; the fact that relationships to more distant kin were more valuable to Mohedja than that with her sister-in-law; the responsibility of mothers rather than fathers to make these decisions and to bear the brunt of their consequences; the maintenance of an official front of freely agreeing to requests for child transfers despite the evidently mixed feelings; and the way in which Mze Nuru rose in order to speed up Mwanesha's transfer, thereby resolving Mohedja's ambivalence in a definitive stroke. However, Mohedja did not leave all difficult decisions to her spirits.

Mwanesha spent less than a year in S—. In 1985, Mohedja gave me two accounts of what happened. In the first, she said she did not visit Mwanesha for six or seven months. But once she went, Mwanesha would not stop crying and so she was returned home to Lombeni. In the second, she said that every time Tumbu returned from visiting he reported that the woman had been complaining about Mwanesha; there was always something. Mohedja figured that she was no longer really interested in raising her. She went one day to see for herself. There she heard complaints – for example, that Mwanesha did not want to study (yet she was very young at the time). Three or four days later, Mohedja returned to S— and simply took Mwanesha home. Mwanesha was delighted to return. Mohedja did not know whether the woman felt angry inside (*meluku añatin rohu*), but Mohedja believed she no longer wanted to raise Mwanesha.

Mohedja added that she would not have been concerned if the news that something was wrong had come only from third parties gossiping about the woman mistreating Mwanesha; there was always such gossip among "Black people" (*ulu mainting*) when there was fosterage. For example, there was gossip when Tumbu's cousin took Haza and Mohedja warned the cousin to ignore it.

Mohedja later reflected that Mwanesha had spent about a year in S— but never really adjusted or felt at home there.

Maulida, Second Living Son

Maulida is Mohedja's youngest living child, born in the early 1980s. After Mwanesha, Mohedja thought she was finished giving birth and by this time she was a little embarrassed to be still having children.

> *10 July 1985.* Mohedja and a friend were chatting on her veranda today, comparing their birth experiences and describing times when they had each given birth quickly and without help. Mohedja said she was embarrassed to be pregnant at the same time as her daughter Mariam. In fact, she gave birth to Maulida some twenty days after Mariam gave birth. It was also the very night that Hamidu, Nuriaty's youngest son, died. He died suddenly. Mohedja sent a messenger to Tumbu in his field and began arrangements for the body. But then, shortly after hearing the news, she went into labour. It was evening. She went to bed with labour pains. When Tumbu came, and when Nuriaty looked in on her, she denied it was labour because she felt compassion for Nuriaty and was embarrassed to be giving birth when people were mourning her grandchild. Tumbu must have seen that she was really in labour because he kept coming back to check on her.
>
> Mohedja resolved the situation by giving the new son to her bereaved daughter to raise. Nuriaty took Maulida some three days after his birth.
>
> In 1985, Mohedja said she was certain that Maulida knew who his real parents were even though everyone still maintained the fiction. She thought he would want to come live with her if he knew the truth, so she shouted at him a lot so that he would go home to Nuriaty's. It wouldn't be fair to Nuriaty for Mohedja to take him now; Nuriaty suffered a lot with him, having looked after him since right after his birth. Maulida eventually learned who his parents were from talk among his age-mates. Over the years, I observed how Maulida shifted his allegiances from Nuriaty to Mohedja and Tumbu, fully identifying as their son.

Mohedja's last child was a daughter who died as an infant.

Concern for children continued well after and beyond the early years, including the formal responsibilities of holding circumcisions for boys and weddings for girls, events which were often complex and costly but central to the parental role – in effect, a second phase of reproduction.

After listing her children on her taped life story, Mohedja went on to say that she and Tumbu married off Nuriaty, and then Mariam, then they circumcised Ali, and then married off Haza, and then after a long period they married off Amiaty and then Mwanesha. This was complete now, she said. She emphasized that as Maulida was raised by Nuriaty, his circumcision had been her responsibility and achievement, though Mohedja and Tumbu had helped; Maulida was circumcised along with Nuriaty's own sons, thus at a very early age.

They had completed their responsibilities towards their children, and it was now the adult children's turn to sponsor the circumcisions and weddings of the grandchildren. Mohedja and Tumbu's participation was optional, she said; having completed their own events, no one in the community could demand another cow or a large meal from them. In fact, they had completed their obligation to the community (their *shungu*) long ago (around 1966), at Nuriaty's wedding. Now, said Mohedja, she and Tumbu could relax. But she then began to list in order the older grandchildren whose ceremonies would need arranging. She emphasized the role of grandparents in advising and explaining how to produce the complex events, much as her mother had helped her. They would also help materially when they could. "If you have a little money or perhaps a mosquito net or sheet, you give it to your child who is marrying off a daughter. But it is not forbidden [*haram*] not to get too involved. Now you can take it easy," she laughed. "But for as long as we are still alive, we will help and offer advice. Once we are gone, they will know how to do it on their own."

There was a pause as she talked to a young granddaughter who had just arrived having purchased a pumpkin. Why did she buy a not-so-nice one when there were nice ones for sale? Mohedja asked. She told her to put it in the kitchen and asked to see the other children's hands. There could be no dirt on them if they were going to study Qur'an. She asked, "Have you finished eating? Have you put the legumes [*ambatry*] in the pot?"

Settling children entailed more than sponsoring their ceremonies. In the past, people reported, marriages were entirely arranged by older adults. They could force young people to marry against their will and sometimes did not even inform them until the engagement itself. Conversely, if the parents did not like their child's prospective choice, they could simply forbid the marriage. Things changed slowly. Rae Samba was simply told whom she was marrying, but she in turn deferred to Mohedja's choices. Nuriaty simply had to accept the man Tumbu's mother picked for her. Nuriaty kept quiet and did not fight the decision, but the marriage itself lasted only a short time. Each of Nuriaty's younger sisters married men they liked and both Mariam and Amiaty stayed with their first husbands.

In 1975, Mohedja was attempting to ensure a good marriage for her daughter, Haza, and improve the placement of Haza's two children from a failed first marriage. These events show both the potential and the limits of drawing on spirits to intervene in the welfare of offspring.

Settling Haza and Her Children

As mentioned, Haza was raised by a cousin of Tumbu's. But when it came time to sponsor her first wedding, Mohedja and Tumbu went to as much trouble and expense as did the foster parents. When Haza's first husband turned out to be a ne'er-do-well, it was Tumbu and Mohedja who made sure everyone was fed. Haza gave birth at a young age to two children who were quite independent-minded. When Mohedja saw them running around at the far side of the village she decided she ought to raise them, and she took them from Haza. They remained with her for several years and then split their time between their mother and grandmother.

Mohedja and Tumbu remained concerned about Haza's welfare. They helped her make a definitive separation from her first husband and find a second one. This man was raised in the village of M— by an aunt who was a client of Ndramboeny. The aunt had started coming from M— to consult Ndramboeny in Mohedja before her nephew "happened" to see Haza working in a field and decided he wanted to marry her. The trumba consultation became one of Mohedja's first big cases (chapter 7). Mohedja thus ended up strengthening the patient-healer relationship with a marriage and backing up her daughter's new marriage with the therapeutic relation.

The connection was denser than this. The aunt was the granddaughter of a woman who had also been possessed by Ndramboeny and from whom Mohedja had inherited Ndramboeny's spear. The family had called the trumba "Grandfather" and he had taken care of them. So when the aunt was sick, she looked around for the same trumba to treat her and found Mohedja. In all likelihood, the aunt was becoming possessed by the same spirit herself. Hence it was the links to Ndramboeny among otherwise unrelated people that led to relationships of therapy, and these, in turn, forged the basis for the marriage alliance.

Tumbu and Mohedja each used their specialized knowledge to support Haza's well-being. Prior to the wedding (a simple affair for a woman's second marriage), Mohedja gave Haza protective medicine, and her spirits rose to protect the wedding from the ostensibly ill-timed scheduling proposed by the husband's astrologer.

When Haza prepared to go live with her new husband in his village, she received lectures from both Mohedja and Ndramboeny about how to behave. On 26 December 1975, the aunt arrived for treatment and to fetch Haza. At the conclusion of the therapeutic interview, Ndramboeny rose in Mohedja and admonished the woman not to hesitate to scold Haza if she misbehaved. Ndramboeny then called for Haza and sternly told her in front of the client to treat the woman like her own mother, to visit with her, and to listen to her. The trumba said that if one wanted to make friends in a new place one had to be open, to greet people and show an interest in them. (To my great astonishment, Ndramboeny used me as an example.) Ndramboeny concluded by telling the client to return if she suffered any more problems with her health, even if she did not have the money to pay. The conversation ended with the client telling Haza good-humouredly that they would do each other's hair.

In this way, by means of the authority of Ndramboeny, with whom the woman already had an intimate relationship, Mohedja was able to ease Haza's entry to her new place of residence, prepare a positive beginning for the mother-in-law and daughter-in-law relationship, and ensure that Haza's conduct and welfare would be monitored. Indeed, Haza was going to a setting in which she could expect to find the trumba who cohabited with her mother also appear in her mother-in-law.

The next morning, before Haza left for M—, Mohedja took her aside and spoke privately, telling her to behave herself. This was different from the words of the trumba. Tumbu made her an amulet (*hiriz*) and performed a blessing (*shijabu*) over Haza and her brother, Ali. The blessing for Ali was to offer him success in his training to become a *guarde indigène* (an occupation he never took up).

Haza and her new husband settled in M— where they had several children together and did very well. The first daughter Haza conceived with her new husband lived for some years with Mohedja, but she continued to see her mother and there were regular visits between the two villages.

Perceptions about these matters can be subjective and adults do not always reveal how they feel about things. It is interesting in this regard to compare the way my wife, anthropologist Jackie Solway, and I separately described the same incident in our respective fieldnotes.

14 October 1985 (ML). Haza visited and appeared to have a very good time with lots of sisterly chatter with Mariam and Amiaty. She wanted to bring her daughter back home with her, but the little girl didn't want to leave, cried, and ran off to sleep. I asked, wasn't Haza sad to leave her? Amiaty said no, but Mariam said yes, only that Haza was afraid to force her lest Mohedja think Haza really didn't want her to raise her children.

14 October 1985 (JS). Haza's daughter cried uncontrollably when her mother left for M— and wanted to go with her. Haza says her daughter always wants to leave with her when she goes but that once she is in M— she cries that she wants to return to Lombeni. What was interesting was the rather dispassionate way (to my mind) in which Haza left her screaming – very little comforting or sympathy.

Mohedja's autonomy was never absolute and there were times when she acceded to situations without bringing in the spirits to intervene. This is significant to my argument. Spirits are not automatic instruments that magically overcome anxiety or conflict. Whether a spirit rises to address a particular issue is as much a matter of (implicit) judgment on the part of the host as is what the spirit says when he does rise. In either case, it is a matter of practical wisdom to know when and how to speak and when and how to remain silent.[1]

When Haza's husband decided he wanted to raise Haza's two children by her first husband, Mohedja said she had little option but to let them go to M— as well. Perhaps because it was in the children's interests to get schooling in their stepfather's village, or perhaps because Mohedja did not feel strongly enough about it, she accepted the request. So far as I know, the spirits did not rise either to place any obstacles in the way of the transfer or to ease it. The children continued to visit Mohedja periodically and felt at home in both households, but they lived primarily with Haza. It was Haza and her husband who took primary responsibility in arranging a marriage for Haza's oldest daughter.

This daughter, who in 1975 at the age of about three was one of the only children unafraid of me, had been my companion and used to hang around my door and correct my mistakes in speaking. In 1992, she was a high school student. Although many of her peers were married, especially those who had not received a French education, she caused a fuss when she arrived at Mohedja's with a boy whom she referred to as just a "brother." When Tumbu found out that this "brother" had spent the night in his compound, he at once sent word to her parents. The next day, Tumbu and Mohedja went to M— to join Haza and her husband in a visit to the boy's parents to seek an engagement. They were married shortly after and began married life in M—.

As Mohedja grew from young adulthood to middle age, she developed greater control over the disposition of the younger children, although this was never complete; her daughters and daughter-in-law also had something to say. When her daughters were young mothers themselves, Mohedja sometimes intervened in their child-rearing practices, and this applied to me as well. In 1985, I returned to Mayotte with my wife, Jackie, and our two-year-old daughter, Nadia, for a four-month stay. Jackie had conducted her own lengthy ethnographic fieldwork in Botswana before we were married, and now we were spending time in each other's field sites. People told us that being married and bringing a child to the field would bring us closer to our respective communities, but in fact we experienced the reverse. We lived in one of the two rooms in Mohedja and Tumbu's house and it was difficult to have any privacy and likewise to maintain sanitary conditions with a pit latrine. Moreover, our ideas of tending to Nadia differed from those of Mohedja, who sometimes attempted to take charge.

As her mother and mother-in-law grew elderly, children once under their care shifted back to Mohedja and Tumbu. When Tumbu's mother died, Mohedja took charge of Tumbu's brother's daughter whom the old woman had fetched from Madagascar to raise. Mohedja said she cared for her "like a real daughter"; she married her off with her own money and labour and looked after her when she was pregnant and gave birth. Tumbu built her a house, as well as houses for his two youngest daughters, adjacent to his and Mohedja's. Mohedja's offspring who had been fostered elsewhere gravitated back towards her household as they grew up. Nuriaty chose to build nearby, and although living in M—, Haza too constructed an additional house adjacent to Mohedja's. Mariam was a daily visitor. The emotional and social links among the children and their parents were very strong.

Here is a summary of the child transfers within Mohedja's extended family as they appeared in 1980. Tumbu and Mohedja were then looking after two daughters of their own as well as a son and daughter of Haza's. Nuriaty was looking after her two sons plus a daughter of her sister Mariam and her own youngest brother, Maulida, the younger son of Mohedja and Tumbu. Mariam was looking after two sons and two daughters of her own as well as her brother Ali's oldest son. She took him because he was ill and nursed him together with her own young son. Another of Mariam's daughters was being raised by the girl's father's sister. Haza was raising her two children with her second husband and shared support of the two older children with Tumbu and Mohedja.

By 1985, Mariam had returned Ali's son to his birth mother. Mariam felt sorry for her because she had had no further children of her own and often needed help in the household. The mother accepted after ascertaining that Mariam would not be angry. The boy still felt comfortable visiting Mariam. In 1992, Mohedja was raising one of Ali's daughters. She had felt lonely without a daughter to raise. When Mariam refused to give one of her daughters, Mohedja asked Ali, who in turn said to ask his wife. Mohedja then invited the wife to choose which girl to send her.

In 1995, Mohedja and Tumbu had thirty-eight live grandchildren (Nuriaty had two live offspring, Mariam eleven, Haza eleven, Ali nine, Amiaty three, and Mwanesha two). By then, the daughter of Mariam's whom Nuriaty had raised had a daughter of her own, who Nuriaty also took in. All Haza's children, from both marriages, lived in M— and Mohedja continued to raise Ali's daughter. The children of both Amiaty and Mwanesha, raised by their respective mothers, lived adjacent to Mohedja and were continuously around. Nuriaty's unmarried sons were also regularly present at the houses of both their mother and grandmother, as was Maulida.

Since then, child transfers appear to have lessened as children became less a labour asset than a financial liability. Schooling became universal and schooling costs (books, clothing, lunches) rose rapidly. Adult women who used to rely on girls for domestic assistance found that more of the domestic labour rested on their shoulders, although they drew increasingly on labour-saving devices, relied entirely on husked store-bought rice, and purchased frozen fish and meat. Subsistence agricultural labour declined for everyone.

Mohedja's parental links extended to others. In 1985, she developed a kinship tie with one of the schoolteachers, a man from S— who, after looking around, asked her to be his "mother." As a result, she spent three days visiting his actual mother in S— and there were several visits back and forth. At least one other uxorilocally married man asked for kinship ties and made Mohedja his mother.

In the same year, a migrant from Anjouan asked Tumbu for a place to live. Tumbu lent him his shed and helped arrange a marriage for him. The man often dropped by to chat. Tumbu remarked that since he and Mohedja first married they had never ceased to have people living with them. They enjoyed and placed a high value on it.

Sociability was very important. People should engage in conversation, Mohedja once observed. "It's not good to remain silent."

Mohedja always kept an eye out for her grandchildren and did not hesitate to intervene if she thought they needed support or reprimand. While taking full responsibility to raise a grandchild required relating to them as a parent rather than a grandparent, the normative relationship between grandparents and grandchildren was one of joking. This humour did not shy away from aggression or sexual innuendo and could often turn quite sharp. Here, in brief, is a side of Mohedja I do not often portray.

> Once I overheard Mohedja ask a very young grandson, "So, am I your spouse?" "Yes," he replied. Mohedja: "I thought you no longer loved me." Grandson: "I love you." Mohedja: "Okay, so what will you give me?"
>
> Another time I heard Mohedja scornfully teasing two of her six-year-old grandsons for not yet having built their own houses (one-room structures that boys generally accomplished in their early teens).[2] The boys normally slept at Mariam's but were going to house-sit for an older boy while he lived in town to study. She then turned to another grandson and said that he was just like his father, incapable of finishing a house on his own. The boy replied with good humour: "I'll build one of the government-sponsored houses or I will hire someone to build it." Mohedja retorted, "What will you hire them with, your penis?"

To maintain dignity and social competence in Mayotte one had to develop a Muslim persona; hence socializing children and grand-children included ensuring they received a basic Islamic education sufficient to recite a variety of sacred verses. As children, Mohedja and Tumbu each learned to recite the Qur'an and as young parents they eagerly began teaching it to their own children as well as other children in the village. In 1975, I joined Mohedja's class in elementary recitation held in the early morning before breakfast. Small children sat on the ground around her, printed primers or wooden boards marked with letters in charcoal on their laps. Mohedja held a stick over a granddaughter to make her cooperate. The girl cried but Mohedja just increased the pressure until she stifled her tears and started reciting. Mohedja had the greater responsibility as Tumbu often left early for the fields, and she found it hard. I did not last long (Lambek 1993).

Mohedja contrasted the Qur'anic classes to the French primary school, which by 1985 all the village children had begun to attend.

There were no *vacances* in Qur'anic school, only Fridays off. Mothers tried to get their children to the public school every day and no longer kept pushing them to attend Qur'anic class. Some children did not appear for a week at a time. As a result, she lost her motivation as well and declared she was fed up; children no longer listened, and she could not apply the switch like she used to. Other women in the village had started classes so there was opportunity for children who wanted it.

Mohedja knew how to recite the entire Qur'an and thought that girls and boys had an equal desire to learn it. She and Tumbu listened avidly to Islamic instruction on the radio given in Shimaore. However, she explained it was insufficient to learn the interpretations orally; you had to be able to write and read a text to know it properly.

Mohedja explored the religious roles open to women. She was an active singer in the women's performance of the Maulida Shengy, a popular ode in honour of the Prophet, and she studied how to wash the dead and did so. However, she got sick because she had forgotten to ask permission of her trumba first. One of the main oppositions between Islam and trumba is that the former encourages active participation in mortuary ritual while the trumba, even those who manifest as Muslims, being themselves in an ambiguous relationship with death, expect their hosts to avoid funerals and corpses. Conversely, while the public pronunciation of Muslim blessing rituals was not an act available to women, the patros Mze Nuru did so.

In 1985, Mohedja and Tumbu were improving their Islamic knowledge by learning from their daughter Amiaty who could read fluently a basic primer known as the *Safina*. Amiaty explained that a couple of years earlier, the entire village (i.e., the women) became interested in studying and brought a scholar to the house of a woman elder every Tuesday and Saturday for lessons. But the aging teacher found this too hard and told people to come to him in S—. Only Amiaty and one other girl took him up on the offer. A blessing was held for them, and they started studying. The other girl soon quit because of her public schooling. Amiaty, who did not have the benefit of French schooling, continued going to S— over a period of two years. She bought a book at the market and wanted to keep learning. But once she married, her husband forbade it, afraid she would talk to men en route.

Tumbu said that he would have preferred Amiaty not to marry so soon and to have kept studying for another two or three years. She had a good head and was learning quickly but had not progressed very far. But she wanted to marry. Tumbu knew her husband would be jealous and would forbid her to continue going to S—.

In July 1985, Tumbu and I discussed circumcision. Tumbu explained that before a circumcision, one called up the parents' cohabiting spirits, if there were any, or those of the grandparents, to inform them. If not, the spirits might take it as a slight or insult they were not told about the circumcision of a child whom they had helped to raise. Spirits easily had their feelings hurt and could cause a boy to faint or bleed excessively.

Several boys were circumcised together, on an auspicious day in the dry season. The boys were washed and oiled and teased by their grandmothers the day before. They looked clean, shiny, and proud. In the past, a drum was beaten from the start until all the boys were cut so that people would not hear any cries. Tumbu said the mothers and fathers were frightened, their hearts (*rohu*) beating hard. Some boys were frightened, some not, but all the parents were. Tumbu himself preferred to stay far away when the boys were cut. Spirits sometimes spontaneously entered their female hosts and shrieked outside the enclosure where the cutting was taking place.

Male circumcision was compared to a girl's first marriage and defloration.[3] Both were preceded (by days or months) by a ritual in which demons were smoked out of the child's body. Children were often smoked together, boys and girls. Tumbu emphasized how unpleasant and overwhelming the smell was. You gasped for air and just inhaled more smoke. The children emerged stinking. Everyone had to undergo the treatment although the period of smoking was shorter in 1985 than in Tumbu's youth (and has since been dropped entirely). Tumbu remembered he was smoked together with his older brother. I asked whether he remembered his circumcision; was he scared? He said yes but said that depending on how stretchy the foreskin was and how the cut was done, it was more or less painless. It was always very quick and easier to bear than the smoking. It was the smoking that remained memorable.

In 1995, Amiaty was planning the circumcisions of her sons. She went one night to Mohedja's room to call up Ndramboeny. Amiaty explained to me that she had no special spirit of her mother's that she used regularly; the spirits have told them they can call up any one of them and that what was spoken to one would be passed on to the others. Amiaty sat on the floor to call up Ndramboeny as Mohedja and Tumbu reclined on the bed. Ndramboeny began by saying to Jackie and me not to be strangers and that we would all hold this event together. He then told Amiaty to fetch medicine from the bush, and to do a *fatiha* and wash the boys in medicine after the smoking. The main thing Amiaty wanted from Ndramboeny was confirmation of what the astrologer she had consulted told her would be an auspicious time for the smoking. The astrologer, who was relatively young, had told Amiaty he was afraid to advise a family that cohabited with such big fundis. Amiaty assured him she trusted him; after all, they both put their faith in God. But the astrologer asked her to confirm his findings with the spirits. Ndramboeny accepted the astrologer's findings but said that the extra medicine he was asking Amiaty to fetch was a secret and not to be mentioned to the astrologer. The medicine was to protect the boys from attacks of sorcery and Ndramboeny worried that the astrologer might withdraw from overseeing the smoking if he knew they were using additional protection. All this was stated in a whisper. The spirit then turned back to Jackie and me and confirmed that we were having only two children (who were with us in Lombeni then). Unlike so many villagers who could not understand our decision not to have more, Ndramboeny said that was good. He added, "May the children grow well; may God bless them. We are all kin even though not of one womb [*kibu*, i.e., not biologically related]."

Chapter Ten

Treating Mariam's Baby

Although the spirits are strange Others, noteworthy for their difference from human beings, when they are established as cohabiting with particular hosts, they are drawn into the family circle. As Mohedja says in what follows, the spirits help parent the host's children. Spirits play a significant role in the family and are instrumental in articulating and resolving problems. As no family is without conflict, the spirits also play a role, whether in mediating or in taking sides. This chapter and the next two explore three instances of domestic issues faced by Mohedja and the role of the spirits in helping to resolve them. There is conflict in each of them.

7 June 1976. Mariam came to her mother for advice. Both she and her baby had been ailing off and on for some time. The previous Tuesday the baby had become much worse, with a high temperature through the night. Mariam took the initiative to seek medicine from the senior trumba healer, Musy Matwar.

That night, Tumbu privately called up Mze Nuru in Mohedja who said that Mariam's problems were caused by a patros. The next night, they arranged a small, private ceremony to encourage the spirit, Mariam's first, to rise. Present were Mohedja and Tumbu, Mariam, Mariam's older sister, Nuriaty, and a cousin of Mohedja's who was also her apprentice. The cousin prepared the medicine and washed Mariam in it, then we all entered the small room, lit incense, and sang and clapped in order to coax the spirit to rise. Mariam's husband sat silently in the doorway. Only the cousin's spirit rose. Mariam wept softly and uttered a few cries now and then, but the others complained that the spirit kept coming and going and never stayed long enough so that they could talk to him. After they had encouraged him gently and at length and the spirit still failed to properly appear, the cousin's spirit said, "Maybe it's me he doesn't like?" "No," said Mohedja firmly, "maybe it's us." Mohedja began a long speech, first to the absent spirit and then to the company as a whole, but directed, I think, primarily at Tumbu. Mohedja appeared quite agitated. She told the absent spirit that she wanted to be friends. "Let's hear what you have to say and then make friends—. We're waiting for you to come and speak, to tell us what's bothering you, what you don't like—. Don't you like any of us? If we wanted to fight you, we wouldn't have called you up like this but would have gone for donkey shit [whose smoke was used in forcible exorcism]. If you keep coming and going like this, how can we talk?"

Giving way to anxiety, she asked irritably why Mze Marwan, Tumbu's patros, didn't come and help. She complained that she didn't know any more what to do about the situation, that Mariam and her baby were continually sick, that things could not continue like this. "Why aren't any of the patros fundis rising? There is not a single thing right here! *Tsisy ata kabar araiky manzary.*" She called directly to Mze Marwan to come and help.

The baby had been asleep on Mohedja's lap and now woke and cried and was passed to Mariam to nurse. Mohedja complained about Mze Marwan not rising and said she was sad that none of the fundis were coming to help. She was less upset about the recalcitrance of Mariam's spirit. The arrival of a spirit was often a very slow business the first time round. What bothered her was that the family fundis were not giving any advice.

Tumbu said something about Mze Marwan speaking to him yesterday and saying he would arrive today on his own accord. "Stop always speaking about 'yesterday,'" retorted Mohedja irritably. Tumbu suggested that maybe his spirit wasn't rising because they had used ground wood, from only one kind of tree, instead of fetching fresh herbal medicine. Tumbu admitted he had forgotten to go pick fresh medicine.

While Mohedja's complaint was directed explicitly to Mze Marwan, in fact it was Tumbu she was angry with. One might ask why Mze Nuru did not arrive in Mohedja herself. Nothing was said, but I suspect it was because it was Mze Nuru they anticipated would appear in Mariam. It was also possible that Mohedja was menstruating and therefore not able to enter trance at this time.

At this point, the group broke up, declaring they would repeat the attempt the next night. Ultimately, they did not, Tumbu having suggested they try giving Mariam the medicine for a few days first. Mohedja was clearly very worried about the baby's condition and wouldn't leave the village even for a couple of hours to go to the fields. The baby's sickness and that of her mother were kept quite separate, the mother's illness simply making it harder to care for the baby. Only the mother's condition was related to the patros.

8 June. The following day, Mariam seemed fine and cheerful. Both she and the baby had taken nivaquine the previous two days although Mohedja asserted the baby's condition was not a case of *la fièvre* (malaria), but that her whole body was affected (*neñin jaby*) and that she had something graver. The baby continued to cough at night.

Mariam decided on her own initiative to call up Kos Vola, the trumba then still cohabiting with Mohedja's aged mother, to get advice about the baby. This was a strong move as the trumba was rarely called in the old woman anymore. In fact, Mohedja had the same trumba and I suspected that Mariam would one day as well. Mariam explained that she was calling Kos Vola in her grandmother rather than in her mother since the trumba had been cohabiting with Rae Samba for a much longer period and was a much more experienced curer in that locus. (Mariam and her grandmother also had a particularly strong relationship.) This was done early in the morning with only Mariam, her mother, and grandmother present. I suspected Tumbu did not know about it and related this to the tenseness in his relationship with Mariam during that period. I was not present either, but Mohedja told me later what happened. The spirit took a little time to rise. When Kos Vola appeared, Mohedja asked whether she should take the baby from Mariam and start raising her herself since it appeared that she was not flourishing under Mariam's care. (This was not a criticism of Mariam's parental abilities, but suggested there might have been something incompatible in their respective destinies [*nyora*].) Kos Vola replied that the infant would continue to fare badly if Mariam raised her, but that she should go to Mariam's older sister, Nuriaty. Nuriaty had in fact asked for the baby some time earlier since she had no daughters of her own and Mariam had refused to part with her. This time Mariam accepted. Wednesdays and Thursdays were inauspicious, so the transfer would take place on Friday.

9 June. This evening, Nuriaty's patros was called to advise him of the transfer and to ensure he was agreeable. Mohedja pointed out that it would be the patros as well as Nuriaty herself who would be raising the child and hence his permission had to be obtained. Only the two sisters, their husbands, Mohedja, and I were present. Tumbu did not attend. The two men sat on the bed, the women on a mat on the floor. Incense was lit and Nuriaty, already an experienced host, rapidly entered trance and the spirit shook hands with all of us. However, the spirit appeared more interested in teasing Nuriaty's husband than in discussing the subject at hand. When Mariam failed to explain the issue, Mohedja took over, saying that they had called the spirit in order to check with him about sending the baby to live with Nuriaty, that it wouldn't be proper to do so without asking, and that they wanted to make sure that the patros was agreeable. If he had any special concerns or requests, he should make them known immediately and not wait until later to make someone sick. The spirit assured them that it was fine but didn't seem very interested. Mohedja repeated her remarks in order to make sure. The spirit nodded and went on to his main concern, which was negotiating with Nuriaty's husband about the production of the formal curing ritual (*azulahy*), that is, the public presentation of the spirit and the announcement of his name. "Next year," said the husband. "Next year, next year" (*mwak'an*, *mwak'an*), retorted the spirit, "that's my name, *mwak'an*" [referring to the fact that the spirit's name only becomes officially known in the course of the ceremony].

Mohedja said they planned to transfer the baby on Friday and asked whether that would that be a good day. The patros replied mischievously that they should ask Nuriaty's husband. The patros went on like this for some time, refusing to commit, until finally the husband confirmed that Friday was fine and that the baby should be brought early in the morning. He added that since Nuriaty was taking the baby, it was appropriate for her to come to Mariam's house to fetch her, rather than having Mariam bring the baby to her. Mohedja then added trumba incense (*embuku*) to the fire and addressed Nuriaty's trumba over the smoke, repeating the statements spoken directly to the patros. The trumba was assumed to hear and acquiesce even though he was not present. The patros had private things he wished to discuss with Nuriaty's husband and the two of them went off together.

In contrast to the measured demeanour that Mze Nuru displayed when he entered Mohedja, the patros present in Nuriaty did not appear to be taking things very seriously. This was because, unlike Mze Nuru, the spirit was a youth and because he was impatiently awaiting the ceremonies that would firmly establish his identity and presence in Nuriaty. Furthermore, Nuriaty was concerned about her relations with her husband and wanted him to show his commitment to her by sponsoring the ceremony and to the baby by setting the date of transfer.

I mentioned to Mohedja that I thought it was an unfortunate time to stop the baby from nursing since she was so thin. She agreed but said it had to be done. Friday morning, early, Nuriaty came and fetched the baby. And the baby improved; the nightly fevers stopped, a fact which they accepted as a matter of course, although they were still worried the infant was underweight. Mariam said she missed her terribly for the first few days, but the baby was brought around and able to interact with her. The baby was fully raised by Nuriaty. By 1995, she was a mother herself and Nuriaty was raising one of her children.

Child transfers were not uncommon but, as we have seen, they were not always straightforward. Nuriaty was probably envious of her sister's fertility and badly wanted a daughter. Mariam did not want to give up the baby until the seriousness of the illness recontextualized the issue. But neither of the sisters ostensibly made the decision. Rather, there was a whole cast of players within the family circle who played a part. So expected was the participation of the spirits that at the beginning of the crisis their absence was the occasion of surprise and dismay. When her parents' spirits proved unable to make a decision, Mariam took the matter to Kos Vola in her grandmother, where the spirit was distant enough from the situation to be objective, yet close enough to take a sympathetic interest. Kos Vola's decision carried authority among all family members, though it is worthy of note that no action was taken until the acquiescence of Nuriaty's cohabiting spirits were reached. As for Mohedja, she was absolved of the responsibility of having, in effect, to choose between her daughters.

Mariam's husband, the baby's father, appeared to have little say in the disposition of the child. Nuriaty's spirit did bring her husband into it, but the main concern there was the nature of their own marriage, which had been a stormy one, and support for the spirit's ceremony.

The events also showed that the host must be well disposed if the spirit is going to rise and offer help – that there must, in a sense, be a unity of purpose between them. At the time, Tumbu was annoyed with Mariam and that was preventing the arrival and support of Mze Marwan that Mohedja was complaining about.

The conflict extended back some months. On a Tuesday in April, when Mze Nuru had risen in Mohedja to treat a neighbour's child, he was accosted by Mariam. They retreated to the privacy of Mohedja's house where Mariam said, "I'm sick."

"Sick how?" responded Mze Nuru.

"Sick. My belly (kibu)."

"Your belly?"

"Below the navel."

Mariam proceeded to say that she suffered at night from dreams of fighting with people. The previous night, her adversary, a village man slightly older than Mariam, even died. Mze Nuru said that Mariam had attracted a harmful spirit while carrying food out in the country in the evening (which she should have known better than to do). The spirit followed her home and had been with her ever since. "The trip from S—!" exclaimed Mariam, "It's from then that I started having the dreams." The adherence of the bush spirit, which was bothering both Mariam and her baby, was like a form of sorcery and Mze Nuru advised Tumbu to extract a *sairy* (sorcery packet) from Mariam the next day and to take a small chicken out to the spot in the woods where she had been infected.

Tumbu protested that this was his ylang ylang day (the timing of which was critical) and that nothing could interfere with it. This in turn upset Mariam, who said she only wanted to get well. But the demand touched a chord in Tumbu. There was never enough time to get his work done and no one ever helped him anymore, he grumbled. His real complaint lay with Mariam's husband. He went to all the trouble and expense to marry off his daughter and now her husband wouldn't do any work. Not only did Tumbu have to support Mariam, but he didn't get any assistance from his son-in-law. He said the son-in-law should perform Mariam's cure. Mariam replied that in that case maybe she should kick out her husband; every time Tumbu needed assistance she had quarrelled with her husband, trying to get him to go and help. Tumbu stomped off angrily and Mze Nuru then advised Mariam to try and talk things over with her husband and ask for his help. Mariam replied despairingly that she just wanted to get well and added sadly that maybe her husband no longer loved her.

The issue here was complex. In turning to ylang ylang production, Tumbu's needs for labour had become acute. Ylang ylang oil earned a good price and Mariam and her husband reaped some of the benefit. Tumbu's other daughters were married to men who had incomes of their own and supported their wives well, but Mariam's husband was rather lazy and did only the bare minimum in subsistence cultivation. Whereas his other sons-in-law were beyond Tumbu's reach and his reproach, Mariam's husband had in fact been working for him and was rather dependent on him, yet Tumbu was annoyed that as his labour needs grew, so his son-in-law withdrew. Tumbu resented the fact that he did not support his daughter well and even more that he did not take the opportunity that would have been to their mutual material benefit to work with him. But if Tumbu could not control his son-in-law's labour power, and thereby left Mariam caught in the middle, it was clear that the women, in part by means of the spirits, controlled the reproductive power and the allocation of offspring.

In the end, Tumbu extracted the sorcery packet on the Thursday and Mariam's husband then took the chicken to the woods, luring the spirit back from where it had come. Tumbu also prepared medicine for Mariam and a day later she reported she was no longer troubled by bad dreams. That day, her husband helped Tumbu with the heavy job of distilling the ylang ylang flowers. Tumbu then sent him down to the beach with money to purchase fish for the two households.

At one point in the original discussion, Tumbu testily asked Mze Nuru, risen in Mohedja, why he did not perform the cure himself. The spirit replied sadly that he considered them to be as one person (*ulu raiky*), or didn't Tumbu think that way too? Tumbu quickly replied that he did. And despite his bad humour, he performed the cure as rapidly as he was able. The unity of the group of spirits and humans was precisely what made them such a decisive force in confronting misfortune and resolving conflicts. At the same time, it was the differentiation into multiple voices within the extended family that provided the enabling condition. There is ambivalence in any family relationship. Possession helps to cut through this ambivalence, both by splitting contrasting or contradictory emotions into multiple loci and by granting a certain authority to the most disinterested voice.

In conclusion, I want to highlight two points. The first is the way Mze Nuru spoke of himself, Mohedja, and Tumbu as "one person" (*ulu raiky*). The second is the way Mohedja pointed out that the spirits who cohabited with Nuriaty would also be raising the child who was transferred between the sisters. What these remarks indicate are not merely Mohedja's rhetorical powers, but also the real sense in which the spirits are incorporated into the family and seen to work with family members and on their behalf. Nuriaty's spirits participate in her parenting, sharing the responsibilities for raising her family. And Mze Nuru is explicit about the interests he shares with Tumbu and Mohedja and that they share with each other. While speaking about being *ulu raiky* is not uncommon – and might be translated as "one people" rather than the stronger "one person," as I have done – I take the statement to refer to a deep process of identification. The identification between Mohedja and her spirit Mze Nuru is explicit. Moreover, despite her irritation with Tumbu and Mze Marwan, it is used to reinforce the identification between Tumbu and his wife and ultimately the family as a whole. It is noteworthy that Tumbu immediately concurred. Conflicts internal to the family are transcended by intense identifications between what might otherwise be emphasized as discrete individuals with competing interests. Cohabitation clarifies the fact that the members of the family are all part of one another.[1]

Mohedja herself was often caught up in the immediacy of her relations with significant others, whether with Tumbu or with one of her children, with anxiety about them, or simply a positive identificatory emotional flow. Mze Nuru provided some distance. Via Mze Nuru, Mohedja actualized her concerns for the welfare of her family. His interventions furthered her own concerns, albeit under another voice and another agency. Mze Nuru brought authority, efficacy, and dispassion in a way that Mohedja herself could not always do. It was not that Mohedja's personal emotions or intentions were muted, inverted, or transformed, but merely that they were held at arm's length. Basic intentions do not change, but they are put into perspective by an additional voice, and this tempers their immediate manifestation. Thus, while possession is often viewed by outsiders as a kind of emotional intensity or excess, of being carried off by one's passions (ecstasy), in fact what we have seen here is the reverse: issues are explored rationally and dispassionately. We can also say that the spirits help overcome impasses.[2]

One final point to note is that while the cohabiting spirits were brought in to intercede in child transfers and to advise treatment for ill children, they were never considered the source of serious harm, nor were they invoked to discount human responsibility. The following anecdote makes this explicit.

20 December 1975. Mohedja and Tumbu were invited to a patros ceremony for Zalia in S——. Amiaty and Mariam expressed surprise that Zalia had a spirit. Mohedja responded that she had had it a long time but until now the family had not cared to do anything about it. "Perhaps that's why she's had so much trouble keeping children," Amiaty ventured. Mariam replied scornfully, "Can a patros cause trouble with keeping children?" I asked what this "trouble" they were referring to was. Apparently Zalia had refused to nurse her babies, not because she had no milk, but because her breasts were sore. "And if their own mother won't nurse them, another woman certainly won't take over!" said Mariam. "Is this caused by the patros?" I asked. Amiaty said perhaps, but Mariam exclaimed, "Nonsense, it's her own *rohu* [soul, character] that is stopping her. Any woman who would go reef fishing the day after her baby died just doesn't like children."

Chapter Eleven

Ali's Marriage

This chapter turns to events within the family that greatly concerned Tumbu and especially Mohedja but in which the spirits with whom they cohabited played a relatively insignificant role. The couple had several sons who died in infancy or childhood. Until Maulida's birth in their middle age, Ali was their only son and they had great emotional as well as practical investment in him. He was an adolescent during my first year in Lombeni. Shortly after I returned in 1980, Mohedja narrated some dramatic events concerning Ali that had taken place during my absence.

12 July 1980. A young woman of Lombeni Kely named Amina was engaged to a young man from A— but the groom and his mother walked out on the first night of the wedding when they discovered Amina was not a virgin. They were within their rights to do so. However, Mohedja added parenthetically, Amina's family could have talked the boy from A— into staying in the marriage if he hadn't brought his mother along. Amina announced that Tumbu and Mohedja's son, Ali, was responsible for her defloration. Mohedja claimed she said this because she liked Ali and hoped he would marry her. The elders warned her about the consequences of lying, threatening her with a *fatiha* [in this case, pronounced to bring out the truth and punish liars]. At this, she changed her story and named a young man from S— who then paid a cow in compensation.

The grandmother who had raised Amina and was sponsoring her marriage was embarrassed but not terribly disconcerted or angry. She sold the cow and used part of the money to buy Amina gold combs (such as a virgin bride would receive from her husband). Amina's father had left the village after her mother died and had not raised her, but he came and just took the rest of the money, claiming the right as her father.

A month later, Mohedja considerably developed the story of Amina and Ali. She spoke at length about something that was obviously of grave concern to her.

After the wedding fiasco, Amina quietly married a different man from S—. One day this man followed Mohedja to her fields and there he complained that Ali was "stealing" his wife [i.e., committing adultery with her]. Every night she went off to his house. Ali was a bachelor at the time and bachelor youths maintained single-room houses on the fringes of the village where they slept and entertained women. The husband asked Mohedja to tell Ali to desist. Mohedja was very upset and on her return home she immediately confronted Ali. She said she had told him all along never to go after someone's spouse (*vady n'ulun*); the husband could do sorcery or was in his rights to utter a *fatiha* that would seek out and punish the interloper. Mohedja was frightened for his life.

Ali didn't listen. Amina's husband soon left her over the affair. Amina continued to visit Ali every night until finally Ali fell very sick. He was ill for some three months. During this time, he stayed at his mother's house.

Mohedja went to an astrologer for divination. He told her that Ali was suffering from sorcery and said they needed a healer from the north (*kibula*, the direction of Mecca) to treat him, that local healers would be ineffective. After some thought, Tumbu and Mohedja went to a spirit medium in T—. He performed divination and then his spirit rose and prescribed medicine. The medium came to Lombeni to administer it. Ali had to inhale the steam and wash in it every day. But he got no better, not even after Tumbu's second trip to T— for more medicine.

Mze Nuru then rose in Mohedja and told Tumbu there were two *sairy* (packets of sorcery) to be removed – one at the spot where Ali was wont to roast bananas and drink palm wine in the bush and the other in Ali's body. Tumbu asked his son for the location of his picnic spot and went and removed the sorcery there. Then he removed sorcery from Ali's body. However, Ali remained sick.

Mohedja suggested another diviner. This woman said the sorcery was over, but that Ali still suffered from *tsiku* (wind), an illness for which she provided medicine. She said that if he vomited the medicine, it was a sure sign of wind. He vomited. After a while, he got used to the medicine and was able to keep it down. He also kept on applying medicine from the first medium. Soon he was well again.

The first night that Ali was back in his bachelor house, Amina joined him. Ali was frightened because Mohedja had warned him of the consequences. Concerned as well about his mother's feelings, Ali went over to Lombeni Be to sleep. But Amina kept calling him and after a few days he couldn't resist. They started sleeping together again. Amina became pregnant and named Ali as the father.

Amina's two grandmothers came to Mohedja to say that she and Tumbu should support Amina during the pregnancy. They replied not until the baby was born and they were sure Ali was the father. After the birth, Ali's sisters went to examine the baby; they all saw the likeness, though Mohedja remained sceptical for a while. Signs of paternity included the shape of the hands and feet, the nails, ears, forehead, and also the face.[1]

The family accepted the paternity and started to support Amina. In fact, Ali had been stealing soap and kerosene for her from his parents all the while she was pregnant. After a time, the baby became ill. They were worried that Amina was bothered by a spirit of the sort that kills infants and so Ali's older sister Mariam took the baby to raise. Ali continued to bear certain responsibilities towards his son. For example, he bought him new clothes at the end of every Ramadan. Mariam had many children of her own and could not afford the clothes.

From the time that Amina's previous husband left, her grandmothers had been talking about a marriage with Ali. They set a Friday for the engagement. Ali went to the fields that day. His sisters brought money on his behalf, as did Tumbu. But Ali didn't show up. Maybe God didn't want the marriage to take place, said Mohedja to me. Mohedja herself didn't want the marriage because, she said, it would look like she had helped to break up Amina's previous marriage. She agreed not to disrupt the process but refused to participate.

Two months later, Ali fell ill again. When he recovered, Mze Nuru rose at night in Mohedja and said not to go ahead with the marriage, that it wouldn't work. Tumbu went to two different diviners, one in Lombeni, the other Samba, Mohedja's elder brother in F— to check this. The results of each divination confirmed Mze Nuru's statement. At that, Amina's mother's sister went to her own diviner in A—. He too said the consequences of the marriage would be negative, elaborating that while it would not be harmful for Amina, it would have a deleterious effect on Ali. But the two grandmothers continued to say that as long as the couple wanted to marry, they should go ahead with it. They were angry and said Mohedja just didn't want the marriage. Amina's grandfather, normally a close friend of Mohedja and Tumbu's, even tried to refuse the rice they offered for Amina's post-partum period [a traditional prestation]. But Mohedja was adamant in rejecting the marriage, since "there's no shop for souls [i.e., you can't buy a new life]; when you die, that's it, *rohu tsisy dukan; naka maty, bass.*"

Mohedja was concerned because of the sorcery placed on the relationship and because of the findings of the divination. She asked Ali to stop seeing Amina. He said it was Amina who came to him. So Mohedja asked Amina to stop. Was she trying to kill her son? Mohedja told her that she should have married Ali at once if that was whom she liked; she should never have married the man from S— first.

Ali continued to receive Amina in his house although Mohedja was upset. And Amina's grandmothers continued to press for the marriage, despite Tumbu and Mohedja's objections. In fact, the grandmothers were furious with Mohedja. One of them was Musy Matwar, Mohedja's trumba fundi, towards whom Mohedja normally showed a good deal of respect and friendship. The grandmothers went to the senior astrologer and elder kinsman in the community. He said he could only marry them if Ali went to Amina's house and not vice versa. Privately, the elder advised Tumbu that if the parents married them off, this might serve to cool their desire.

Mohedja said that the grandmothers worried that if Amina did not marry Ali, she would never find another husband; Amina cared only for Ali. On the grandmothers' advice, Amina stopped coming to Ali's house for three nights. Finally, she told him to come to her house. Then she ran off to her grandmother, who called in the male elder. They burst in and forced an engagement in the middle of the night. Mohedja dreamt she saw women coming from A— for a wedding in Lombeni. She woke and heard the elder telling Mariam to go fetch her new sister-in-law. Mohedja was very upset and confronted the elder. He said that he was not behind it; it was the grandmothers' doing. Mohedja replied that he knew perfectly well the marriage couldn't work – he had seen it through his divination.

Mohedja thereby not only risked her relationship with her trumba teacher but now stood up to a male authority figure who was universally respected and feared.

That day, Mariam called over Ali and told him he was committing suicide. "You are trying to do something impossible [or forbidden]" (anao mila mañan kabar tsy mety). Next morning, Ali left for K— to stay with a friend. Amina kept calling him back to Lombeni. When he returned, Mariam asked Tumbu's sister, who happened to be Ali's next-door neighbour, to watch his house and call her if he went off to Amina's. That night Ali got up. His father's sister followed him to Amina's then ran to wake Mariam and Nuriaty. The three women went to Amina's, calling Ali to come out. They marched him back to his house. Ali was very angry and returned to K—. Amina called him back and the whole series of events was repeated, this time with an additional sister in on the action. Mohedja was not included in Mariam's plans and said she knew nothing about it until later. During this time, she and Tumbu were despondent.

Finally, Mariam asked her aunt to enter Amina's house [cross-sibling avoidance relations, which were already close to having been violated, forbade the sisters from doing so]. The aunt entered and removed Ali. They went and woke Tumbu and Mohedja and all went over to Ali's. There Tumbu and Mohedja told him to stop being suicidal. They said they would get him married, if that was what he wanted, but to someone else. He was silent. In the morning, he went off to K—. A few days later, he returned with the names of three possible fiancées.

That night, Mze Nuru rose in Mohedja and told Tumbu which of the three young women it should be; the other two wouldn't work on the grounds of astrological incompatibility. Mohedja did not believe what Mze Nuru had said. She went to an independent diviner the same morning after Tumbu told her. The diviner gave the same results. Tumbu went off to another diviner in M— who again said the same. Sometimes, remarked Mohedja, it was good to go far to seek a divination.

Mohedja added that it was good thing that Amina's first husband did not utter a *fatiha*. Ali would have died, as he was indeed at fault. Mohedja had told him over and over again that men who stole wives or who deflowered virgins would suffer for their acts. It was very dangerous.

She also pointed out that throughout the process they never performed medicine (*audy*) on Ali [i.e., tried to change his mind by working with medicines and the like behind his back], but only tried to convince him verbally. Eventually this worked.

Amina blamed Mohedja for not letting her marry Ali. For a long time, she refused to speak to her. But, Mohedja said, "Was it me or was it that the marriage was simply impossible, *vadiaña tsy mety*?"

Here is Tumbu's independent recounting of the events to me.

Ali slept with Amina. She even left her husband to go to his house. The husband came to Tumbu about it. Tumbu told Ali to desist but he didn't. The man left Amina and Ali got very sick; they thought he would die. They tried all kinds of treatment. Tumbu extracted sorcery. They went to Mohedja's older brother in F— for help. He directed them to another astrologer. The latter cured Ali, who then went right back to Amina. Amina's husband had done sorcery so that Ali would be sick if he married her. Tumbu refused to allow the marriage. Ali was angry and moved away to K— where he stayed for two months, although Tumbu had told him to go somewhere he had kin rather than a village where he had no relations. Ali returned to Lombeni and told his father he would stay away from Amina if his father married him off to someone else. Contrary to Mohedja, Tumbu said that he did do medicine so that Ali would no longer crave Amina. Ali did not know this.

Many years later, Ali's younger sister Amiaty recounted the story and laughed over the way her parents had not known that Amina visited Ali while he was living in K—. The house owner told Tumbu he had not seen Amina – at the very moment when they were inside together. When Amina became pregnant, Mohedja denied Ali could be the father since he had been away in K—. It was only when the baby was born that they saw it was Ali's. The parents then rushed Ali, who was too young, into a marriage.

It is interesting that in their respective accounts, neither Mohedja nor Tumbu played up the role of their spirits. As Mohedja said, in cases like this it is better to seek help at a distance. Mze Nuru was ineffective on his own and needed the support of numerous diviners. Even so, Amina suspected Mohedja's lack of objectivity. That the spirits appeared to have little sway over Ali may also be connected to Tumbu's certainty, expressed in another context, that Ali himself would never be possessed (an observation that proved correct). When Mohedja appeared unable to proceed further, her daughter Mariam took over and, in effect, carried out her mother's wishes. Tumbu pointed to Mariam as the strongest of their children.

It is possible that Mohedja's extreme anxiety about Ali's original dalliance with Amina drew on Mohedja's unconscious concerns with respect to her own original engagement in F— that was abruptly broken off and that seemed to shape her response to later unwanted suitors (chapter 8).

Ali's Marriage

Ali's aunt wanted him to marry his cross-cousin in her village. Ali did not want this, and had he made the marriage, the bride would have had to come live in Lombeni since all Ali's work was there. Mohedja explained that she and Tumbu depended on him: he went daily to look after the cows in the bush and also cooked their ylang ylang. So they did not want him to marry even as far as the next village. When Ali brought his parents the names of three potential brides, they took them to diviners, who approved only one of them, a distant relative in Lombeni Be. This girl had been engaged to a man who had died quite suddenly. So Mohedja went to the young woman's grandmother (mother's mother) who had raised her. The grandmother said another boy was supposed to come finalize things very soon. She told Mohedja to wait a couple of days and said she would speak to the girl's father in the meantime. The other boy did not turn up. Mohedja returned to the grandmother, who was interested but had not yet spoken to the girl's father. So Mohedja went directly to the father who said he preferred Ali over the other suitor because the latter already had a wife; he did not want a polygynous match for his daughter's first marriage. Soon after, an engagement was held, with senior kin from Ali's side going to the girl's family. Ali's father-in-law requested a relatively low amount for the *mahary* (Arabic *mahr*; prestation in cash from the groom's to the bride's family).

Tumbu paid the *mahary*. Then he bought gold, clothing, and soap to fill Ali's "suitcase" (*valise*), the customary prestation that a groom brought his wife on the last day of what was a virgin wedding. This was a public event. Mohedja elaborated the contents of Ali's suitcase: twelve *saluvaña* (full-length tubular cloth wraps with matching head scarf), three dresses, two skirts, six blouses, two pairs of sandals, one necklace, one brooch, earrings, one gold bracelet, three gold hair combs and a gold pin, silver bangles, lipstick, powder, a hair-parting implement, one large and four small bottles of cologne, shampoo, and brilliantine. The contents of the suitcase had been subject to inflation. Nuriaty had received only three *saluvaña* when she married a decade or so earlier. A couple of decades after Ali's wedding, the "suitcase" had expanded to include a freezer, television, and other appliances. Mohedja and Tumbu filled Ali's suitcase well because they had heard rumours that they could not fill it.

In effect, Mohedja and Tumbu did more for Ali than they had to. As Tumbu put it, he had put aside 10,000 francs towards a pilgrimage to Mecca. But Ali got into trouble and had to be married off. Parents had the duty to feed, dress, and circumcise their sons and to feed, dress, and marry off their daughters and build houses for them. The groom himself had the primary responsibility for accumulating the wealth necessary for marriage, but parents often helped and, as they indicated, the shame of a small gift fell on the groom's parents as much as on the groom. Mohedja and Tumbu also made the commitment to fill the suitcase because they badly wanted to see Ali married. They had genuine concerns for his health and depended heavily on his labour. Moreover, in participating in the ylang ylang production, Ali had earned their financial support.

And so, Ali married and moved to his wife's place in Lombeni Be. In 1980, the marriage was still in its early stages and the young people were not yet accustomed to one another. I noticed that Tumbu and Mohedja no longer had their radio. Ali had taken it, Tumbu explained. Before he was married, Ali would borrow it, but Tumbu could ask for it back whenever he and Mohedja wanted it. But now they were embarrassed to ask for it because of the daughter-in-law. The future of the marriage was unclear. Mohedja commented that she wanted to tell Ali to build a house of his own in Lombeni Kely in case he was thrown out by his wife – not that it was likely, but "just in case."

In 1985, Ali's marriage was not untroubled. His wife complained about his staying out late drinking. Mohedja knew he would not change his habits quickly and advised her daughter-in-law that as long as Ali gave her enough food and money she should just eat and go to sleep.

> Ali himself had a lot to tell me. He felt that his in-laws interfered too much and that they rebuffed his mother's attempts to make closer ties with them. He said they were unable to get accustomed to others, *reo tsy mety zatra ulun*. Mohedja took Ali's wife home with her for the birth of one of their children and looked after her during the ensuing period. But on the fortieth day exactly (the minimal time of post-partum seclusion), Ali's wife and her kin insisted on her returning home. When she bore her first son, the infant was very sick. The custom was for an ailing firstborn son to be cared for by the father's kin until he could walk and then return him to his parents. Nuriaty and Mohedja went to discuss this with Ali's in-laws and the latter agreed. The baby was placed in Nuriaty's care. Three days later, Nuriaty was woken at dawn as Ali's wife and father-in-law came to take the baby home. Ali said his family had been shamed. He himself had been sleeping at the time and knew nothing about it, nor did his mother. Yet his wife's kin had discussed it among themselves. If there had been an astrological problem, they should have included him in their deliberations instead of just fetching the child. As it was, he felt, they made his mother a laughingstock.
>
> Ali was very angry and said he withdrew interest in his son because his wife's family were acting as though he weren't the father. In addition, they had embarrassed his mother, his father, and his older sisters. He stopped buying clothes for his son or looking after him when he cried or was sick, saying it was his father-in-law's obligation. Eventually, his in-laws complained about him to Tumbu and Tumbu scolded him; they might have insulted him, but the boy was his son, after all.
>
> At one point, Ali brought his belongings home to Lombeni Kely. His wife complained to Tumbu and Tumbu talked him into going back. But he left his goats under his nephew's care at his father's and planned to build his hen house there as well.
>
> Ali summed up the problem. It was very hard to marry into his wife's family because they wanted to be in control. His wife listened to her parents instead of to him and then, following their instructions, tried to tell him what to do. A wife and a husband should come to an agreement between themselves before listening to outsiders. Moreover, Ali's in-laws expected him to deposit all his savings with his wife, not acknowledging his own

financial responsibilities. If they had not given birth together, he would have left permanently, but his parents wanted him to stay to ensure his children's welfare. If his parents were able to take the children, that would be another matter. Mohedja wanted to raise one but did not dare ask.

He concluded that he only felt comfortable in Lombeni Kely and only felt able to think, plan, and get ahead here. His mother had also withdrawn from his in-laws. She used to visit regularly, but they never made her feel comfortable.

Here we see the problem of child transfers from another angle. If one side changed its mind, there could be great insult and damage done to the relationship. Breaking off or turning down a child transfer required great delicacy and tact. Ali also described what an ideal marriage might be like, an ideal which his parents' marriage resembled much more closely than did his own. In any case, most of the negotiations appeared to take place between his parents and his wife's parents. When Ali neglected his role as father, the matter was taken to his own father, that is, to Tumbu. It appeared that Tumbu and Mohedja's remonstrations with Ali played a large part in maintaining the marriage.

Ali also showed discomfort with uxorilocal residence. He spent most of his time and conducted all his business in Lombeni Kely. The small shop that he then shared with Mariam was located near their parents' house. One of his wife's and her family's biggest complaints was that Ali showed up only at night. It seemed that each party to the marriage, not only the wife, as Ali implied, was still more closely tied to their respective families of orientation than they were to each other.

One reason that Ali had strong ties at home has been mentioned before. He was his father's junior partner and Tumbu needed him to look after their cattle and to keep the ylang ylang production going. At the time, he was Tumbu's only grown son. Presumably, Ali listened to his father as much as he complained that his wife listened to hers. This was a structural problem implicit in family constitution and bilateral affiliation in Mayotte. Uxorilocal residence was the norm, but there were no strict rules about it. In Ali's case, as in many, there was a tension between residential proximity to one side and economic cooperation with the other. Ali's father-in-law also produced ylang ylang and would have liked his help. Every household struggled as a new economic unit with the obligations they had to other households, as well as their dependence upon them.

Ali's father-in-law was a well-known diviner from a family that cohabited with many spirits. Presumably the baby was withdrawn from Nuriaty as a result of divination or the message of a spirit on their side.

As Ali said, this could have been handled diplomatically, and certainly the communication should have been accomplished before the transfer rather than after, but the divination process was the "wild card" in this.

Complementary to Ali's account, both Mohedja and her daughter Amiaty told me that Ali's wife did not like them much. She seldom visited and when she did it was usually no more than a quick hello and goodbye. As a result, her children were not accustomed to being there. Mohedja used to visit them frequently but stopped when it was not reciprocated.

In sum, there was a sense that both parties to the marriage were still somewhat immature – a result of marrying so young – and thus subject to their respective dependency on their own parents. It appeared that each of them felt unease at being in a "strange" setting and thus unable to fully cope with the structural problem with which the marriage presented them.

A few years later, the situation resolved itself somewhat in Ali's favour. He built his wife a house on a plot belonging to her family but on the other side of Lombeni Be from her parents. He also took up with a second wife in Lombeni Kely whom he married during a short period when he divorced his first wife. They reunited but he was unable to give up the new wife (with whom he had not had children). This gave him a base in both villages.

Ali had also taken over management of his father's fields and thereby controlled distribution of the income from the ylang ylang. However, ylang ylang no longer fetched the prices it once did, and the cost of living had risen significantly over the decade. Ali managed to purchase a truck and supplemented his income by hiring out the vehicle for the transport of goods. He resented the fact that he had never received a school education and could not compete with younger people for the more secure and better-paying jobs, which lay in the white-collar sphere. He continued to own his shop jointly with two of his sisters rather than with either spouse. By 1995, one of his daughters was living with Mohedja.

Nevertheless, Ali also became somewhat disaffected from his natal family and resented what he considered his parents' favouritism towards his youngest sister, Mwanesha. Tumbu complained that he often did not stop by to greet his parents for two to three days in row, even though he parked the truck close by. When he did appear, he had little to say, yet Tumbu could see that he was a lively talker with his friends outside the family. Mohedja was concerned that he did not attend the circumcision of his sister Amiaty's sons.

In later years, Ali suffered in a number of manual jobs. He worked for a time as a night watchman in town until that grew too dangerous and Mohedja insisted he quit, and then as a night watchman at the elementary school that had since been built in Lombeni. This was not hard work but meant he had little time for sleep.

Ali's marital trajectory was very different from that of his parents. Eventually he found some happiness in taking a third wife, this time in Madagascar. He visited her every few months; life there was cheap for people on a French salary and the new wife appreciated the income. He had children with this woman and also with an Anjouanais migrant in Mayotte and was proud that he was arranging French citizenship papers for all his offspring.

Chapter Twelve

Mohedja and Her Mother-in-Law

As previous chapters have shown, cohabitation is not always fully harmonious, but consists of an ebb and flow of what Bhrigupati Singh has aptly described as "agonistic intensity" within "a continuum in the play of life" (2015, 162–3). There are various modes and channels for expressing aggression, ranging from overt shouting or cursing and threats of physical violence – as expressed, for example, by Tumbu's mother – to the threats entailed in pronouncing a *fatiha* to reveal or punish a guilty party, to more modulated and indirect forms made possible by drawing on the voices of spirits. Sometimes the spirits made their feelings known by making the host ill or by refusing to speak when called upon. Sometimes they were able to subtly turn things to the interests of their host at the expense of others. For the most part, Mohedja and Tumbu were supportive of one another and worked to define and pursue their common interests, along with the spirits. Yet Mohedja's spirits sometimes said things she would not have allowed herself to say or that Tumbu would not have readily accepted if she had, leading Tumbu in a direction or to conclusions he might not have chosen for himself. The spirits were able to do so without unduly implicating Mohedja and indeed partially concealing from Mohedja herself her own acts of aggression.

Tumbu's mother, Dady Nuriaty, was a feisty, crotchety person with a sharp tongue. We were next door neighbours and, if she confessed to sleeping uneasily in my proximity during the first weeks after my arrival in 1975, I sometimes felt reciprocally. But we soon got used to each other and, in my books, she was not a bad sort. She died a few years later and was fondly remembered by her children and grandchildren, who like to tell humorous stories about the old lady's strong disposition.

28 March 1976. Mohedja had never spoken ill of her mother-in-law, Dady Nuriaty, but today she let me know how she felt. "There's not one thing right or decent about her, *tsisy ata kabar araiky manzary am nazy!*" she exclaimed.

The immediate cause for Mohedja's expostulation was a quarrel between Mohedja's oldest daughter, Nuriaty, and her grandmother. Nuriaty, who was about twenty-six years old at the time, had been named for her grandmother, who was known as Dady Nuriaty, meaning at once both "Granny Nuriaty" and "Grandmother of Nuriaty." Nuriaty was raised by her grandmother, lived adjacent to her, and regularly cooperated with her in domestic activities. Mohedja heard about the dispute from Nuriaty, but seeking a more balanced account, went to hear what Nuriaty's husband, Kolo, had to say, and discovered, as Mohedja told me, that the two versions were identical. Kolo said he had been astonished that Nuriaty had been continually sick since their recent marriage. He went to a diviner and was told that it was not a case of sorcery but only that Nuriaty's patros wanted to hold his ceremony. So Nuriaty and Kolo called on her grandmother to let her know that they were planning the ceremony for after the next rice harvest and to say that they should all begin accumulating the things they would need for it. It was proper to alert one's elders to one's plans.

Instead of acquiescing, Dady Nuriaty began a tirade, saying that Nuriaty couldn't do anything right and was always causing problems. When Nuriaty started to respond, Dady Nuriaty threatened to hit her. Nuriaty fell silent but her grandmother hit her anyway. Kolo led her back to their own house. They said they had called on her to consult about one thing but all she wanted to do was insult Nuriaty so they might as well go home again. Later Nuriaty brought her grandmother a peace offering of food. Dady Nuriaty refused it but eventually softened up.

Mohedja's anger at Dady Nuriaty led her to recall a series of incidents in which her mother-in-law had been at fault. It will be obvious that her account is partisan (though another daughter-in-law told similar stories) and does not speak well of either woman. It was delivered when Mohedja was in the grip of high emotion. Nevertheless, the incidents are of interest for the light they shed on domestic politics, and they continue to illustrate how Mohedja processed, constructed, and reconstructed the events of daily life.

We have already seen in chapter 9 the circumstances under which Nuriaty was transferred as an infant to the care of Tumbu's mother and the resentment this produced. Now Mohedja was outraged that Dady

Nuriaty had asked how Nuriaty could act in such a way after she had given her the breast as an infant.

> This was an outright lie, said Mohedja; she had never breastfed her. Dady Nuriaty had also lied, Mohedja said, when she told me that she had sponsored Nuriaty's wedding. Dady Nuriaty had contributed very little, whereas Mohedja herself had worked extra hard in the fields and sold her surplus rice to buy dishes and glassware for Nuriaty. Shortly after her marriage, when Nuriaty followed her husband for a period to live in his village, she left the dishes packed in a box in her house. Dady Nuriaty took them one by one, each time she broke one taking another, until they were all gone. Mohedja watched this silently but felt very upset inside. "And now Dady Nuriaty complains when Nuriaty doesn't fetch her water! Well, Nuriaty should do it when she can but not worry about it if she doesn't feel up to it. She certainly has done enough for her grandmother. Dady Nuriaty has her own children, and she should ask them instead of taking advantage of her grandchildren. And if even her own children don't like her, her grandchildren can hardly be expected to!"[1]
>
> Mohedja said the incident was typical of Dady Nuriaty; she couldn't talk to her kin without criticizing them and telling them they were no good. Yet even though her children disliked or were afraid of her, they all tried to do the right thing by her. They each visited her every day to ask after her welfare.

One of Mohedja's grudges against Dady Nuriaty went back to a time when she had urged Tumbu to leave Mohedja. When Tumbu said he could not do so, she argued with him. Hadn't she left his father for other husbands, and hadn't his father acted in the same way? Tumbu replied that his father's affairs were his father's business and that he had to judge his own case for himself.

Up to this point, Dady Nuriaty's conduct, while not particularly generous regarding Mohedja, had remained within accepted norms. Many people felt that long-term commitment to a single marital relationship was less desirable than engaging in a variety of relationships and founding several sets of siblings. A mother had the right to advise her son.

> But Dady Nuriaty overstepped the bounds when, as Mohedja claimed, she determined to do something about it. Dady Nuriaty announced she was going to D— to visit kin but actually went instead to a fundi in B— and asked for medicine to separate husband and wife.
>
> Mohedja learned this from a dream that night. On waking, she told Tumbu not to eat anything his mother brought back from her journey, but she didn't

elaborate. They were out planting ylang ylang at the time. Dady Nuriaty arrived with cakes and meat and, despite Mohedja's warning, Tumbu ate some. Mohedja kept quiet, only refusing a serving for herself. Later when they cooked their noon *batabata* (boiled manioc and starchy banana), he ate more of his mother's treats. In the evening when they returned to the village, Tumbu became very ill. Returning from the latrine, he fainted.

Mariam was sleeping in her fields. That night she dreamt that her father was very sick. The next day, as she worked in the fields, her mind (*rohu*) began to bother her and she rushed home to find her fears confirmed. Meanwhile, Tumbu's patros rose and asked for Tumbu's apprentice, Hasan Mena, to be sent for. Tumbu's son Ali left a message with Hasan's wife: "Tell my 'uncle' (*baba hely*) that my father is very sick." Hasan Mena arrived the next morning before it was light. His patros rose and said the problem was sorcery. He named the perpetrator as a dark woman (*viavy mainting*) but said no more. He extracted the sorcery and then treated Tumbu with herbal medicine for a week. When Tumbu recovered Hasan Mena told him that the source of his trouble had been his own mother. Although she had asked for medicine to make the couple separate, she had somehow received medicine to kill him instead.

From that time forwards, declared Mohedja, Tumbu had been frightened of his mother. He never ate food she gave or sent him unless he had observed it cooking. He told his children to be quiet when she started an argument and not to get her more excited. Since she was his mother, he went to see her every day, but he said that had she been his *nindry hely* or *nindry be* ("little" or "big" mother, i.e., mother's younger or older sister) he would have greeted her only when they happened to meet on the path. When I remarked on Tumbu and his siblings' solicitousness towards Dady Nuriaty, Mohedja replied, "Well, she is their mother, isn't she?"[2]

When Dady Nuriaty's first attempt at breaking up the marriage failed, she tried again, asserted Mohedja. She called up a trumba in a host in S— and asked for medicine to separate her son and his wife. The trumba replied that this would be difficult and that the only way to succeed would be to call up Mohedja's spirits, any one of them would do. Mohedja had a dream that night in which her spirits told her that if Dady Nuriaty came and asked her to call them she should refuse, because, once called, they would do her bidding, they wouldn't be able to resist the reward she would offer them.[3]

These remarks point to something essential about spirits; however well disposed they were towards their host, they were always ready to follow their own self-interests. Mohedja simultaneously acknowledged their assistance (in warning her), incorporating them towards her own ends and interests, and also indicated their autonomy from her.

Mohedja said she awoke the next morning thinking the story an unlikely one. She observed her mother-in-law leave for S—. She returned around noon and went straight home. In the evening, she came to their courtyard as Mohedja was cooking. She called out that she wished to speak to Mohedja and asked her to step into the house for a minute. Dady Nuriaty said she was worried about all the sickness there had been among the children in the family lately and that she wanted to call up the spirits to consult about it.

Mohedja remembered her dream. She replied, very well, that she would go to her mother-in-law's house later that evening. She said she needed to finish cooking first and still wanted to bathe and go to the mosque. After doing those things, however, she just returned home, had dinner, and went to bed. The next day, Dady Nuriaty said she had waited for her and Mohedja replied that she had been too tired. "Let's do it right now!" said Dady Nuriaty. "I'm too hungry," replied Mohedja. Then she had to go to the fields, and on her return, she was too tired and dirty, and so it went. Dady Nuriaty pursued her for a full week before she got tired of her excuses and gave up.

Mohedja compared her situation to that of her *rahavavy*, the wife of Tumbu's younger maternal half-brother. There too Dady Nuriaty tried to break up her son's long-standing marriage in favour of a new polygynous one he had initiated. She refused to preside over a reconciliation and threatened to withdraw her parental blessing if he returned to his first wife. Tumbu's brother disregarded her and negotiated with his first wife and her brother. He paid his brother-in-law a fine of 2,500 CFA francs and the latter passed it on to his sister. Although the couple were reconciled, the wife couldn't help but overhear her mother-in-law reviling her daily. Finally, she got so angry she went over and started talking back and there was a loud and long argument that everyone in the village overheard. After that, things quietened down. But the tail end of the story, concluded Mohedja, had happened just the other day. Tumbu's brother and his wife were having trouble finding a spouse for their daughter. They went to the diviner, who happened to be Dady Nuriaty's brother, and someone who had been involved in the marital reconciliation. He discovered that the bad things Dady Nuriaty had said to them was what was blocking an engagement. So they all went over to Dady Nuriaty's house, lit incense and listened to her recite sacred liturgy and take back her words. Mohedja happened to be passing and witnessed the scene…

The incident that made Dady Nuriaty most notorious, said Mohedja, concerned a quarrel between her daughter and the daughter of one of Dady Nuriaty's sisters.

Following the quarrel, Dady Nuriaty attended a religious dance at B— and she and her daughter supposedly asked the presiding fundi to perform a *fatiha* on their behalf. The latter did so, a standard procedure, without knowing that the *fatiha* was aimed at killing someone, even someone as close as the client's own sister's daughter. Shortly after that, another daughter of Dady Nuriaty's sister entered labour. Rae Samba (Mohedja's mother), who was a midwife, was called and she was gone all that day and night. During the night, the baby was born dead, and the mother died soon thereafter. In the morning, they buried the baby and then held the funeral for the mother. People began to say it was Dady Nuriaty's doing. She denied everything, but the fundi of the religious dance confirmed that she had asked him for a *fatiha*.

That night, someone in the village dreamt that Dady Nuriaty's house was on fire. People tried to put it out, but they were unsuccessful, and the house burned to the ground. Meanwhile, the fire crawled across the clearing to the adjacent house of Dady Nuriaty's daughter [Tumbu's half-sister] and began to consume it as well. The daughter was inside and didn't think to run out. Soon all the walls were in flames. Someone came to tell the dreamer, and she went back and heard Tumbu's sister's screams for help within the house. The house burned down and the woman with it.

When Tumbu heard the dream, he said the implications were too disturbing to keep silent [i.e., that his mother and sister were at risk of divine punishment] and he called a family conference to inform them. If Dady Nuriaty and her daughter did not hold a *kafara* (sacrifice to take back the *fatiha*), this would be their fate. In the dream, the spirits had said that they would have to provide a red cow. So they took Dady Nuriaty's red cow, slaughtered it, and called the original fundi to come and eat. They invited Dady Nuriaty's sister and her remaining daughters and gave them meat. They came in tears and refused to eat.

Although Dady Nuriaty and her daughter protested their innocence they participated in the *kafara*. Everyone in the village believed them guilty, said Mohedja.

Part of the significance of the dream was that it indicated that it was more Dady Nuriaty's responsibility than her daughter's. When the daughter first told her mother she was thinking of holding a *fatiha*, her mother, as her responsible elder (*ulu be*), ought to have talked her out of it or simply forbidden it instead of going along with it. And the case was particularly bad because it was her own kin she killed, indeed a classificatory daughter.

Mohedja was embarrassed at first to tell me that she herself had been the dreamer.

PART FOUR

Scenes from a Marriage

Chapter Thirteen

Playing and Working: Kalu and the Kakanoru

Two additional spirits shed further light on how Mohedja and Tumbu cohabited with one another, adding further strands to their relationship, and providing additional perspectives on their lives. Kalu offers reflections on their domestic activities and the kakanoru on their cultivation of subsistence and cash crops on the land they were able to purchase. These spirits enriched their experience, offering interludes for playful regression in their working lives and positive dependence on one another.

Kalu, the Child Spirit

29 August 1975. During the night, Mohedja's child spirit, Kalu, rose and announced it was time to hold a trumba ceremony for Mohedja's niece. Mohedja had raised this woman, who lived in an adjacent house and who had recently suffered a stillbirth. In the early morning, even before prayers, Kalu called together all the women of the compound as well as other women in the village who were hosts to senior trumba. They came, lit incense, clapped, and washed the young woman in medicine, but all to no effect. No spirit rose in the niece. (Nor had one fully risen some twenty years later.)

Kalu then asked for a chicken from an older cousin of Mohedja's and rice from the niece's mother. Having acquired both, the spirit left. Mohedja was herself again until mid-afternoon when the spirit returned to cook her food. Kalu is a small child and acted like one. She lisped heavily and said funny things, calling people by various "wrong" kinship terms. There was much joking, most of it too fast for me. Mohedja's own small children and grandchildren looked taken aback. Kalu cooked the chicken and rice (the standard meal for child spirits), fed herself first (in other contexts this would have been exceedingly impolite), and then offered food to others.

I was told that if you ate her food, Kalu would come to your house and cry until you gave her another chicken and more rice to cook. Pretending to be Mohedja, Kalu tried to trick passers-by into eating, but her adult daughters warned them off. In fact, all of us in the compound were fed, including Tumbu and me, after Kalu had eaten her fill. Mohedja herself was not allowed to eat chicken as it was forbidden by her senior trumba.

The one person to whom Kalu showed respect was Musy Matwar. When the senior trumba fundi went by, Kalu asked her if she needed any work done, perhaps water to be fetched. Musy replied in a motherly way and joined in the laughter.

Several women in Lombeni Kely were possessed by child spirits (andify). The child spirits were all female and they appeared with the highly exaggerated and caricatured manners of small girls, although no girls actually acted in such uninhibited and provocative ways. The child spirits each had particularly warm and affectionate relations with their respective host's husband, as Kalu did with Tumbu. They placed men into two classes: potential sexual predators and trusted friends. A man became a friend of a child spirit once he had offered her the means to prepare a festive meal for herself and a few of her friends. Until he did so, the child spirits were exceedingly coy with him, but at the same time, such men were suitable victims for the spirits' pranks.

Child spirits were playful and given to the enjoyment of the senses. They behaved precisely in the way mothers were always telling their young children not to: acting greedy, dirtying their clothes, and so on. By inverting age-related behaviours and the locus of propriety, their appearance was inherently comical. The comical element was played up by both spirits and onlookers, who used the opportunity to make lots of jokes about kinship, selfishness, relations between the sexes, and relations between the generations. In addition, the child spirits acted as tricksters deliberately attempting to con unsuspecting people to partake of their food and hence become indebted to them. Their presence was the occasion for much laughter.

If domestic visits of the little trumba were occasions for joking and play with kinship and age transformations and transgressions, for the hosts themselves they were times for sanctioned regression to childishness, giggling, and much silliness. The trumba made a point of selfishness, rendered explicit in the comedy, but eventually transcended by their acts of kindness, such as feeding the actual youngsters of the household. In fact, Kalu's visit may have been designed in part to cheer up Mohedja's niece. Adults, in turn, were very fond of these children who appeared in their midst and treated them with generosity and good humour (often better than they treated actual children). Kalu's timing may have also been affected by the fact that Mohedja had been complaining for some days how tired she was of eating bananas; moreover, Kalu appeared the day after the cat had stolen the fish put aside for supper.

Events like this demonstrated the quality and multiplicity of ties people had with each other and the way lines of intimacy were laid down. Mohedja felt comfortable enough to host Kalu, knowing that she had the support of her family and friends. The child spirits often came to cook and play together and showed camaraderie.[1] Despite the public joking, there was a highly intimate quality to this kind of lowered inhibition.

Although of course I never reached the degree of intimacy that Tumbu had with her, Kalu referred to Tumbu, to Mohedja's eldest son Ali, and to me each as brothers (*anadahy*; male cross-sibling). That is, in contrast to most men, we were all identified as supportive male kin who were not sexually threatening. As noted, men entered this category when they provided the child spirit with a meal. Kalu placed me in this category ahead of the fact, in light of my relations with Mohedja, my intimacy in the household, and the awkwardness that would have ensued had lunch been withheld from me. This committed me to holding a feast for Kalu in turn, which I did some nine months later.

Other men were not only threatening but threatened by the little trumba. Mohedja once described an incident which she referred to as extremely embarrassing. Her little trumba cooked a chicken and offered some to a young man who was passing by. He did not know enough not to accept the food and after he had eaten Kalu made a terrific fuss, following the man home to his mother's, crying, and saying he had eaten her food and she wanted to be reciprocated. His mother (a friend of Mohedja's) gave Kalu some rice and a chicken. Mohedja raised the chicken, which had many offspring. All of them belonged to Kalu and were ultimately cooked by her.

Towards men who were not "brothers," the spirits displayed a precocious sexual interest. On the one hand, they described themselves as afraid of sexual advances, while on the other, they joked coyly and aggressively at men's expense. On one occasion, Kalu interjected that Tumbu's younger brother had done something or other she did not like and declared that she would "pinch his penis" if he tried it again. "That will stop him; if one attacks a man anywhere else, they pay no attention!" she said. Tumbu laughed in response.

While thus alluding to the battle of the sexes more generally, at the same time, the child spirits contrasted potential sexual relations, characterized by an uneasy material exchange and lack of complete trust, with the solidarity and generalized reciprocity (in Sahlins's sense) ideally characteristic of relations between brothers and sisters. What this meant in concrete terms was that the strength of a marriage like Mohedja's and Tumbu's was based precisely on the degree to which elements of siblingship were brought into the conjugal matrix. What was expressed over and over between Tumbu and his wife's spirits (and between Mohedja and her husband's spirits) was a relationship of mutual trust. This sibling-like quality was not unique to Mohedja and Tumbu's marriage but characteristic of a significant proportion of stable conjugal unions in Lombeni, whether or not cohabitation with spirits was directly involved.

The play of the child spirits both reflected and set up reflection upon relations between the sexes in general as they were established in May-otte at the time. In brief, a woman's sexuality was understood as her resource and something she transacted with men in return for mate-rial goods (labour, food, cash, or commodities). In contrast to North American morality, no self-respecting woman would sleep with a man without some expectation of material return. The marital relationship also partook of this model of exchange. The precocious interest in sex, and yet also the fear of it, expressed by the child spirits referred, I think, not only to sexual desire per se or to internal conflict about it so much as to anxiety around its deployment so as to receive fair return. Salient in peoples' minds was the desirability for a girl to balance sexual and material exchange in such a way that she could retain her virginity for her first marriage and use her sexuality to ensure security thereafter. In this direction lay social honour, self-respect, and material well-being for a woman, but the temptations from men and their wavering com-mitment to the exchange process were troubling. It was no accident, I think, that a number of divorced women who were having trouble find-ing and keeping a husband in the rapidly changing marital economy of the 1980s seemed devoted to the child spirits risen in their friends. It was likewise no accident that all the child spirits and all their hosts were female. The spirits were also expressive of a kind of feminist solidarity.

There was another side to the little trumba that deserves mention. In addition to serving as a means of regression and a vehicle for per-formance of domestic comedy, the child spirits had a particular place in the hierarchy of trumba. They were sometimes called the offspring of the senior trumba and Kalu herself was sometimes referred to as the daughter of Kos Vola, but they appeared as well to retain the memory of stratification in the Sakalava polity and to evoke the female slaves asso-ciated with the monarchs. Thus, when the little trumba rose, they did so not only to play but also to work. The reason Kalu offered to fetch water for Musy Matwar has to do with the fact that Musy was the leading trumba medium in Lombeni and host to Ndramañavakarivu, the most highly regarded senior trumba in Mayotte. Musy was well respected by the women of Lombeni Kely, yet she was a poor and aging widow; like their hosts, the child spirits sometimes went to husk her rice or help her with other chores. At the public ceremonies for the senior trumba, the child spirits often ran to do their bidding, washed their feet, and showed other signs of subservience. The senior trumba were pleased and paid them. It should be noted, however, that the hosts of the senior and child spirits tended to be one and the same, the women in question shifting identity over the course of the night and thus being both the givers and recipients of such attention.

There was some ambivalence and uncertainty about the status of the child spirits. One day Mohedja told me they were slaves (*andevu*); on another, she denied this and explained that as children of the senior trumba they merely treated them with the respect due to parents. Foot washing was the custom of their kind of people (*kabila*), she said, just as people in Canada had different customs from those in Mayotte. An implicit but unmentioned aspect of slavery and the frequent allusions to sex was that such women could have been concubines and hence not able to preserve their sexuality.

In associating servitude with childhood, the little trumba preserved a sense of the dependent status of slaves. They appear to exemplify the sort of "slave morality" that philosophers from Aristotle to Nietzsche have understood – one in which they are not free to take disinterested action or make mature moral judgments. In this way, they contrasted strikingly with the dispassion characteristic of Mohedja's senior spirits like Ndramboeny or Mze Nuru. But it is less a slave morality per se than the performance of one. The child spirits are conscious they are acting; they let all kinds of attitudes and intentions tumble out and render them the stuff of comedy. Perspectivism reigns, and because the junior and senior spirits are in the end cohabiting with one and the same host, there is room for exploration and acknowledgment of conflict, ambivalence, contradiction, and playfulness.

The child trumba served to set off a contrast through which the full virtues and responsibilities of free adulthood could be appreciated. The issue here includes, but also transcends, gender. As framed performances, the child trumba marked precisely the moral autonomy and agency of their hosts and reminded them of their autonomy and responsibility to deploy mature moral judgment. In addition, the shifts between voices provided a means whereby ambivalence about bearing the responsibilities of adulthood and parenthood could be subjectively recognized and worked through.

There is one final important feature of child spirits. Whereas the presence of other spirits was evident when the hosts were in trance – and indeed, that was the point – Kalu herself sometimes tried to conceal her presence, to pretend that she was not there, in order to fool her interlocutors and potential victims. In other words, the spirit was pretending to be the host, Kalu performing as Mohedja. So, whereas Kalu's presence was predicated on her differentiation from Mohedja, she sometimes pretended that she *was* Mohedja – a pretence that eventually had to collapse if Kalu was to be recognized. This comedy was in effect a kind of meta-commentary on possession from within possession itself.[2]

Kalu first entered Mohedja when she was nursing her second daughter, Mariam, in the early 1950s. Mohedja's mother did not have a little trumba, although they were present in her day. Mohedja explained that the little trumba (*trumba madiniky*) made you sick upon entry. But they gave their names the first time they rose and immediately stopped making the host sick. They came in conjunction with senior trumba and often turned up during the ceremonies of the big spirits. Having been in active possession by a child spirit in such a big crowd, the host was embarrassed afterwards when she reflected on what her behaviour must have been like. When the cow for the major ceremony was slaughtered, the little trumba came to collect their share of raw meat and carried it back in their clothing, "like children," and getting themselves and their clothing all bloody.

Tumbu said that when Kalu first entered Mohedja, she rose frequently in order to talk to him. She also worked very hard in the fields, so hard that Tumbu felt sorry for her. They would be clearing land, Kalu at a terrific pace, until Tumbu asked her to leave so that Mohedja could have something to eat. After the meal, Kalu rose again and worked hard. Mohedja said she suffered a lot from this – afterwards she would be exhausted. The intense labour ended with the harvest. Tumbu then gave Kalu a large basket (*vurohu*) of unhusked rice. Over many years, he offered her a chicken and rice from her supply in the granary whenever she turned up.

Then, one year when Kalu asked for her bushel of rice to be set aside, Tumbu regretfully told her he could no longer afford to give her so much and said that instead she should come and take from the common stock whenever she wanted some. Kalu insisted on the basket, Tumbu refused, and so she stopped coming so frequently. Soon she was hardly visiting him at all, appearing only at ceremonies or on days when someone offered to feed her. In 1976, she become active again once I invited her for a meal; she liked to make friends.

I do not know what lay behind this shift in the fields. Perhaps it had to do with lower rice yields, greater household expenses, and the increasing encroachment of the cash economy. Perhaps it had to do with Mohedja's age and Tumbu's concern for her welfare. He said that Kalu's visits were a nuisance to Mohedja, both because they left her in some pain and fatigue and because of the potential embarrassment. Perhaps Mohedja and Tumbu had simply outgrown this kind of relationship. Finally, it was possible that Kalu's demands were simply getting out of hand. Like small children, these spirits did not always know when to stop asking for things (as I was shortly to experience for myself); perhaps this was why Tumbu had to be firm.

Questions of property were always at issue so long as the spirits were understood as distinct persons. Thus, in 1985, Kalu was incensed when the chicken she had received from one of Mohedja's sons-in-law was eaten by the household. Mohedja put aside another chicken as Kalu's. When Mohedja had to kill this chicken as well during a daughter's wedding feast, Mohedja remarked that Kalu would be very angry when she found out. Mohedja said she would have to find her another.

In 1993, Tumbu emphasized again how hard the child spirits worked. Kalu would sweep, put water in the bathing enclosure, husk rice, wash laundry – in effect, do all the housework and then work in the field until Tumbu begged her stop. She would be tired! But you had to give her a chicken and rice to cook. The child spirits were also very sociable and would call their friends to cook and eat together.

While drawing on a host's psychic resources, their inner memories or qualities of immaturity, the little trumba were not a direct, unmediated expression of them. As a class they had qualities pertaining to a particular phase of psychic life. Yet this does not mean that inner needs or essential personal immaturity determined the emergence of the little trumba. They were first and foremost stock characters and as stock characters they drew on general psychic resources and qualities. In evaluating the psychological state of any given host, we have to consider many more factors.

In Mohedja's case I would note, first, that the child spirit was but one of many spirits by whom she was possessed. Second, Kalu was not necessarily the spirit she favoured. Third, over the course of her life the proportion of time she was possessed by Kalu relative to other spirits declined. Finally, as people in Mayotte themselves observed, there was a good deal of variation in the way different hosts were possessed by one and the same spirit.

The child spirits were lascivious. When Kalu rose in Mohedja she performed a complex play of furtively avoiding men and breathlessly describing her fear of them, yet simultaneously attempting to trap and trick them. She said she was afraid of men's penises yet referred often to them. Yet her behaviour was too childish and droll to be seductive. At a ceremony in C— we observed Kalu rise in another woman where her behaviour was quite different. She pursed her lips, made kissing motions in the air, squirmed, and wriggled her hips. Mohedja was sitting next to her, possessed by Ndramboeny. This grandfatherly figure immediately turned to Kalu and warned her of the men present, but Kalu ignored the advice. A few days later, after Mohedja had been visited by Kalu as well, I asked about this. She replied that the same trumba acted differently in different people, based partly on the character of the host. In addition, she said, it was a matter of the astrological "fit" or balance, that is, whether the *nyora* (astrologically established "character") of the host was compatible with that of the trumba. If it was a good fit, everything would be calm and there would be no untoward behaviour.

Kalu herself explained that here at Mohedja's the atmosphere was good. In other people, conditions might be uncomfortable and so the trumba would act up and behave differently from her host, as was probably the case with the woman in C—. Kalu's expression of ease suggested that Mohedja's portrayal was positive. The relations among the various persons in her social configuration were harmonious. For Mohedja, performance as Kalu was playful in the best sense of the word; her regression was comfortable and good-humoured rather than forced or over-determined. What was apparent was a kind of joyous flexibility and openness rather than compulsion or psychic conflict.[3]

Tumbu's relationship with Kalu having peaked in intensity some time before I first arrived in Lombeni, much of what I know about Kalu comes from her relationship with me. During spring 1976, I saw a good deal of her. I enjoyed Kalu's visits and the humour and warmth of our relationship. Moreover, Kalu was often an excellent source of information because she could speak with the knowledge of a spirit but without having to maintain the authority or propriety of an adult. For example, when I was sponsoring a trumba ceremony for another woman, Kalu advised me it was prohibited (*fady*) to purchase the liquor on a Tuesday or Thursday. But, she added, it would not weaken the medicine and since no one had told me about the prohibition, I could ignore it. She, Kalu, would keep quiet and it wouldn't harm anything. This illustrated the attitude of servant spirits to the demands of the senior ones, both a form of resistance and an expression of their own lack of prohibitions.

I had mentioned a couple of times to Mohedja that I wanted to offer Kalu a festive meal (*festa*) and eventually did so. One Friday morning, although Tumbu wanted to be off to distill his ylang ylang, he stayed around long enough to set things up. He caught two chickens and arranged three bottles of soft drinks and a loaf of bread I had purchased. Although Tumbu loved bread, he refused my suggestion that he take half for himself. He brought out 4 kg of rice from the granary, lit the incense, and called Kalu. When she arrived, he showed her the ingredients and asked if there was anything else she needed. When she asked for onions and spices, Tumbu immediately pulled out some cash and sent a young daughter to the shop. Tumbu then left for work and Kalu went off to Mohedja's sister-in-law to call her small trumba to join her. They then tried to coax other women. One laughed and asked what were they doing coming to play in a period when there was so much work to be done. The two child spirits played and cooked, giggling together and joking with family and passersby. They ate well and fed their hosts' children. Kalu dumped rice in her lap, saying it tasted better eaten from there, and then wondered whether the owner of the clothing (Mohedja herself) would be angry at their dirty condition.[4]

That evening a young man came over and gave Kalu two eggs which she had asked him to find and which she then gave to me. He sat and joked with her. Kalu teased him, saying she knew he had been out hunting for tenrec (hedgehog, a forbidden food) the previous night. He was astonished that Kalu knew about it and said the little trumba must really go about at night looking for food.

My commitment to Kalu did not end with sponsorship of the feast. A few weeks before my departure after the initial year of fieldwork, Kalu rose one night in Mohedja and told Tumbu she wanted to talk to me. So, they arranged for her to return the next evening after dinner. Mohedja sat on the bed and began to go into trance. There was a lot of coughing. She put her left leg up on the bed and stroked her calf for some time. When Kalu arrived she at once complained that the elder trumba had held her back. They were stopping her because she hadn't asked their permission to visit. Tumbu had to ask them to let Kalu through.

Kalu said she had heard there was going to be a large trumba ceremony (*rombu*) and announced that she wanted me to buy her an outfit for it. She explained that Mohedja was always angry to see what she, Kalu had done to her clothes; to avoid this she wanted clothing of her own. She requested a headcloth (*kishaly*) and body wrap (*saluvaña*) and blouse. She and Tumbu estimated this would take seven metres of cloth.

Kalu's next proposition was that she would accompany me to town to make the purchase, or rather, that Mohedja would go and she, Kalu, would rise in the shop. When I reminded her that she was afraid of strange men, she replied that she would keep her presence quiet. She added that she rose in many people in town as well. I was a bit annoyed since this was an unexpected extra expense. I had been planning to display my generosity on parting by surprising Mohedja with a new outfit and found my plans pre-empted. I was also still unused to the fact that people expressed close social relations by demanding things of one another and suspected, to the contrary, that she saw me merely as a source of goods. I accepted with bad grace when Kalu refused to back down. At that point Kalu talked about other subjects.

After I left, Mohedja came out of trance and Tumbu told her about the arrangements. The next day I changed my mind about the day I was going to town and asked Mohedja whether we had to tell Kalu about the change in plans. Mohedja wouldn't give me a clear answer and said it was up to me to decide. I said we had better call her since yesterday, when I had asked whether she would make Mohedja sick if I didn't buy her the cloth, she had said yes. Mohedja expressed no surprise about the cloth but said she didn't know why Kalu insisted on accompanying me to town. She said she would return later so that I could call up Kalu.

Tumbu then came to see me. He expressed no surprise about the cloth either and said that he had already supplied each of Mohedja's other trumba with their clothing; only Kalu remained without an outfit of her own. The clothes sat in the trunk in a corner of the house when the trumba were not present. Mohedja could only use one of these outfits for herself if she lit incense and asked permission of the owner. Thus, the clothing was rarely worn; on the host's death it was passed on to the person who cohabited with the same spirit. Mohedja and her mother each had separate outfits for Kos Vola though at the time they shared her silver-trimmed ebony staff.

Tumbu added that since Mohedja and her trumba had the same taste, Mohedja herself could accompany me shopping. He said that Mohedja was embarrassed at the thought of Kalu rising in public in town. Furthermore, the clothing could be bought just as easily in the large neighbouring village. He concluded there was no reason to call Kalu just to change the arrangements.

A while after Tumbu left, Mohedja came again to my room. I began to speak normally to her and then noticed she was holding her cloth over her mouth and looking at me peculiarly. The cloth over her mouth was a gesture Kalu used when she wanted to pass people anonymously. My visitor was not Mohedja but Kalu. Kalu acceded to the change of plans I put to her. She agreed that Mohedja could choose the cloth. Her only concern was that she be the recipient. I said I wanted her to lend the clothes to Mohedja as well. Kalu replied, "Absolutely not, especially because Mohedja always complains when I borrow her clothes" [and dirtied them with food or blood]. She said that if I wanted Mohedja to have new clothes, I could buy her some as well! I realized that not only was I losing, but I was also probably out of place and just acting cheap. When Mohedja came to, and I explained our plans, she expressed astonishment at learning that Tumbu and Kalu had each said that she and the trumba shared the same taste in clothes.

30 May 1976. For three nights in a row, Kalu had been pestering Mohedja in her dreams because she hasn't received the clothing that I promised her. [In fact, it was only on working through these notes that I realized she must have wanted the outfit for a trumba ceremony we had recently attended in another village.] Kalu thought it was Mohedja who was putting her off. The first night Kalu accused her and took her to trial in front of the senior trumba, where she had her throat squeezed. The next two nights Mohedja just saw Kalu crying. So this morning we went to S— to buy cloth. Mohedja chose white material with clusters of flowers and bought separate cloth for a blouse and skirt. Kalu hadn't asked me for the latter, but Mohedja said she had told her. The trumba did not rise in the shop but Mohedja said we should show her the material before it was sewn.

That night, as Mohedja sat on the bed, Tumbu called on Kalu to rise. Mohedja started coughing and Kalu again complained that the adult trumba were getting in her way. She made her usual comment that perhaps I couldn't fully understand her when she thought she spoke so well (thereby drawing attention to her childish language). She was shown the material, and after giving it barely a glance, thanked me profusely. She said she was the youngest of all the trumba and compared her age to one of Mohedja's granddaughters who was then around five. In fact, she stayed at the same age and had been present for years and years. Tumbu remarked that perhaps she had been around forever; he remembered her possessing someone when he was very small.

Kalu then said she wanted to write a letter to my mother. I was very surprised and laughed. Kalu replied quickly that she wouldn't do it if I didn't want her to, but I said I would be delighted.

Mohedja did not dream of Kalu during the next few nights. Kalu reappeared a few days later and dictated a letter to my mother. It was in the same standard format of greetings that Mohedja herself used.

That same evening, Tumbu took the opportunity to inform Kalu of the recent death of his niece. She had suffered from a post-partum psychosis and many curers, including Tumbu, had been brought in to try and help her, but without success. Because she was young, feeling ran high and there had been a good deal of anxious quarrelling during which someone had accused Tumbu of harming her. This was the first time I heard him feel sorry for himself or bitter about what had transpired. Speaking to Kalu seemed to be a context where he could let down his defenses. Tumbu vented his full resentment towards the man who had accused him of undermining the young woman's cure. Kalu in turn provided Tumbu with sympathy and full agreement.

A few moments later, the Grandfather (Ndramboeny) replaced Kalu and asked Tumbu how the children were doing. He replied that they were all fine except for Mariam who had been suffering from a fever. As Ndramboeny announced he was leaving, Tumbu quickly asked whether Mariam's illness was just what it appeared to be or whether there was something else to it [i.e., sorcery]. The trumba replied, just a fever.

Tumbu had greeted Ndramboeny informally rather than with the normal phrase of respect. I was surprised and asked about it. Tumbu replied he didn't have to speak formally because Ndramboeny had risen in a woman rather than a man. Ndramboeny did not object to this remark. Tumbu laughed and explained that the spirit was his *rahalahy*, his male friend/brother; after all, they were both married to the same woman. The trumba laughed at this too.

By 1992, Mohedja said that she was embarrassed to have Kalu rise. Kalu had not come in a long time and might show up, but Mohedja no longer wanted to call her voluntarily. Her grandchildren were now old enough that they would laugh at her and tell her what had transpired when Kalu was present. The grandchildren said it was she, Mohedja, doing those things, but it was not her. Before, no one had reported back. Her own children would not have made fun of her.[5] Moreover, Kalu no longer had her own chickens. And by this time, Kalu visited Nuriaty, and most of those active with child spirits were Nuriaty's age.

The child spirits were called selfish but actually played with the concept. When Kalu feasted in Nuriaty, she brought Fantas to Mariam's and Amiaty's children. At first, she said they were Kalu's grandchildren, as Kalu had cohabited with Mohedja first. When I queried this, she called them Kalu's younger siblings.

Fanimbaly, the Kakanoru

Kalu came most frequently to play and work in the fields during the time when Mohedja and Tumbu were attempting to build a life for themselves through subsistence cultivation. In those years, Tumbu began to acquire land and engaged in the heavy and somewhat lonely work of clearing it in order to plant more cash crops, mainly ylang ylang. Clearing land appears to have been sensed as a kind of appropriation from or violation of its previous inhabitants. It was during this work that Tumbu encountered one of these inhabitants, a forest-dwelling kakanoru, and began cohabiting with him.

Kakanoru are small humanoid creatures who could sometimes be glimpsed directly in the forest. There were said to be many kakanoru in Mayotte and they lived in Madagascar as well.[6] Many people mentioned having seen one. They were found in the bush, especially near rivers. Mohedja saw one once in her youth, the height of a four-year old but broad, dark skinned, with hair to the ground, collecting freshwater shrimp from a stream. At first, she thought it was a naked woman. When kakanoru rose in a host, they required it be in pitch darkness.[7]

In 1975, I heard from a young man that if a kakanoru made friends with you he might bring you money or warn you if the government were after you for some reason. Likewise, he could give you medicine that would make a storekeeper forget you had not paid for the goods you took. Once a man who had befriended a kakanoru was woken by the noise of the kakanoru carrying in a large chest, which might have been filled with something valuable, like money or clothing. His mother lit the lamp to see what was going on and the kakanoru fled, taking the treasure with him. In return for his friendship, one gives a kakanoru milk and sweet bananas.

Tumbu began to be bothered by a kakanoru as he was looking after his cattle and beginning to clear trees on the property that he purchased on behalf of his brother. This was a dark and densely forested place and Tumbu often worked alone. Tumbu had been collecting undergrowth to feed the cattle that he kept there. He took a nap around noon and saw in his sleep a creature approaching him, a short child-like figure wearing shorts and a red shirt and hat. He watched him approach until the creature saw him and jumped in surprise. The creature asked Tumbu why he was keeping his cows there and told him to leave. Tumbu replied in his sleep, "But where else but in the bush (añala) should one keep cows?" "Ahh," he replied. At that the creature turned and left. Tumbu awoke startled and looked around to see whether anyone was spying on him or his livestock. The cows were eating peacefully. Tumbu was not afraid and then he began to laugh. "Was that a kakanoru?" he asked himself. People said there were kakanoru here in the forest and, well, he had just seen one!

On the second and third days, he saw him again in his sleep. "Let's be friends," the kakanoru suggested, "Let's arrange things." After that he saw the kakanoru often.

Tumbu purchased a smaller second property where he and Mohedja planned to grow rice and other food crops. There was a large tree and a spring at the bottom of the slope. Mze Nuru rose in Mohedja and warned Tumbu that before he began clearing the land he needed to attend to the proprietor (tompin) and to leave some milk, eggs, and honey there for him. Tumbu was told to then go to sleep, and he would see whether the owner was satisfied. He took a small pot with eggs, honey, and a little milk early in the morning and placed them in the large cavity by the tree. He addressed the proprietors saying he had not come to fight, nor to argue, nor to shout, but only to produce food for himself and his family to eat. He asked them not to bother him or his children and promised to continue to bring them food. He never saw the spirts and went ahead and cleared the land for planting but left the large tree standing. And "thanks be to God," the land proved fertile, and everything they planted there – bananas, manioc, rice, taro, pineapples – flourished. Every year, he left eggs and milk for the proprietor. And so they all did well. As he told me years later, "We came to an agreement and have been together since."

During the period when he was establishing his fields, Tumbu dreamt that he was walking naked through the village from his mother's house. He was very embarrassed and tried to cover himself because people would see him as a bad person. (It was shame not at his exposed body but at the negligent or blatant act of exposure.) The dream recurred, and it was only later that Tumbu realized that it signified his cohabitation with the kakanoru. Kakanoru wore no clothes but had long hair that served to cover them.[8]

Eventually the kakanoru rose. Tumbu ignored his request for a ceremony. Then one day when he was alone deep in the forest looking after his cattle, he felt someone pin his arms and he struggled until he fell into a hole. He came out dizzy and arrived home in a bad state. Tumbu became very sick. He was not bedridden and could still work most days, but he ached all over, especially at night when he could feel his body churning (*neñin nakahy mandeha*). This was like the advent of his patros. He called upon a curer to pick the right medicine. When Mohedja applied the medicine, the creature rose and immediately darted into a dark room, so that Mohedja knew at once that he was a kakanoru.

Tumbu explained that each kind of spirit had its own kind of incense. Depending on which kind he lit, the spirits knew whom he was calling and so the others stayed away. However, the kakanoru occasionally rose mischievously when *uban* incense was lit for the patros. "It is their system," Tumbu chuckled.

> *30 May 1976.* Tumbu told me that when he wanted the kakanoru to come to him in his sleep he had to go sleep in the dark half of the house or put out the lamp (people usually slept with a small kerosene flame burning). The other night, the kakanoru rose and told Mohedja he wanted his full treatment; he had been promised this some time ago. As a result, the kakanoru was making Tumbu sick. Where? In the body (*añatin neñin*). Treatment required a sheet under which to inhale plant medicine. The kakanoru told Mohedja he did not want to invite guests or have a party. They anticipated he would give his name on receiving the medicine. Tumbu also informed Mohedja's trumba of his plans. He had seen a curer in S— who would conduct the inhalation. Now it was only a matter of getting the money together.

The installation happened later in 1976, after I had left. It was a simple matter of inhaling medicine, with no public ceremony. After that he was no longer troubled, and he saw the kakanoru every night in his sleep. He used to come often and even Mohedja saw him. By the mid-1980s he rarely appeared. The kakanoru's name was Fanimbaly. He appeared as a fundi (curer) but, said Tumbu, was not as accomplished as the patros.

I asked what Fanimbaly looked like. He had a human face, but not of anyone in particular, nor always the same face, and he was often covered by long hair so as to be unrecognizable. All kakanoru were short like children, but with adult features and long hair that could reach the ground. They spoke through their nose and their left arms were stronger than the right. They drank milk and liked to eat sweet bananas (*ansasaka*, which in Mayotte are very small) as well as sugar and coconut. Mohedja once told me that Fanimbaly was crippled and could not walk.

In March 1976, sometime after Tumbu had completed the installation ceremony for Mze Marwan in his cousin, she had a dream in which a kakanoru approached her and said, "Let's go to X" (the location of the plot of land Tumbu had first purchased and where he had first encountered a kakanoru). The kakanoru told her to bring along some sweet bananas and said he meant no harm; he meant not to cohabit with her but only to visit. She declined because she was sick at the time. But she explained that this kakanoru was Mze Marwan's friend and showed up in all Tumbu's former clients who cohabited with Mze Marwan. He was, in fact, the same kakanoru who cohabited with Tumbu. The proof of his identity was the request for sweet bananas and the place he wanted her to visit. Tumbu told me he did not know whether the kakanoru lived at that spot, but that it was when he first began cultivating there that the kakanoru started to cohabit. Since that time, he had come to own the field outright.

By 1995, the kakanoru had more or less left Tumbu, shifting to his cousin. But Tumbu said that he could still see him, even in daylight, but far off.

Chapter Fourteen

Later Arrivals: Maimuna, Rasua, and the Spirit of the Maulida

Three more spirits came to cohabit with Mohedja after my first year in Mayotte. The first was another patros, this time a female, who arrived sometime before 1980. The male spirit of the Maulida arrived around 1984, and the final trumba, Rasua, also female, between 1985 and 1992. The latter two spirits were kinds that were "fashionable" during that decade, that is, coming to cohabit with several people in Lombeni and neighbouring communities. I briefly discuss Mohedja and Tumbu's situation in 1980, 1985, and 1992.

In some ways, gaining new spirits could be likened to having children, bringing new persons into the household. As in childbirth, their arrival was not without some pain. And just as Mohedja had wished for contraception and to be done with giving birth to children, so she wished she could stop the arrival of new spirits.

Mohedja said she was fed up with new arrivals and yet she succumbed to them and managed to do positive things with them. The new spirits were not as active cohabitants as the earlier ones and did not rise as frequently once they were installed. Yet each had significance for Mohedja and her relations with others. The new spirits danced blissfully at their respective ceremonies. Maimuna especially shows Mohedja at a point of equanimity. Despite the trauma associated with the onset of each of these spirits, there was a sense of a new phase in the life course and of beginning to age gracefully.

I have argued that the arrivals of new spirits are not random and their identities not unmotivated. But nor are they fully determined. Spirits must conform to the genre of which they are a part, and they are socialized to develop trustworthy relations with their hosts and members of their host families, but they also maintain some autonomy, some unpredictability. They hold responsibility for their actions, and they speak in their own voice.

Maimuna, 1980

I first heard of a female patros in 1980. One evening in July, Mohedja told me she had given birth to a daughter since my last visit. She would have given birth at the clinic, but her labour had been too sudden and light to get there in time. Mohedja was sick, with swollen breasts, and they fed the baby with a bottle. The baby died nine days later, in the early evening, but Mohedja continued to suffer with a painful neck, back, and breasts. She grew very sick and went to the clinic, where she received injections and medicine.

Mohedja was sick for over a month. Finally, she went to an astrologer who diagnosed a spirit and provided medicine. As she was inhaling the medicinal steam, she was actively possessed. They called for Safy, a younger male patros fundi to talk to the spirit. The spirit rose and shouted but would not speak except to announce her name – Maimuna bun Zakariya. Only those who were present knew it. Hearing it once she left trance, Mohedja realized from the name that the patros was female (otherwise there were no special signs of gender among patros), but she did not know then whether Maimuna was old or young.

I asked Mohedja why they had not called either Mze Nuru or Mze Marwan during her sickness. She replied that when one is ill one forgets things, and just goes looking for an external fundi. I think, in fact, that a fundi at some arm's length is necessary, both in order to have a more objective perspective and for public acknowledgment and legitimation of the new spirit. In the same way, a psychotherapist would not go to herself or her partner for treatment.

The second time they called Maimuna with Safy present, the spirit began to speak, saying she wanted a small cake and a red cock in the meantime and would ask for other things later. The spirit requested Mohedja's brother, Samba, and his cohabiting spirit Mze Rihu as her fundi. But when Samba visited, Mze Rihu rose and declared that Samba lived too far away to serve as the curer. He said that Tumbu (who also cohabited with Mze Rihu) should oversee the treatment. Maimuna had not returned since and Mohedja ended by saying she hoped she never would. She complained that the spirit would likely make a lot of demands.

The night following our conversation, Maimuna spoke to Mohedja in her sleep and said she would not request her public annunciation ceremony (*azulahy*) until I returned to Mayotte another time. Mohedja explained, as I had told her, that I might never come back. In that case, said Maimuna, she would not require a ceremony at all.

13 August 1980. One evening about a month later, as I was planning to return to Canada, Mohedja spontaneously went into trance. At first, I wasn't sure;

I talked to her normally and she replied. Then she again became distant, yawning, gazing absently towards the wall. Maimuna rose. She was very uncomfortable and said the other spirits were inhibiting her from entering properly. She confirmed there would be no annunciation ceremony until I returned. I agreed to sponsor the ceremony if and when I returned and asked Maimuna for assurance that she wouldn't make Mohedja sick in the meantime. She agreed to the condition. I joked that if I were a long time coming and she wanted her ceremony she should bother me. Maimuna then mentioned two villages from which she would invite people for the ceremony. Maimuna drank from the bottle of cologne I'd brought the spirits and then offered me some. I refused. She splashed some on me, gave Tumbu a drink, and then complained he had taken too much.

Tumbu asked for advice concerning the household and Maimuna told him to recite a *fatiha* the day before their new house went up. He could do it on his own. Maimuna left, replaced by Mze Nuru. Both spirits wished me a safe journey and said they had risen in order to say goodbye.

Tumbu asked Mze Nuru why he was angry with him; he hadn't risen in a long time. Tumbu said he was taken aback (*kushanga*). Mze Nuru retorted, "You know why." Tumbu entreated the spirit to tell him and said he wasn't aware of having done anything wrong. The following day, Tumbu confessed that he was upset that Mze Nuru was angry. They had been very good friends and he used to rise regularly and always warned Tumbu of impending trouble. But, Tumbu said, it was less bad to have a patros angry with you than a trumba; an angry trumba harmed people whereas an angry patros just remained silent. He added that Maimuna was not a good person; she had caused Mohedja much pain. She first entered when Mohedja had a swollen breast and kept her very sick for a long time. Maimuna had been nasty, but he admitted she was better now that they had established a relationship.

Once again, a spirit arrived to make her ill, but in fact turned the adversity of illness (and perhaps the loss of the infant) into something positive, socializing the forces of illness and asserting control over them. This is a kind of self-strengthening.

Maimuna, 1985

I returned to Mayotte in 1985, together with my wife, Jackie, and our two-year old daughter, Nadia. Tumbu told me twice, once on our arrival at the airport and then a couple of days later, how well he and Mohedja were getting along. They discussed household expenses with each other openly; Tumbu kept checking with Mohedja to answer Jackie's questions about the costs associated with the house. Tumbu often told

Mohedja about his day when he got home, and they talked late into the night together in their room next to ours. Tumbu was very solicitous that I not overtire Mohedja.

I was mindful of the promise I had made to Maimuna and eager to have the opportunity to participate in the production of an annunciation ceremony but decided to wait and see if Mohedja brought it up. Mohedja was complaining about a new spirit that had made her sick in the meantime (about which see below). She explained she could not hold the ceremonies for Maimuna and this spirit concurrently because the latter wanted a performance of a Maulida for its ceremony.

Her daughter Nuriaty interjected to ask who Maimuna was.

Mohedja replied, "The spirit that bothered me when I gave birth and Safy treated me." To everyone's amazement, Maimuna had not risen since the time we had talked five years earlier in 1980, nor bothered Mohedja in the meantime. Maimuna's silence had been so complete that Mohedja's adult children had forgotten about her. And yet, her presence had remained latent, and she reappeared and recalled our agreement once I returned. In effect, Maimuna had been "parked" until my return.

Mohedja's adult daughters were taken aback and tried to convince their mother not to hold a patros ceremony, saying it would be embarrassing at her age for Mohedja to dance and carry on in public. I said that I did not want to break my word to the spirit and that it was up to Mohedja to decide whether to go ahead.

As they were about to celebrate the wedding of their daughter Amiaty, Tumbu asked me to postpone discussing the ceremony for Maimuna until the wedding was over and Mohedja was less tired and preoccupied. Incidentally, he also reminded me of my obligations to the child spirit, Kalu.

Finally, after three months had passed and the wedding was successfully celebrated, I asked Mohedja whether we should call Maimuna. She said that she was still too busy and to wait a couple of days. Five days later, mindful that our departure from Mayotte was approaching, I told Mohedja that she was responsible for telling me when to call Maimuna. She said we would do it that very night, and so at 8:30 p.m., when Tumbu had finished supper, we invited Maimuna.

When Maimuna rose, she overrode Mohedja's daughters and insisted her ceremony be held. Preparations began, I took lots of notes, and Maimuna danced blissfully among her fellow patros at the celebration. However, Mohedja did demur on maintaining Maimuna's dietary restrictions, saying, "I'm prohibited so many foods already, what would there be left for me to eat?" Maimuna was willing to compromise on this.

The motivation for the arrival of any given spirit is complex and multi-stranded, and I do not want to overplay my significance, but certainly Maimuna's presence and actions were connected to mine. Through Maimuna, Mohedja offered me the gift of sponsoring and seeing a ceremony from the inside, as it were, much as I was offering her the gift of sponsoring the expensive ceremony, something usually subsidized by a spouse or grown children, that Maimuna's arrival had rendered necessary. As such, it helped confirm and deepen our relationship. I like to think that Mohedja was asserting her participation in my research, that I was doing it *with* her, rather than *on* her. I like to think this as well with respect to Tumbu.

The fact that Maimuna was female may also be relevant. Tumbu laughed, reflecting on how Maimuna only rose in Mohedja when I was around and otherwise was not heard from. He once referred to Maimuna as my friend, in reference to the ceremony I sponsored. And an unrelated spirit practitioner also assured me that I would be well protected by the spirit for having sponsored her ceremony.

However, Maimuna's original arrival had nothing to do with me. She had first appeared before my visit in 1980, in the context of the death of her infant and her own illness. Moreover, the fact that Maimuna had been absent during my own absence had less to do with me personally than with the fact that I had committed to sponsoring the cure; Maimuna could not have progressed in my absence and complaints would not have done her any good if I were not around to initiate the treatment. There were also other strands to Maimuna's identity. She was said to be a sister of Mze Marwan, hence thickening connections with both Tumbu and Nuriaty, who each hosted him. Mohedja had also used the occasion to reach out to her older brother and to Mze Rihu, as well as to Safy, as fellow healers. Maimuna's presence also connected her to other hosts of the same spirit.

I had the sense of a finely articulated sense of control and of common interest between host and spirit. I wrote that it felt to me that Maimuna was Mohedja and Mohedja was Maimuna. The separation between them was a social fiction, while internally there was a strong identification. Throughout the course of Maimuna's embodiment and ceremony, there emanated Mohedja's inner strength.

The Spirit of the Maulida, 1985

Despite her evident love for and dependence upon some of the spirits with whom she cohabited, Mohedja was clear to state that she would have been happier to live her life without them. She remarked regretfully on how many spirits she had and said that was why she was always getting sick (*chafaka marary*).

15 October 1985. Shortly after the ceremony for Maimuna, we were talking about the women who had appeared in a state of possession for the first time during the event. Reflecting on how easily the young women had become actively possessed and begun dancing, Mohedja said ruefully that although she saw that some people's spirits just rose and played during spirit parties, she herself had suffered at the arrival of each new spirit. Darwesh didn't enter her because he liked her but because he had been sent to take her life (*rohu*). Perhaps all her other spirits came because they themselves wanted to. Kos Vola was the only one who didn't make her sick when she first entered. She mused that perhaps she was born with Kos Vola.

I asked about her Maulida spirit (*lulu ny maulida*), the most recent spirit at that time to emerge.

"Stop, enough already!" (*Bass, kiass!*) "I pray that he's gone home." (*Amin izy nandeha mody.*) Like the others, the Maulida spirit made her very sick. "When he arrived last year, my whole body hurt (*neñin jaby narary*), I was sick to my stomach (*narary kibu*) and vomited from evening to dawn. Baba ny Nuriaty [Tumbu] removed a sorcery packet, but that wasn't the cause. He prepared a *singa* [Qur'anic passage written in soot and dissolved in water] to drink, but that didn't help either. Eventually I didn't even have the strength to raise my head. They say that at dawn the spirit rose. After that I was able to rest a little. They followed the spirit's instruction to fetch Dady Musy [Musy Matwar, the elderly medium in Lombeni who treated spirits of this kind as well as trumba] to bathe me and give me medicine to drink. We called up the spirit twice since then. The first time he rose, he said nothing, and left again. The second time we called him, he didn't come at all. Let's hope he has gone for good." However, she suspected that things with him were not yet finished.

In speaking this way, Mohedja was denying that the arrival of the spirit was the product of her own desire or agency, a fact reinforced by his reluctance to speak. It may be that most of her spirits appeared as a response to, or in the context of, physical illness. She was right to contrast this with people who took on possession more lightly. On the other hand, this does not explain why she maintained relations with the spirits long past the original episodes of illness. It does not explain cohabitation.

The new spirit was of a kind called *lulu kimaore* because they spoke an older version of Shimaore and were ancient inhabitants and rulers of Mayotte (Maore), in parallel with the trumba of Madagascar. Like the trumba, they manifest a historical consciousness and, given the history of Mayotte, they were all Muslim. They were often referred to as spirits of the Maulida because they rose in their hosts as they were overcome by the beauty of the Maulida Shengy, a collective recital in song and dance of a poem praising and recounting the life of the Prophet.[1] This was a performance in which Mohedja loved to participate. The popular dance is performed by women; here male spirits rose in female hosts and danced alongside them. Not only did these spirits rise in performances of the Maulida that took place for social, religious, and aesthetic reasons that had nothing to do with spirits, but they also requested a performance of the Maulida as their own initiation ceremony. People without spirits would come to dance as well. Performances of the Maulida thus transcended distinctions between Islam and spirit possession, showing their complementarity rather than contradictory nature.

The individual lulu kimaore who resided with Musy and one other woman in the village was popularly known as Bako Maore. Mohedja did not know his real name. She thought perhaps this was who she had as well since the spirit had asked them to call in Musy. However, he spoke in a deep voice, indicating he was a "grandfather" (*dadilahy*). She dreamt that she was led by an old man (*dadilahy*) into the forest to a place called Handre and they talked together. (Handre was associated with the past of Mayotte; there was a tomb in the bush considered sacred and people who cultivated there maintained the ancient prohibition against working on Wednesdays.) It was after the dream that she fell sick, though, she said, perhaps the family did not believe it at first because she was up and about. One night, on going to bed, she had bad pains in her stomach. She came out and vomited several times. Tumbu removed a *sairy*. At cockcrow, as Tumbu told her later, the spirit rose and announced his presence, saying he had not been sent by anyone (i.e., as sorcery) but came simply because he wanted to. Mohedja speculated that perhaps it was because she had done *fihavañana* (fictive kinship) with a woman who had a spirit of this kind. She had been sick since, but when they had called the spirit earlier, he had not risen. She said she would be delighted if he left and never came back.

When the spirit eventually did rise, he turned out to be an old man with no teeth. He liked cakes and betel nut, the latter a habit that had since died out in Mayotte. As a Muslim, he did not drink liquor.

Note Mohedja's insight here: the arrival of the new spirit was not an attack on her person but a means to articulate the development of her relations with other women in the community who cohabited with spirits of this kind. Some of these women were the ones with whom she had been in conflict with over Ali's marriage; that conflict was definitively over and indeed at the time she fell ill, Mohedja's daughter Amiaty was engaged to a man from that kin group. That was the wedding that preceded the ceremony for Maimuna. Mohedja herself loved performing the Maulida and now, during some moments, she could be transported so that the spirit danced in her place.

~

In 1992, I found Tumbu and Mohedja tired. Each said they no longer had the energy to go to the fields. Tumbu had made the hadj to Mecca sometime during the seven years of my absence and he returned quite depleted. Tumbu said he no longer worked but only prayed, ate, and sat with his family. Every time he went to the fields, he felt sick.

When I first arrived, Mohedja greeted me in an embarrassed high-pitched voice. She brought me into the house, away from all the curious onlookers, and asked me whether I would prefer to wash in hot or cold water. After supper, she proposed that she and I together with Tumbu go up to a somewhat removed and empty house where we could talk in private, just the three of us.

I was quite unprepared when Tumbu launched into a long account of his pilgrimage and unable to grasp most of it. But the gist was that he had become separated from his companions and guide. As a result, he missed their flight home. Tumbu said he put his hands in God. All he wanted was God's blessing (*rady*); God would do what he liked with him. He was not afraid of being molested by people in Mecca, but he was full of regret and anxiety at losing the others. This was his *hadj*. But he added that the hadj was difficult for everyone because there were so many people, all crushed together. If God had wanted him to die on the hadj, he would have taken him then and there.

Tumbu concluded that anyone who fully performs the hadj will return depleted; many people who go to Mecca pay others to do the hard parts. If you perform them all yourself, it takes a lot out of you. This is especially because of the heat; the sun shone so strongly!

Tumbu was most impressed by the huge numbers of people. "You'd think they must be everyone in the world. But once you are there you lose all fear. We're all Muslims. You'd die if you fell in the crush, but people aren't afraid."

Mohedja was distraught when the group from Mayotte returned without him. Crowds gathered at the house, speculating about what had happened, and she could not get away from it. Everyone was crying and asking God for mercy. The veranda was full of the curious. Many assumed Tumbu had died, and one rumour even said that his hand had been cut off. Every day, Mohedja told me, you heard something new, as if the villagers had been there and seen for themselves. And when Tumbu did return, people came by to see whether his ear or his hand were still there. Mohedja sighed at the way "people are trouble" (*ulun belu mashaka*).

During his absence, one of her nieces went to a diviner who said Tumbu was missing because he had failed to call up the family spirits to tell them he was leaving for the hadj. She advised Mohedja to call her spirits to ask forgiveness. Mohedja acknowledged they had not advised the spirits, but thought the rest was untrue: why would spirits be angry that Tumbu was following what God wanted? She reflected that "once you go for divination there's nothing that won't come out." In any case, she said, she had too much grief to call the spirits.

Mohedja did go on the first day for divination at Tumbu's uncle's. The senior astrologer said he was not dead and would return after some days. To her immense relief, this was what happened.

Tumbu must have had extreme resilience and sagacity to manage the trip home with little money and only his minimal French to go by. He brought gold watches for himself and Ali and several items of clothing. However, he was quite sick, with a high fever. Happily, Tumbu had made friends with a male nurse's aide who had recently married into the village. This man, whom Tumbu referred to as a grandson, looked after him. He assured me that Tumbu's blood pressure and heart were fine. He assumed Tumbu had suffered heat stroke and he applied ice packs for the high fever, gave him a shot of pain killer, and assured he received a tetanus vaccination. Tumbu told me he was sent to the clinic where he received multiple injections in his legs and both arms, though he did not return for the subsequent doses once he no longer felt sick. The nurse's aide was also supplying Mohedja with eye drops. Tumbu and Mohedja were both very pleased with their new relation and happily took the medications he offered. I was pleased too, but worried that there seemed to be too many medicines floating around without prescriptions and follow-up.

Tumbu said that he was now ill only when he exerted himself. He had built and furnished the houses of his two younger daughters before going on the hadj, and having completed his parental obligations, he felt he could now let his children look after him. At the same time, Tumbu confessed himself both saddened and taken aback not to be working. He had always worked and, while his grown children now helped, it was not the same thing. He wished he had a motor vehicle that would render easier access to his fields.

Mohedja and Tumbu said they had seen neither Darwesh nor Mai-muna since their respective ceremonies and that they had not wanted to call them. Mze Nuru came of his own accord whenever he saw some-thing that needed addressing in the family or when someone came with a problem. Mohedja said, "We're used to Mze Nuru, and he doesn't trouble us." She thought the other spirits were probably still there in the background and indeed Maimuna did rise once to treat a client who asked for her specifically.

Tumbu's spirits rarely appeared. But once, after visiting someone in the hospital where he tasted the potato gruel they served the patients, his patros rose and said, "Never give me hospital food!"

Mze Marwan rose in Tumbu only if he were called for, but he rose regularly in Nuriaty. Tumbu said he no longer engaged in much cur-ing. On his return from Mecca, he began to teach Nuriaty how to extract sorcery. He called her to watch him as he performed extractions and then oversaw her doing so. Eventually, Marwan rose in Nuriaty to announce he would extract sorcery from her and Tumbu began to send her his clients. Only the kakanoru remained somewhat active in Tumbu. The kakanoru was currently advising a man who had worked in the metropole in telecommunications and wished to be relocated back in Mayotte. Somehow, the creature from the bush was able to help the cosmopolitan client.

Mariam was jealous of her sister. She said jokingly that Nuriaty had taken the inheritance (*mwaratha*) of all the spirts who cohabited with each of their parents. She said perhaps the spirits preferred Nuriaty because she was larger; Mariam herself was too thin, with not enough blood for the spirits to eat.

Tumbu said that removing *sairy* was hard work and he was only pre-pared to do it for close kin. Clients often failed to give him anything in return and extraction made him sick. He said, "I've become too old" (*Rohu nakahy fabakoku*). He approved of Nuriaty's decision to set a fee of 100 francs per extraction (whereas in the past their clients gave only what they felt like). "Everything costs now," he said. On the other hand, he said he did not mind accepting much less from people whom he knew had little to spare.

Rasua

17 June 1992. Mohedja had been sick all night, complaining of pain in her left eye and temple, and then her whole side. Tumbu was taken aback and early that morning went to his uncle the diviner to see whether he should take her to the clinic. But the diviner said it was "someone in her head who was angry with something Mohedja had done." As he had to leave for the fields (he *did* still work!), Tumbu asked Mariam to call up the spirit and find out. Mariam in turn asked Nuriaty to join them.

Mohedja had seen in her sleep that it was her latest spirit, Rasua, who was bothering her. Nuriaty declared it was an inopportune day of the month to call the spirit and they should wait for the fundi from S— who would come on Friday. But sometime after Nuriaty left, Mariam disregarded her older sister's opinion, lit incense, and spoke over it as Mohedja lay on the bed listening. Mariam asked the spirits what the trouble was. "If we've bothered you, rise and tell us. We don't even know if the source is a patros or trumba. Even if it is not from you, we are asking for your help." She spoke for several minutes before putting the incense away.

The new spirit had arrived sometime between 1985 and 1992. Mohedja said she had been very sick. She felt as though she had a stone in her chest and coughed up blood. But the French doctor said he could find nothing wrong. He gave her a thorough check-up and, after two visits, told her not to return. He said she wasn't sick, but she knew she was. That was why she didn't want to go to the clinic now; the doctors cannot see the illnesses produced by trumba.

Tumbu added, "These illnesses are like the wind; they blow but can't be seen. Have you ever seen the wind? But you can feel it!"

The doctor refused to give her any medication. The nurses did give her something when she asked, but it had no effect. Sometimes when she ate, the food just didn't go down. She coughed and the food came up together with blood. She was sick like that for four years. Local medicine didn't help either.

They didn't realize the problem was something else entirely.

After a long period, she returned to the clinic, but the doctor still didn't see anything. She went many times, to different doctors but none of them saw the disease. By the time they realized it was a trumba she had already suffered a good deal. She called in Musy Matwar to treat her. "That trumba was a bad one."

I asked, "Didn't the other trumba tell you what the problem was?"

"Maybe they don't like to reveal the secrets of their fellows."

The day they were finally able to call up the trumba, "everyone cried. It rose in a bad way, as if I had lost my *rohu* [as if I had died]. It was really bad."

The spirit told them what it needed for treatment. At that time, they had to postpone arrangements for Mwanesha's wedding as Mohedja was so sick. It was a new kind of medicine and the trumba instructed them what to do. They put Mohedja on a platform, higher than the table. She climbed up and was bathed in the medicine there.[2] After the medicine, they requested permission to hold the wedding before the *rombu* (main ceremony), but the spirit refused, and they had to hold the *rombu* first. Only once Rasua gave her name could they hold the wedding. Once the *rombu* was held, most of her symptoms dissipated. Her body had been hot, day and night, and even now her body still felt hot all the time.

Mohedja continued, "I've been sick with trumba and patros, but nothing like this. I was so thin, people were shocked. For four years I lost blood, from my vagina as well, blood like at childbirth. I couldn't fast during Ramadan." Once she received a shot and medicine at the clinic, but it would have been better not to; she felt faint and had more bleeding. She thought it was the end.

Mohedja said the spirit had arrived of her own account and not as the result of sorcery. She didn't know when it first arrived, only that she was very sick, and in a way different from all previous spirits, and that all her goats died.

And so, the family held a large trumba ceremony (*rombu*) for the new trumba. The trumba had requested Ndramañavaka, a senior spirit in Musy Matwar, as her fundi, but Musy professed herself too old and sent her to Mohedja's cousin in S— who also cohabited with Ndramañavaka. In fact, this cousin had been Mohedja's client, and had held her own *rombu* under Mohedja's supervision. The trumba announced her name as Rasua but Mohedja referred to her as a Betsiuku. Although I did not know it at the time, Betsiuku (Betsioko in Malagasy orthography) refers to a cemetery in Madagascar where recent generations of the northern Sakalava royal clan have been laid to rest. Their trumba were very common in Mahajanga and they had begun to be so in Mayotte as well. They were members of the royal clan who had lived during Merina and French conquest of northwest Madagascar and hence had colonial traits. They entered their hosts quite dramatically, as though emerging from under a burial shroud, and many of them required accordion music and straw hats. Wet kaolin was applied to the parts of the body that were involved in their original demise; in Mohedja's case, this included her hands, face, feet, and legs.

When Tumbu returned from the fields, he declared he wanted to call Rasua that evening. He was very worried about Mohedja's condition and felt badly she was suffering so much. He did not want to wait for the cousin from S— who had enough on her plate. Mohedja listened silently as Tumbu asked me whether it was better to call the spirit before or after dinner. When Nuriaty and Mariam lit the incense, Ndramboeny rose and said forcefully that Mohedja's suffering was their fault.

They all looked down at the ground and Tumbu nervously lit matches as Ndramboeny lectured them. "Didn't you see that Mohedja's feet were swollen when a goat was tied nearby? You all committed an error [*kosa*] and then everyone just went about their business [*kula ulun niaraka shiguliny*]. And then you blamed us [i.e., the trumba]. But it's not our fault, it's yours. If you did the right medicine, Mohedja would be cured."

Tumbu: "But we don't know which kind of medicine."

Ndramboeny: "Sure you do, everyone does."

Mariam: "Up on the platform?"

Ndramboeny: "No!"

Tumbu: "We want to speak to her [Rasua] directly; to get the truth."

Nuriaty brought in a white plate with a large, silver coin, white clay, and a white sheet. The coin was a French 5-franc silver piece, dated 1873, that belonged to Kos Vola and had been passed on from Mohedja's mother. Though I didn't understand their significance at the time, such coins were central to trumba practice in Madagascar.[3]

Ndramboeny: "We can't drink for each other; we're not the same ancestry [*razaña*]."

Tumbu: "So we are asking the other spirit to come."

They lit more incense. Ndramboeny held Mariam's baby upside down by his feet (a common act on the part of spirits) and then asked for a mat to recline on. Mariam took her baby back and the spirit stretched and began coughing. Nuriaty moved the incense out of the way and covered Mohedja's body with a sheet. Mohedja fell flat on her back as Nuriaty fluttered the sheet over her face and applied white clay to her forehead and raised her head to apply some to her mouth. Mohedja's body shook under the sheet. Tumbu shut the door to keep out the children. They lifted her up and held her head to drink from the white plate and tied a new white cloth around her waist, as an older woman dressed in a similar white cloth entered.

The transition was dramatic, but it was one I would see many times over once I began fieldwork in Madagascar. This was the way that trumba who were buried at Betsiuku emerged from under their shrouds and were installed in their hosts.

The spirit sat on the mat shaking her head from side to side with a cloth over her face. They applied the white clay paste to her feet. The spirit took the silver coin to rub more paste on her face and asked to have her cloth belt tied very tight. Once dressed, she sat on the bed and began to drink a Fanta that Mariam brought her.

Only then could she begin to speak. She told me she was a young unmarried woman, named Rasua, the daughter of Malala and Rafutsy, and that her *rombu* had required an accordion. She then instructed me to fetch her an additional Fanta. She answered some questions concerning Mwanesha's current illness, but the gist of her conversation was that contrary to what Tumbu had said, it was not her [Rasua's] fault that Mohedja was sick. She wasn't trying to be difficult; she couldn't help being prohibited (*fady*) goat. And when she, Rasua, was sick from proximity to goats, so was Mohedja, since they shared one body. Nor was it Tumbu's or their children's direct fault that there were goats and goat shit around, so there had been no reason for her to rise and complain. She just suffered.

Rasua then prepared to leave. She drank a bit more of the water infused with white clay and Mariam put more on her head, arms, and legs to ease her transition. She lay back on the bed and the sheet was held over her. She hiccupped and moaned and Nuriaty reminded them to undo the tight belt. Mariam massaged her as she groaned in pain and then sat up, Mohedja again.

An hour later, Mohedja said she was feeling much better, less heavy. She said she had swept up goat feces and should not have. Since the arrival of the trumba, she and Tumbu had not been able to raise goats; when they tried to do so the goats died. But her children living adjacent raised goats. When Maulida neglected to feed Nuriaty's goats, they had wandered into Mohedja's kitchen shed, eaten some morsels, and left excrement on the ground, which Mohedja had subsequently swept up.

If her daughters ate goat at their houses, it would not bother her, but she could not eat from the same dishes until the smell was gone, some days later. All the spirits from Betsiuku, of whom several had arrived to cohabit with villagers, were prohibited goat. One neighbour developed mouth sores whenever she ate goat.

Now that the spirit had explained the problem, they had to treat it.

Friday, 19 June. The cousin from S— arrived and set about bathing Mohedja with three buckets of water in which medicinal leaves had been mixed and strained. Honey, cologne, and a piece of gold or silver was added to each bucket. Mohedja sat on a chair on the back veranda, her body smeared with white clay and the buckets were poured over her as Amiaty rubbed her.

They went inside and the cousin sat facing Mohedja over incense, calling Rasua to say that if the family had made a mistake, it wasn't intentional; we were now asking for pardon and washing away the pollution. Mohedja was tended by several women; Tumbu sat on the veranda just outside. Rasua entered as on the previous day. Mohedja's cousin then held her leg, saying gently that her trouble would soon be over. She rubbed a gold earring in the wet clay and water and then washed her face with it and massaged her fingers, saying they were washing out the bad.

Rasua asked how we all were.

"We're fine."

Rasua: "Aha."

"We've come to ease the restrictions, right?"

Rasua: "Right."

"We come to ask that our mother get well."

Rasua: "No problem; I've had the medicine."

Rasua then asked the cousin about her own clients. Then she explained that the prohibition against goats wasn't simply to cause trouble but came from her ancestors [applying to all their descendants] and could not be avoided. Mohedja's ankles were swollen when the goats were kept nearby.

The cousin explained that the gold, silver, and white clay purified Mohedja from the restricted substances.

Tumbu then entered and said it was Nuriaty's fault for raising goats close by.

The cousin repeated eloquently that the restrictions were ancestral.

Tumbu said he couldn't force his children to do things, but they had now seen and understood the situation.

The cousin said they should keep the goats elsewhere, and periodically apply medicine. She turned to Rasua, smiling, and said, "Isn't that it?"

They said goodbye and the trumba went under the cloth as Mariam rubbed her back.

At this point, the situation changed. A pair of clients entered the room to seek advice about the forthcoming circumcisions of their sons and the need to remove the restrictions associated with trambuñu medicine from Kos Vola via Mohedja. Ndramboeny rose and gave them elaborate instructions as to how to proceed.

Once the clients had left, Ndramboeny and Mohedja's cousin held a private conversation concerning their respective apprentices or former clients who didn't properly respect or reimburse their fundis. By this time, Mohedja had supervised the ceremonies of several other people with trumba, including her cousin, who now supervised ceremonies on her own, but always brought the proceeds to Mohedja to divide between them. It was a matter of the apprentice acknowledging the master.

In sum, Tumbu had been solicitous of Mohedja but angry at Rasua for making Mohedja sick without telling them what the problem was, what they were doing wrong that she did not like. Rasua replied that it was not a matter of liking or disliking, and therefore of anger on her part, but that she simply could not help being sick from contact with goats.

The next day Mohedja was up, sweeping and cooking again. She continued to apply white clay to her eyes and hands every night.

Rasua acknowledged that her concerns had been met. Since the performance of her *rombu*, she no longer made Mohedja sick deliberately, and once purified of the pollution caused by the goats, Mohedja was well again. When I returned in 1995 (together with Jackie, Nadia, and our then eight-year-old son, Simon), Mohedja was no longer bothered by goats near the house. The only prohibitions were against eating goat or food from a pot in which goat had been cooked. They said that Rasua was now cooperative and no longer objected to the presence of goats.

In 1995, Mohedja remarked that most of her spirits no longer visited. Ndramboeny and Mze Nuru did most of the curing and had effectively displaced the others. Kos Vola still rose for her remaining clients seeking *trambuñu* medicine with her, but Ndramboeny took over this work for new clients. Maimuna had not risen, nor bothered Mohedja, since the ceremony we had held a decade earlier. Rasua treated clients who came to Mohedja with a Betsiuku spirit. Mohedja concluded that she herself was no longer bothered by her spirits. "When I'm sick, I'm simply sick, with an illness coming directly from God" (*Ka marary, marary tu, areting bokan' Ndrañahary*). Since the spirits have all had their ceremonies, they no longer bother me."

Tumbu and Mohedja viewed their spirits with some ambivalence. In May 1976, Mohedja had told me that if she had the chance, she would rid herself of all the spirits she had, every single one. She said they brought nothing but pain and sickness. Tumbu said he would do the same; if the spirits asked for a parting gift, he would even be willing to give them a cow in order to be rid of them. He was prepared to do so even if it meant abandoning his career as a fundi. A person with spirits continuously fell sick because of their quickness to anger and their whims. This was especially true if the cohabiting spirits were themselves fundis; if not, they might leave their host in relative peace.

Mohedja said that any of her spirits could act up at any time. There were times when she coughed for a month on end. This was caused by the spirits and cough medicine only aggravated it. There were times when a spirit simply chose to be angry, and this left the host in a good deal of pain.

These remarks were borne out by the many times I saw Mohedja ill and her symptoms relieved by spirit medicine. And yet they were also belied by the spirits' actions. Tumbu and Mohedja specifically said that the fundis were the worst spirits to have; yet it was precisely these spirits who interceded on behalf of the family and who looked out for their welfare. There were many times in their respective accounts where Tumbu and Mohedja were explicit about this and others where the beneficent intervention of the spirits was merely implicit. Moreover, the spirits' anger could be appeased, they could be addressed, and they could be challenged, their more reasonable requests met, and the others negotiated. Living with spirits was like living with kin and neighbours. Quarrels arose but they were resolved. There was love between people, but also ambivalence.

Mohedja and Tumbu used their suffering, albeit not deliberately, as a way to legitimate the autonomy and disinterest of the spirits, to distinguish the spirits from their own identities, feelings, and motivations. This is the way in which, at one level, possession works. But it is equally true to say that the spirits are a means by which people like Mohedja and Tumbu turn their physical suffering and emotional or interpersonal ambivalence into something meaningful and into something which, in the end, works on behalf of themselves and their families. Cohabitation is a means by which one's own pain works for the welfare of one's children and other consociates. But it also affords a kind of working through and generates equanimity for the hosts.

Probing more deeply, one could also follow the arguments of Herbert Fingarette and others who say that psychic pain is a necessary step for growth, that we cannot overcome our internal conflicts until we expose and confront them. This hurts. But sometimes, in the right people and in the right therapeutic context, this is also the means to transcend them, to leave them behind. I think cohabiting with spirits can do this and I think it largely did this for Mohedja and Tumbu. By 1995, Mohedja said the spirits no longer caused her pain. Instead, Tumbu and Mohedja were soon to face more severe obstacles.

PART FIVE

Final Matters

Chapter Fifteen

Decline, Death, Succession

In 2000, I found Tumbu and Mohedja preoccupied with illness. Tumbu's feet were swollen, and he had no feeling in one of them. He walked poorly with a stick and fell frequently, unable to support himself. Tumbu had been in hospital with two successive prostate operations; somehow, they had botched the first. He also suffered from arthritis, and he had asthma and used a puffer. Nuriaty massaged him with a green plant every morning and Mariam bathed him. Ever since he had returned from Mecca, Tumbu had stopped dressing "like a boy" (i.e., wearing trousers and shirt) and dressed like an adult (*ulu be*) in a Muslim gown (*ankanzu*). But at the same time, he had shifted decisively in social status and stage of life from an elder (*ulu be*) to a frail old man (*bakoko*).

Mohedja suffered from high blood pressure and diabetes. These were called respectively the diseases of salt and of sugar and had become quite common in Mayotte. Mohedja took them seriously; she claimed she could feel the effects if she ate even a little salt or sugar. She could no longer support the spirits rising in her body and did not attend trumba ceremonies. She was too weak and, as she said, she had to look after "my comrade" (*havaku*). During the day she left Tumbu to her daughters, but I could hear them conversing at night, albeit now from separate beds.

Mohedja was also preoccupied with finances. There was an electricity bill due for 600 francs she did not know how to pay. When Tumbu was sickest, they had phoned Mariam in La Réunion and she had returned right away. Maulida called asking for a ticket home as well and Tumbu had to go into debt for it, which he had now paid off with the pension money that came every four months but that was not enough to last them in the best of times, they said. Everyone struggled to pay electricity and water. Water used to be free, but no one wanted to go back to carrying it or to using kerosene lamps. In addition, people kept the electric light on at night. The other big expense was schoolbooks – and the grandchildren also needed snack money and clothing.[1] Mohedja regretted the loss of cash since she had stopped working as a curer.

Ever trying to look ahead, Tumbu had plans to build a house on one his fields and start a chicken farm. By the following year, he had put up a tin house that was used by his daughters when they collected manioc and other products. Tumbu was generally positive about the state of things in the present; he appreciated the changes in infrastructure and all the nice new objects – cars, electric lights, more substantial houses, refrigerators, etc. However, what had been better in the past, he said, was access to food; everyone could eat. Now you needed money to eat. In addition, you could no longer grow crops without irrigation or fertilizer. From the moment children first opened their eyes, Tumbu said, they needed money. "The country has been fixed up [*tany voadzary*]," he concluded, "but we have become poor."

Mohedja wanted to tell me right away about their youngest daughter Mwanesha having been ill, "crazy" (*adala*), she emphasized. Mwanesha had grown gradually sicker after giving birth. By the end of four months, she was manifestly schizophrenic, and this lasted for three months more. They tried all their own fundis but found they needed someone from afar. These fundis too proved ineffective until a local healer finally restored Mwanesha by hiding medicine in her food. Within a few days, Mwanesha reached out to Mohedja and begged her forgiveness (*rady*) for swearing and saying horrible things, insisting the family were poisoning her. For the first month of her illness, she had lived with Tumbu and Mohedja, but then had moved back to her own house and would have nothing to do with her parents, accepting only food that her husband had cooked.

The healer attributed the source of Mwanesha's problems to Tumbu, namely, that he had not given his deceased older brother's daughter the plot he had purchased with his brother's down payment. The sign of this was the fact that Mohedja and others had seen the recently deceased husband of Tumbu's niece in their sleep and even in broad daylight. The healer claimed this to be the source of Tumbu and Mohedja's illnesses as well; she described it to me as like a broken promise. This seemed unfair, as I had repeatedly heard Tumbu remind his children that the field belonged to their cousin and to look out for her interests. Ali herded his cousin's cattle there along with his own and was the one to pay the annual tax, which she could not afford. Eventually it became apparent that Mwanesha suffered from psychosis and during her worst moments threatened violence against her parents. Once placed on anti-psychotic medication, she showed little affect until some years later when the dosage was better adjusted. Her sister Amiaty lived next door and looked out for her children.

It was sad to find people I had known in their prime no longer as capable as they once had been. This extended to Mohedja's brother Asman, who died during my stay in 2000. His final weeks were not without drama. When he became very ill, Asman decided his adult children were not looking after him properly and he determined to move to his kin in F—. His children said he was too sick and should stay put. They told drivers to refuse to take him, but eventually he found a willing driver and made his escape. Asman stayed in the house of a niece in F— and told everyone there that people in Lombeni had not looked after him properly. He even went to the *cathi* (Muslim judge) to make a statement to that effect and to declare that he wished to be buried in F—.

The family in Lombeni were outraged. They asked for him to be sent home, but to no avail; he refused to budge. Eventually Mohedja advised Asman's children to go to F— and, without speaking to anyone, simply scoop him up and bring him home, which is what they did. On Asman's death, the kin in F— were not certain whether they would be welcome at his funeral in Lombeni. One of Samba's sons came with an offering, saying it was from his wife for fear it would not be accepted from him. Mohedja, now head of the family, had to convince him to stay for the funeral. She said the family were no longer angry once they had Asman home again. Two further nephews arrived, asking her forgiveness (*rady*) and anticipating the need for a peacemaking (*suluha*), but Mohedja assured them none was necessary.

One day I accompanied Mohedja to the weekly clinic held by a French doctor, Jean-François. He explained that hypertension and diabetes were caught much later in Mayotte than in the metropole and hence could do more damage. He figured that Mohedja must have gone two crucial years without medication, causing irreversible damage to the kidneys. He suggested it had also affected her brain, which, seeing her sensitive handling of her brother's funeral, I seriously doubted.

Mohedja was prescribed dalfagan for pain and adalat for hypertension. She told me she used to get something stronger that dissolved under the tongue. It seemed to me that her medications could have caused side effects that she had attributed to her spirits. Conversely, however, Mohedja had once claimed that her spirits did not like her taking the medicine for high blood pressure as it made her dizzy. And so she had stopped taking it for a couple of years, much as the doctor had said. The biomedical practitioners should have checked on her and regulated the dose. I also suspect they had not caught whatever medical problems she suffered from in the years prior to 1992 when Rasua appeared.

Tumbu had responded to his deteriorating condition differently. Ali told me that when it first began and he could still walk, Tumbu heard second-hand that his mother's brother, a powerful astrologer, was doing sorcery against him. In a moment of panic, and quite uncharacteristically, he tried to escape to La Réunion (where many people from the village were then living temporarily to access the higher government benefits available there). Without telling anyone, Tumbu sold a cow, went to town, and purchased a ticket for a flight the same day. He set out from town for the airport on foot, in his dirty clothes, but telling his niece, whom he ran into in the central market where she worked. She called home and Ali rushed after him. He found his father on the road, pulled him into the taxi, and brought him home. The implication was that the uncle had made medicine to get Tumbu to set off unthinkingly, whereas Tumbu had seen himself escaping the uncle's clutches. He had no address in La Réunion; it was a crazy thing to do, said Ali. But once Ali brought him home, Tumbu grew worse. On one occasion he saw his uncle approach the compound and stand at the banana trees looking at him at three o'clock in the afternoon. He was convinced his uncle had caused his illness. Ali was afraid to confront the uncle as he could have been attacked as well. Why would his uncle want to harm Tumbu? I asked. Ali said he was threatened by Tumbu's authority and wanted to be the sole leader in the village. When Ali told me all this in 2007, long after Tumbu had died, he was still afraid of the old man.

In 1999, Tumbu made another attempt to make sense of his condition and restore his health. Tumbu announced his sickness was caused by a new patros. He insisted they do medicine to call him up. According to Ali, a new spirit appeared to rise, declaring that he was the cause of Tumbu's inability to walk and that if they held an annunciation ceremony for him Tumbu would be cured. Ali did not believe it; there was no spirit (*lulu*). He said, if you are really a lulu, show it by letting Tumbu walk now. Mariam explained her father's illness as a consequence of his having worked so hard all his life. He had continued with dogged determination to work in his fields and attend to his cows, even after returning physically depleted from Mecca.

Ali said that they had spent a lot of money trying to treat his father. But Tumbu eventually came to his senses and told them to stop and just take him to the hospital. According to Jean-François, whose interest in Tumbu and Mohedja I tried to cultivate, they had never removed the prostate but only scraped enough of the tumour to let him urinate.

He said the operation was too complex for someone of Tumbu's age and condition. Furthermore, at that time the hospital was still under-resourced, and they did a triage. I wondered whether Tumbu's appearance and lack of French worked against him. Clearly, the treatment would have been better in metropolitan France.

In 2000, concerned for Tumbu, I asked whether he should not return to the hospital. Nuriaty was vehemently opposed. Her main reason was his and their shame (*aibu*) at his having to urinate and defecate in public since he could not walk to the toilet. At the time, there were no private rooms or curtains in the wards, and everyone watched everything. Moreover, none of his children had the time to stay at the hospital and care for him.

Jean-François suggested that if Tumbu went to hospital they could tell whether the problem with his leg was phlebitis, but they could not cure it if it was. He admitted that Tumbu had received an infection during their first attempt at scraping the prostate. I repeated Tumbu's complaint of pain in the lower back and down his legs. The doctor now further admitted that Tumbu suffered from prostate cancer and thought this could be the cancer metastasizing. But in any case, they had decided some time ago not to remove the prostate and it was probably too late, even if he and his children could tolerate further time at the hospital.

I had thought I was helping but I was merely discovering what the family already knew. I learned that Tumbu had been told and accepted that he would never recover. I turned to the question of pain management and Jean-François sent over some codeine. In the following years, Tumbu's immobility and pain grew worse, and his care remained a constant strain on the family.

What of the spirits? In 2000, Tumbu observed that Mohedja's trumba rose only when specially called and they never stayed for long. Mohedja no longer conducted *trambuñu* medicine and Maimuna had not been heard from at all. But the spirits continued within the family. Mze Marwan worked as a healer through Nuriaty, and she now managed her practice with a cell phone. Kos Vola, Ndramboeny, and a child spirit were all cohabiting with Nuriaty as well, although they had yet to hold their ceremonies and announce their names. Kos Vola had also begun cohabiting with several of Mohedja's nieces. When the daughter of Samba, whom Mohedja had raised, was given some patros medicine, my venture that she might be receiving Mze Rihu was greeted with laughter. Some years later Mze Rihu, along with several of Mohedja's spirits, was active in this woman's son.

In a quiet conversation, Tumbu told me that Mariam now had a patros, but one who rose infrequently – only when he was very happy or to warn people who were doing something wrong, and never at a public ceremony. When medicine was being performed on a family member, the patros might rise suddenly to point out a mistake or stop the proceedings. Once, when one of Mariam's grandsons was being circumcised, he rose to guide the hand of the cutter. The spirit often talked to Mariam in her sleep, and she would come to tell her father about it the next morning. Tumbu then admitted he knew the spirit was Mze Nuru. The spirit never said so directly, but once when Mze Nuru had risen in Mohedja to treat Mariam, he requested a red chicken (Mze Nuru's color) as an offering. At some point he would have to rise in Mariam herself to call for medicine. But Tumbu could see that he was Mze Nuru. "I've seen it. Her spirit is a strong/reliable one. Mze Nuru is strong/reliable" (*Fa hitaku. Hodary lulu nazy. Mze Nuru hodary*). Tumbu was assured there would continue to be a very strong fundi watching over the family (*mraba*). "Mze Nuru is really strong [*hodary swuf*]."

It is evident from Tumbu's account that Mohedja played a role in ensuring the succession, not least by Mze Nuru speaking through Mohedja to indicate the kind of offering the spirit in Mariam would need. Mohedja herself told me that Mariam was in the process of receiving all her spirits though none had fully risen in her yet. As far as she knew, neither of her three younger daughters or her sons were hosting spirits. Nor had Mze Nuru passed on to any descendants of Malidy Juma (her former fundi).

I briefly revisited the following year (2001). In the early mornings, Tumbu sat on his veranda reciting from the Qur'an and listening to cassette sermons. His daughters told me that the spirits would remain with him until his death but that his old age rendered any medical treatments initiated by them ineffective.

Tumbu had overseen the planting of lychees, a new crop, on one of his plots, and the family continued to harvest manioc and coconuts. Tumbu's two cows, along with those of Ali and other family members, were looked after by an informal migrant from Mwali whom they had befriended. He was responsible but asked for cash rather than calves in recompense due to the risk of being sent home if he were caught by the police. They paid him 500 francs per month.

Mariam had been sick on and off. A spirit rose in a woman in S— telling Mariam that she and her mother should each bathe in trumba medicine to remove inadvertent offenses to the spirits. I watched the elaborate preparations, including crushing fragrant medicinal leaves and adding white clay, the silver coin, rose water, honey, and incense. Amiaty poured three buckets of the medicated water over Mohedja who vigorously rubbed herself. Then Mohedja bathed Mariam and daubed her nose and forehead with white clay, adding lines down each arm, and around her neck, back, and ankles. Mariam drank medicated water from the plate and Mohedja passed the incense around her head seven times as she recited softly. Mohedja then requested all the spirits, trumba and patros, to look after Mariam. The interaction between mother and daughter exhibited their intimacy and Mohedja's acquiescence to Mariam's reception of the spirits.

On my departure in 2001, I was overcome with emotion as Mohedja produced gifts for me to bring home. I knew she was planning a T-shirt for my son, but she pulled out a pair of gold earrings and combs for Jackie, as well as a woman's wrapper and headcloth. She asked that Jackie pose for a photo in the get-up and send it to her. She included a cloth and costume jewellery for our daughter. It was the last time I was to see her or Tumbu.

Mohedja died suddenly 19 April 2004, and eight months later, on 24 December, Tumbu followed, after the long illness that had left him bedridden for seven years. After each death, I was notified by letter. I sent condolences, saying that I might participate in the *mandeving*, the ceremony held sometime after death with a religious performance and prayers to support the deceased. Their children were eager to perform it sooner than later but agreed to wait to hold a joint observance for both parents (as well as on behalf of Tumbu's older brother who had died in Madagascar) when I could return. They did so out of kindness and in acknowledgment of my relationship with their parents. Eventually we confirmed a date. I reached Mayotte the evening of Tuesday, 12 July 2005, as preparations were in full swing. We began the event (*asa*)[2] the following morning and the main acts, including a performance of the women's Maulida, that had been Mohedja's favourite, took place 15–16 July.

Observance of the event was first on my agenda. I understood it as a way to honour and pay my respects to these remarkable individuals but – ever the ethnographer – also as an event about which to take notes (albeit less comprehensively). As both participant and observer – or rather, as observer in both senses of that word – one matter that inevitably arose was the difference in the ways in which my siblings in Mayotte and I anticipated, experienced, and expressed what it meant to separate from and commemorate someone. This was a personal as well as an ethnographic lesson, albeit transcended by a sense of our common grief. Conducting the ritual together brought us closer than we had been before. In truth, I had not had a particularly strong connection with the siblings. But by the end, they took me aside and affirmed they would honour and maintain the bond that their parents had forged – that I would always be welcome there. I have visited four times since.

Mohedja and Tumbu had seven children to reach adulthood. Unlike most adults of their generation, neither of them had children with other people. Of the live children, they had three daughters followed by a son, two more daughters, and a last son.

In 2005, Nuriaty and Haza were each living in the communities of their respective husbands, but Nuriaty retained a house in Lombeni and moved back for the duration, while Haza commuted. By this time there were paved roads and many cars. The other siblings lived in the village, Amiaty and Mwanesha in houses immediately adjacent and Maulida temporarily in the house of the parents. Each sibling was married with children; Nuriaty, Mariam, and Haza were already grandmothers themselves.

In the interstices between our intense efforts to acquire, prepare, and distribute food and cash to the performers and other guests, each sibling took me aside to speak in relative privacy about the occasion of each death. Because the conversations were personal, I realized only after the fact that their recitations were a kind of local speech form. Each account was very precise about details, with dates and times. Nevertheless, the narratives were individual and intimate, and I was very touched that the siblings shared them with me. They thought it important that, as a fellow sibling, I should know the way our parents died; how to do that took the form of a first-person witnessing.

Their responses were shaped by the fact that Mohedja had appeared to be in good health whereas Tumbu had long been in very poor condition. Mohedja suffered from hypertension and the only symptom she expressed was fatigue, possibly exacerbated by her worries. In fact, Jean-François had recently noted improvement and even permitted some salt. Tumbu himself was devastated by the fact that Mohedja predeceased him.

The siblings each told me how acutely they felt the loss of their mother, especially because of its suddenness. They cried a lot and for a long time could not eat. They each described her final morning. She rose, told Amiaty not to make a fresh pot of rice for breakfast as there were leftovers, checked in with Tumbu, and walked a small grandchild up the steep hill to the nursery school (*maternelle*) that now served the village, a strenuous but habitual path.

Ali gave me his version of his mother's last hours, as follows.

In the morning, Mother took a grandchild to nursery school, then went down to the beach to inquire about fish. It was lucky that she didn't die there, in the midst of people. She came home. Father called out from his sick bed, "Who's there?" Mother replied and said she was hungry. She got out leftovers, ate maybe three or four bites, and then collapsed on the veranda and lay unconscious, breathing laboriously. Father heard her fall and called for help, but he couldn't get up himself. Eventually, Father's sister came by, wanting something from Amiaty's shop. It was shut and she called for Amiaty. Father heard her and managed to get her attention. Later, Mariam drove with Mother to the clinic, and I followed on foot. I found Mariam crying outside the room, entered, felt my mother's hand, and realized she was near death. Then I saw her die. I couldn't convince the staff; they scornfully told me to move away but eventually acknowledged her death. She was laid out at home. Father took it very hard; he cried and cried and couldn't understand why it wasn't him taken.

We all grieved heavily. I saw Mother every night in my dreams. It was because I was the only one who didn't cry; I tried to act like a man and held it in. It was the first time I saw death happen.

No one could believe it, especially the people who had talked to her in the village that morning. Everyone thought it must be "Baba of Nuriaty," not "Mama of Nuriaty." Many people attended the funeral. Mother had more people at her funeral than did Father and more money was collected.

A few days later, Mariam provided her version of events.

On Saturday, Mother went to the neighbouring village to ask her cousin to look out for her children, to become our mother. On the weekend, she told me she felt odd, and that no food was appetizing. I suggested fish but she said she didn't feel like fish or meat, that she no longer felt like eating anything. On Monday she died.

On Saturday, when I came as usual to care for Father, Mother said to me, "I feel so sorry for you" (*kuskunia anao ataa*), and began to cry. Mother told me, "No one will care for you, you must find comfort in your own family, your children and grandchildren." She came down to my house later and repeated this. On Sunday, I found her crying and heard again, "I am so sorry for you." I guess it was because I was then the only one still looking after Father and I told her it was God's will.

Mother said she had too much on her mind and had hardly slept the past two nights with worry, mainly over the serious illness of Mwanesha and Father's deteriorating condition. On Monday she rose and went to arrange papers for Maulida's daughter at the nursery. Mother chatted with people about buying fish and returned home. The night before, she had eaten leftovers for supper, not feeling like cooking. Now she was very hungry. Father asked who was there and she replied. He heard her fetch food and sit on the veranda. She ate a spoonful or two and then stood up to get some water. Suddenly Father heard her cry out "*La Ilaha Illa Allah,*" three times and then a thud. He called out to ask what was wrong, had a child hurt themselves? There was no answer. Father struggled and managed to raise himself and by means of the chair to push himself out on the veranda and saw her. He called out, but no one was around, and he banged with his stick. Finally, his sister appeared looking for Amiaty to open the shop.

I had seen Mother on the path to the nursery and greeted her, but I didn't notice her return. Father's sister came and told me to follow quickly but not to run so as not to make onlookers curious. I thought that Father had died. When I got to the house, I found it was Mother; she was barely alive. We sent Amiaty to find transport. She got to the mayor's and said her mother was very sick and needed transport. The mayor replied he had just seen our mother and she was fine. But luckily, he acquiesced. I rode with Mother to the clinic in the next village, where they immediately gave her serum and said if she wasn't better in an hour, they would take her to the hospital. The staff wanted me to leave the room, but I refused; it was my mother! I stood nearby and watched. An hour later, Mother was still unconscious and breathing oddly; after another hour, at 10:00 a.m., she was dead. The doctors wanted to take her body to the hospital, but I refused. What could they want with a dead body? Ali rushed back to the village to prepare, and I brought Mother in the ambulance. We laid her out at home, as Father insisted. She was buried at 3:00 p.m.

I am terribly sad when I remember my mother. We used to talk. I cried a lot after her death.

Maulida told me that he had turned down Mohedja's request to name his daughter after her. On her death, he regretted it and cried a lot. That night he addressed his daughter by his mother's name.

Mariam continued:

Father was on his sick bed for seven years. Everyone was tired of caring for him. I was the only one who kept up regularly. Nuriaty had moved away.

Father told me I was the one who really stuck by him. He said he wished he could simply die like everyone else. Near the end he was covered in bedsores and the stench was bad. Those of us who cared for him slept on the veranda of the shop – me, Nuriaty, and Haza in turns. [Ali had done so until his job as a night watchman prevented him; Amiaty and Mwanesha looked after young children.] At some point, he told me he felt his life force had changed and that he wouldn't last much longer. Father asked to be taken to the hospital in town, but it was difficult to convince the clinic staff. Father confided that he didn't want there to be talk after he died that his children hadn't looked after him properly.

At the hospital the doctors criticized us harshly for his bedsores and for not coming earlier. Father lay there many days, barely conscious, taking only sips of water. One day Nuriaty told him she was going to La Réunion to care for a daughter-in-law who had given birth there.[3] He replied with grunts, which Nuriaty interpreted as acquiescence, but I found ambiguous. We took turns spending nights with him. Late one night when Haza was on watch, he opened his eyes and asked where he was. The hospital, she said. He asked about Nuriaty, where she was. Haza told him, La Réunion. "Ah," he said. It was during Haza's rotation that Tumbu died; she phoned and told us to prepare at home for the corpse.

We cried when Father died but not as much as for Mother. Her death was so sudden, and she had been a relatively healthy person, except for high blood pressure.

I (ML) said I remembered being told one shouldn't cry at a death.

"Yes," Mariam replied, "In Islam people who cry accrue sin [damby], but we can't help it. God wants us just to utter the Shahada, he has merely taken back his thing [zavatrany]. But we can't help it and we cry."

Father died on Thursday evening and was buried at 8:00 a.m. on Friday. After that, people went to Friday service.

Nuriaty cried during the performance of the Maulida, remembering her mother and how she had died so suddenly. Before dawn, she recounted her version to me, which I summarize here. Mohedja had gone down to see the visiting doctor about a grandson who was ill. She returned home hungry, fetched some food, and then collapsed. Tumbu cried a lot. They had been taking turns looking after Tumbu. She had a ticket to La Réunion to attend to her daughter-in-law's post-natal care (mañapataña) but postponed it. Tumbu then spent a long time in the hospital, barely conscious. He lay there refusing all food and drink with his eyes closed. One day he opened them and asked Nuriaty if she had returned from La Réunion. She told him she had not gone. He told her to go and, because he seemed to be doing a little better, she did. [The doctors were rehydrating Tumbu and preparing to send him home.] A few days later he died, and she could not return in time for the funeral. He was laid out at Mariam's.

In 2007, Ali recalled how sick his father had been; Tumbu's only luck was in having had children to look after him. "He suffered so much that you [Michael] wouldn't have recognized him at the end. However, he never lost his reason." Ali was more shocked at his mother's death; it was so sudden and unexpected. He said he cried whenever he looked at the photos I'd brought.

These narratives were very moving in their circumstantial detail and precision. They described how each death happened (not the "cause," which was a matter for God) as each speaker experienced it. They manage to be both objective and deeply personal, but they were by no means the end of the matter.

~

Tumbu and Mohedja were strong, responsible people. When they were healthy, they exuded quiet confidence and authority; singly and together, and along with the spirits, they affirmed the coherence and protection of the family. But they were overcome by the brute facts of disease. Their adult children had remained psychologically quite dependent on them and now needed to find their own way, including how to relate newly to each other in the face of their loss.

At the beginning, they suffered an absorbing amount of grief. Ali told me they had so much sadness after their mother died that they eventually underwent collective treatment to remove grief (mañaboka hamu). Everyone in the family took the medicine, including the grandchildren. Village elders had to go calm Tumbu and remind him things were in God's hands.

They had also to deal with anger. Not only distraught over his wife's death, Tumbu was in his last years often angry and impatient. Mariam explained this was because he suffered so much: dependent, bedridden, declining, and in constant pain. She would wash and feed him and not respond. But even after death Tumbu remained in pain. Mariam dreamt of him angry. Mohedja's mother, Rae Samba, had been like this too, ill in the afterworld and expressing it through angry dreams to her daughter. The dreams had stopped but the family were mindful they should hold an additional prayer on Tumbu's behalf.

In the period between Mohedja and Tumbu's death, Mwanesha had suffered a relapse and Ali hired a very expensive curer from the Grande Comore to treat her. Eventually Ali admitted the curer's efforts came to nothing, but Mwanesha gradually improved with medicine from the hospital.

Following Tumbu's death, the family remained troubled, with much illness. And so Ali engaged another expensive healer from a distant village. Shortly before my arrival in 2005, they held a prayer (*badry*) to ward off aggressors and underwent treatment to remove an evil spirit (*shetwan*) that had been making everyone sick and that was lurking somewhere around the parental courtyard. These acts were conducted secretly at night in their fields. They sacrificed a black cow belonging to Ali and a red goat of Amiaty's. Ali explained proudly that there were very many prayers; family members were circled in incense and bathed in water in which Koranic verses had been dissolved. Each of Tumbu and Mohedja's children and grandchildren and their spouses received the medicine, and they sent the sanctified water to those who could not be present, including grandchildren in France.[4] They ate the meat during the night and were home before dawn. The secrecy was imposed by the healer so that the sorcerer would not know they had removed the evil spirit; otherwise, s/he would send another.

Ali worried they would continue to suffer because Tumbu had always known what to do to protect them. The previous year, his vanilla had blossomed well but then birds ate virtually all. Tumbu told him to remove sorcery from the field and the birds left. But now when they had problems there was no one to provide advice or remedy. Ali lamented that Nuriaty, who was a healer, had lost interest, and Mariam, an aspiring healer, did not yet know enough. For her part, Mariam was insulted that Ali disregarded her. She went along with the treatment in the fields but had little faith in Ali's judgment and suspected that the expensive healer was a charlatan. Mariam's criticism of Nuriaty is evident in her account of Tumbu's death above.

The *mandeving* (memorial ceremony) certainly had positive effects. The siblings cooperated in an activity that was important to all of us and that went well. They told me they were getting along (*kuparan*). Before her death, Mohedja had stated that she wanted her possessions to be distributed and used. Following the fortieth-day ceremony (*arbain*) of her death, her children divided her clothing and household items among themselves equitably, including an informal migrant from Mwali whom Mohedja had recently taken in as a daughter. Later they did the same with Tumbu's goods. Use of the fields was easily shared. Mohedja and Tumbu's house belonged to all the siblings. They decided to let the youngest son, Maulida, use it until he was able to build his own house. The house plot was reserved for one of Ali's daughters whom Mohedja had raised since she was small. In their last years, she had cared for her grandparents and done the cooking and cleaning. The siblings agreed she deserved something, and they all wanted to do this for her. Eventually the house would be torn down and Ali would build her a new house on the plot. In the meantime, following Mohedja's wishes, the girl was placed in Amiaty's care.

The acute issue facing the siblings was the loss of both their parents. "How can we get by without our elders [*ulu be*]?" they lamented. "Our mother is gone; our father is gone." This sense of unmet dependence was not resolved by the *mandeving*, and it was the source of future conflict among them.

During the *mandeving*, they deferred to several older kin as elders, but they found none of these people reliable enough to stand in their parents' place. An alternative was to make one of themselves parent or elder to the others. Sometimes in Mayotte an older sibling took on the parental role as mother or father to the others. In this family, the oldest sibling (*zuky be*) had, from the perspective of the other siblings, abandoned them. In late middle age, Nuriaty had remarried her first husband and moved to his village. Their two remaining children were delighted but in Lombeni she was widely criticized. Amiaty told me that Mohedja and Tumbu had each begged Nuriaty not to move away while he and Mohedja were so weak. Tumbu said that as the oldest sibling she should set an example. Her further removal to La Réunion during Tumbu's final days and her absence from his funeral added to the sense of her irresponsibility. The siblings felt bereft of their oldest sibling, who should have been at once their parent and fundi.

Nuriaty was, in any case, in difficulty because of her own ill health, the serious illness of her two sons, no daughters to care for her, and no financial means. Mariam was in a much stronger position both socially and financially, with many offspring, several holding good jobs. Mariam was eager to be the parental figure but felt unacknowledged by the others, especially by Ali, and envied by her older sister.

In 2015, Mariam told me that they had held a *fatiha*, a short prayer at which they killed a goat and served milk and fish as well, for their parents every year since Mohedja died. When they attempted to discontinue it, their parents appeared to them (in dreams) and asked them to carry on. They did so, but at the *fatiha* in 2015 (a decade after the deaths) the siblings told their parents that this was the last year, that they could not do it anymore. They asked their parents to understand that things had become too expensive.[5]

Tumbu and Mohedja had not bothered them since, Mariam said, so they must have accepted it. But relations among the siblings had deteriorated further.

Mohedja and Tumbu were gone but the spirits continued to cohabit with the family. The spirits were central to the ongoing tensions, especially between the oldest two daughters. No one had expected Mohedja to die so soon except possibly Mohedja herself. Before she died, she tried to ensure succession of her spirits. At a trumba ceremony elsewhere, Mohedja's spirits had risen and asked a male relative to pass on the message to Mohedja that she should give all their clothing and accessories to Mariam. At the time, Mariam said, she thought this was because Mohedja was no longer interested in trumba matters. In retrospect, the implication was that she knew she was near death.

Mohedja had evidently felt closer to Mariam than to Nuriaty. Recall that for many years Mariam had not received any spirits, but that the parents knew that Mze Nuru would shift from Mohedja to Mariam shortly before her death. This came to pass exactly as predicted. Mariam told me that Mze Nuru first fully rose in her some four months before Mohedja died. That would have been December 2003. Mze Nuru had first risen at home, revealing his identity to Mohedja. He said that as he was not a stranger or newcomer to the family, there was no need to keep his name secret. Mohedja oversaw Mariam's treatment but called in Nuriaty to manage the annunciation ceremony (*azulahy*) at which Mze Nuru gave his name in public. Nuriaty did so, expecting, I think, only Mze Nuru to rise. She was taken aback to find that virtually every spirit who had cohabited with Mohedja made an appearance, one after another, and those who had cohabited with Tumbu announced themselves as well. All this seemed to Nuriaty to put Mariam in the limelight and push herself to the background.

This took place shortly before Mohedja died. There was no time to complete all the ceremonies for either the patros or the trumba and Mariam came to feel as though the spirits were not properly installed. Moreover, she had trouble getting the family to recognize Mze Nuru's presence as robustly as they had when Mohedja was hosting him.

Both sisters were ambivalent. In 2007, Mariam first told me that the spirits had died along with her mother. Then she admitted she had received each of her mother's spirits, except for Kalu, who was cohabiting only with Nuriaty. But Mariam claimed she did not want any of them, that she was too young, and that she did not like the idea of shouting in public. She could spend all night at a ceremony, and they would not rise. If clients asked for any of them, she denied their presence. Mze Nuru occasionally rose at home.

Nuriaty laughed and said too casually that the spirits had all shifted – every one of them – from Mohedja to Mariam before Mohedja's death. Others reported that Nuriaty had been angry that Mariam had "taken" all the spirits, to which Mariam retorted, "I didn't ask for them." No doubt the suspicion that she had "taken" them was behind her stringent denial of interest in them. I suspect Nuriaty was also resentful at her mother's favouritism. Another fundi who was present at the ceremony told me he had observed Nuriaty in tears.

Before her death, Mohedja told Mariam to go to her cousin in S— to complete the trumba ceremonies. She could not practise as a fundi until the trumba had their full ceremonies and announced their names in public. Mariam had no time to follow up while Tumbu was still alive. Then the trumba rose and said the first phase had not been completed correctly because Mohedja had been ill at the time. The cousin redid the first ceremony, but the spirits complained she made some mistakes. When Mariam sought help to arrange the following ceremonies, the cousin kept putting her off. Mariam was surprised and increasingly frustrated. After three years of this, she told her cousin she would find another fundi. She was Tumbu Vita's daughter, after all! Tumbu had told her that if someone said they would cure you but kept putting it off, you should let it go.

In 2005, once the memorial ceremony had concluded, I asked Mariam if I could pay my respects to the spirits. She was agreeable but uncertain how to proceed. She asked me how I used to call them in her parents. She said they would not be angry or make her sick if I did not greet them. I said it need not be all the spirits, that I could greet one on behalf of all. She asked me whom I most wanted to see, and I replied Mze Nuru.

Mariam decided we should include Amiaty, who would know how to reach the spirits, but otherwise she wanted us to be discreet. Amiaty and I were to go to Mariam's house separately so as not to raise attention. We met in Mariam's back room and Mariam closed the shutters. We sat on the clean linoleum floor where Mariam had placed incense, white clay, cologne, and Kos Vola's silver coin. I observed Ndramboeny's spear and Kos Vola's staff standing in a corner behind a cupboard. Amiaty instructed me to place incense on the brazier and I clumsily invited Mze Nuru. Amiaty smoothed and rounded out my speech, saying there were no outsiders here, that we all knew each other (*tsisy mugyen, jaby fañkahay*). Mariam reached for more incense, closed her eyes, and slowly rubbed her hands.

A spirit entered without a lot of commotion. Mariam shuddered and opened her eyes, looking slightly different, with a different smile. The spirit shook our hands in greeting, introducing himself as Mze Nuru and naming his parents and home village. He asked how I was and wished me well. I said I hoped he would continue to look after the family.

In response, Mze Nuru began to complain, saying the family "don't believe this is really me and so I no longer care (*za fa tsy shiguly*)." I had provoked an emotional outburst. Mze Nuru went on at length how Mohedja had never had to tell the family to call up the spirits and people did so of their own accord, yet they no longer called the spirits in Mariam. And Mariam herself didn't care, so why should he? They didn't even call him for their big event, the memorial (*mandeving*) for their parents, not even simply informing him about it over incense. So why should he rise and help them or send them messages? "They trusted (*kuamin*) that I [Mze Nuru] was present in Mohedja, but not here [in Mariam]."

Amiaty tried to defend the family and appease Mze Nuru, saying that in Mohedja the spirits had just visited of their own accord. She said that Mariam pushed the family away when they wanted to ask for the spirits. Mze Nuru responded, "We are never informed of anything anymore." He compared their efforts to my own, saying that I had persisted until Mariam gave in to our rendezvous.

Mze Nuru explained that when he realized that Mohedja was soon to die he rushed into Mariam and pushed through the ceremony, so that he would continue to be there for the family. But then they did not call upon him. He mentioned the expensive ceremony Ali had organized with another curer, bitter that the cohabiting spirits had been displaced by a stranger. The family performed a major treatment but never called him. And now Mariam's children were ill. Mze Nuru began to cry.

Amiaty listened, somewhat nonplussed; she admitted that they had ignored the spirits, but she insisted they did trust them. And she added that they really needed the spirits' help. Their eldest sibling (*zuky be*) had gone elsewhere and in the absence of their parents they lacked guidance and did not always do the right thing. They would rectify this. She added that the spirits used to rise in Tumbu and Mohedja and look after their children and grandchildren so that they did not suffer. "But now we suffer, with no elders left in the family."

Mze Nuru retorted that they treated his presence in Mariam as a joke; no one took Mariam's cohabitation seriously. Ali had even gone to ask the advice of a spirit in a different host.

Amiaty then requested help with her sons; they rarely showed up or spent time with her and they had started smoking. Mze Nuru retorted that Amiaty had forgotten he had told her to do some medicine to cleanse her compound of sorcery. She had been told to do this back when Tumbu was still alive.

The litany of complaints was interspersed with moments of ease and laughter between Amiaty and Mze Nuru. In closing, he asked for a gift. I placed a five-euro note in his dish and he used the opportunity to point out to Amiaty how depleted his dish was.

The conversation showed that Mariam had failed to consolidate her authority as a host to her mother's spirits and, specifically, how resentful she or they had been that Ali had gone ahead and organized treatment for the family without consulting them. It was as if there was a competition between the two siblings as to who would take charge. While Amiaty assured Mze Nuru they would do better, she could hardly make promises on behalf of her siblings. Nuriaty was aggrieved, Ali mistrustful, and the other siblings not very interested. Amiaty also failed to mention that she herself had consulted a spirit in another host.

Mze Nuru withdrew and after a brief transition another spirit rose, shook hands, and announced himself as "Lord Unknown" (Ndramtsihay). Because Mariam had yet to conduct the full trumba ceremony and slaughter a cow, he could not give his true name, Ndramboeny.[6] He moved up to a chair and said he knew I had wanted to see more of them than just Mze Nuru. He asked after me and then continued in the same vein as Mze Nuru: the spirits did not visit because they were not welcome.

Amiaty replied, "But we *do* care. And we are suffering. Our children get sick."

Ndramboeny retorted, "You don't even leave incense. But we continue to help you anyway." He said the family members no longer loved them. He too mentioned the event that Ali had organized without informing the spirits or asking their help. He described the family as having become reformist Muslims (*jaula*) for whom spirits were *haram*. And there was fighting among family members, even in this house. Ndramboeny was concerned that Mariam had not bathed properly after the pollution from attending her daughter's childbirth. The spirit cried, holding his scarf to his eyes.

He then turned to Amiaty and said, "I pity you; I pity all of Tumbu and Mohedja's offspring." Ndramboeny continued that since Mze Nuru's ceremony not one of them had called any of the spirits now cohabiting with Mariam. Mariam herself had said they were dead. "What are you waiting for?"

During the conversation, one of Mohedja's grandsons had walked in. He saw what was going on at once and sat quietly listening to Ndramboeny who sometimes turned to him but was more interested in engaging Amiaty. He had his small son with him, and Mariam's youngest daughter had been sitting on the far side of the room listening as well.

Ndramboeny said goodbye, and after a brief transition, Maimuna introduced herself, and declared herself the sister of Mze Marwan.[7] She greeted me and asked me to greet Halidy [Mariam's husband] for her as well. Mariam could have her *kafiry* (non-Muslim) things and he could do his reformist Muslim (*jaula*) thing. But the spirits would stay in the house; they could all get along, each with their own religion (*diny*).

Maimuna then recalled how close she and I had been and told me to bring her food next time, that she was hungry. She spoke briefly with the grandson who was concerned about getting turned down for a job. She then called over Mariam's little daughter, felt her pulse, and told Amiaty to tell Mariam to fetch medicine and bathe the girl for seven days. Maimuna looked into the girl's eyes and asked her if she saw bad things in her sleep, to which the girl replied no.

Maimuna departed and Mariam appeared in some pain coming out of trance. I left for another appointment and presumably Amiaty told her what had transpired. Our interaction had lasted some ninety minutes.

The next morning, Amiaty told me that I had acted like an elder and provided an example for how she and her siblings should proceed. She said that she would be calling the spirits again, that they could not abandon them now, and that they needed the spirits to look after them. Amiaty was looking for guidance and the spirits were eager to offer it. Amiaty concluded that Mariam needed to be less stubborn and not push people away.

I realized that Mariam could not beg her siblings to come either. She needed them to come of their own accord, much as the grandson had done. The spirits were disturbed at having been neglected in Mariam. They had not been told or asked for help about the children's exams or minor illnesses and were insulted not to have been informed about the treatment that Ali had organized or about the commemoration for the parents. All this was a challenge not only to continuity in the family, but specifically to Mariam's legitimacy as an authoritative host when the spirits spoke through her. The spirits made this explicit by saying that none of the siblings "believed" or "trusted" in their presence in Mariam. The point was that family members remained uncommitted to the spirits as they cohabited with her and, presumably, they were ambivalent about shifting their relationship with Mariam from one of sister to family elder. Amiaty was the closest and she showed concern for both the welfare of her children and the feelings of the spirits. She was comfortable with the spirits and not frightened or cowed by them.

I passed on Maimuna's greetings to Halidy. He said the spirits just wanted to be fed all the time. I mentioned what the spirit said about two religions in the house. He said that could not be, there was only one religion. If the spirits were not Muslim, they would accrue sin (*damby*). But he acknowledged their presence and said he did call them up on occasion – though not as much as they liked. He knew that Mariam would become a fundi, but also that she did not want to be pestered by external clients.

An irony that no one mentioned was that Mariam herself was somewhat attracted to reformist Islam, as were two of her daughters, and they had all started wearing closer head coverings when they went out in public.

As for Nuriaty, she told me she was no longer interested in spirits (*fa tsy shiguly kabar ny lulu*) since her mother died. When clients arrived, she turned them away. She did not want to be in active possession (*menziky*) anymore; she was "tired, tired, tired" (*vaha, vaha, vaha*). However, when a niece came to ask for medicine she agreed, saying she would continue to assist family members but not external clients. She was now thinking of the afterlife (*kiyama*). "I don't want to continue, so what can the spirits do about it? I've dropped it all." Nuriaty seemed sad and discouraged and the force of her words betrayed her. But she did not want to reveal what had led her to this.

Nuriaty later added a practical reason for laying off. She suffered from sciatica. Her leg had hurt for some time and the pain medication Jean-François gave her offered no relief. She was hoping to be treated in the hospital in La Réunion but in the meantime could not walk far or collect medicinal plants.

Things continued to unravel. Mariam felt her original treatment had not been correctly performed and went through a year of very troubled behaviour and emotions, which she attributed to the spirits not entering her fully on account of intervention by Nuriaty.[8] At one point, she was so disturbed and even "crazy" (*adala*) that she had to be tied down for the trip to a distant curer. The spirits themselves rose in Mariam and revealed that at the original ceremony, Nuriaty had given them poison (*sum*) and that Mariam would only be cured when they were. To declare that a curer had deliberately adulterated the medicine or tried to undermine the client was to accuse them of sorcery, and that is what Mariam did, through both her symptoms and the words of the spirits. In addition, Mze Nuru said through Mariam that Nuriaty had gone to his home to ask him to be her friend and come live with her but that he had refused. Nuriaty was humiliated and left abandoned in her deceased husband's village, unable to return home without the confession demanded by Mariam and that Nuriaty refused to give.

Kos Vola, who had always looked out for Ali ever since Mohedja had conducted *trambuñu* medicine under her supervision at his birth, now spoke through Mariam to indicate her withdrawal from him. Ali, conversely, became alienated from his sisters. He refused to allow his daughter to take up the plot adjacent to their houses that Mohedja had set aside for her. Amiaty said her parents were upset and visited her at night. As was her wont when she was alive, said Amiaty, Mohedja did not say anything but only gave her a sad look. In 2009, the house was inhabited by the unmarried sons of Amiaty and Mwanesha. Amiaty often cooked there, having dreamt that Mohedja was sad the kitchen shed was not in use. In 2015, it was rented by a family of unofficial migrants and the plot was designated for one of Mwanesha's daughters.

By 2015, Mayotte was a French department and several of Mohedja and Tumbu's grandchildren were studying or living in the metropole. Mariam had visited the metropole twice. Nuriaty remained apart, now married to a man without papers and suffering from diabetes and hypertension as well as from abandonment. Given her illness, it had become physically too difficult to receive the spirits.

Mariam had been twice to Madagascar and successfully completed her trumba ceremonies with a healer in Majunga.[9] The Zanzibari mrewa, who had cohabited with Rae Samba and had not appeared since, received her ceremony. She turned out to be a female, named Zabibu. I did not have a chance to meet her; but, as Mariam observed, since she spoke Swahili, we would not have been able to communicate with one another.

I called up Mze Nuru a final time, in the presence of Amiaty and Mwanesha. Mze Nuru began by saying that Mariam had become a reformist Muslim and no longer liked the spirits. He said the problems within the family were large as they lacked an elder. He became agitated when I tried to take up Nuriaty's cause and very angry when I said I doubted she had committed sorcery. If I did not trust him, he would leave immediately! When I apologized, he continued heatedly that Nuriaty had made Mariam sick, had refused to acknowledge her actions, had not helped Mariam when she was ill, and had not taken the maternal leadership expected of an older sister. He was much more direct than Mariam in saying that the mediation (*suluha*) I was then trying to set up between the siblings was unrealistic and that many preconditions would have to be met first. He stated that Tumbu and Mohedja had given Nuriaty all their knowledge, and he concluded that I had trusted him only when he had appeared in Mohedja but not now in Mariam. When Mariam came out of trance, she pronounced herself amenable to trying to make peace with Nuriaty, but thereafter she made excuses to avoid doing so.

Our interaction was intense and unsatisfactory. Mze Nuru was resentful and angry, not at all like the person I remembered cohabiting with Mohedja. Amiaty and Mwanesha each looked down at the floor, saying nothing. Mze Nuru expressed stronger emotions and said things more explicitly than did Mariam herself. Amiaty observed that "the spirit follows the principal (*lulu mañaraka tompin*). If the host (*tompin*) is angry, so is the spirit; if the host is sad, so is the spirit. The spirit will always stand by the host."

Amiaty had tried to reach an objective answer with respect to the problems in the family. She went first to an astrologer who told her the family spirits were bothering them. When she called the spirits in Mariam they just cried and would not speak clearly. She then sought Mze Marwan in a granddaughter of Mwana Sidy who lived in a distant village. Marwan pointed out that Tumbu and Mohedja's family was evidently protected by strong spirits. No outsider would be able to attack them; hence the problem had to come from within the family. It could not be spirits from afar who were bothering them, but only their own spirits. Amiaty then sought her mother's spirits as well. She could not find anyone with Mze Nuru, but she tracked down Ndramboeny in a medium in town. She had to leave fifty euros in his dish, and Ndramboeny rose and cried, saying he had turned into an amorphous and evil spirit (*shetwan*) within the family.

It seemed as if the spirits so carefully cultivated by Mohedja and Tumbu for the protection and continuity of the family were no longer cohabiting smoothly. Mze Nuru had shifted from Mohedja to Mariam, but he was no longer the quietly observant and disinterested person I remembered. Mohedja and Tumbu would have been perplexed and distraught by the spirits' inability to establish good will and authority.[10]

On a brief visit in 2023, I learned of two major developments. On the one hand, I was sad to see that there was no longer any cohabitation with spirits among the siblings. Those who had been present in Mariam had all withdrawn. She professed to be much happier without them.

At the height of the quarrel between Mariam and Nuriaty, Amiaty had sought out each of the family's major spirits in hosts living in distant villages, asking for advice and help. They all said the same thing, that the trouble came from close to home and that the spirits could no longer work within or for the family (*mraba*). When Amiaty reached Kos Vola, the spirit cried and cried.

During this period, Mariam was in a bad way. She said she spent five months in metropolitan France for medical treatment, including two months in hospital, and an operation in which they removed something from her abdomen. When she returned home, she still felt ill. She wanted the spirits to leave, and they agreed. She dreamt that a smelly old man was chasing her, and she woke just as he was about to jump on the bed. She then became very ill so that people had to look after her. Finally, she found a fundi who said that once she threw away her spirits' paraphernalia she would be fine. He was a fundi who worked entirely by means of the Qur'an and other Arabic writing.

Mariam told the spirits she no longer wanted them, and they rose in her to say they could no longer help the family. Then they just made inarticulate noises. Mariam sent Kos Vola's staff and Ndramboeny's spear, along with the white dish and silver coin, to Mahabu, the central trumba shrine in Mayotte, so that they might find a host with whom the spirits wanted to cohabit. She gave the spirits' clothing, inherited from Mohedja, to other hosts of trumba. The remaining implements of the patros she threw out on a rocky promontory. Ever since, she has felt fine. As her daughter remarked, the fact that she did not develop a psychosis on getting rid of the spirits' possessions (as happened to some other hosts who discarded their paraphernalia) proved that this was the right thing to do. Mariam herself rationalized her actions, saying that Nuriaty had sent the spirits only to have them turn against her and the family. It was as if an experiment had been conducted and when it failed Mariam moved on.

The spirits who had once cared for the family were gone. But they were not alone in abandoning each other. There was perhaps less cohabitation in the community overall, and certainly, fewer public ceremonies. People attributed the decline to the pressure of reformist Islam and the way it shamed participants in spirit ceremonies.[11] Most people said they were not reformists at heart but were tired of the criticism they received from reformers telling them that interacting with spirits was forbidden. So most spirit activities no longer took place in public, but privately, behind closed doors. When a patros ceremony did take place, young people were astonished, never having seen one before. Some unfortunate people were caught between having spirits who wanted to rise and not being able, or willing, to go for treatment and hold their ceremonies. Visiting one old friend, I happened to mention that I thought it was a shame that his wife's grandparents' legacy of sponsoring patros ceremonies seemed to have disappeared. As I uttered the name of one of her family's cohabiting spirits, the wife, who was lying indisposed on the sofa, suddenly twitched and teared up. It was over in a moment, but my friend looked down and I apologized if I had embarrassed them. "That is why I'm so sick," said the wife. She had several spirits who wanted to rise but her husband, who had leanings towards reformist Islam, refused to agree to hold the ceremonies. Nevertheless, spirit activity certainly thrives elsewhere in Mayotte (Heslon 2023).

With the departure of the spirits from Mariam, Ali concluded that the extended family no longer had spirits to protect them; it was each of them on their own now. However, the family did continue to matter. The second development I learned about was that around early 2022, and after the spirits had left Mariam, the quarrels among the siblings had been more or less resolved. Even if underlying resentments remained, they were at least all talking to one another. Mariam's oldest son (who also happened to be Tumbu and Mohedja's first grandchild) arrived from La Réunion where he had lived for many decades, determined to bring his mother and her siblings together. His diplomacy worked. They gathered at Mariam's and agreed to go on to Nuriaty's, where they took her by surprise. They held a tearful reunion and agreed that henceforward they would attend each other's family events (weddings, funerals, etc.). Shortly after, they held a picnic at the family's field. Everyone contributed fifty euros and they bought a goat to roast. All the children and grandchildren participated.

Chapter Sixteen

Reflections on Voice

This book has recounted Mohedja and Tumbu living their lives together. It offers one response to the following questions: What constitutes a life or lives well lived? What is it to live a life?[1] My intention has not been to explain the course of their lives as the consequence of earlier experiences or inner conflicts. But I have been interested in exploring their motivations, which may be more or less unconscious. What I show is the scope that cohabitating with spirits and with each other provided them for action, intimacy, growth, maturity, and experience of various kinds.

Cohabiting with spirits in Mayotte and Madagascar is at times painful. Cohabitation is hard work and intrinsically open, as are all relationships within a family. But in the long run it enriches life. Spirits afford all kinds of possibilities – social and psychological, aesthetic and intellectual, practical and ethical, ludic and therapeutic. They open channels of communication, overcome impasse, and thicken life, adding layers of meaning, relationships, and possibility.

Given the presence of spirits and conventional codes and modes of interaction with them – constituting what could be called, after Wittgenstein, a form of life – it is simply wrong-headed to try to explain their presence, either at large, or in particular, as though one were tracking and explaining the manifestation of a disease or a specific and relatively rare social practice, like polyandry, or form of bad behaviour, like plagiarism. Likewise, it is manifestly absurd to reduce spirits to some kind of positive function. A better comparison is with something like playing and enjoying classical or popular music or an intellectual pursuit like anthropology or philosophy. We do not explain the presence of these practices in functionalist terms, but account for their emergence and presence historically. We do not explain individual attention to or participation in them with respect to a single function or narrow motivation. Rather, the presence of certain musical genres and instruments enables people to draw on their capacities and to enlarge them, by learning to play or cultivating an ear, perhaps even to compose. When accounting for why one person likes classical music, or prefers Bach over Brahms, or plays the oboe rather than the piano, or no instrument at all, why they became an anthropologist rather than a sociologist, engineer, or postal carrier, carried out fieldwork in Madagascar rather than Mali or Montreal, we do so in terms of their biography. Context, character, and contingency each play a role, and each act enables or constrains subsequent ones. We understand such practices and preferences as part of that person's life as a whole and in relation to other persons. We listen to what they tell us and observe what they do, but we also consider factors they may not have taken explicitly into account, such as the way taste is shaped by class, opportunity by gender, and choice by unconscious conflict or identification, as well as simple fortuity. Most of all, we attend to *how* they live – with music, with their instrument, with their calling – and how these activities enrich their lives. Sometimes we might say that certain people are consumed by a particular form of music, sport, or academic pursuit.

Human beings are subjects in the various ways post-structuralist theorists have put it, but they are also creatures with complex motivation and imagination, pouring their subjective concerns and creations into the world as much as they are subjected to or shaped by their worlds. Properties of mind and body that we could call capacities or affordances are each taken up more or less in any given society and by any given individual. Some of us have greater innate capacities of certain kinds than others. Some people are musically gifted, as we say, others less so; some can compose, play an instrument, sing, or dance or simply enjoy listening. Others are relatively tone-deaf. Some affordances are universal, some capacities are cultivated, and between these are the cultural genres and forms of life people live with and within.

Insofar as dissociation springs from a general human capacity and yet manifests in culturally particular genres and forms of life, it can be exercised in some societies and not others, shaped variously in different societies, and taken up variously by distinct individuals within a given society. There can be no general explanation for why it is a practice available in certain societies or taken up by certain individuals. Causal and functionalist explanations are widespread, but they are often inappropriate and misguided.

Active cohabitation with spirits is one of the means through which some people in Mayotte have lived their lives. Cohabitation becomes understandable in the context of these lives, just as these lives are better understood when the place of cohabitation within them is acknowledged.

Spirits cohabit with the people I call their hosts, but also with their hosts' spouses and offspring. They become members of families, an intrinsic part of kinship. Spirits can articulate and transcend the ordinary relations between spouses and between members of different generations. It would be difficult to describe marriage or kinship in Mayotte without including the spirits, just as it would be difficult to describe the spirits without considering kinship and marriage.

If spirits are part of the web of social relations, we can also ask what to make of the selfhood of the hosts. Are hosts mature or immature, psychologically fragmented or integrated? We can ask both what cohabitation expresses about the selves of the hosts and what the affordances of cohabitation are for further constituting and strengthening (or possibly disintegrating) the self. Certainly, the presence of spirits implies that the self is always and only a self in relation to others. I look at cohabitation as a technology of self rather than a pathology of self.[2] Indeed, I go further and suggest that the most successful mediums are people with a strong ego and that the most successful cohabitations generate further maturity and insight.

By "technology" I mean to go back to Aristotle's concept of *techne* – knowledge used in production. There is a kind of creative production in cohabitation – the creation of a character, a performance, a career, of refigured social relations. Ultimately, the subject of production is the life of the host in her relations with others. As lived, cohabitation is also praxis. Cohabitation is not simply the poietic embodiment and enactment of cultural texts; it addresses the contingent, the particular, the immediate, the personal. It requires, exhibits, and possibly enhances what Aristotle termed *phronesis*, practical judgment or wisdom.[3] What spirits say and do, and what humans say and do with respect to spirits, has an ethical dimension.

As a mode of living, or a form of life, we can put cohabitation with spirits in conversation with both philosophy and psychoanalysis. I draw on arguments developed in these fields to show their resonance with cohabitation, not to explain the latter by means of the former, and precisely not to see cohabitation as something anomalous, but rather as fully part of our common condition. In this chapter I focus on the question of voice, leaving psychoanalysis to the postscript.

In the spring of 1985, an Air India flight out of Toronto exploded over the mid-Atlantic. This was one of the rare items concerning Canada to be announced on the radio in Mayotte. The news was received with some consternation by Mohedja and Tumbu because the crash took place at approximately the date on which I had written that my family and I were leaving Canada en route to visit them. Being unaware of the volume of air traffic from Toronto, they were very worried. However, as in many a crisis and anxious moment before, a spirit well known to the household arrived to offer his assurance. Rising in Mohedja, Mze Nuru told the family that we were fine and would arrive on schedule. Once we had arrived safely and Mohedja was telling me the story, she admitted that she herself had not fully believed what Mze Nuru had said.

In the moment of uncertainty, we could say that Mohedja spoke or thought in two voices: the confident, self-assured, calm, encouraging spirit and the uncertain, worried human. Insofar as these voices have, in some sense, a single locus within Mohedja, this raises complications both for the explicit view held in Mayotte concerning the autonomy of spirits as distinct beings, and for dominant Euro-American views of the healthy self as a unitary, internally coherent, well-integrated individual. It is the nature of this polyphonic selfhood that has been an implicit subject of this work. And it is the positive aspects of this polyphony as it is cultivated by some people in Mayotte – the force, reach, and multiplicity of perspectives that it provides – that have formed a main argument.

The presence of cohabiting spirits who periodically interrupt or irrupt and speak through the bodies of their hosts manifests an ontology comparable to, but distinct from, those described as animism or naturalism. It affords a kind of perspectivism, but one quite different from that depicted by Viveiros de Castro (1998) for Amazonia. The perspectives here are those of multiple persons, an articulation of distinct voices. Rather than one's perspective of the world being understood as a function of the kind of body one has (as in Amazonia), here the perspective varies according to who is speaking through a human body at any given time – in effect, the kind of mind one has. The multiplicity of perspective here is analogous to that of different characters in a drama as orchestrated by the playwright or in a novel by the author. Kenneth Burke (1945) calls the former dramatic irony and Bakhtin calls the later polyphony. The voice of the spirit may also be seen to exemplify Bakhtin's (1981, 324) corresponding concept of heteroglossia, that is, the use of another's voice "serving to express authorial intentions but in a refracted way." In each case, the product is more than the sum of its parts.

In drama or fiction, the voices in the text, the characters produced therein, speak to each other, but they also speak for the author, and to the audience or readers, sometimes long after the act of reading is finished.

This informs my view of cohabitation as a kind of art. Moreover, cohabitation is an art that happens in the midst of everyday life; it is, in effect, an art of living. Voicing is consequential, carrying practical, ethical import. More than the writing or reading of fiction, or of life lived thereafter with memorable authors or characters, as one might live with Jane Austen or Madame Bovary, the spirits with whom people in Mayotte cohabit have a direct impact on, and interest in, their bodies, their relationships, and their well-being.

Throughout the book, I have described a very good marriage. In closing, I will depict an incident that departs somewhat from this picture, but also illustrates how the polyphony afforded by the presence of Mze Nuru helped resolve things. One evening in 1995, one of Mohedja's grandsons, Siaka, a young man then in his early twenties, sitting on the stoop arm in arm with Mohedja, began teasing her by telling me the story of Tumbu's second marriage. He began by calling Tumbu a *Bonjour Madame*, the kind of man who does everything his wife wants. To prove his masculine autonomy, Tumbu went off to S— and took a second wife (a previously married woman). When four days later he returned home, Mohedja handed him his clothes and told him to leave. Tumbu then had *ngoma* (regret, sadness). The next morning, he told the new wife he was going down to the beach to purchase fish. But instead, he rushed home. His clothes remained in S— "to this day."

Siaka explained that he was telling me only what he knew of the event, but that his grandparents did not like to explain things to him clearly (*mzury*). It had happened a couple of years before my first visit twenty years earlier.

In response, Mohedja took up the story, which, in fact, she had told me once before, in 1976. Tumbu did not tell her his plans to marry, but she knew and kept silent. Then he went off to S— for three days. On his return, she told him he should have stayed there and not come back. One of their daughters and one of their grandchildren were very sick at the time and Mohedja took them to the hospital on the other side of the island, where they stayed for four days. Transport was difficult back then and there was no road all the way to Lombeni. So an uncle carried their grandson the rest of the way home. Tumbu had not visited them at the hospital and did not know they had returned. He set off for town but learned en route that they were back in Lombeni. So he turned around and came right home. Mohedja was really mad and said, "Stop right there; don't move your feet one step forward!" She was furious because of his neglect of the children. Even Ali was angry with his father.

Mohedja continued to recount the story to Siaka and me. She struggled at the hospital, day after day, in crowded conditions with two very sick children and no help. She had to feed and bathe them and care for them at night. She said, "It was I who divorced him, not the other way around."

It was rice harvest time, and after returning from the hospital she went to their field and found the crop overripe. This only incensed her further. She returned to the village and told her mother she would sleep at their hut in the field to get the harvest done. Tumbu followed her there. She refused to speak to him and just kept harvesting. She worked in one spot, he in another. Rice was harvested by cutting the stalks with a small knife or the sharp rim of a shell. Tumbu kept trying to speak to her. He told her not to spend the night there, but she paid no attention and he left. In the evening, she cooked and went to bed. At midnight she heard a noise getting closer. It was Tumbu. He entered and kept talking to her, but she remained silent. They harvested for five days, she not speaking to him or serving him food. Then she was called home because their daughter Mariam was giving birth. That evening, Mohedja asked Tumbu, "What are you doing here? I'm not afraid to sleep alone at home. Go back to your wife." He stayed up talking to her, pouring out his feelings (*ata hetsaka rohu nazy*). This went on for four days and then he went to S— to collect his belongings.

Later the woman came and asked Mohedja to be her friend (*rahavavy*, also the word for co-wife) and they cooked together when she came to the village for events. Siaka teased his grandmother, saying that Tumbu and the woman had never really split up, that he had seen the two of them together in the fields, that they would meet there. Mohedja retorted that he was too young at the time to know anything about it.

Mohedja relished the story, insisting that what had made her so angry was not the marriage per se but being left with two very sick children and conditions in the hospital being so difficult. When she first told me about it, she laughed a lot. However, when I asked her then if she thought Tumbu might try again to take a second wife, she seemed a bit uncertain. But she said he knew what he could expect: she had no intention of sharing a husband and would divorce him.

Here is how Tumbu recounted the matter in 1976, a couple of years after it happened. He saw a pretty divorcée in S— and married her.

Such marriages are very easily arranged and enacted. Tumbu pointed out that Islam permits up to four simultaneous marriages if a man can properly support each of his wives. However, Mohedja reacted badly. She said she was not going to put up with being a co-wife and that Tumbu had to choose between them. He tried to reason with her and then to wait out her anger, but all to no avail. After some reflection, he realized that his life was anchored in Lombeni; all his children were there and so were his interests. If Mohedja expelled him from the household, he would lose his home base. Reluctantly, he gave up his second wife. He joked though that were I to give him the money he would make a second marriage again; he had several prospects already in mind.

Tumbu said the marriage lasted for fourteen days. Siaka insisted it was only four days; the days when Tumbu and Mohedja were harvesting their rice and thereafter in Lombeni did not count. Tumbu spent these days talking to Mohedja, but she did not speak to him. For several days, they harvested silently in the fields. Mohedja cooked for herself, but in fact she left enough in the pot for him to eat after her.

This all seemed fairly straightforward. But what Siaka, and possibly Tumbu, was not privy to was Mze Nuru's account of events, which he told me privately.

27 January 1976. Mze Nuru and I were discussing whether spirits could be hired to commit sorcery on behalf of others. Mze Nuru said that although both he and Mze Marwan were sometimes prepared to harm others when they were asked to do so by clients, neither Tumbu nor Mohedja would ever agree to do so. The petitioner would have to raise the spirit without telling the host what he wanted, or it would be a no-go. Mze Nuru added that he would only do it for someone who was a close friend and had a legitimate gripe and also was willing to pay. Once, a woman in the village asked Mze Nuru to make her husband temporarily impotent when he was seducing other women. Nothing could be easier for Mze Nuru, who professed himself willing, but when he asked what he would get out of it, whether a chicken or something else, the woman didn't want to give anything and so Mze Nuru turned her down.

Mze Nuru then said that he did make someone impotent once. Tumbu had affairs with other women but when he went so far as to have one with someone in the same village and Mohedja found out about it, she was very hurt and asked Mze Nuru for help. Mze Nuru talked to Tumbu, and he promised he would never have sex with other women again. Then he married in S—. Mze Nuru knew of it ahead of time and came to warn Mohedja in her sleep, but Mohedja wouldn't listen. Mohedja seemed to have made up her mind that if Tumbu married another woman, she would leave him.

When the marriage took place, Mze Nuru was very angry – not that there is anything wrong with second marriages in themselves, but because Tumbu had broken his word to his male friend, the spirit. While Mohedja told Tumbu to make a choice and waited him out, Mze Nuru took immediate action. He said he entered Tumbu's belly, chuckling that he was curious to see Tumbu sleeping with this new woman. His presence made Tumbu impotent.

Tumbu was naturally upset and though it was nighttime he went off to find his fundi Malidy Juma for treatment. But Malidy was living in his distant fields at the time. Tumbu returned to the wife in S—. She fed him, and he rested, but he was still unsuccessful. Finally, he returned to Mohedja, with whom Mze Nuru did not prevent him from having sex.

Mze Nuru added that another time he made Tumbu ill was when Tumbu was reluctant to hold his (Mze Nuru's) original ceremony [chapter 5]. This was done at Mohedja's request, and it also proved successful.

Mze Nuru was evidently someone who felt in control of things, followed his own principles, and took responsibility for his actions.

Although active possession is a vigorously embodied phenomenon, the central puzzle, in large measure, is one of voice. If, following Stanley Cavell or Veena Das, our language is not descriptive of ourselves but expressive of ourselves, whose voice is speaking when, of whom is it an expression, and with what implications? Does the voice of the spirit strengthen or weaken the voice of the host, enhance, complement, or counter it?

Questions of distributed voice and agency can be described by means of G.H. Mead's dialectic of the I and the me, and by Erving Goffman's concept of footing and his distinctions among the animator, author, and principal of any utterance. With Mead (1967), in relation to the continuous and transcending "I" are the various alternating social instances of "me" of which the I is composed. With Goffman, there is the I who voices an utterance (the animator), the I who has composed the words expressed (the author), and the I in whose name the utterance is spoken, whose position is established thereby, or who is accountable (the principal) (Goffman 1981, 144). In ordinary conversation, these are generally one and the same, but cohabitation uncouples them and renders the relations between them ambiguous.

This is, in a sense, the inverse of the gap Das (2007) observes between voice and speech. It is not as though the voice is hollow, the speech mechanical or empty, as might sometimes appear in a dissociated state. In Mayotte, when the spirit is fully present in the body of the host, there is no mistaking his voice, which is full, firm, and forceful, wanting to be heard. The voices of spirits are strong. The question is whether to consider the spirit as merely the animator, and the host as author or principal, in Goffman's terms, or how the "me" of the spirit (explicitly a "not-me" of the host and a "not-one-of-us" of the human community) is established to the satisfaction of the I, in Mead's terms.

"One important aspect of voice (as distinct from, say, speech acts) is that the voice must belong to me, be mine, not in the sense in which I own a piece of property but in the sense that it acquires life within my history" (Das 2020, 4).[4] Thus we can ask whether and how cohabitation entails having or adding a voice, or relinquishing one, and how that voice is mine (acquires life within my history) even if it is marked as not mine. Even were the voice of the spirit to be understood (as I do not) as an artificial one, a stage voice, is it not expressing something that is mine, stemming from my history, as Das puts it, or from my unconscious, as a psychoanalyst might put it? Is it mine in the way the characters in a novel are voices of the author, voices that, as Bakhtin calls it, are polyphonous?

In some instances, the voice of the spirit could compensate or offset the loss of voice as oneself, or simply serve as a means to be heard more forcefully or to communicate more intimately. Having a voice requires having someone you can trust to hear you, as Mariam discovered to her detriment. As Das (2020, 17) summarizes Cavell, voice concerns "the problem of making oneself intelligible, finding someone … to whom I might trust my words."[5] When spirits first appear in a given host, they demand acknowledgment of their autonomous voice – acknowledgment provided by the host and the host's significant others, such as a spouse, parents, offspring, neighbours, fellow spirits – through pursuit of the ceremony. They demand to be heard. When this acknowledgment is not forthcoming, there is shame and frustration, a threat to reality, and a denial of voice.

A striking fact about Mohedja and Tumbu is that they each recognized the importance of private, one-on-one conversations. They often held these with each other and with each other's cohabiting spirits. I was very fortunate that sometimes they each held these with me. I am left to wonder why I was selected to be Mze Nuru's confidante and to whom else he had recounted his actions concerning Tumbu's second marriage, perhaps directly after the event itself.

If cohabitation produces continuity and attunement of voice, active possession also indicates the power of interruption, of an unexpected voice breaking through. As Peggy Kamuf writes, after Derrida, we need to be vigilant for interruption, not expecting it, but ready to receive it, and ready to listen to a new voice when it appears. We must pay "vigilant attention to all that interrupts the unity of tone or voice and pluralizes the routes along which meaning is sent" (Kamuf 2010, 14).[6]

Interruption carries both indeterminacy and potential. Allowing oneself to be actively inhabited by a spirit requires enormous trust – trust in the human others who are encouraging us to go forwards and trust that they will look after us in our absence, but above all, trust in oneself, that one will not be shamed or mute, that one will find a distinct voice, and that one will find one's way back. In this act, vulnerability is at once both greatly heightened and overcome by the new voice.

Das indicates that her "signature theme [is] finding one's voice in one's history" (2020, 21). That is, in effect, what I describe for Mohedja and Tumbu, albeit they do so through multiple voices; their voices are, in the end, a kind of orchestration. Such attunement or orchestration suggests that philosophers such as Cavell or Bernard Williams may make too much of the necessary *singularity* of voice as a measure of personal integrity. As another philosopher, Kierkegaard, exemplifies in his polyonymous authorship (i.e., writing under multiple names), authentic voice need not always be singular or unitary in its expression. Ambivalence, irony, and the playful but serious desire to speak otherwise can all be true of and to voice.

The example of Kierkegaard suggests that the practice of dispersing voice is not as far from a Euro-American way of life as it might look. As Jonas Tinius remarks in his ethnographic study of German theatre production, "Reckoning the cultivation of character through characters as a way to insert fiction into our lives then means allowing all of those implied human beings, and their traits, to become readily available for our own potential future self-making. Characters and the fiction they imply then become part of our *repertoire* of being" (2018, 357, his emphasis). The phrase "repertoire of being" is a wonderful one.

Tinius continues:

> I am arguing that it is plausible and enriching to consider imagination and multiplicity, incoherence and friction rather than only stability and authenticity, coherence and narrative, as informing the formation of character, both on and off the stage.... We can think of characters as dynamic repertoires of actions and traits that allow us to become otherwise; characters in this sense could then be described as *creative appropriations of other fictions*. In order to cultivate character, then, we need, perhaps counter-intuitively, to include the idea of detachment from stability, steadiness, singularity and to incorporate a sense of capacity for being other and multiple. (357, his emphasis)

Stage actors can serve as metonyms for responsive and creative readers or responders to fictions (in the sense of things made) of all kinds. Hosts to the spirits exhibit quite literally what Jeanette Winterson calls, with respect to the arts, "the paradox of active surrender."[7] Actively surrendering to or appropriating fictions produces further artistry. Directors and actors are themselves artists. And so are the hosts cohabiting with spirits. The concept of the artist is not an exact fit and hosts are not the equivalent of actors on the stage, but like artists, hosts are masters of the art of noticing lives, using dissociation like a poet composing verse or an actor portraying character, holding a perspective on the everyday and infusing it with an energy that in turn incites imaginative and appreciative response from others (including ethnographers).[8] In producing great art, artists draw on acquired skills in the media and genres at hand, but their primary material is themselves. Painfully or joyously, artists draw out from themselves to produce works in the world. At the same time, to live as an artist is not to rest with finished products but to continue to notice, appropriate, transform, and transcend. Without wishing to romanticize, this is what strong hosts do. (Weaker hosts remain caught in their preoccupations or their enjoyment, without working on their characters or working through them.)

To the aesthetic dimension raised in the comparison with writers of fiction or actors on stage, I add the ethical one.[9] The temporary displacement of one person by another raises questions concerning action and character. Through cohabitation, things are said and done; who is accountable? Who, in Goffman's language is, in the end, the principal? Is the state of ostensible patiency not also one of agency? Is not the action of the spirit a product of the host's passion?[10] The practice of both hosts and spirits speaks to questions of dignity and responsibility and to the varieties of ways they can be played out. Cohabitation is not the manifestation of a slave morality in Nietzsche's sense. It does not propose rigid boundaries between good and evil, moral absolutism, or a code that must be followed. It is open and generous.[11]

This book has described Mohedja and Tumbu's practical judgment as they engaged in the first instance with matters affecting their family and themselves. Following Pierre Bourdieu's influential elaboration of practice theory (1977), practice follows from habitus, the inculcation of embodied dispositions from childhood onwards, dispositions that come to seem natural and that are difficult to change. Bourdieu's analysis is profound, and it goes a long way towards explaining how it is that people come to cohabit with spirits, how it appears to happen outside their hands, and perhaps why, in certain social milieux, such as Mayotte circa 1975–95, the possessed were preponderately of a particular age and gender, namely post-adolescent women. We can draw on Bourdieu to understand how people come to feel at ease cohabiting with spirits, how active possession is no mere or deliberate "performance."

However, this is insufficient as an account of the practice of someone like Tumbu or Mohedja. Cohabitation is not simply a matter of succumbing to habit. Hosts and spirits are continually forced to address particular circumstances and exercise their judgment. They do so with regard to a sense of what is important in life, with an understanding of the right relationship of means to ends, and with consideration for others and a sense of their own dignity. Such practice is profoundly ethical, and it transcends distinctions between the rational and the embodied. One's practice as a medium, even with respect to such things as the timing of a given act (say, entering or leaving a state of active possession), is open to moral evaluation. Mohedja's irritation at the non-appearance of Mze Marwan when Mariam and her daughter were sick (chapter 10) illustrates the point. Embodiment and naturalization notwithstanding, people subject their practice to ethical scrutiny.

While there are certainly elements of self-interest, the practice of both Mohedja and Tumbu (as well as other people) is marked by a concern for respect – self-respect, respect shown them by others, and the respect they show to others. They operate according to criteria concerning equality, justice, well-being, responsibility, truth, and excellence; they are virtuous people.

Anyone can write or act (theatrically) but only some people are skilled and responsible writers or actors, or great ones. Interpreting is not something passive, but creative; an actor throws herself into her character and an anthropologist interprets his tradition in the act of practising anthropology. Hosts can be said to interpret, in this sense, the spirits they come to embody and cohabit with. Cohabitation is practical; spirits intervene, warn, mediate, advise, and treat household members and other clients. The spirits are artistic characterizations, and both spirits and hosts are accountable agents; skilled hosts like Mohedja and Tumbu enable their spirits to perform with a high degree of seriousness, attention, judgment, verve, and sometimes fun.

Cohabitation with spirits encompasses or transcends the domains through which we commonly distribute things: art, therapy, kinship, religion, self, other, fantasy, reality. It is simply, in Wittgenstein's terms, its own form of life.

I have emphasized the singularity of cohabitation, but the argument is also about what we all share. Cohabitation renders undisguisable certain general aspects of human existence. We are all subject to episodes of dissociation, more or less strong; all subject to issuing disclaimers or acknowledging the limits of our agency; all subject to identifying with characters in our milieu; all open to ironic recognition of the stubbornness yet opacity and contingency of the self. And we all move between our different personas (ethnographer, teacher, parent, etc.) without great inconsistency. Of course, in articulating persons as it does, cohabitation shapes experience in particular ways. If the choice between universalism and relativism is a false one, it is because claims to the universal cannot rest on our initial assumptions or prejudices, but are reached only through deep understanding of other forms of life.

Someone in Mayotte once said to me that everyone has a spirit (*lulu*) in their head, but not all spirits emerge and render their hosts in states of active possession (*menziky*); in most people, including children, they have "respect" (*ishima*) and do not rise. In its explicit form, this is an anomalous position in local theory. Nevertheless, it implies a basic point: anyone has the potential – it is an inherent human capacity.

I began to understand cohabitation better when I shifted from asking why (some) people cohabited with spirits to asking why they cohabited with specific spirits (rather than others). This enabled me to begin to see that cohabitation was not an illness or a stratagem, but a densely textured moral and aesthetic vehicle, one whose individual manifestations emerged from and addressed relational issues.

I have shown throughout the complexity of the question of motivation and I will discuss it further in the postscript. But to summarize in gross terms, it seems that Tumbu's engagement with spirits was originally motivated, at least in part, by Mohedja and the spirits already cohabiting with her. She encouraged him to work alongside her and he wanted to do so. After much resistance, he began hosting a spirit distinct from those cohabiting with Mohedja, but he and Mze Marwan then collaborated closely with Mohedja and Mze Nuru. Later he received Mze Nuru's older brother, who also cohabited with Mohedja's older brother, Samba. Tumbu became an active and successful healer but as he grew old, he gradually relinquished active possession as it became too strenuous, albeit keeping up strong relations with the spirits directly cohabiting with Mohedja. Mohedja drew from her mother and from Samba to grow and to become active in new ways, watching over her family and working as a healer. She was receptive to a variety of other spirits as well, while continuing her main engagement with her senior spirits. None of this occurred without ambivalence and perhaps some irony.

Both Tumbu and Mohedja were agents of their own growth. Cohabiting with the spirits and with each other, they addressed adversity and opportunity. They lived full lives with integrity, engagement, vitality, attentiveness, responsivity, and self-awareness.

Psychoanalytic Postscript

What happens if instead of translating these stories into the alien categories of social and cultural theory, we say that these lives are this way, just as our lives are, or may be, another way, whatever way that is? "Interpretation," [Adam] Phillips writes in a discussion of "truth" in psychoanalysis, "can be a refusal to listen." The aim is to enlarge our understanding of what happens to the world as a result of these ties between heaven and earth. This entails a struggle between their categories and the categories available to scholars of religion in history and culture in which neither is given primacy. Otherwise it will be said of the study of religion, to borrow from Jean-Paul Sartre's critique of Marxist social and psychological theory, that "it situates but no longer discovers anything."

Robert Orsi[1]

Consciousness, in the everyday psychological sense (awareness, intent, and the giving of meaning to experiences) is inadequate to account for agency. One does not have to subscribe to a full-blown Freudianism to see that instinctive reaction, the docile body, and the unconscious work, in their different ways, more pervasively and continuously than consciousness does. This is part of the reason why an agent's act is more (and less) than her consciousness of it.

Talal Asad[2]

The unity [of self] that is genuinely available to us is, I think, marked by disruption and division. This is not the well-known view that whatever psychic unity we achieve will always be vulnerable to disruption, but rather a view that whatever unity is genuinely available *partially consists* in certain forms of disruption. The aim of unity should not be to overcome these disruptions, but to find ways to live well with them. Ironically, the unity that is available to us is a peculiar form of disunity.

Jonathan Lear[3]

Insofar as human hosts are involved in the manifestations of spirits, and insofar as they genuinely deny that fact and complain that they wish they had not been singled out for cohabitation, it seems that we cannot understand what is going on without some recourse to the unconscious, and that takes us inevitably to psychoanalysis. The question I ask is, What is it to perform as, and to live with, spirits? Living with others is at once social and ethical; psychoanalysis complements the social by supplying the dimension of subjectivity and acknowledging the contribution of unconscious factors and forces.

In theoretical digressions throughout the narrative, I have acknowledged psychoanalysis and here I want to make its relevance explicit while avoiding that "refusal to listen" of which Orsi and Phillips speak in my epigraph. Cohabitation in Mayotte is an autonomous, historically constituted cultural genre, technology, practice, and form of life, not directly a projective system. As such, it is not a proper object for psychoanalysis. However, the ways in which specific individuals draw on the possibilities cohabitation affords are.[4]

I bring psychoanalysis into the picture not in order to explain, reduce, or subsume living with spirits within its webs of interpretation, but to enable the two discourses to speak to each other. The aim is not the replacement of one by the other, the dissolution of possession within psychoanalysis, but rather, in the terms of Hans-Georg Gadamer ([1960] 1985), the opening and fusing of horizons. At the individual level, I draw on the language of psychoanalysis to help describe how persons may be motivated to receive particular spirits and how they then cohabit with them. At the cultural level, I suggest that cohabitation provides a means comparable *to* psychoanalysis for enabling psychic growth. The mode of communication set up by cohabitation shares certain features with the analytic relationship and provides a space for the internalized conversation that is a path to insight. In sum, I draw on psychoanalytic thought not to diagnose pathology or single out distress, but, on the contrary, to enrich description of motivation and human flourishing. I cannot demonstrate cause and effect and it would be wrong to try to do so.

Caution is necessary. Cohabitation and psychoanalysis do not translate directly into each other; they are genuinely different – different forms of life. They are incommensurable – they can speak to each other but not be reduced to or measured against each other. I use psychoanalysis to enhance the reading of cohabitation rather than as a language to translate it into. The exercise is essentially a comparative and hermeneutic one. I think cohabitation is something genuinely new for psychoanalysis, much as psychoanalysis is new to cohabitation.

Additionally, dissociation is not the same phenomenon as the Freudian unconscious. In Freud, the unconscious is a deep part of the psyche, based on a metaphor of horizontal layering. Dissociation, by contrast, can be conceived in the image of a vertical split, in which the distinctive consciousness exhibited by the spirit who speaks and interacts with others is paired with the unconscious of the human host.

The redescription of possession as cohabitation resolutely does away with the deterministic language found in some psychoanalytic arguments.[5] Clearly, not everyone who cohabits with spirits (in Mayotte or elsewhere) does so for identical reasons or with the same underlying motivations or even in the same way over time. Nor does a given host enter relations with spirits out of a single or overdetermined motivation. Nevertheless, cohabitation with a particular spirit is not random either. As we have seen, Mohedja and Tumbu have distinctive relations with each of their spirits and once the spirits arrive, they act over time with a variety of motivations and interests. Similarly, when a painter or writer masters a given technique, they can produce a variety of works of art.

In a lucid essay, Lionel Trilling (2001) refutes the idea that illness is the source of artistic greatness. He points out that with respect to neurosis we are all stricken; it is rather a question of what we make of or do with our neurosis, not what it does to us, that counts. Cohabitation is analogous. Psychoanalysis and cohabitation have in common that they each transcend any supposedly objective distinction between health and illness or between action and passion.

Contrary to common perception, psychoanalysis is not merely a theory of psychopathology or form of treatment, but rather a mode of conceiving the human condition as a whole. It understands conflict as inherent in human experience but attends also to how stasis can be overcome. Psychoanalysis and cohabitation each involve a kind of narrative construction and a transformation of self by the story in which one places oneself. They each raise profound questions about self-knowledge, attachment, ambivalence, responsibility, and their limits. Neither claims to offer final answers. While each is constituted by means of suffering and a therapeutic idiom, they provide the means for ethical questioning, action, and possibly growth for the subject, that is, the subject always in relation to herself and to significant others.

On ethics, Aristotle has the first (and perhaps last) word. Freud and Aristotle come together in at least two respects. First, both see psychic health and ethical discrimination as intrinsic to each other. Both link ethics to character and happiness, and both are concerned with the conditions for human flourishing. Both see living well as the end and means of life. However, where Freud emphasizes the inevitability of conflict and unhappiness, Aristotle idealizes harmony (cf. MacIntyre 1981,147; Hampshire 1983). One could say that Freud is pessimistic whereas Aristotle is optimistic. In any case, Freudian thought implies an ethical viewpoint, much as Aristotelian ethics draws on a theory of character.

Second, both thinkers focus on practice, on life as it is lived, rather than idealized rules. Ethics and happiness are not things we can legislate or realize in the abstract, nor are they conditions we can complacently assume we have reached for good. Rather, they require continuously addressing the exigencies of life in all its contingency, ambiguity, and temporality. The central moral issue raised by psychoanalysis, says Herbert Fingarette, is that of accepting responsibility not only for guilty wishes which may come into conscious focus, but for what happens next. "Guilt is retrospective, but responsibility is prospective…. To accept responsibility is to be responsible for what shall be done" (Fingarette 1963, 165) and such acceptance is a necessary condition of maturity (167). Once the spirits fully arrive, they too are expected to take responsibility for their actions, and they demand their hosts do so as well.

Although the tension between conscious reason and underlying desire is differentially expressed by the two thinkers, and perhaps never systematically resolved by either of them,[6] they offer parallel accounts of how to act. For Aristotle, phronesis entails "the exercise of judgement in particular cases" (MacIntyre 1981, 144), whereby virtue is the mean between two opposing vices in given circumstances (for example, courage between fearfulness and foolhardiness). Ricoeur compares the Freudian reality principle to "the 'prudence' [phronesis] principle, in the full Aristotelian sense" (1970, 279) of finding the mean. The ethics of psychoanalysis, Ricoeur suggests, lies here. The ego must mediate between the demands of the id and the "false idealism" and destructive condemnation of the superego.

This has implications for the therapeutic encounter. Through her abstention from judgment, the analyst provides the neutral space in which patients learn to exercise practical wisdom. The spirits offer a similar neutral space to their clients, as we saw, for example, in Mohedja's therapeutic practice as Ndramboeny in chapter 7.[7]

Freud's view of the patients suffering from hysteria with whom he worked at the beginning of his career is similar in one respect to what I would say about Mohedja and Tumbu. Freud writes that hysteria "can exist in conjunction with gifts of the richest and most original kind." He writes of Frau Emmy von N. that she "gave us an example of how hysteria [cohabitation] is compatible with an unblemished character and a well-governed mode of life. The woman we came to know was an admirable one. The moral seriousness with which she viewed her duties, her intelligence and energy, which were no less than a man's [*sic*], and her high degree of education and love of truth impressed both of us [Freud and Breuer] greatly; while her benevolent care for the welfare of all her dependents, her humility of mind and the refinement of her manners revealed her qualities as a true lady as well" ([1893–5] 1955, 103–4). Of Fräulein Elisabeth von R., Freud writes: "I have described the patient's character, the features which one meets with so frequently in hysterical people ... her giftedness, her ambition, her moral sensibility, her excessive demand for love which, to begin with, found satisfaction in her family, and the independence of her nature which went beyond the feminine ideal and found expression in a considerable amount of obstinacy, pugnacity and reserve" (161). I could hardly describe Mohedja's character any better (though I certainly do not consider her to have suffered from hysteria); I would only add her sense of humour.

Freud speaks to the ethical quality of these women's illness, arguing that it was the defence against certain ideas which are incompatible with the ego that resulted in the conversion to physical symptoms. While the inability to face the situation might be regarded as "an act of moral cowardice" (123), at the same time, the defence against the uncalled-for desire rather than the acting upon it was "evidence of ... moral character" (157). While I do not consider cohabitation either as hysteria or as primarily a defence, the point is that to understand peoples' practice, we have to be fully open to their ethical concerns and not only their selfish, aggressive, cowardly, or instrumental ones. Moreover, even if there are elements of defence, and perhaps narcissism, the spirits themselves are expected to acknowledge their actions and are held accountable.

Psychoanalytic theory is by no means homogenous but composed of many intertwined lines of thought emerging from and since Freud's original corpus. I draw selectively and somewhat eclectically on a number of positions within the broad tradition, not in order to make a definitive argument, but to suggest what light each might shed.

Cohabitation entails action, not merely representation, even though a component of the action could be understood as the act of disclaiming it. The ostensible paradox of displacing acts onto spirit alters does not seem so unusual when it is placed alongside psychoanalyst Roy Schafer's description of how people use the body to make both claims and disclaimers. Mental actions are frequently corporealized, as in phrases like "I don't know what's gotten into me." Schafer calls this narrative action. For speakers of English, Schafer notes, "As body-centered beings, we corporealize our mental actions from the first; the learning of ordinary figurative language facilitates and consolidates this apparently unavoidable way of constructing experience" (2018, 242–3).

Schafer argues that the psychoanalytic cure requires acknowledging one's agency. "By attributing agency to impulses and thoughts rather than to oneself, the analysand disavows responsibility. Thereby the analysand attempts to preclude the experiencing of his or her actions in an anxious, guilty, ashamed, or otherwise disturbing manner. Through such disclaiming, one simply appears as the victim or witness of happenings whose origins and explanations lie entirely outside one's own sphere of influence – outside the 'self,' as some would say" (242). Reconstructing the disclaimer in action terms "changes the mode of constructing experience" (242), transforming rather than merely translating it – thus, from "it slipped my mind" to "I forgot it even though I did not want to." In the latter, "one is narrating that one has been performing contradictory actions and does not understand why one has been doing so" (242).

Schafer describes the dense world of the disclaimer. "I inhabit a world of autonomously acting mental activities. These entities include thoughts, feelings, desires, attitudes, impulses, prohibitions, and judgments. They act on me or on one another, and these actions take place in me or around me in space. The actions of these entities are more evident at some times than at others. They cause my suffering and my gratifications. At best they are only sometimes or partly subject to my influence or control ... [they] do not seem to describe the personal life of a unitary, fully responsible agent" (246).

Schafer refers to this thinking as "animistic" (246). My point in making the comparison with cohabitation is not to liken the thought of analysands to something "primitive," but rather to show the ordinariness of disclaimers.

For Schafer, disclaiming action is a form of fantasizing, people "imagining their selves or their minds as spatial entities existing in a split up and split off way" (243). Cohabitation offers a literal exemplification. But if cohabitation strengthens the disclaimer by constituting a whole other character to whom action can be attributed, it also provides a strong means for transforming the experience. First of all, the subject has the opportunity to speak as the agent, to claim the action, albeit in another voice. Second, much of the therapy surrounding possession concerns negotiating with spirit alters and acknowledging the claims of each agent by both parties. Third, the alters perdure in the subject's life and they are repeatedly called upon to claim their agency. Fourth, the repetition of this communicative process between agentive voices leads ultimately to a greater consistency in their actions and claims, and hence to greater insight and unity. Here I follow Schafer in understanding insight in a practical rather than a discursive or intellectual sense.

Schafer's argument is reasonable as far as it goes. Yet it seems to depend upon – and reassert – Western notions of the self as an autonomous, defensive, bounded agent. It emphasizes individuality at the expense of relationality and values action at the expense of passion. By contrast, agency in cohabitation occurs by means of relationship. The subject does not acknowledge full agency, but she accepts the presence of powerful others and her need to play a part in acknowledging, shaping, and maintaining her relationships with them. Sometimes agency is denied in order to better later reincorporate it. Over time, the interests of hosts and spirits converge and there is ever-closer identification, but always with the sense that agency is diffused, and that the host's responsibility lies in addressing and responding to the spirits. She exercises her practical wisdom in this process of interlocution. Agency is critical, but it is never autonomous and, as Asad notes (1993, 15), it is both more and less than the agent's consciousness of it. One becomes a stronger and more powerful self by folding in more and more relational aspects, not by denying them.

Moreover, if bad faith is constituted as an over-identification with a given role, and hence the relinquishment of choice or judgment, cohabitation is the very opposite.[8] Because there is always more than one voice, because persons keep intruding on one another, there is always room for alternatives. The very change of voice is itself an act and hence a form of choice. The disclaimer of agency has to be distinguished from the agency of the disclaimer.

Finally, the disclaimer of agency may be seen as the claim of passion, as a positive act of receptivity or submission and an acceptance of being moved. As described by historian Lorraine Daston, "In the root sense of the word 'passion' (from the Greek *pathema*, the Latin *passio*; cf. the German *Leidenschaft*), passions are suffered like an illness (they have the same root as 'patient'), things that befall rather than move us, not so much states as sieges of the soul. In contrast to the emotions ... *passions don't belong to us; we belong to them*" (2019, 34, my emphasis). Autonomy need not always be the primary value.

My portrait departs from most psychoanalytic applications to anthropology in that it is not primarily about illness, weakness, deviance, or crisis, but about growth, strength, and integration. When I began thinking about the psychic strength of spirit mediums, I was unaware of the remarkable work of Herbert Fingarette comparing psychoanalytic therapy and mystical enlightenment as forms of self-transformation and growth. Tumbu and Mohedja are not mystics, but they have the kind of strong egos that Fingarette describes. Fingarette writes that "the psychoanalytic quest for autonomy reveals the Self in greater depth; it reveals it as a community of selves" (1963, 180). "Archaic selves" are closely woven with the adult conscious self. Psychoanalysis offers "a special, startling kind of intimacy…. It calls for me to recognize that I suffer … for the deeds of those other selves…. I must assume responsibility for the acts and thoughts of those other persons as if they were I. Finally and paradoxically, in the morally clear vision which thus occurs, there emerges, as in a montage, a new Self, a Self free of bondage to the old deeds of the old selves" (181). Fingarette draws on the concept of "regression in the service of the ego" (from Ernst Kris) as a positive "letting go" of defensive anxiety;[9] the resulting energy produces creativity and joy (330–4). He even suggests that "doctrines of possession" are "antecedents and analogues of the concepts of regressive and sublimative eruptions of the unconscious" (185). We have seen to what degree the various spirits, albeit culturally shaped, appear as such eruptions, whether partly regressive, like Kalu and Darwesh, or sublimative, like Mze Nuru and Ndramboeny.

Fingarette argues that the person is a "plurality-in-unity" (227) such that people everywhere live vicariously through several selves. In the West, art lets us realize these "unseen selves," objectifying what has previously been "fugitive and subjective" (188). "The artist evokes highly charged fantasies in a controlled fashion – controlled as to the pattern, the relative intensity of the drives mobilized, and the degree of consciousness of the fantasy" (188). However, "the secularization and isolation of the arts in the West reflects our ideological orientation. It is an orientation which excludes the acceptance of the world revealed by art as a real world. Instead of being conceived as an elaboration of worlds and lives which, in some mysterious way, really belong to us, the arts are subordinated to the waking, utilitarian world…. They are disarmed by being classified as 'play,' 'diversion,' and 'imagination,' rather than as real life…. Thus genuinely creative art is insulated from 'life' for most Westerners. It is, for the regnant ideology, a dis-ease" (189). The only alternative to live out creatively our secret lives is psychotherapy.

Fingarette continues, "The vicarious living of other lives is not merely a desirable experience, it is essential. There can be no development into a human being without the incorporation into the total Self of a variety of lives and part-lives. The more these are fully lived, the more rich and deep a Self. Indeed, we know from psychoanalysis that we must live the lives of others around us as we perceive them (identification) in order to develop even that minimum unique blend of lives and past-lives which can establish us as individuals" (190). Moreover, "There is a remarkable ability – which we tend to take for granted until we recall the case of the psychotic – to keep a variety of conscious and closely interrelated lives entirely unconfused" (191). *"The living of many lives enables the Self to work through, existentially and creatively, various moral tendencies potential in its nature. To learn by experience and eventually to profit by insight into these experiences: this is the way to spiritual progress and human freedom"* (198–9, my emphasis).

It is evident how all this approaches a description and even a validation of cohabitation.

Fingarette offers a culturally informed and philosophically sophisticated account of ego psychology. However, insofar as he focuses on the ultimately autonomous individual, his ideas need to be expanded by developments in psychoanalytic thought that can be broadly characterized as relational (Mitchell 1988a). This is partly because his account of self-transformation may be overly optimistic,[10] but more because a relational perspective, with its concern for separation and connection, provides a better way to describe the place of cohabitation in psychic life. Unlike ego psychology, the focus is not on individual autonomy so much as on growth through relationship and on the necessary permeability of selves.[11]

As Stephen Mitchell describes the relational model,

We are portrayed not as a conglomeration of physically based urges, but as being shaped by and inevitably embedded within a matrix of relationships with other people, struggling both to maintain our ties to others and to differentiate ourselves from them. In this vision the basic unit of study is not the individual as a separate entity whose desires clash with an external reality, but an interactional field within which the individual arises and struggles to make contact and to articulate himself [sic]. Desire is experienced always in the context of relatedness, and it is that context which defines its meaning. Mind is composed of relational configurations. The person is comprehensible only within this tapestry of relationships, past and present.... In this perspective the figure is always in the tapestry, and the threads of the tapestry (via identifications and introjections) are always in the figure. (1988a, 3)

A relational model sees "mind as fundamentally dyadic and interactive; above all else, mind seeks contact, engagement with other minds" (3). In sum, for Mitchell, the creation of the subjective world is an interactive process (255).

The relational approach stems from the work of British psychoanalysts such as Ronald Fairbairn and Donald Winnicott, themselves deriving ideas from Melanie Klein. It is often called object relations, "objects" here referring to persons.[12] It has roots in Freud, whose theory of narcissism "sustains the view that we are all incorporations and extensions of – take in and provide aspects of – one another" (Chodorow 1989, 147).

Although the relational approach has its origins in attention to the pre-Oedipal stage, the main interest for my purposes is not the aetiological origin of selfhood in infancy but rather the understanding of the self as a product of relationships developed throughout the life course (albeit building upon the foundation established during infancy). As Mitchell puts it, "In each relational-model account the passions depicted characterize human longings and fears at all ages. The struggle between destructiveness and hopeful benevolence [Klein], the search for all-embracing love [Balint], the tension between self-expression and pandering [Winnicott], between autonomy and a longing to fuse [Mahler], the need for supportive recognition and admired heroes [Kohut] – these are fundamental dimensions of human relations, from infancy through senescence" (1988a, 134).[13] Mitchell continues, "Being a self with others entails a constant dialectic between attachment and self-definition, between connection and differentiation, a continual negotiation between one's wishes and will and the wishes and will of others, between one's own subjective reality and a consensual reality of others with whom one lives" (149).

A critical feature is the grounding of selfhood in relations with psychic representations of others rather than bounded corporeal autonomy. Hence, "If a person is to develop at all, the self must come to include what were originally aspects of the other and the relation to the other.... We become a person, then, in internal relation with the social world....

People inevitably incorporate one another; our sociality is built into our psychic structure and there is no easy separation of individual and society or possibility of the individual apart from society" (Chodorow 1989, 149). Put in other terms, there is a dialectical flux of projections and introjections. Self-other relations become internalized, part of the self. We become, as Joan Rivière memorably put it, "members of one another" (as cited by Chodorow 1989, 158). This is what I described in particular with reference to Mohedja, whose internalization of relations with her mother and brother were mediated by the presence of particular spirits.

A newly arrived spirit is initially understood as a not-me. This not-me helps to set off by contrast who "I" am.[14] But as the spirit is negotiated with on the social plane and internalized on the psychological plane, so the not-me is increasingly absorbed into the "I" and the "I" expands thereby, to encompass both "me" and "not-me." This can be understood as a growth in maturity, but this is does not mean a more strongly bounded ego. Indeed, to gain spirits is to be increasingly connected with others. While spirits are in one sense alien beings, they carry with them the histories of their relations with humans; to receive the spirit is to introject aspects of this history. Hence, a break in the unity of the conscious self is at the same time a bridge to sharing identity with others and thickening relationships with them.[15] Consider the density of relations between Mohedja and her mother and her mother's former clients, or her relationships with Tumbu.

"On a psychological level, then," says Nancy Chodorow, "even the apparent boundaries of the individual do not separate in any simple way the pristine individual from the rest of the world." Among other things, this means that any depiction of "strong ego" has immediately to be qualified to note that "strong" does not mean "strongly bounded."[16] It should be evident that openness characterizes the receptivity of hosts towards their cohabiting spirits.

For relational theorists, self-construction through identifying and relating with others is not a matter of passing successively through a series of developmental stages, but characteristic of ongoing daily life (Chodorow 1989, 149).[17] Where for Fingarette the "community of selves" refers to successive stages of psychic development, for Mitchell plurality is found in the modes of relating with significant others that are addressed throughout the life cycle. Where Fingarette sees a succession of selves and the issue of how we deal with our earlier selves, Mitchell sees conflicting, or at least divergent, modes of relating which are present side by side continuously. I am not in a position to adjudicate between them, but happily I do not have to choose. Cohabiting spirits are understood locally as distinct selves, with some of their traits drawn from childhood and adolescence and others from adulthood and old age, but they can cohabit with one and the same host and manifest in their distinctive modes of relating with others. Cohabitation adds a layer to the ongoing human dialectical process of externalization and internalization. It enables both the internalization of self-objects and their externalization as distinct persons.

Additionally, the relational model suggests a comparison between the practice and experience of cohabitation for some mediums and the practice and experience of psychoanalysis for some analysands. Each can be understood as a kind of dialogical working-through process in which the subject gradually comes to internalize the therapeutic interlocutor and a mode of relating. Much as a goal of psychoanalytic treatment may be to cultivate the ability for self-analysis, such that patients continue what Freud called the "interminable" process on their own, having perhaps introjected features of the analyst, so some hosts come to internalize their own curers, as both Mohedja and Tumbu do with Malidy Juma and – quite literally – with Mze Nuru and Mze Marwan, respectively.

Here I can add to the table an idea from Heinz Kohut concerning self-objects, namely others who are not fully differentiated from the self, like a parent from the infant's perspective. They are "objectively separate people who serve functions that will later be performed by the individual's own psychic structure" (Greenberg and Mitchell 1983, 353). An arriving spirit could be considered a kind of self-object (or representation of such).

As spirits are "worked through," via a dialectic of differentiation and identification, so hosts grow in practical insight. As hosts internalize their cohabiting spirits, so the spirits become more like their hosts. Psychoanalyst Masud Khan (1974) has suggested that the other becomes in effect a close friend in the progression of that dialogue with an internalized other that might be necessary to define self-experience. Tumbu once told me that the spirits with whom he cohabited would only do what he himself would consider right and would dislike what he himself disliked.

As Chodorow puts it, "Paraphrasing Freud ... where fragmented internal objects were, there shall harmoniously related objects be; and where false, reactive self was, there shall true, agentic self be, with its relationally based capacity both to be alone and to participate in the transitional space between self and other self that creates play, intimacy, and culture" (Chodorow 1989, 159).

However, we should not exaggerate or idealize the fully unified self as a desired end point. Jonathan Lear makes the insightful point that unity is itself partly constituted by forms of disruption, and that we should learn to live well with them. As noted in the epigraph, and as illustrated in the lives I have recounted, "Ironically, the unity that is available to us is a peculiar form of disunity" (2011, 43).

Play, Fantasy, Enlivenment

In her reference to transitional space and play, Chodorow signals another major contribution of the relational tradition and one that is central for appreciating cohabitation. A key figure here is Donald Winnicott, for whom mental health is the capacity not (only) for work and love, as Freud put it, but for play. Cohabitation with spirits is serious and sometimes painful. Yet it can also be understood as play in the sense that psychoanalysis understands it.

As Robert Orsi summarizes it, "playing ... is the 'intermediate area of experiencing' (in Winnicott's words) that exists in between 'the inner reality of the individual and the shared reality of the world that is external to individuals.' Moving between the 'subjective and that which is objectively perceived' is a source of human creativity" (Orsi 2016, 235).

In *Playing and Reality*, Winnicott "points us to the transitional space between mother and infant that is neither me nor not-me and that becomes the creative arena of play and culture" (Chodorow 1989, 10). Winnicott writes famously of "transitional objects," like a child's favourite teddy bear, that are present in the objective world, yet have a subjective meaning created by the individual. "The transitional object thus inhabits a transitional space where boundaries are and aren't, where the world is both subjective and objective, where [originally] mother and child accept this lack of definition" (Chodorow 1989, 152–3).

The significance of play extends well beyond childhood. "Playing is no inner psychic reality. It is outside the individual, but it is not the external world.... There is a direct development from transitional phenomena to playing, and from playing to shared playing, and from this to cultural experiences.... Playing implies trust.... *Playing is essentially satisfying*" (Winnicott 1971, 51–2, his emphasis).

As Chodorow observes, "Winnicott's view ... shows how childhood experience and the childhood subjective world come to be integrated into the adult's creative life and culture as a whole without seeing creativity as simply a return to childhood wishes, fantasies, and fears" (Chodorow 1989, 153). In a later work, she writes, "For the musician, the instrument is created.... The violin or guitar is made of wood and has gut or metal strings.... But the musician, in playing, also creates her instrument from within. It is part of her self, and, in a chamber group, orchestra, or jam session, she creates a transitional space with other players. An instrument (or paintbrush) extends and is part of the self and the self's creativity, creates a connection to others, and is out there and separate. Me and not me" (2020, 259).

Cohabitation is a form of play in this sense. It offers a transitional space between the objective and the subjective. And the spirits are me and not me, or perhaps, not-me and not-not-me.

Play is not simply a matter of pleasure. As Orsi write, for Winnicott, "it is also 'liable to become frightening.' There is a precariousness to play. New ways of experiencing and moving the body may be tried in play. The boundaries of self and other are explored, transgressed, and reestablished. There is the prospect of absorptive solitude in play without fear of impingement. Unfamiliar sensations and novel possibilities for life and relationship arise. 'On the basis of playing,' Winnicott says, 'is built the whole of man's [sic] existential existence'" (2016, 225–6, citing Winnicott 1971, 64).

As Thomas Ogden (2010, 335) writes, for Winnicott this "capacity to live imaginatively in an intermediate space between reality and fantasy" is "crucial to psychological health."

Cohabiting with and acting as the spirits may also be understood by means of the related psychoanalytic concept of (healthy) narcissistic illusion. Such illusions occur throughout the life cycle and are not necessarily negative (Mitchell 1988a, 194). In healthy narcissism, one enjoys illusions, say, of grandiosity, but readily relinquishes them; in pathological narcissism, illusions are taken too seriously. Cohabitation provides a means for what Mitchell considers the negotiation of the delicate balance between illusion and reality, succumbing to the exclusivity of neither. The frame of possession – shifting between voices and responding to them – provides a means for such negotiation and a protected space for illusion.

Albeit far from considering cohabitation per se, Hans Loewald offers perhaps the strongest argument for its richness. Loewald considers the unconscious as a source of the vitality of life, including the imaginative and intuitive dimensions of experience. "For Loewald, a meaningful human life is founded not on replacing unconscious life with consciousness or secondary-process thought, or on overcoming the influence of the unconscious, but on the infusion of unconscious life into, and its integration with, consciousness. Unconscious fantasies expressed in dreams and transferences enrich life and give it meaning" (Chodorow 2020, 104). Central for Loewald is not enlightenment but enlivenment,

Loewald writes, "the integration of ego and reality consists in, and the continued integrity of ego and reality depends on, transference of unconscious processes and 'contents' on to new experiences and objects of contemporary life ... there is neither such a thing as reality nor a real relationship, without transference. Any 'real relationship' involves transfer of unconscious images to present-day objects. In fact, present-day objects are objects, and thus real, in the full sense of the word ... only to the extent to which this transference, in the sense of transformational interplay between unconscious and preconscious, is realized" (1980, 252–4, as cited by Chodorow 2020, 105).

For Loewald, "fantasy is unreal only insofar as its communication with present actuality is inhibited or severed. To that extent, however, present actuality is unreal too. Perhaps a better word than 'unreal' is 'meaningless'" (1980, 362 as cited by Chodorow 2020,106).[18]

For Loewald, "only the enchanted life is worth living" (Mitchell 1988b, 854).

The twin goals of this book have been to put what was called spirit possession under the new description of cohabitation and to narrate certain aspects of the lives and world of Mohedja Salim and Tumbu Vita, a married couple of twentieth-century Mayotte. I have drawn on psychoanalysis to indicate the relevance, reality, and value of cohabitation for those who live with spirits to those readers who live without them.

While exploring an ostensibly radically different form of life, my agenda has been to render explicit how much we share, while leaving Mohedja and Tumbu their individuality and their particular and intense humanity, vitality, creativity, and responsivity. I have wanted to show their complexity, not strip it away – less to account for their practice than to appreciate it.

Photo 1. Ndramboeny with his spear advising some of Mohedja's relatives, 1975–6.

Photo 2. Tumbu preparing medicine, 1975–6. The Qur'anic verse will be rinsed off and then drunk by the client. Note the sack of plant medicines.

Photo 3. Mohedja with a granddaughter and friends, 1975–6. The women are measuring dry rice for a ceremony.

Photo 4. Tumbu cutting into the hillside to prepare his house plot, 1980.

Acknowledgments

I have lived with this material for a long time and many people have contributed to my thinking about it. I will not recapitulate all the thanks recorded in previous books and articles in which many of the ideas here were first presented, but simply note the original provocation on the part of Gananath Obeyesekere to take psychoanalysis into account, long and productive conversations with Paul Antze, and later responses from Marsha Hewitt. Rogaia Abusharaf and two anonymous external reviewers offered extremely generous and insightful comments, and Jodi Lewchuk, as usual, proved the perfect editor.

My first year of fieldwork (1975–6) was supported by a Canada Council doctoral fellowship and an NSF grant award to Conrad Kottak and Henry Wright. I subsequently received a grant from the National Geographic Society and several consecutive grants from the Social Sciences and Humanities Research Council of Canada, including a two-term tier 1 Canada Research Chair, during which time I was also supported by the University of Toronto Scarborough.

My latest visit to Mayotte (in 2023) was financed by the French National Research Institute for Sustainable Development (IRD) in conjunction with the Future Maore Reefs project and was greatly facilitated by fellow anthropologists Georgeta Stoïca and Marta Gentilucci. I have learned a great deal from Sophie Blanchy and from more recent research in Mayotte on the part of Sophie Bouffart, Mathilde Heslon, and Damien Riccio.

Jackie Solway and I have cohabited for over forty years. She has twice accompanied me to Mayotte (along with our children) and offered countless valuable insights and support along the way.

I owe enormous thanks to all my friends in Mayotte and especially to the children and grandchildren of Tumbu and Mohedja. As is evident on virtually every page, my greatest debt is to the protagonists of this book, Mohedja Salim and Tumbu Vita (along with their cohabiting spirits) for sharing their remarkable lives. I deeply regret I cannot honour them with their true names, but I need to leave them this vestige of privacy.

Notes

1. Cohabiting

1 I have laid out some of the grammar of possession in Mayotte in Lambek (1981). Not everyone who cohabits with spirits does so grammatically – that is, their interactions with spirits do not always work out in a harmonious or socially recognized fashion. I do not discuss here cases in which hosts remain seriously troubled by spirits.

2 Aisha Beliso-De Jesús (2014) speaks of "copresences" with respect to Afro-Cuban Santería, a concept that also overlaps with cohabitation, albeit in a more fully embodied form as she understands it.

3 In her excellent account of spirit mediumship at Sidi shrines in western India, Jazmin Graves Eyssallenne suggests that "embodiment" is a term preferable to "possession" (2023, 106).

4 This is analogous to the French mode of speaking of "possession" rather than "spirit possession."

5 Kibushy is primarily an oral language that draws on words that have different orthographic conventions when written in Malagasy, Shimaore, or French. For the most part, I have written them as they sound in English, notably replacing a Malagasy "o" and a French "ou" with a "u." The "ñ" is pronounced as the "ng" in "sing."

6 Work that resonates with cohabitation includes Crapanzano (1985), Crapanzano and Garrison (1977), Kapchan (2007), Masquelier (2002), Motta (2019), Obeyesekere (1984), and Zempléni (1977). On performance and experience, see, inter alia, Kapferer (1983, 1997) and Espírito Santo and Matan (2022). A classic work that integrates embodiment and self-reflection is Boddy (1989). Collections that compare similar phenomena in Europe, Atlantic America, and globally are, respectively, Pócs and Zempléni (2022), Johnson (2014b), and Schmidt and Huskinson (2010). Boddy (1994) and Zempléni (2022) provide intelligent and comprehensive

reviews of the vast literature. Kramer provides an overview of possession in Africa from an aesthetic perspective, concluding that it is "always both more and less than therapy, art, entertainment, social criticism, profession, fashion, or ethnography" (1993, 240), while Masquelier (2001) provides an exemplary account from one location (Niger). Ochoa (2020) offers a lively account of multigenerational cohabitation in Cuba, and Bacigalupo (2016) the life history of a shaman in Chile.

7 For a full account, see Lambek (2018).

8 This book can be read in conjunction with my earlier work, but that work is not necessary for the comprehension of this one. I describe my first encounter with spirits in *Human Spirits* (1981) and explore the grammar and public dimensions of spirit cures and performances there. In *Knowledge and Practice in Mayotte* (1993), I follow Mohedja and Tumbu in their practice of curing others in much greater depth than I present here, as well as show the articulation of spirit possession with Islam, astrology, and sorcery. *The Weight of the Past* (2002) moves the account to northwest Madagascar, where the senior spirits have their shrines and tombs and where the spirits, manifestations of deceased historical figures, have political significance and explicit historical resonance.

9 The relevance of Mze Rihu's remarks will become evident in chapter 6.

10 Robert Orsi (2005, 145). Among many other examples, Tanya Luhrmann (2012) writes of Protestant Christians who think of Jesus as their friend, and Bhrigupati Singh (2015) writes of living with deities in India.

11 "Person-centred ethnography" is a term deployed by Levy and Hollan (1998). There is excellent work, such as that by Boddy (1989), Crapanzano (1985), Kapferer (1983), Motta (2019), Obeyesekere (1984), and Ram (2013), that attempts to link possession to the subjectivity of mediums. This book follows their lead but takes a direction of its own.

12 When I first conceptualized the book, I planned to include the lives of two younger and unrelated hosts but eventually decided it would make the account too long.

2. Acknowledging Spirits

1 The verb is *mianzaka* (*mianjaka*), used more commonly in Madagascar, with the root, *jaka*, meaning "burden" in the sense of burdening or ruling over.

2 As quoted in Mervyn Rothstein (1996).

3 Sandra Bamford argues with respect to the Kamea of Papua New Guinea, that instead of marking a difference, a shared taboo establishes "*essential sameness*" (2007, 94, her emphasis).

4 As Janice Boddy astutely argues in the case of northern Sudan, "Zar ... is a medium for the cultivation of women's consciousness" (1989, 345)

and "provokes those it claims to think about themselves via their inverse spirit counterparts" (306). She continues, "All the implicit functions and significances of the zar seem to work, gradually and cumulatively, toward developing in the possessed a mature, considered perspective of herself and her life situation" (308).

5 In a given genre of possession, either the ambiguity between me and not-me is maintained in performance, as appears to be the case in Sudanese *zar*, and perhaps even highlighted (Boddy 1989), or disambiguation of the me and not-me is deemed critical to the felicity of the performance. The latter can indeed be an aspect of the underlying structure that renders possession meaningful, such that the collapse of the distinction becomes a failure of performance (as is the case in Mayotte and Madagascar). At some level, possession is everywhere both ambiguous and unambiguous, constituting both one entity and two.

6 See Berger and Luckmann (1966); Hacking (1999).

7 Geertz (1968, 111–12), as cited in Rosaldo (2013, 137n1).

8 Other aspects of scope are discussed in Lambek (1993). Overall, the public scope of cohabitation is narrower in Mayotte than in northwest Madagascar (Lambek 2002).

9 The speech of a spirit is not simply an unmediated or involuntary expression but tacitly framed and marked. The dissociative state of a possessed host cannot be called simply unconscious, nor is speech under dissociation the same as psychotic speech.

10 See Critchley (2005).

11 The initiation and the partial socialization are discussed in Lambek (1981).

12 Gadamer would speak of a widening of the horizon ([1960] 1985).

13 The classic argument is found in Berger and Luckmann (1966). Obeyesekere (1984) provides a different, but equally brilliant, model and one directed specifically at possession. However, his interlocutors were much unhappier than mine and took paths that removed them from the ordinary life of householders. Moreover, Obeyesekere himself took a stronger and more orthodox Freudian line of interpretation than I do here.

3. Tumbu: The Search for Livelihood and Land

1 More on their Muslim practice is found in the final section of chapter 9.

4. Mohedjai Kos Vola and the Line of Women

1 In 1995, Mohedja told me she thought that Kos Vola was the wife of Ndramañavakarivu (Andriantsoly in life), the Sakalava monarch who fled Madagascar for Mayotte, converted to Islam, and was purported to have

ceded Mayotte to the French in 1840. He is considered the leading trumba in Mayotte and has a shrine (Mahabu) on a promontory near Mamutzu where annual performances of the Maulida are held on his behalf. Kos Vola did not accompany him to Mayotte, said Mohedja, and is buried in Madagascar. She is the mother of Ndramihotsy, another Sakalava prince and trumba. A different spirit medium told me many years later that Kos Vola was the sister of Ndramboeny; if that is the case, Mohedja was possessed by a brother and sister pair, ones who lived during the establishment of the Sakalava kingdom in northwest Madagascar, several generations before Ndramañavakarivu.

2 Neither Mohedja's father nor her stepfathers directly cohabited with spirits.

3 On the significance of the first engagement, see chapter 5.

4 Attending to the public announcement of the name also supports the mystification whereby the reality of possession is established. While the annunciation of the name is an illocutionary act in which the identity of the spirit in the host is constituted, the event is understood by participants as also locutionary in nature. From the local point of view, in giving his name, the spirit is also speaking referentially, revealing a given identity rather than producing it. See Lambek (2006).

5 Women in Mayotte did not wear veils; they loosely covered their hair on most public occasions.

6 Tumbu had also pledged to sacrifice a goat if Mwanesha got well. This was fulfilled the following April, with some twenty adult kin invited to help prepare and consume the meal and recite prayers for the well-being of Mwanesha and the entire extended family. Two weeks later, Mwanesha was sent to live with foster parents (chapter 9).

7 For Tumbu, then, Kos Vola is a "wife." See the discussion in chapter 6.

8 Trumba wands are smooth staffs or canes made of hard wood (*famelung*), blackened by being buried for a time in mud, and tipped and decorated with silver.

9 Despite the Islamic prohibition on alcohol, palm wine was a source of tension in many marriages. Young men drank but were supposed to stop by the time they married. Many did not or could not stop and their wives were upset at the consequent decline in economic activity, the frequent absence of their husbands, the smell and general unpleasantness, and the public embarrassment. Most men did stop drinking by middle age. Tumbu and Mohedja explained that in Mayotte people drank not when they were depressed, feeling regrets or worries, but when they were in a good mood.

10 Sometimes it was the wife's cohabiting spirit who pushed the husband to stop drinking.

11 Trawick (1992, 60). Trawick's model is Lacanian and not one that I pursue here.

12 As Mitchell's use of pronouns makes clear, this understanding is not restricted to feminist theories, nor does it apply only to women as some social science applications of relational psychoanalysis might lead one to believe.

5. Mze Nuru: Affirmation and Identification

1 At the time, women gave birth at home, without medical assistance. Post-partum infection, fever, and delirium were a part of many women's experiences. While I was present in 1976, a woman became psychotic shortly after giving birth and died about a week later.

2 In Mayotte, as both Tumbu and Mohedja told me, it was considered stupid to explicitly wish for a spirit and dangerous to encourage one to enter on one's own.

3 All this is discussed in *Human Spirits* (1981).

4 For the psychoanalytic model underlying these remarks see the Postscript.

5 These identifications are not explicit or literal. Another time when I asked Mohedja in 1976 about Mze Nuru's appearance in her dreams, she reported that she saw him as a man, dressed in trousers and a shirt. She did not describe his features or identify him specifically with anyone she knew.

6. Mze Marwan and Mze Rihu: Consolidation and Cooperation

1 Their curing practice is described at length in Lambek (1993).

2 A fascinating aspect about this is that both Tumbu and Mohedja knew full well the immediate source of the material *sairy* itself and indeed it was Tumbu who had taught this healer how to produce and extract it. See *Knowledge and Practice in Mayotte* (1993) for further discussion.

3 While the spirits here support Tumbu and Mohedja's marriage, I am not offering a functionalist explanation for their presence (see also Lambek 1980, 1981).

7. Ndramboeny: Mohedja as a Curer

1 The music at trumba ceremonies was provided by clapping, rattle, guitar, and sometimes accordion. It was sharply distinguished from patros ceremonies, which made extensive use of drums. Indeed, the very names of the two ceremonies, *rombu* and *azulahy*, refer to clapping and drumming, respectively. See Lambek (1981, 1993) for extended descriptions of trumba ceremonies managed by Mohedja.

2 Ndramboeny's willingness to forgo the cow was not unusual. In 1985, I was told that most people hosting more than one senior trumba held their *rombu be* concurrently and slaughtered a single cow.

3 See Lambek (2002) on Ndramboeny in Madagascar, and for a comparison of his cohabitation in three different hosts, see Lambek (2014).

4 This was an extension of the joking relationship that Tumbu and Mohedja engaged in with the young woman.

5 "Privileged discourse" is a concept that Paul Antze and I developed in an unpublished paper by that name (1983). The uncoupling of the ordinary, habitual, conventional, or normative links between message and meta-message is one of the primary positive affordances of possession. The work that is done within the frame may then come to permeate ordinary life outside it. We held the same to be true for psychoanalytic therapy.

6 While she recovered from the psychosis, Ruby suffered internal pain for some seven years, followed by an operation in which they "opened her from breast to stomach."

7 One could think here of the conjunction of the transference and the therapeutic alliance in psychoanalysis.

8 For further discussion of the work of therapy and therapists by means of spirits, see Lambek (1981, 1993).

8. Darwesh and the Suitors

1 Such visits were not characteristic of trumba, who are deceased humans, mostly royalty, located in tombs.

2 For an example, see Lambek (1988).

3 On the impact on those accused of practicing sorcery, see chapter 12 and Lambek (2021).

4 See the complementary account in chapter 6.

5 This is an instance where Mohedja seems to identify the spirit as herself.

6 The psychoanalytic model I'm drawing on here is one of object relations rather than drive theory. See the postscript for further discussion, but in brief, I argue that unconscious projection was exchanged for introjection. In introjection something functioning as an object-representation shifts to become a self-representation; projection is the reverse. Identification results from a series of introjective-projective processes (Fingarette 1963).

9. Raising Children

1 Compare my writing on ethical judgment (Lambek 2015).

2 Boys and girls had different childhood experiences. Boys were nursed for as long as two years if their mothers did not get pregnant in the meantime,

whereas girls were said to be weaned at a year or when they started walking, whichever came first, lest the fat from the milk descend and block the womb, leading to fertility problems in maturity. Girl babies were likewise placed in a sitting position earlier than boys. People said that for girls, one wanted soft flesh whereas boys were going to have to work hard. While infants were treated with great affection and attention, toddlers of both sexes had a rough time of it. They straggled after their mothers and were often teased or left to cry. A slightly older sibling was often the one to provide a kind word or a helping hand. Boys had a more carefree existence than girls, who were roped earlier into a regular routine of domestic tasks. Yet boys were also pushed out earlier and made to be more responsible for themselves. Girls were not entirely housebound and played on the village square at night when their work was done. In addition to Qur'anic class and French schooling (once it became available), girls could join *debaa* dance teams, dress up, and perform in other villages. They also gathered periodically with their age-mates for *festa*, when they each brought food, cooked together, and danced to the radio. A group of fifteen girls gathered one day in 1985 with six chickens, fish, tinned sardines, and twelve kilograms of rice to cook for themselves. After eating, they fed their younger siblings and fixed each other's hair. Then they went home to change and returned to dance until after 9:00 p.m. *Festa* also described the gatherings of child trumba (chapter 13).

3 Only boys were cut. People were astonished and horrified when I mentioned the practice of female circumcision.

10. Treating Mariam's Baby

1 This resonates with what Marshall Sahlins (2013) refers to as the mutuality of being characteristic of kinship.
2 I am indebted to a referee for making this point.

11. Ali's Marriage

1 Infants were said to take on characteristics of both parents.

12. Mohedja and Her Mother-in-Law

1 The account says much about notions of intergenerational reciprocity and obligations. It also shows the kinds of conflict towards which child fosterage can lead because the process is not a definitive one. Each parental or grandparental figure continues to maintain rights, interests, and responsibilities in the child.

2 Mohedja herself addressed Dady Nuriaty as *mama* rather than *rafuza* (mother-in-law).

3 Mohedja did not bother to distinguish which spirit was the source of her information. It was the information itself rather than her relationship with a particular spirit that was crucial.

13. Playing and Working: Kalu and the Kakanoru

1 The name "Kalu" was sometimes replaced by "Somo," a term of mutual address among the child spirits and sometimes an exclamation of pleasure. Among the Sakalava of Analalava, it was one of a series of words used between women to mean "friend" (Feeley-Harnik 1991, 265).

2 See Lambek (1981, chapter 12). One could say this comedy offered an insight into the performative nature of gender, and indeed of all forms of identity, resonant with the theoretical formulations of Erving Goffman and Judith Butler.

3 The concept "regression in the service of the ego" developed by Ernst Kris is appropriate here. See the postscript for further discussion.

4 The negotiations leading up to the feast and the amusement of the feast itself are described in greater detail and under different names, in *Human Spirits* (Lambek 1981, 173–6).

5 She is referring to the fact that children had to be respectful, but grandchildren were entitled to tease grandparents.

6 Kakanoru is a Kibushy transformation of *kalanoro*, as they are known in Madagascar. In Shimaore-speaking villages there were creatures with virtually identical traits to kakanoru known as *Mwana Issa*, which translates literally as "child Jesus."

7 In this they contrast with trumba, who require moonlight and who want to be seen.

8 This was a more common descriptor than the shorts and shirt in which Tumbu first glimpsed a kakanoru. Tumbu's nakedness could also have been a sign of his insecurity at not yet being an "owner" in the village (chapter 3).

14. Later Arrivals: Maimuna, Rasua, and the Spirit of the Maulida

1 For an excellent account of the related women's musical genre, the *debaa*, see Bertuzzi (2021).

2 This is similar to treatments for spirits found in the distant southwest of Madagascar.

3 See Lambek (2001).

15. Decline, Death, Succession

1 The government did supply a modest allowance for those in school.

2 "Event" is here a barely adequate translation of *asa*, which means literally "work," or in this case, "a work" or an "affair." *Asa* in this sense is not in contrast to "play" (*soma*) since it includes enjoyment, but it conveys a serious and formal undertaking that embraces ritual and hospitality.

3 At the time, many villagers had relocated temporarily to La Réunion, and it was a common practice for mothers or mothers-in-law to assist after childbirth.

4 They did not include me. The medicine went exclusively to kin through procreation but no doubt they also assumed I was living comfortably and invulnerable to sorcery. People said sorcery worked only on those who believed in it.

5 Nuriaty and Ali did not attend the final *fatiha*. Each sibling continued independently to perform the *maitimia* prayer held annually during the month of *dilhedj* by every family on behalf of their deceased kin.

6 In their parents' day, patros and trumba would not have arrived on the same occasion.

7 This was never an explicit point when Maimuna cohabited with Mohedja.

8 This could be considered an extreme form of mourning her mother's death.

9 Many hosts from Mayotte did the same. Travel to Majunga was cheap, as was life there with euros, and the Malagasy healers had greater expertise and stronger reputations than those in Mayotte.

10 I have analysed the conflict among the siblings as well as my failed attempts to make peace elsewhere and desist from going further here (Lambek 2011, 2021).

11 Challenges to spirit activities on the part of reformist Islam are widespread in much of Africa; see, for example, the excellent account in Masquelier (2001). The zar has also virtually disappeared in northern Sudan (Janice Boddy, pers. comm.). Across the Atlantic, forms of fundamentalist Christianity are also challenging spirit activities (e.g., Selka 2014).

16. Reflections on Voice

1 Here I closely paraphrase Jonathan Lear (2021, 79).

2 Here then is a radical distinction between cohabitation and what has been called multiple personality disorder.

3 As James Faubion has indirectly warned me (via anonymous refereed comments on Lambek 2022), I may be untrue to the way Aristotle applies these concepts. Rather than maintaining sharp distinctions between

poiesis or techne and praxis as different kinds of activity, I draw on them as different but complementary frames or descriptions with which to see cohabitation.

4 Das adds, "One of Cavell's great achievements is to have shown that subjectivity is expressed in the discovery and loss of one's voice in one's history" (2020, 16).

5 Das herself suggests this is the "female" side of scepticism. The passage continues, "Skepticism is thus taken in the realm of the social and is one site where we can see the culturally specific transfigurations that provide the context for living with such issues. Cavell famously argues that the answer to the skeptic's doubts lies not in providing more information, or more evidence, but simply in acknowledging the flesh and blood character of the other who is before me. The theme of skepticism and the uncanny – accepting one's separateness from the other and yet being able to articulate how one's life might be staked in this other…." (Das 2020, 17).

6 Kamuf here is drawing on Derrida writing on Gadamer writing on Celan – multiple voicing indeed.

7 Jeanette Winterson, *Art Objects: Essays on Ecstasy and Effrontery*, as cited by Popova (2014).

8 Michel Leiris (1958) offered an early and insightful comparison of spirit performances in Ethiopia with theatre. See also Kramer (1993).

9 The active, ethical dimension is where the analogy with theatre partly fails.

10 These are puzzles I have addressed in essays concerning the continuity of person or self; the condition of being of one or two (or more) minds; the individuated interpretation of a stock character; and whether the question might be considered through the lens of irony rather than self-deception.

11 I discuss its generous, if sometimes sly, response to Islam in Lambek (1993).

Psychoanalytic Postscript

1 Robert Orsi (2016, 110), citing Phillips (1997, 27) and Sartre (1963, 57).

2 Talal Asad (1993, 15), as cited by Schaefer (2020).

3 Jonathan Lear (2011, 43).

4 Compare Obeyesekere's masterful account (1984), in which he makes a closer connection between public idiom and personal meanings than do I.

5 It also helps wrest analysis away from deviance, deprivation, and marginality.

6 See, for example, Leys (1996) on Freud and the essays by Kosman and Sorabji in Rorty (1980) on Aristotle.

7 I abstain from making further comparison between the two forms of therapeutic encounter, but more could be said.

8 Compare Boddy (1989) on possession as a means of resistance to an "overdetermined" self.

9 Alternatively, if anxiety is produced by a conflict between conscious will and unconscious motivation, cohabitation can reduce it by placing both side by side.

10 A weakness of ego psychology is its optimistic can-do quality. Critics may be correct to say that this American ideology undermines the core of psychoanalysis, whose strength lies in its unflinching pessimism, or at least realism. I am no advocate of the vulgarization of Freudianism found in the North American self-help movement. But the ideological effects of ego psychology on American society need not be confused with its value when applied to non-Western subjects – people who too often have been viewed as the inverse of the American ideal – as passive, devoid of agency, lacking moral sensibility, and so on.

11 A relational approach may also blunt the critical edge associated with drive theory, with respect to the asocial qualities within the human makeup. See Murphy (1971) for an anthropological celebration of psychoanalytic negativism. In *Human Spirits*, I gave a reading of possession that was informed by this view. For one thing, it helps make sense of the types and attributes of spirits available in the cultural repertoire in Mayotte, including portrayals of sexual precocity, gluttony, and aggression. It is noteworthy that these regressive features, associated with spirit types portraying particular stages of the life cycle, are characteristic of spirits in a wide range of cultural contexts. For a work that draws primarily on Freudian views of symbolism as propounded in *The Interpretation of Dreams*, see Obeyesekere's application of psychoanalysis to spirit mediums in the Hindu/Buddhist interface of Sri Lanka (1984). In addition, and despite its possible relevance, I have not wished to juxtapose an incommensurable Lacanian approach to the object relational. For Lacanian perspectives on cohabitation in South India and on madness and Islamic thought in Morocco, see respectively Trawick (1992) and Pandolfo (2017).

12 As Chodorow explicates, "The unfortunate locution 'object,' in object-relations theory seems to be a holdover from a psychoanalytic theory centered on drives, which have, in Freud's view, 'objects' and 'aims.' In this model, the personhood of the object is not stressed, nor need the object be a person. Object-relations theorists tend to mean 'other'" (1989, 220n9).

13 The references are to psychoanalysts Melanie Klein, Michael Balint, Donald Winnicott, Margaret Mahler, and Heinz Kohut.

14 The terms are G.H. Mead's as noted in the previous chapter. In a sense, relational psychoanalysis is the counterpart of sociological interactionist or dialogical theories of selfhood such as Mead's.

15 In this respect, cohabitation is radically different from multiple personality disorder, in which dissociation is alienating and distancing of social connection. Moreover, whereas cohabitation is based on a central self for whom the spirits are alters, multiple personality disorder is constituted by alters in the absence or fragmentation of a core self. The spirits are not fragments of the self, broken splinters, but semi-autonomous parts of a functioning "whole." They are parts added to the whole rather than split from it.

16 This distinction is a major contribution of Chodorow who also links it to differences of gender. She has argued that "the selves of women and men tend to be constructed differently – women's self more in relation and involved with boundary negotiations, separation and connection, men's self more distanced and based on defensively firm boundaries and denials of self-other connection" (1989, 2). The comparison of Mohedja and Tumbu appears to be an instance of this. The distinction is, of course, relative, and may be culture specific.

17 It is worth noting that the identifications and introjections refer to other persons in the relational matrix. Compare accounts of possession in terms of mimesis with respect to foreign others and even material objects (Boddy 1989; Kramer 1993; Taussig 1993).

18 Loewald is also famous for describing overcoming neurosis as a matter of transforming hungry ghosts (unresolved conflicts) into benevolent ancestors. The spirits in Mayotte are not literally ancestors but, as we have seen, they can be identified with them or subjectively experienced as parental or grandparental. In his seminal account of Tallensi relations with ancestors, Meyer Fortes noted that ancestors were not exclusively benevolent, but rather "comparable to externalized representations of conscience" (1987, 197). Like Tallensi ancestors, spirits in Mayotte can be both nurturant and constructive and threatening and destructive, but more often the former. Indeed, the spirits themselves often talk about raising (*mitarimy*) future hosts, in the sense of looking after them.

References

Anscombe, Elizabeth. 1963. *Intention*. Ithaca, NY: Cornell University Press.

Antze, Paul, and Michael Lambek. 1983. "Privileged Discourse: The Construction of the Self in Spirit Possession and Psychoanalysis." Unpublished paper delivered at the annual meeting of the American Anthropological Association, Chicago.

Aristotle. 1976. *Nichomachean Ethics*. Harmondsworth: Penguin.

Asad, Talal. 1993. *Genealogies of Religion: Discipline and Reasons of Power in Christianity and Islam*. Baltimore: Johns Hopkins University Press. https://doi.org/10.1353/book.16014.

Austin, J.L. 1970. *Philosophical Papers*. New York: Oxford University Press.

Bacigalupo, Ana Mariella. 2016. Thunder Shaman. Austin: University of Texas Press.

Bakhtin, M.M. 1981. *The Dialogic Imagination: Four Essays*. Edited by Michael Holquist. Translated by Caryl Emerson. Austin: University of Texas Press.

Bamford, Sandra. 2007. *Biology Unmoored: Melanesian Reflections on Life and Biotechnology*. Berkeley: University of California Press. https://doi.org/10.1525/9780520939479.

Beliso-De Jesús, Aisha. 2014. "Santería Copresence and the Making of African Diaspora Bodies." *Cultural Anthropology* 29, no. 3 (August): 503–52. https://doi.org/10.14506/ca29.3.04.

Berger, Peter L., and Thomas Luckmann. 1966. *The Social Construction of Reality*. London: Penguin.

Bertuzzi, Eléna. 2021. "*S'imposer en dansant : Créativité et prestige des femmes de Mayotte*." PhD diss., Université Paris Nanterre.

Boddy, Janice. 1989. *Wombs and Alien Spirits*. Madison: Wisconsin University Press.

– 1994. "Spirit Possession Revisited." *Annual Review of Anthropology* 23:407–34. https://doi.org/10.1146/annurev.an.23.100194.002203.

Bouffart, Sophie. 2009. *"La possession comme lieu et mode d'expression de la complexité sociale : Le cas de Mayotte."* PhD diss., Université Paris Nanterre.

Bourdieu, Pierre. 1977. *Outline of a Theory of Practice*. Translated by Richard Nice. Cambridge: Cambridge University Press. https://doi.org/10.1017/CBO9780511812507.

Burke, Kenneth. 1945. *A Grammar of Motives*. Berkeley: University of California Press.

Cavell, Stanley. 1996. *A Pitch of Philosophy*. Cambridge, MA: Harvard University Press.

Chakrabarty, Dipesh. 2000. *Provincializing Europe*. Princeton, NJ: Princeton University Press.

Chodorow, Nancy J. 1989. *Feminism and Psychoanalytic Theory*. New Haven, CT: Yale University Press.

– 2020. *The Psychoanalytic Ear and the Sociological Eye*. London: Routledge. https://doi.org/10.4324/9780429026393.

Comaroff, John, and Jean Comaroff. 1992. *Ethnography and the Historical Imagination*. Boulder, CO: Westview.

Crapanzano, Vincent. 1985. *Tuhami: Portrait of a Moroccan*. Chicago: University of Chicago Press.

– 2010. "At the Heart of the Discipline": Critical Reflections on Fieldwork. *Emotions in the Field: The Psychology and Anthropology of Fieldwork Experience.* Edited by James Davies and Dimitrina Spencer. Palo Alto, CA: Stanford University Press.

Crapanzano, Vincent, and Vivian Garrison, eds. 1977. *Case Studies in Spirit Possession*. New York: Wiley.

Critchley, Simon. 2005. "Cavell's 'Romanticism' and Cavell's Romanticism." In *Contending with Stanley Cavell*, edited by Russell B. Goodman, 37–54. Oxford: Oxford University Press. https://doi.org/10.1093/oso/9780195175684.003.0004.

Csikszentmihalyi, Mihaly. 2008. *Flow: The Psychology of Optimal Experience*. New York: Harper.

Das, Veena. 2007. *Life and Words: Violence and the Descent into the Ordinary*. Berkeley: University of California Press. https://doi.org/10.1525/9780520939530.

– 2020. *Textures of the Ordinary: Doing Anthropology after Wittgenstein*. New York: Fordham University Press. https://doi.org/10.5422/fordham/9780823287895.001.0001.

Daston, Lorraine. 2019. *Against Nature*. Cambridge, MA: MIT Press. https://doi.org/10.7551/mitpress/12267.001.0001.

Espírito Santo, Diana, and Matan Shapiro, eds. 2022. *The Dynamic Cosmos: Movement, Paradox, and Experimentation in the Anthropology of Spirit Possession*. London: Bloomsbury. https://doi.org/10.5040/9781350299351.

Eyssallenne, Jazmin Graves. 2023. "Wonder: Spirit Mediumship and Devotional Music at a Mumbai Shrine of the Sidi Ancestor Saints." In *Wonder in South Asia: Histories, Aesthetics, Ethics*, edited by Tulasi Srinivas, 103–22. Albany: SUNY Press. https://doi.org/10.1515/9781438495293-007.

Feeley-Harnik, Gillian. 1991. *A Green Estate: Estate: Restoring Independence in Madagascar*. Washington, DC: Smithsonian Institution Press.

Fingarette, Herbert. 1963. *The Self in Transformation: Psychoanalysis, Philosophy, and the Life of the Spirit*. New York: Basic Books.

Floyd, Juliet. 2020. "Wittgenstein on Ethics: Working through *Lebensformen*." *Philosophy and Social Criticism* 46, no. 2 (February): 115–30. https://doi.org/10.1177/0191453718810918.

Fortes, Meyer. 1987. "Custom and Conscience." In *Religion, Morality, and the Person: Essays on Tallensi Religion*, 175–217. Cambridge: Cambridge University Press. https://doi.org/10.1017/CBO9780511557996.009.

Freud, Sigmund, and Josef Breuer. (1893–5) 1955. *Studies on Hysteria*. Standard Edition II. London: Hogarth.

Gadamer, Hans-Georg. (1960) 1985. *Truth and Method*. New York: Crossroad.

Geertz, Clifford. 1968. *Islam Observed*. Chicago: University of Chicago Press.

– 1973. *The Interpretation of Cultures*. New York: Basic Books.

Goffman, Erving. 1981. "Footing." In *Forms of Talk*, 124–59. Philadelphia: University of Pennsylvania Press.

Greenberg, Jay R., and Stephen A. Mitchell. 1983. *Object Relations in Psychoanalytic Theory*. Cambridge, MA: Harvard University Press. https://doi.org/10.2307/j.ctvjk2xv6.

Hacking, Ian. 1999. *The Social Construction of What?* Cambridge, MA: Harvard University Press. https://doi.org/10.2307/j.ctv1bzfp1z.

Hallowell, A. Irving. 1955. *Culture and Experience*. Philadelphia: University of Pennsylvania Press. https://doi.org/10.9783/9781512816600.

Hampshire, Stuart. 1983. *Morality and Conflict*. Oxford: Basil Blackwell.

Heslon, Mathilde. 2022. *"Rituels d'initiation et construction de la possession."* Paper presented at an internal seminar at the Musée du Quai-Branly, Paris, 5 April 2022.

– 2023. *"Trouver sa vie à Mayotte : Dispositifs et pratiques de soin de jeunes personnes en situation d'affliction."* PhD diss., EHESS Paris.

Ingold, Tim. 2018. "One World Anthropology." *HAU: Journal of Ethnographic Theory* 8, nos. 1–2 (Spring/Autumn): 158–71. https://doi.org/10.1086/698315.

Johnson, Paul Christopher, ed. 2014a. *Spirited Things: The Work of "Possession" in Afro-Atlantic Religions*. Chicago: University of Chicago Press. https://doi.org/10.7208/chicago/9780226122939.001.0001.

– 2014b. "Toward an Atlantic Genealogy of Spirit Possession." In Johnson 2014a, 23–46.

Kamuf, Peggy. 2010. "Introduction: Watchwords." In *To Follow: The Wake of Jacques Derrida*, 1–19. Edinburgh: Edinburgh University Press. https://doi .org/10.3366/edinburgh/9780748641543.003.0017.

Kapchan, Deborah. 2007. *Traveling Spirit Masters: Moroccan Gnawa Trance and Music in the Global Marketplace*. Middletown, CT: Wesleyan University Press. https://doi.org/10.1353/book.114153.

Kapferer, Bruce. 1983. *A Celebration of Demons*. Bloomington: Indiana University Press.

– 1997. *The Feast of the Sorcerer*. Chicago: University of Chicago Press.

Kelly, Ray. 1977. *Etoro Social Structure*. Ann Arbor: University of Michigan Press.

Khan, M. Masud R. 1974. "Montaigne, Rousseau and Freud." In *The Privacy of the Self*, 99–111. London: Hogarth. https://doi.org/10.4324/9780429482830-8.

Kosman, Louis Aryeh. 1980. "Being Properly Affected: Virtues and Feelings in Aristotle's *Ethics*." In Rorty 1980, 103–16. https://doi.org/10.1525 /9780520340985-010.

Kramer, Fritz. 1993. *The Red Fez*. London: Verso.

Lambek, Michael. 1980. "Spirits and Spouses: Possession as a System of Communication among the Malagasy Speakers of Mayotte." *American Ethnologist* 7, no. 2 (May): 318–31. https://doi.org/10.1525 /ae.1980.7.2.02a00060.

– 1981. *Human Spirits:A Cultural Account of Trance in Mayotte*. Cambridge: Cambridge University Press.

– 1988. "Graceful Exits: Spirit Possession as Personal Performance in Mayotte." *Culture* 8, no. 1 (July): 59–69. https://doi.org/10.7202/1078798ar.

– 1990. "Exchange, Time, and Person in Mayotte: The Structure and Destructuring of a Cultural System." *American Anthropologist* 92, no. 3 (September): 647–61. https://doi.org/10.1525/aa.1990.92.3.02a00060.

– 1993. *Knowledge and Practice in Mayotte: Local Discourses of Islam, Sorcery and Spirit Possession*. Toronto: University of Toronto Press. https://doi .org/10.3138/9781442676534.

– 2001. "The Value of Coins in a Sakalava Polity: Money, Death, and Historicity in Mahajanga, Madagascar." *Comparative Studies in Society and History* 43, no. 4 (October): 735–62. https://www.jstor.org/stable/2696668.

– 2002. *The Weight of the Past: Living with History in Mahajanga, Madagascar*. New York: Palgrave Macmillan. https://doi.org/10.1007/978-1-349-73080-3.

– 2006. "What's in a Name? Name Bestowal and the Identity of Spirits in Mayotte and Northwest Madagascar." In *The Anthropology of Names and Naming*, edited by Gabriele vom Bruck and Barbara Bodenhorn, 116–38. Cambridge: Cambridge University Press.

– 2007. "On Catching Up with Oneself: Learning to Know that One Means What One Does." In *Learning Religion*, edited by David Berliner and Ramon

Sarró, 65–81. Oxford: Berghahn. https://doi.org/10.1515
/9781782382133-006.

– 2011. "Kinship as Gift and Theft: Acts of Succession in Mayotte and
Ancient Israel." *American Ethnologist* 38, no. 1 (February): 2–16. https://doi
.org/10.1111/j.1548-1425.2010.01288.x.

– 2014. "The Interpretation of Lives or Life as Interpretation: Cohabiting with
Spirits in the Malagasy World." *American Ethnologist* 41, no. 3 (August):
491–503. https://doi.org/10.1111/amet.12089.

– 2015. *The Ethical Condition: Essays on Action, Person, and Value.* Chicago:
University of Chicago Press. https://doi.org/10.7208
/chicago/9780226292380.001.0001.

– 2018. *Island in the Stream: An Ethnographic History of Mayotte.* Toronto:
University of Toronto Press.

– 2021. "On Sorcery: Life with the Concept." In *Living with Concepts*, edited by
Andrew Brandel and Marco Motta, 215–42. New York: Fordham University
Press. https://doi.org/10.5422/fordham/9780823294268.003.0010.

– 2022. "Nowhere and Everywhere." In *Where is the Good?*, edited by David
Henig, Anna Strhan, and Joel Robbins, 46–59. Oxford: Berghahn. https://
doi.org/10.1515/9781800735521-004.

Lear, Jonathan. 2011. *A Case for Irony.* Cambridge, MA: Harvard University
Press. https://doi.org/10.4159/harvard.9780674063143.

– 2021. "Brief Encounter." In *Concepts and Persons*, by Michael Lambek,
72–86. Toronto: University of Toronto Press. https://doi.org/10.3138
/9781487539597-006.

Leiris, Michel. 1958. *La Possession et ses aspects théâtraux chez les Ethiopiens de
Gondar.* Paris: Plon.

Levy, Robert, and Douglas Hollan. 1998. "Person-Centered Interviewing and
Observation in Anthropology." In *Handbook of Methods in Cultural Anthropology*,
edited by H. Russell Bernard, 333–64. Walnut Creek, CA: Altamira Press.

Leys, Ruth. 1996. "Traumatic Cures: Shellshock, Janet, and the Question of
Memory." In *Tense Past: Cultural Essays in Trauma and Memory*, edited by
Paul Antze and Michael Lambek, 103–45. New York: Routledge.

Loewald, Hans W. 1980. *Papers on Psychoanalysis.* New Haven: Yale University
Press.

– 2000. *The Essential Hans Loewald.* Hagerstown, MD: University Publishing
Group.

Luhrmann, Tanya. 2012. *When God Talks Back.* New York: Vintage.

MacIntyre, Alasdair. 1981. *After Virtue: A Study in Moral Theory.* South Bend,
IN: University of Notre Dame Press.

Mahler, Margaret. 1986. "On the First Three Subphases of the Separation-
Individuation Process." In *Essential Papers on Object Relations*, edited by
Peter Buckley, 222–32. New York: New York University Press.

Malara, Diego. 2022. "Angels and Demons: Notes on Kinship and Exorcism at an Ethiopian Orthodox Shrine." In *The Dynamic Cosmos*, edited by Diana Espírito Santo and Matan Shapiro, 21–34. London: Bloomsbury. https://doi .org/10.5040/9781350299351.ch-1.

Masquelier, Adeline. 2001. *Prayer Has Spoiled Everything: Possession, Power, and Identity in an Islamic Town of Niger*. Durham: Duke University Press. https://doi.org/10.2307/j.ctv1134dsp.

– 2002. "From Hostage to Host: Confessions of a Spirit Medium in Niger." *Ethos* 30, nos. 1–2 (March): 49–76. https://doi.org/10.1525/eth.2002.30.1-2.49.

"Mayotte Guerlain for Women." n.d. Fragrantica. Accessed 4 June 2024. https://www.fragrantica.com/perfume/Guerlain/Mayotte-5399.html.

Mead, George Herbert. 1967. *Mind, Self, and Society from the Standpoint of a Social Behaviorist*. Chicago: The University of Chicago Press. https://doi .org/10.7208/chicago/9780226516608.001.0001.

Mitchell, Stephen A. 1988a. *Relational Concepts in Psychoanalysis: An Integration*. Cambridge: Harvard University Press. https://doi .org/10.4159/9780674041158.

– 1988b. "From Ghosts to Ancestors: The Psychoanalytic Vision of Hans Loewald." *Psychoanalytic Dialogues* 8 (6): 825–55. https://doi .org/10.1080/10481889809539297.

Motta, Marco. 2019. *Esprits fragiles : Réparer les liens ordinaires à Zanzibar*. Lausanne, Switzerland: Bsn Press.

Murphy, Robert. 1971. *The Dialectics of Social Life*. New York: Basic Books.

Nehamas, Alexander. 1998. *The Art of Living: Socratic Reflections from Plato to Foucault*. Berkeley: University of California Press. https://doi .org/10.1525/9780520925519.

Obeyesekere, Gananath. 1984. *Medusa's Hair*. Chicago: University of Chicago Press.

Ochoa, Todd Ramon. 2020. *A Party for Lazarus: Six Generations of Ancestral Devotion in a Cuban Town*. Berkeley: University of California Press.

Ogden, Thomas H. 2010. "On Three Forms of Thinking: Magical Thinking, Dream Thinking, and Transformative Thinking." *The Psychoanalytic Quarterly* 79, no. 2 (April): 317–47. https://doi.org/10.1002/j.2167-4086.2010 .tb00450.x.

Orsi, Robert. 2005. *Between Heaven and Earth*. Princeton: Princeton University Press.

– 2016. *History and Presence*. Cambridge, MA: Harvard University Press.

Pandolfo, Stefania. 2017. *Knot of the Soul: Madness, Psychoanalysis, Islam*. Chicago: University of Chicago Press. https://doi.org/10.7208 /chicago/9780226465111.001.0001.

Phillips, Adam. 1997. *Terrors and Experts*. Cambridge, MA: Harvard University Press.

Pócs, Éva, and Andras Zempléni, eds. 2022. *Spirit Possession: Multidisciplinary Approaches to a Worldwide Phenomenon*. Budapest: Central European University Press. https://doi.org/10.1515/9789633864142.

Popova, Maria. 2014. "The Paradox of Active Surrender: Jeanette Winterson on How Learning to Understand Art Transforms Us." *The Marginalian*, 27 October 2014. https://www.themarginalian.org/2014/10/27 /jeanette-winterson-art-objects/.

Ram, Kalpana. 2013. *Fertile Disorder: Spirit Possession and Its Provocation of the Modern*. Honolulu: University of Hawai'i Press. https://doi.org/10.21313 /hawaii/9780824836306.001.0001.

Riccio, Damien. 2022. "*La condition clandestine : Une ethnographie des travailleurs migrants à Mayotte*." PhD diss., University of Bordeaux.

Ricoeur, Paul. 1970. *Freud and Philosophy: An Essay on Interpretation*. Translated by Denis Savage. New Haven, CT: Yale University Press.

Rorty, Amélie Oksenberg, ed. 1980. *Essays on Aristotle's Ethics*. Berkeley: University of California Press.

Rosaldo, Renato. 2013. *The Day of Shelly's Death*. Durham, NC: Duke University Press.

Rothstein, Mervyn. 1996. "The Conductor: Daniel Barenboim." Cigar Aficionado, Summer 1996. https://www.cigaraficionado.com/article /the-conductor-daniel-barenboim-7616.

Sahlins, Marshall. 2013. *What Kinship Is–And Is Not*. Chicago: University of Chicago Press.

– 2017. "The Original Political Society." *HAU: Journal of Ethnographic Theory* 7, no. 2 (Autumn): 91–128. http://doi.org/10.14318/hau7.2.014.

Sartre, Jean-Paul. 1963. *Search for a Method*. Translated by Hazel E. Barnes. New York: Vintage Books.

Schaefer, Donovan O. 2020. "Talal Asad's Challenge to Religious Studies." *Religion and Society* 11 (September): 20–3. https://doi.org/10.3167 /arrs.2020.110102.

Schafer, Roy. (1983) 2018. "Action and Narration in Psychoanalysis." In *The Analytic Attitude*, 240–56. New York: Routledge. https://doi .org/10.4324/9780429481024-15.

Schmidt, Bettina, and Lucy Huskinson, eds. 2010. *Spirit Possession and Trance: New Interdisciplinary Perspectives*. London: Bloomsbury.

Schneider, David. 1968. *American Kinship: A Cultural Account*. Chicago: University of Chicago Press.

Selka, Stephen. 2014. "Demons and Money." In Johnson 2014a, 155–75.

Singh, Bhrigupati. 2015. *Poverty and the Quest for Life*. Chicago: University of Chicago Press.

Sorabji, Richard. 1980. "Aristotle on the Role of Intellect in Virtue." In Rorty 1980, 201–19. https://doi.org/10.1525/9780520340985-015.

Taussig, Michael. 1993. *Mimesis and Alterity*. New York: Routledge.

Tinius, Jonas. 2018. "Capacity for Character: Fiction, Ethics, and the Anthropology of Conduct." *Social Anthropology/Anthropologie sociale* 26, no. 3 (August): 345–60. https://doi.org/10.1111/1469-8676.12531.

Trawick, Margaret. 1992. "Desire in Kinship: A Lacanian View of the South Indian Familial Self." In *Psychoanalytic Anthropology after Freud*, edited by David H. Spain, 49–62. New York: Psyche Press.

Trilling, Lionel. (1950) 2001. "Art and Neurosis." In *The Moral Obligation to Be Intelligent*, 87–104. New York: Farrar Straus Giroux.

Vérin, Pierre. 1986. *The History of Civilization in Northern Madagascar*. Rotterdam: Balkema.

Viveiros de Castro, Eduardo. 1998. "Cosmological Deixis and Amerindian Perspectivism." *Journal of the Royal Anthropological Institute* 4, no. 3 (September): 469–88. https://doi.org/10.2307/3034157.

Winnicott, D.W. 1971. *Playing and Reality*. London: Routledge.

Wittgenstein, Ludwig. (1967) 2020. *The Mythology in Our Language: Remarks on Frazer's Golden Bough*. Edited by Stephan Palmié and Giovanni da Col. Translated by Stephan Palmié. Chicago: Hau Books.

Zempléni, Andras. 1977. "From Symptom to Sacrifice: The Story of Khady Fall." In Crapanzano and Garrison 1977, 87–139.

– 2022. "Discerning Spirit Possession." In *Spirit Possession: Multidisciplinary Approaches to a Worldwide Phenomenon*, edited by Pócs, Éva and Andras Zempléni, 1–50. Budapest: Central European University Press.

Index

Anthropological Horizons

Editor: Michael Lambek, University of Toronto

"Being Alive Well": Health and the Politics of Cree Well-Being/Naomi Adelson (2000)

Irish Travellers: Racism and the Politics of Culture/Jane Helleiner (2001)

Of Property and Propriety: The Role of Gender and Class in Imperialism and Nationalism/Edited by Himani Bannerji, Shahrzad Mojab, and Judith Whitehead (2001)

An Irish Working Class: Explorations in Political Economy and Hegemony, 1800–1950/Marilyn Silverman (2001)

The Double Twist: From Ethnography to Morphodynamics/Edited by Pierre Maranda (2001)

The House of Difference: Cultural Politics and National Identity in Canada/Eva Mackey (2002)

Writing and Colonialism in Northern Ghana: The Encounter between the LoDagaa and "the World on Paper," 1892–1991/Sean Hawkins (2002)

Guardians of the Transcendent: An Ethnography of a Jain Ascetic Community/Anne Vallely (2002)

The Hot and the Cold: Ills of Humans and Maize in Native Mexico/Jacques M. Chevalier and Andrés Sánchez Bain (2003)

Figured Worlds: Ontological Obstacles in Intercultural Relations/Edited by John Clammer, Sylvie Poirier, and Eric Schwimmer (2004)

Revenge of the Windigo: The Construction of the Mind and Mental Health of North American Aboriginal Peoples/James B. Waldram (2004)

The Cultural Politics of Markets: Economic Liberalization and Social Change in Nepal/Katharine Neilson Rankin (2004)

A World of Relationships: Itineraries, Dreams, and Events in the Australian Western Desert/Sylvie Poirier (2005)

The Politics of the Past in an Argentine Working-Class Neighbourhood/Lindsay DuBois (2005)

Youth and Identity Politics in South Africa, 1990–1994/Sibusisiwe Nombuso Dlamini (2005)

Maps of Experience: The Anchoring of Land to Story in Secwepemc Discourse/Andie Diane Palmer (2005)

We Are Now a Nation: Croats between "Home" and "Homeland"/Daphne N. Winland (2007)

Beyond Bodies: Rainmaking and Sense Making in Tanzania/Todd Sanders (2008)

Kaleidoscopic Odessa: History and Place in Contemporary Ukraine/Tanya Richardson (2008)

Invaders as Ancestors: On the Intercultural Making and Unmaking of Spanish Colonialism in the Andes/Peter Gose (2008)

From Equality to Inequality: Social Change among Newly Sedentary Lanoh Hunter-Gatherer Traders of Peninsular Malaysia/Csilla Dallos (2011)

Rural Nostalgias and Transnational Dreams: Identity and Modernity among Jat Sikhs/Nicola Mooney (2011)

Dimensions of Development: History, Community, and Change in Allpachico, Peru/Susan Vincent (2012)

People of Substance: An Ethnography of Morality in the Colombian Amazon/Carlos David Londoño Sulkin (2012)

"We Are Still Didene": Stories of Hunting and History from Northern British Columbia/Thomas McIlwraith (2012)

Being Māori in the City: Indigenous Everyday Life in Auckland/Natacha Gagné (2013)

The Hakkas of Sarawak: Sacrificial Gifts in Cold War Era Malaysia/Kee Howe Yong (2013)

Remembering Nayeche and the Gray Bull Engiro: African Storytellers of the Karamoja Plateau and the Plains of Turkana/Mustafa Kemal Mirzeler (2014)

In Light of Africa: Globalizing Blackness in Northeast Brazil/Allan Charles Dawson (2014)

The Land of Weddings and Rain: Nation and Modernity in Post-Socialist Lithuania/Gediminas Lankauskas (2015)

Milanese Encounters: Public Space and Vision in Contemporary Urban Italy/Cristina Moretti (2015)

Legacies of Violence: History, Society, and the State in Sardinia/Antonio Sorge (2015)

Looking Back, Moving Forward: Transformation and Ethical Practice in the Ghanaian Church of Pentecost/Girish Daswani (2015)

Why the Porcupine Is Not a Bird: Explorations in the Folk Zoology of an Eastern Indonesian People/Gregory Forth (2016)

The Heart of Helambu: Ethnography and Entanglement in Nepal/Tom O'Neill (2016)

Tournaments of Value: Sociability and Hierarchy in a Yemeni Town, 20th Anniversary Edition/Ann Meneley (2016)

Europe Un-Imagined: Nation and Culture at a French-German Television Channel/Damien Stankiewicz (2017)

Transforming Indigeneity: Urbanization and Language Revitalization in the Brazilian Amazon/Sarah Shulist (2018)

Wrapping Authority: Women Islamic Leaders in a Sufi Movement in Dakar, Senegal/Joseph Hill (2018)

Island in the Stream: An Ethnographic History of Mayotte/Michael Lambek (2018)

Materializing Difference: Consumer Culture, Politics, and Ethnicity among Romanian Roma/Péter Berta (2019)

Virtual Activism: Sexuality, the Internet, and a Social Movement in Singapore/Robert Phillips (2020)

Shadow Play: Information Politics in Urban Indonesia/Sheri Lynn Gibbins (2021)

www.ingramcontent.com/pod-product-compliance
Lightning Source LLC
Chambersburg PA
CBHW031139020426
42333CB00013B/448